Bits and Pieces of Cragsmoor

Including a History of the Carroll Butler Brown House

By Marie Bilney and Christina Clark

AuthorHouse™
1663 Liberty Drive
Bloomington, IN 47403
www.authorhouse.com
Phone: 1-800-839-8640

First published by AuthorHouse   8/26/2010

ISBN: 978-1-4520-6196-2 (e)
ISBN: 978-1-4520-6195-5 (sc)

Library of Congress Control Number: 2010911748

Printed in the United States of America
Bloomington, Indiana

This book is printed on acid-free paper.

COVER ACKNOWLEDGEMENTS

Bear Hill Overlook by Emily August - 2006

The Carroll Butler Brown House by Marie Bilney - 2003

Most photos within by Marie Bilney between 2001 and 2006

TABLE OF CONTENTS

A TIME TO GIVE THANKS

READ ON

PREFACE

The Cragsmoor area has been of great interest to us for over fifty years, beginning on November 21, 1951 when Kenneth and Helen Clark purchased a home there, presently still under Clark ownership, although it is used primarily as an occasional vacation home.

Over the course of the past ten to fifteen years, a few of our lady friends have joined us for R and R weekends in this beautiful mountain home, which is what led to our deep interest in the history of Cragsmoor and related subjects.

And so, it was this home which began our research. Many, many hours have been spent in Cragsmoor and Ellenville Libraries, Wawarsing Town Hall, trips to the Ulster County Building in Kingston, looking through tomes and tomes of data, viewing microfilms and microfiches and speaking with anyone who would help us to fill in the gaps. Lots of information has been gathered from previously printed materials, as noted or enclosed within. Much of the information may be repetitive.

We, the authors, are currently pursuing contacts who are family related (by marriage) and who are familiar with Carroll Butler Brown's works of art. If anyone has any knowledge of the artist and/or his descendants, we would appreciate gaining any further information.

Our story begins "way back when' and covers mostly the areas of greatest interest to us. Let us begin.

Early On

IN THE BEGINNING

Some 400 million years ago, Cragsmoor and area were at the bottom of a shallow sea. Over time, large amounts of weathered quartz were carried by streams from a southwest mountain range and deposited here and in surrounding areas.

Glacial periods, ending ten to twelve thousand years ago, eroded the rock to a smoothly polished surface as seen at Sam's Point.

As soil formed, many varieties of plant growth appeared including the scrub pine barrens which are quite unusual in this area.

Over one hundred types of wild flowers are known to grow (or have grown) in Cragsmoor. But not true of Lake Maratanza, a spring-fed lake which boasts neither plant nor fish life.

People began coming to the mountain in the last quarter of the 1700's. The Gonzalus, Ferguson and Lilly families were already living "on the mountain" when just prior to the Revolutionary War came the Mances and Coddingtons (around 1770).

About this time the lush forests gave way to lumbering by many, the Mance family being the largest. John Mance owned 782 acres. And...now that an abundance of lumber was available to build with, it added even more to the influx of people.

Clearing the land led to farming, which produced greater quantities of food than needed and so some land was sold for additional income.

Huckleberries and cranberries now grew profusely and so "the pickers" (who were migrants) came to harvest them. Pickers wages were extremely low and the work was quite tiresome. Mountain fires often were set by the huckleberry pickers and this helped to maintain the famed Shawangunk berries since burning off the older plants did not affect the roots.

Bees were raised for honey, sheep for wool, flax and food. Potatoes grown "on the mountain" were the "very best". Note: Much of the preceding paragraphs was based on information from "Cragsmoor, an Historical Sketch" by Margaret Hakam and Susan Houtaling.

In the summer of 2000 the very first blueberry festival was held in Ellenville, New York and has been celebrated annually since then, traditionally in late August and named the Shawangunk Mountain Wild Blueberry and Huckleberry Harvest Festival. It is well attended by all to enjoy the many treats available, such as pies, pancakes, bake sales, and so much more.

Celebrate the Berrypickers!

by **Marc Fried**, *author/historian/naturalist*

Across the street from the **Chamber of Commerce**'s **Berme Road** office, some distance behind the *Kimble Hose* firehouse hall and *Wawarsing Highway Dept.* building, an old road appears unexpectedly at the foot of the **Shawangunk Mountain** and commences a seven-mile ascent to **Lake Awosting** in **Minnewaska State Park**. I say "old road," but it was actually called by some the "New Road" when built over 100 years ago by the Minnewaska resort to shuttle hotel guests to and from Ellenville's *O&W* rail station. Today it is designated as **Smiley Carriageway** on state park maps, but it was known through most of its life and is still known today by the older, and more history-minded residents of the valley, as the **Smiley Road**.

Were the state park folks worried that the word road might encourage unauthorized vehicular traffic? The roadbed, long abandoned, is in deplorable condition, and any attempt at motor access would probably prove perilous, not to say expensive. But until the great floods of 1955, and especially during the decades preceding World War II, the Smiley Road was in fact bustling with vehicular and pedestrian traffic, and was the lifeline of a thriving homegrown industry. We are talking, of course, about...

This early 20th Century picture, which is in Marc Fried's book **The Huckleberry Pickers**, *is from a glass plate negative in the collection of Phil Aaron, formerly of Ellenville, and reproduced here courtesy Mr. Aaron. Note the berry box worn by the fellow on the left.*

HUCKLEBERRIES.

Now before we get into an argument about whether they were *huckleberries* or *blueberries*, let me say that the term in nearly universal use by those who picked, measured, bought, and sold them was the *h*-word, not the *b*-word, the latter generally being reserved for the horticulturally-hybridized and propagated varieties, quite inferior in all respects except size. Ours were wild berries: unsprayed, uncultivated, and helped along by human intervention only in the form of (very wild) mountain fires that raced up the slope and spread explosively across the pine barrens, the "tangled thickets and hell of broken gorges that form the crest of the Shawangunks --a devil's own playground for a fire," in the words of one mid-century forest ranger. It was the periodic fires that helped maintain the famed Shawangunk Mountain berries that found their way into produce markets, bakeries, dining rooms, and palates from New York City to Albany.

The fires no longer occur. The Shawangunk huckleberries today are just as tasty, but far fewer. The many hundreds of pickers who summered in tents or tarpaper shanties along the **Smiley Road** and at **Sam's Point** are long gone. But their history, their stories, their folkways and lore are preserved in prose, poetry, song, and human memory, and we celebrate them today in our annual late summer Festival.

As we prepare for the celebration, let us be sure to retain the core of history and authenticity that attracts former berrypickers and their descendents to Ellenville for this festival. It is their special day, a day that should be dedicated, above all, to honoring and remembering those who actually lived the rustic, independent, hardworking (sometimes hard-drinking), and often adventurous life of the Shawangunk Mountain berrypicker.

IN CASE OF RAIN: Please remember that all history- and mountain-related exhibits, events, and performances, as well as bake sales, pie judging, etc., scheduled for the **Market Square** behind the Town of Wawarsing offices, will move indoors to **1 Bogardus Place** (near the post office); all other festival exhibits and activities will be postponed to the rain date, Sunday, August 24th.

For more info, contact: Marc B. Fried, 766 Sand Hill Rd, Gardiner, NY 12525-5633.

Wawarsing.Net Magazine · 2003 August
Issue 9   page 12

Forward, into the Past

"... the blueberry, Meenahga"

by **Marion M. Dumond**
Former Town of Wawarsing Historian
and Ellenville Public Library Director (Retired)

In the late 1800s, long before the days of air conditioning, Ellenville residents used to camp in nearby higher elevations to escape the more oppressive heat in the valley. One of the favorite locations was the lower part of the **Shawangunk Mountains**, before the turn to go on up into Cragsmoor. The men would commute each day into Ellenville by horse and wagon.

Young U. E. Terwilliger, a successful insurance and real estate agent in the village, decided that more people would enjoy "the Mountain" if they had cottages equipped with some of the 19th Century's amenities in which to stay. To that purpose, he purchased more than one hundred acres from Casper Fisher and his son Charles. He adapted the Fisher home to a small boarding house and erected four cottages, which were ready for the summer of 1882, and built an additional cottage the next year.

U.E. Terwilliger (*see photo below*) was no stranger to "the Mountain." His grandfather Cornelis (or Cornelius) had purchased land between the schoolhouse (District 11) and the **Gully Road** to Cragsmoor. He and his wife Maria raised their ten children there. One son, Eli D., was one of the Town of Wawarsing's leading citizens and owner of the famous *Terwilliger House* in what is now known as **Liberty Square**. Another son, Jonathan C., was a respected builder. U.E. was Jonathan's son. Coincidentally, the land which U.E. purchased from Casper Fisher had itself been purchased by Fisher from David Haight who had bought it from Abraham and Martin Terwilliger, a different branch of the Terwilliger family.

Mr. Terwilliger was a literate gentleman, largely self-educated, who enjoyed reading and he chose as the name for his boarding house and cottages an Indian word from Longfellow's "Song of Hiawatha." In the part of the poem

when Hiawatha wandered fasting in the forest, he "Saw the blueberry, Meenahga." Mr. Terwilliger chose to incorporate the availability of mountain blueberries with his appreciation of Native American culture and named his enterprise *Mount Meenahga House and Cottages*.

The cottages were very popular and U.E. (he preferred to use his initials, rather than his given name, Uriah) had so little trouble in keeping them filled that he purchased more land and, within ten years of the original project, built a large boarding house with public rooms and large bedrooms. Although untrained in architecture and landscaping, U.E. designed his estate and supervised its development. Charles Fisher worked as a carpenter for U.E. for many years, building the summer houses (*photo, next page*) which added so much to the charm of *Mount Meenahga*.

Carriage drives and paths were installed. Terwilliger was an early environmentalist who preserved as much of the natural habitat as possible; trees were cut judiciously, usually only to open up roads and views. A large recreation building provided space for a bowling alley, pool and billiard tables, a children's playroom, and a large room for amateur theatricals and dancing. Two tennis courts and a croquet court were options for outdoor exercise and, long before golf was available at many places, Mr. Terwilliger hired the expert Thomas Bendelow to lay out a nine-hole course that was completed in 1899. It was a difficult course, more up-and-downhill than level, but *Meenahga*'s guests enjoyed it. In addition to a reading room in the main house, supplied with newspapers, magazines and books, U.E. built a separate library building so that readers would not be bothered by the noise of normal residential traffic and/or conversation in halls and on porches.

Somehow, U.E. found the time to run *Mount Meenahga* and develop his Ellenville business simultaneously, but not alone. His wife and his two children, Bert and Louise, worked at the hotel, but also enjoyed the social life. Carriage or surrey rides around the estate or to **Sam's Point** or Cragsmoor were always popular. Hayrides on summer evenings appealed to the young people, as did trips to the *Ulster County Fair*, the *Sun Ray* bottling plant, and similar Ellenville attractions.

The Terwilliger children grew, went away to school and returned summers to help at *Meenahga*. Son Bert returned permanently to share in both the insurance business and *Meenahga* and, in 1899, married Florence Tone, a graduate of Wellesley College who had come to Ellenville for a position at the *Ellenville High School*. The guest list at *Meenahga* included artists, financiers, business tycoons, statesmen, judges and many family groups with no particular fame. The guest register was signed by John W. Foster of Washington, DC, soon to be Secretary of State. Rev. and Mrs. Allen Dulles were accompanied by their son, John Foster Dulles. John Vernou Bouvier Jr. was a guest in the late 1880s as a young man just out of college (his future granddaughter, Jacqueline Bouvier

Kennedy). John D. Rockefeller Sr. and his family were guests in 1893, and Louise Terwilliger became very friendly with the Rockefeller daughters.

Guests came by horse and carriage or, later, by train and were met by *Meenahga*'s carriages. Some brought maids, or their own coachmen or chauffeur. Guests were more than business; many became personal friends of the Terwilliger family. So, too, did employees, who generally came from the area, both the valley and the upper regions of "the Mountain." The Terwilligers took great pride in enumerating the names of young people who came to work as chambermaids, in the laundry, on the grounds, or in the office and went on to found their own hotels or restaurants, or to hold very responsible management positions in other resorts.

Mount Meenahga's final season ended in October 1921, and the complex was sold in June 1922. Katharine T. Terwilliger devoted six columns of "Before Today's Headlines" to a very personal, warm and detailed history of *Mount Meenahga*. U.E. Terwilliger was K.T.'s paternal grandfather; Bert and Florence Tone were her parents; her brother Robert was born at *Meenahga*; and, Katharine spent her summers as a child and young adult helping with various appropriate responsibilities at her summer home.

"Before Today's Headlines" is available at **Terwilliger House**, the local history center of the *Ellenville Public Library and Museum*. The *Museum* collection also includes an impressive group of postcards showing *Meenahga* scenes. In addition to learning more about *Mount Meenahga* at the *Museum*, visit the display case in the Gallery/Link between the *Library* and the *Museum* to see a berry basket and a picker's box from the heyday of huckleberry picking on "the Mountain," as well as a variety of newspaper clippings. And pick up a copy of Marc Fried's irreverent *The Huckleberry Pickers*, subtitled: "A Raucous History of the Shawangunk Mountains."

At the Ellenville Public Library

Huckleberry Picker Oral History Project
by Heidi Wagner, *Preserve Manager, Sam's Point*

Photograph from "Shawangunk: Adventure, Exploration, History and Epiphany from a Mountain Wilderness" by Marc B. Fried

A project sponsored by The Nature Conservancy to collect and interpret stories about the lives and experiences of huckleberry pickers and their families on the **Shawangunk Ridge** during the nineteenth and early twentieth century is being launched at a get-together in the **Community Room** of the *Ellenville Public Library,* **40 Center Street**, Ellenville, New York on **Saturday, April 3rd** at **1:00 PM**. One-time huckleberry pickers, their families and descendants or anyone who would like to share information regarding the huckleberry pickers is welcome to attend.

(We want to learn all we can about the **Shawangunk Ridge** huckleberry pickers. Any information regarding the berry pickers is welcome. Let's hear your story! Bring along photos and memorabilia if you have them.)

Information that will be gathered will be used to develop an interpretive oral history exhibit. The exhibit will be installed in the new *Sam's Point Preserve Conservation Center*, which is now under construction at the entrance to the Preserve, located in Cragsmoor. The Nature Conservancy staff, assisted by students from Marist College and other volunteers, will document stories and reminiscences on video tape, which will be used to inform people about the cultural history of the *Preserve*. The Nature Conservancy has received $10,000 in funding from the office of New York State Senator John Bonacic in support of the project. "We are excited about this project and know it will add a very important dimension to our exhibits at the new *Conservation Center* at *Sam's Point*," said Cara Lee, Director of the Conservancy's *Shawangunk Ridge Program*.

In addition to *Sam's Point*'s extraordinary ecological significance, the Preserve has a rich and varied cultural history. Beginning in the mid-1800s and aided by the expansion of the railroads, a market developed for the huckleberries that still grow in great quantities along the ridge. Initially a family activity, gathering huckleberries soon developed into a thriving business. Semi-permanent encampments and lively summer communities developed in the vicinity of *Sam's Point*. The ruins of these encampments still remain, containing a handful of standing structures, structural remains such as foundations and building materials and refuse middens. Several photographs of the workers and their families also remain, providing valuable information about a vanished regional agricultural and the culture associated with it.

As part of the interpretive plan for the *Conservation Center*, The Nature Conservancy, working with the *Cragsmoor Historical Society*, plans to collect and archive

8

Continued –

the oral histories of the huckleberry pickers and their families and combine these histories with photographs and artifacts to fabricate a museum quality exhibit that will tell the history of the Shawangunk huckleberry pickers.

Sam's Point Preserve, comprised of nearly 5,000 acres, is owned by the Open Space Institute and managed by the Nature Conservancy. The preserve is located in the southwestern portion of the Northern **Shawangunks**, which is recognized as one of the most important sites for biodiversity conservation in the northeastern United States and is considered by The Nature Conservancy as one of the earth's "Last Great Places."

For more information about this event or the oral history project contact Heidi Wagner, Preserve Manager, at 647-3123 or **hwagner@tnc.org** or **Sam's Point Preserve, PO Box 86, Cragsmoor NY 12420**. The *Ellenville Public Library & Museum* is located at **40 Center Street**, Ellenville, New York. Tel: **647-5530**

Blueberry Festival August 28th

The *Shawangunk Mountain Wild Blueberry/ Huckleberry Harvest Festival* for 2004, sponsored by the *Ellenville-Wawarsing Chamber of Commerce*, is in the early planning stages. The *Festival Committee* is using the successes of last year's event as a base and attempting to add even more exhibits, artisans, craftspersons, entertainment (Bob Lusk, The Carl Richards Band, the Brats, and Looney Ballooney have all agreed to return performances), food, and vendors. Again, a *Blueberry Pancake Breakfast* will precede the festivities

Rain date for street festival is Sunday the 29th, 12 – 6 PM, but folk music, conservation exhibits, and pie sale will be held rain or shine on Saturday (indoors if it's raining), with the option to return Sunday. Over 3000 persons attended in 2003.

Since the core of this festival is the celebration of the heritage of the blueberry/huckleberry pickers and their environs, plans are to expand the Blueberry cultural exhibits and the Shawangunk Mountain exhibits. (If you have something you would like to contribute or would like to participate, please contact the committee.)

The committee would also like to revive something like the old *Art in the Square* as a separate exhibit of local artists and/or of local subject to be held in conjunction with the Festival. If anyone would be interested in coordinating this project, assisting with it, or contributing to the exhibit please contact the committee. This exhibit could add so much to our event.

Festival Committee meetings are held the **third Wednesday** of each month at **5:45 PM** at the *Chamber of Commerce* office on the **Berme Road, 647-4620.** Join us.

Co-chairpersons are Dianne E. Turner, 647-4700 or **motherblueberry12428@yahoo.com** , and John Adams, 647-5626 or **PortBenFarm@webtv.net** .

Huckleberry Memories

by **Marion M. Dumond**
*Former Town of Wawarsing Historian
& Ellenville Public Library Director (Retired)*

"I think we always ate more than we brought home," said Terry Canceleno, reminiscing about picking huckleberries on the mountain as a child, "We picked a lot of berries, but most went into our mouths."

Terry remembers spending her summers in a cabin just off **Ice Caves Road** where her grandmother took care of Terry, her sister, and cousins *(perhaps like one of the cabins in this 1990 picture, below, by Eric Krieger in an article in the Times-Herald Record)*. Both her parents worked during the day (her father was a plumber at *Rose & Douglas*), so a young aunt often "kept an eye" on the children. There weren't summer recreation programs to entertain children during the July-August school vacation, so the children occupied themselves with simple pleasures. A frequent time-filler for the children was to take a walk up the road, often with metal pails and buckets in their hands in case they found a bush or two loaded with huckleberries. "Yes, we always called them huckleberries back then," Terry added. "Now, everybody calls them blueberries."

"I remember the berries being much larger when we picked them ourselves, but when you buy them now, you are lucky if there are a couple of big berries in a box," she commented. "We picked for fun and food. Grandma (Doris Avery) used what we brought home for baking."

Terry was Vernon and Evelyn Avery's second daughter, her father being one of Doris Avery's eleven children, so there were many aunts, uncles, and cousins as part of her childhood memories.

She remembers the many deer who were completely unafraid of the berry pickers and "Yes, we met up with a couple of snakes, but my aunt always went first, throwing stones so the rattlers would know we were coming, and get out of our way."

"We always waved to the Ranger up in the **Fire Tower** as we walked down the fire road, and he always waved back," Terry reminisced. "And I remember an older man up on **Ice Caves Road** who had a lot of animals; he had a cabin on the left, further up than ours, and he didn't really know us, but he would always wave. I'm sure that if he didn't see us coming back by a certain time, he would have checked with my grandmother."

"We had fun days up there, and to this day, blueberries are still my favorite food, believe it or not."

It was pleasant to talk with Terry Canceleno at *Village Cleaners* on **Canal Street**, which she owns and operates with her husband, John. Perhaps her most poignant comment was uttered when she talked about the extended

Continued next page

9

Continued –

Avery family, "We all took care of each other." What a wonderful memory of growing up in the Ellenville area in the late 1950s and early 1960s!

Much older memories of huckleberrying are recorded at the *Ellenville Public Library & Museum (including all the photos or artifacts in this article, such as the 1906 picture above)* where there are two berry pickers' boxes in the collection *(photo below)*. The one most people remember is a large, decorated box which was presented to the local history collection by William Fahy, who had used it for many years, as did his father before him, and before that, the original craftsman who made the container. Mr. Fahy had owned the box for fifty years before presenting it to the *Library*.

The box, now at least 125 years old, was made by Will VanSchaick, who was a friend of Mr. Fahy's father (also a William). When VanSchaick became too old to pick huckleberries, he gave the box to the senior Fahy and told him to pass it on to "little Willie."

The box is a prime example of folk art. It measures 25 inches high, eight inches deep, and 15 inches wide, with canvas straps to hold it on the picker's back. It is padded where the box would meet the picker's shoulders. The yellow painted sides are striped for a wooden effect and the front is lettered "Little Willie V," probably identifying Willie VanSchaick as a boy. The front contains a fanciful scene of birds, ships, sea and lighthouse, but nothing to ➚

represent huckleberries. White porcelain knobs held berry baskets which, when full, were dumped into the box via a square hole in the blue top.

Experts have commented that the box couldn't possibly have been used while picking, because it was too heavy and too cumbersome. It was more likely used to carry the berries from the picking area to the buyer. A smaller, plainer box, also in the museum collection *(the smaller green box, on the right in the photo)*, is a more appropriate size to have been used while picking, but less is known about it.

Pat Clinton, the author of an "Underground Museum" article for the *Ellenville Public Library & Museum* in 1973 about Fahy's gift, went on to interview Mr. Fahy and record his memories. The Museum has a transcript of the two tapes.

William Fahy began picking berries at the age of eight. He recalled that "people would talk all winter about what they would do when huckleberry time came around." Many winter debts were paid off with berry proceeds. "Families of four or five kids would pick, and turn over all their money to their parents toward buying a house," Mr. Fahy said. "You could buy a nice home for around $500 or $1,000 at the turn of the century."

"Little Willie" Fahy picked eight quarts his first official day as a picker. He said he picked into baskets or pails and then poured them into the box. A basket held two or three quarts; the box held 36 to 38 quarts. The first berries picked early in the morning would be wet with dew, so they would be poured on a clean cloth to dry before dumping them into the box.

The Fahy family sold berries to "old Tom" Yarrow, who had a cider mill at the base of the mountain where **Canal & Center Streets** meet. Yarrow, who also distilled wintergreen oil, stored huckleberries in his mill until he sent them by train to New York City.

In those days, berries sold for as much as 10 cents a quart at the start of the season, dropping to as little as a nickel a quart in the height of the season. Buyers would use six-quart measures when purchasing berries from pickers.

In 1879, special huckleberry cars were used by the *O&W Railway* to transport the blue fruit to the New York markets. Pickers at that time earned 6-8 cents per quart.

To put that number in perspective, blueberries from New Jersey, priced to move, cost a consumer 99 cents a pint, or more, in 2004.

As you visit the *Ellenville-Wawarsing Chamber of Commerce*'s *Annual Blueberry Festival* on **August 28th**, take a moment to think about the memories shared in this column. Thanks to Terry Canceleno for taking time from her business to chat about her memories, to Mr. Fahy for his wonderful gift to the local history collection, and to Pat Clinton, now a Florida resident, who wrote publicity for the *Ellenville Public Library & Museum* while on staff in the Museum. Her "Underground Museum" articles record the history of many items in the collection and add to the accumulated treasure of local historical knowledge. 🏠

10

FREE! TAKE A COPY!

Published by the
Ellenville-Wawarsing
Chamber of Commerce
Also Online at
www.Wawarsing.Net

Issue #33 **2005 August**

Wawarsing.Net

SHAWANGUNK MOUNTAIN

Huckleberry Pickers on the Smiley Road

At the Four Mile Post, 1944

WILD BLUEBERRY AND
HUCKLEBERRY FESTIVAL

Ellenville, N.Y. August 27, 2005

11

Blueberry Festival Schedule

Saturday, August 27th, 2005

☞ *Blueberry Pancake Breakfast:* 7:30 to 11:00 AM (with all the fixin's) Fundraiser for *Pioneer-Engine Co. #1* (**Norbury Hall, Center St.**)

The Blueberry Festival — 9:00 AM to 4:00 PM
"Command Center" for information and assistance is at the **Chamber** Booth at *Lighthouse Deli* on **Canal St.** Official Commemorative Festival Shirts available here.

Shawangunk Mountain Wild Blueberry & Huckleberry Festival Cultural Area Venue–
(*located behind* **Town Hall** / M&T Bank *with access from* **Canal and Liberty Streets** – *follow the signs*)

☼ *Catskill Native Nursery* – native plant sale
☼ Historian/Naturalist Marc Fried – author of *The Huckleberry Pickers, Shawangunk Place Names,* tales, book sales, and signing.
☼ *Rusty Plough Farm* – local grower of wild blueberries
☼ *Rondout Valley Growers* – cooking demonstation
☼ Photo-op at "Blueberry Shack" – Bring your camera

☞ *Shawangunk Mountain Exhibits:*
☼ *Sam's Point Preserve*
☼ *Minnewaska State Park*
☼ *Friends of the Shawangunks*
☼ *Cragsmoor Historical Society*
☼ *NY-NJ Trail Conference*
☼ *Shawangunk Mountains Scenic Byway*
☼ Sierra Club
☼ Hudson River Sloop "Clearwater"
☼ *D & H Canal Heritage Corridor Alliance*
☼ *D & H Historical Society*
☼ *Catskill Center for Conservation and Preservation*
☼ Catskill Watershed Corp.
☼ Hudson Valley Raptors – Birds of Prey
☼ *Ellenville Public Library & Museum*
☼ *Cragsmoor Free Library*

☞ *Music and entertainment in the cultural area:*

10:00 to 10:30 AM and 1:00 to 1:30 PM
    Folk Musician *Bob Lusk*
11:00 to 11:30 AM and 2:00 to 2:30 PM
    Bob Lusk and *Marc Fried* perform together
3:00 PM *Dance Emporium* students – Tap Dancing

☞ *All-Blueberry Bake Sale* – **from 9:00 AM** until they're gone… Come early so you don't miss out… scrumptious homemade goodies including blueberry pies from *Cohen's Bakery* and *Saunderskill Farms,* blueberry tarts from Maury Rubin's City Bakery (author of *The Book of Tarts*), cake from Mohonk Mountain House.

☞ *Walking Tour of* Maple Avenue – **10:00 AM**
Irwin Rosenthal – narration about historic homes and area. Tour assembles in the cultural area.

☞ *Blueberry Pie Judging for the Best Pie* – 12 Noon
Prizes awarded by *Cohen's Bakery* and *Wilson's Market* (Entries Accepted Until 11:00 AM)

Free Off-Street Parking: Follow signs
Ellenville Central School, **Maple Avenue**
Top Shelf Jewelers, **Canal St.** East *(toward Shawangunks)*
Optimum Window, **Canal St.** West *(toward Catskills)*
UCAT (Ulster County Area Transportation) will be providing a shuttle bus for the Festival.

Canal & Market Streets, Liberty Square Venue –

☞ *Street Fair* – Artisans, craftspersons, and vendors of general merchandise, including handmade items, puppets, ceramics, woodworking, needlework, jewelry, collectibles, stained glass, dolls, plastercraft, T-shirts, leather goods, skin care, soaps, florals, trading cards, and more. *Many local churches and organizations use this festival for community awareness of their services as fund-raisers for their organizations.*

☞ *Art at the Festival*
(**Hunt Memorial Building**)
A one-day Art Exhibition and sale of works (paintings, sculpture, mixed media) by artists of the Cragsmoor art community. Percentage of sales help pay festival costs.

☞ *Fun at the Festival*
(*Children's Entertainment Area located in the municipal parking lot after* **Canal & Liberty** *intersection*)
Scooby Doo Bounce, Castle Maze, *Kimble Hose* children's games of skill and "chance," *Youth Commission* putting contest, face painting, photo ops at the castle, fairy wands & crowns, sand art, and more.

☞ *Dunking Booth Fundraiser*
Our community says Thank You! Proceeds to our "Miracle Marine" Cpl. Eddie Ryan, who was severely wounded on April 12, 2005, while serving in Iraq, now recovering in the USA.

☞ *Main Stage Music* – Free all-day entertainment
(**Hunt Memorial Building, Liberty Square**)
9:00 to 10:00 AM
    Graham Vest – blues & folk acoustic guitars
10:00 to 11:00 AM
    Amy Laber – voice and acoustic guitar
11:00 AM to 1:00 PM
    Carl Richards Band – country, blues, rock
1:00 PM to 2:00 PM
    The Outpatients – blues-based quartet
2:00 PM to 4:00 PM
    Prof. "Louie" & The Crowmatix – blues music, rompin' rock & roll, and down home country

☞ *Chamber Fundraisers* (toward *Festival* expenses)
(Main Stage)
50/50 Drawings: **Noon and 3:30 PM**
Everything-Blueberry Basket: **3:30 PM**

☞ *Cruise-In Classic Car Show*
(**Canal** toward **Yankee Place**)

☞ *Good Food!*
(throughout the *Festival*)
Blueberry ice-cream, baked goods, jams & jellies, *CYM* Perogies, and it's not all blueberry!! *AAMA* BBQ Chicken & Ribs, *UMC* Sausage & Peppers, **Chamber** Dogs, Pretzels, *Christ Ministries* fabulous fish sandwiches, and more.

☞ *Health Fair* (*Wawarsing Council of Community Agencies*)
(**Market Street**)
Free health screening & information on services and health care. Prizes, balloons. County and regional organizations participating.

☞ *Post-Festival Theatre Performance* – **8:00 PM**
The Devils Music – The Life and Blues of Bessie Smith, Shadowland Theatre, **Canal St.** (647-5511 for info.)

WHAT'S IN A NAME?

Shawangunk -- what a strange word that is!! The following explanation is from the Cragsmoor Journal, Volume X, Number 4 of Ausust 15, 1912.

"Shawangunk Mountains: From "Shawan" meaning white in the Mohican and Lenape (Delaware) speech, and "gunk", a large rock or mass of rocks. Said to have been applied to a precipice of white rocks of the mill-stone kind near the top of these mountains and facing the east. So writes Horatio Gates Spafford in A Gazetteer of the State of New York, Published in Albany in 1813, except that he derives the words from Mohegan. The Mohegans and Mohicans were both Algonquin tribes, the first living in Connecticut and the second along the Hudson where on the west bank they mingled more or less with the Minisinks (Munsees), also an Algonquin tribe with a similar speech. The Minisinks were Lenni-Lenape or Delaware Indians. They ranged here, and doubtless the cliffs of Mt. Lenape, of which Sam's Point is the southern extremity, are the precipice referred to by Spafford in his Gazetteer. The pronunciation now in vogue, namely Shongum, is merely a lazy corruption of Shawangunk."

SAM, THE MAN

Stories of Sam Gonzalus, hunter, trapper and Indian scout have been perpetuated since 1758, during which time Sam had gone out to check on his traps in an area where the terrain was very rugged. The local Indians hated Sam to the point of wanting him dead. The reason being that they felt that he was encroaching upon their hunting grounds and therefore a threat to them.

Since Sam knew these mountainous woods and cliffs so very well, he was aware of an area where there was soft underbrush not far below a certain precipice. One day he was quite mindful of the Indians being in hot pursuit and so he headed toward that very place where he took his legendary leap. Of course, he fell into the treetops which cushioned his fall. Therefore, he landed safely and survived that ordeal.

Naturally, the Indians assumed that Sam died in the fall and they dismissed him from their minds forever and ever.

It is believed that Sam continued his hunting, trapping and scouting until he was a very old man. Question -- Was he never seen again, ever??

This then is the story which has given Sam's Point its name. This landmark offers breath-taking and magnificent views at 2000 feet above sea level.

Note: This, in part, was taken from Katherine T. Terwilliger's book Wawarsing, Where The Streams Wind, pages 9 and 10.

Issue #9   2003 August

Wawarsing.Net

Published by the Ellenville-Wawarsing Chamber of Commerce
Also Online at www.Wawarsing.Net

Blueberry Festival Special!

Cover: Sam's Point, Shawangunk Mts., Town of Wawarsing, Ulster County, New York, USA. Adapted from an early 20th Century postcard. Join us in celebrating the Mountain and the Wild Blueberries (Huckleberries) that grow there! This **Blueberry Festival Special Issue** features the Saturday, August 23rd **Shawangunk Mountain Wild Blueberry & Huckleberry Harvest Festival** in the heart of Ellenville, plus all things Blueberry!

15

Geologic Overview of the Shawangunk Ridge and Surrounding Area
Saturday, June 5th, 10:00 AM – 4:00 PM

Overview: From the formation of the rocks of the Hudson Highlands over a billion years ago to the deglaciation of the Hudson Valley a few thousand years ago, eastern New York State has a long and interesting geologic history. *Ulster County Community College* geologist Steven Schimmrich will examine the geologic features of the *Sam's Point Preserve* and discuss how the **Shawangunk Ridge** fits into the geologic evolution of the surrounding Hudson Valley. This loop hike will start and end at the Preserve parking lot and travel to **Sam's Point**, **Verkeerderkill Falls**, **High Point**, and **Indian Rock** with plenty of stops to discuss what is seen along the way. Terrain: difficult.

For all hikes, please come prepared: bring water, sunscreen, bug spray, sturdy, comfortable footwear and a bag lunch for hikes over three hours. Unless otherwise specified, hikes are approximately 2 hours and are limited to 15 people.

Meet Location: Sam's Point parking lot, *Sam's Point Preserve*, Cragsmoor. Registration: Call 647-3123.

Great Sky Spectacles
Friday, June 11th, (Rain date: June 12), 7:30 PM

Overview: The rare headline-making Venus transit is now over, but fabulous sky spectacles are in store for us during 2004 and 2005. We'll look at the upcoming eclipses, unusually rich meteor showers, and extremely rare planet events that require no knowledge of the constellations. Then, as night deepens, Mid-Hudson Astronomy Association members will set up large telescopes to explore the gaseous surface of Jupiter as well as June's deep-space wonders.

Bob Berman is an editor of both Astronomy magazine and the Old Farmers Almanac, and is the astronomy columnist of Discover Magazine. He is author of three books, has a weekly show on Public Radio, and is adjunct professor of astronomy at Marymount College.

Meet Location: *Sam's Point Preserve*, Cragsmoor. Registration: Call 647-3123.

Dragonfly Display
Saturday, June 12th, (Rain date: June 19), 10:00 AM– 12:00 noon

Overview: Did you ever see dragonflies traveling together in the "wheel position"? Join Karen Strong of DEC's Hudson River Estuary Program for a walk to Lake Maratanza. Learn about dragonfly biology and conservation on a leisurely stroll to dragonfly habitat. Terrain: easy.

For all hikes, please come prepared: bring water, sunscreen, bug spray, sturdy, comfortable footwear and a bag lunch for hikes over three hours. Unless otherwise specified, hikes are limited to 15 people.

Meet Location: Sam's Point parking lot, *Sam's Point Preserve*, Cragsmoor. Registration: Call 647-3123.

16

Sam's Point Preserve is a unique natural resource owned by the Open Space Institute and managed by The Nature Conservancy

Summer 2004 · Volume 1 · Issue 1

Pitch Pine Press

News from Sam's Point Preserve

Our Mission

The mission of Sam's Point Preserve is to use a science driven approach to protect:

- the biological diversity of the landscape, along with
- the wilderness character and spiritual quality it embodies, and
- the record of the relationship between these resources and human beings.

Letter From the Director

It is an exciting time at Sam's Point Preserve, as we watch more than three years of planning and drawings become the reality of a new conservation center. The center will provide a much-needed place to inform people about the Preserve and its unique features, as well as serving as a base for our land management activities. As the building takes shape, its character and style are being expressed, and it will be a wonderful compliment to the setting at Sam's Point.

The project has benefited tremendously from the input of our partner organizations along the ridge, our steadfast advisory committee and the many people who attended our planning charrettes for the building and exhibits that are planned. We are continuing to fundraise for the project, and are coming closer to our goals of both for our capital campaign and the endowment for the Preserve, which total $2.7 million.

With a full slate of public programs, two new Student Conservation Association interns, volunteer workdays and the activity of construction and restoration it will be a high energy summer at Sam's Point Preserve. We hope you will come, see the progress on the center yourself, and head for the ever-peaceful and inspiring places at Sam's Point.

Cara Lee, Director of the Shawangunk Ridge Program, standing amidst the dwarf pitch pines

The Sam's Point Conservation Center taking shape

Letter From the Manager

Welcome to our first edition of the *Pitch Pine Press*. We hope this newsletter will help to keep our supporters and volunteers better informed of all the activities, programs and projects at Sam's Point.

As we reflect on the last three years, we cannot help but be pleased with all that has been accomplished towards achieving the goals outlined in the *Sam's Point Preserve Master Plan*.

In February of 1999, the Sam's Point Advisory Council was formed to assist in preparation of this plan. The council helped to identify and analyze issues facing the preserve and devise management strategies to address these issues.

Through the tireless commitment and advice of the Sam's Point Advisory Council and countless hours contributed by our volunteers and interns we have made great progress in the areas of ecological management and research, fire management, public use management, and education and public outreach.

Sam's Point Preserve represents one of the most unique places on Earth. Its long-term health and protection depends on your continued support.

Heidi Wagner, Manager

Update on the New Conservation Center

The Nature Conservancy®

EASTERN NEW YORK
CHAPTER
Saving the Last Great Places

Interpretive Design and Planning
Yarabbe Associates
Donald Watson, FAIA

Architect:
Matthew Bialecki Associates
Matthew Bialecki AIA

Landscape Architect:
Hudson & Pacific Designs, Inc.
Stefan Yarabek, ASLA

Civil Engineering and Land Surveying:
Medenbach and Eggers, P.C.
Barry Medenbach, P.E.

Construction Well Underway

The Sam's Point Conservation Center is now taking shape and an October, 2004 completion date is anticipated.

The Center is an approximately 3,000 sq. ft. multi-purpose building providing interpretive/ educational spaces, staff offices and visitor facilities.

Designed by Matthew Bialecki, AIA, the building has been designed as a sustainable, green building following the standards of the National Green Building Council LEED building rating system. All of the architectural design, site planning, materials and building systems have been carefully selected to illustrate practical, affordable applications of state-of-the-art sustainable building practices.

The building is constructed of "gunk-crete", a specially formulated concrete and quartzite aggregate mix that evokes the naturally occurring Shawangunk conglomerate. The roof structure consists of heavy timber beams with a wood ceiling. Walls are primarily glass and cement, providing dramatic views of Sam's Point.

The building will be heated with a radiant heating system installed in the floor and is almost entirely passively cooled. The roof system naturally dissipates hot summer heat before it is absorbed into the building.

The landscaping, designed by Stefan Yarabek, ASLA, restores much of the former parking lot to a natural landscape by introducing native plants, limiting hardscape surfaces and incorporating a "bio-swale" to treat storm water run-off.

Interpretive Exhibits Developed

The interpretive displays and educational installations have been designed by Donald Watson, FAIA. A spectacular 40 foot mural representing the natural communities, plant and animal species, and geology of Sam's Point is being developed by artist Linda Thomas.

Other exhibits include a contour model of the Preserve, displays of fire ecology and cultural history, maps, and a series of "discovery" drawers. These educational exhibits will work to explain to the visitor the rare and unique environment of Sam's Point.

"Gunk-crete" planks begin to be assembled and stacked to create the walls of the Conservation Center under the direction of architect, Matthew Bialecki.

Huckleberry Pickers Oral History Project

The Nature Conservancy staff, assisted by students from Marist College and other volunteers, will be collecting oral histories of huckleberry pickers and their families and combining these histories with photographs and artifacts to create a high quality exhibit for the new Conservation Center.

The Nature Conservancy has received $10,000 grant from the office of New York State Senator John Bonacic in support of the project. In addition to Sam's Point's extraordinary ecological significance, the preserve has a rich and varied

Huckleberry Pickers at Sam's Point

cultural history. Beginning in the mid 1800's and aided by the expansion of the railroads, a market developed for the huckleberries that still grow in great quantities along the ridge. Initially a family activity, gathering huckleberries soon developed into a thriving business. Semi-

permanent encampments and lively summer communities developed in the vicinity of Sam's Point. The ruins of these encampments still remain as well as several photographs, providing valuable information about this vanished regional agriculture.

The oral history project was announced on April 3rd at a get-together at the Ellenville Public Library. Former huckleberry pickers and their families shared stories about their summers "on the mountain".

A videographer has been selected to consult and complete final editing of the video.

Child wearing berry box and tin cup for berry picking

The staff at Sam's Point want to learn all they can about the huckleberry pickers. If you have any information to contribute please contact the Preserve Manager at (845) 647-3123.

Fire on the Mountain

Fire on the Mountain   by Frederick Dellenbaugh

Although there hasn't been a fire at Sam's Point in over 50 years, a lot of work is underway regarding fire management.

Specifically, The Nature Conservancy through the Shawangunk Ridge Biodiversity Partnership is developing a ridge-wide fire management plan. TNC, the DEC and the Cragsmoor Volunteer Fire Company are currently working to complete a pre-incident wildfire plan for Sam's Point.

"Firewise" is being introduced as a pilot program in the Hamlet of

Cragsmoor. Firewise Communities/USA is a federally-funded program that informs homeowners about ways to protect their homes from a wildfire before it occurs.

You may ask, why all this concern about fire? Scientists estimate that fire historically swept through the Gunks as frequently as every 5 to 25 years. Fires burn off organic material that has accumulated over the years, thus enriching the soil with nutrient-rich ash. Many of the plants on the ridge have adapted to periodic fire. Pitch pines have the ability to resprout from their main trunk and branches. Plants such as huckleberry, sheep laurel and mountain laurel all produce leaves that contain waxy resin that serves as fuel when a fire occurs. The huckleberry pickers periodically set fire to the berry

bushes to promote growth.

Fire suppression, although necessary to protect life and property, and the lack of fire have resulted in an accumulation of wildland fuels. These conditions may lead to wildfires of devastating intensity that may threaten property, be difficult to control and could actually threaten the natural resources our organizations are trying to protect.

In an effort to reestablish a more natural fire regime, The Shawangunk Ridge Biodiversity Partnership and The Nature Conservancy are planning to use fire in a controlled way to restore the dwarf pitch pines. Working with the DEC, TNC has been conducting controlled burns in the Albany Pine Bush since 1991. Plans for demonstration burns at Sam's Point are now being prepared by a team of fire experts.

Ignition: A member of a burn crew carefully applies fire along a fire break through the use of a drip torch.

"Living with fire is not always hell," says Stephanie Gifford, Director of Ecological Management for The Nature Conservancy, "just ask the numerous species of plants that live in places like the Gunks."

"Applying controlled burns takes planning. First a detailed prescription is produced and approved, then areas are prepared for burning. Then we wait for the right weather and conditions. Only then do we carefully guide fire across the ground."

Hikes and Activities

Jack Fagan

Photo by Rick Levine
Rock scrambling in the Shingle Gully/Ellenville Ice Caves

Please call Heidi Wagner at (845) 647-3123 to register for all hikes and activities. Hikes will occur rain or shine unless notified.

Friday, June11
(Rain date: Sat., June 12)
7:30 PM
Great Sky Spectacles with Bob Berman: The rare headline-making Venus transit is now over, but fabulous sky spectacles are in store for us during 2004 and 2005. We'll look at the upcoming eclipse, unusually rich meteor showers, and extremely rare planet events that require no knowledge of the constellations. Then, as night deepens, Mid-Hudson Astronomy Association members will set up large telescopes to explore the gaseous surface of Jupiter as well as June's deep-space wonders. Meet at the visitor center.

Saturday, June 12
(Rain date: Sat., June19)
10:00AM-12:00 noon

Dragonfly Display: Did you ever see dragonflies traveling together in the "wheel position"? Join Karen Strong of DEC's Hudson River Estuary Program for a walk to Lake Maratanza. Learn about dragon fly biology and conservation on a leisurely stroll to dragonfly habitat. Meet at the parking lot. **Easy.**

Saturday, July 10
9:30 AM-4:00 PM
Orienteering Program: Concerned about finding yourself lost in the woods? Learn map and compass skills with NY State Forest Ranger Rob Mecus. The day will begin in the classroom and then it's out to the field to put your new skills to the test! Bring lunch and water. Meet at the visitor center.

Sunday, July 18
9:30 AM-3:30 PM
Ellenville Ice Caves: Visit the

Visitors wishing to hike in this area must obtain a permit from TNC due the ecological sensitivity of the caves. Groups are limited to 12. Please call Heidi Wagner at (845) 647-3123.

unique terrain and natural communities of Shingle Gully with Rick Levine and Franz Rucker. Begin the hike as a slow steady climb before scrambling up 1000 feet to explore the Grand Canyon and the Labyrinth. Snowballs guaranteed! Pack a flashlight, gloves and warm clothing for a serious temperature drop. Wear long pants and bring along a lunch. Meet at Berme Road in Ellenville.

Celebrate Preserve Day!
TNC's Eastern New York Chapter is celebrating 50 years of conservation success on Preserve Day on October 2nd. Sam's Point will be hosting the following hikes:
Plant Adaptation at Sam's Point: Explore the Ice Caves with ecologist Spider Barbour and learn how plant species have adapted to the harsh environmental conditions at Sam's Point. 9:15 AM
Geologic Overview of the Shawangunk Ridge: Geologist Steve Schimmrich will examine the geological features of the Preserve and discuss how the Ridge fits into the geologic evolution of the surrounding Hudson Valley. 10 AM

Volunteer Opportunities

"Handyman Special"
Do you enjoy working with tools? The staff at Sam's Point need volunteers to help restore the huckleberry shack pictured above. Let us know if you would like to help.

Please call Heidi Wagner at (845) 647-3123 if you would like to participate in any of the following volunteer opportunities:

Sam's Point Volunteer Patrol: Volunteers patrollers provide an official presence within our trail system by informing visitors about Preserve policies and reporting observations to our staff. A great way to exercise and volunteer for Sam's Point at the same time!

Boundary Posting: We need volunteers to assist our interns in posting the Preserve boundaries. Accessing remote areas may be difficult and strenuous at times.

Restoration of Huckleberry Picker's Shack: As part of our cultural history exhibit we plan to restore a huckleberry shack along the Loop Road. We are looking for individuals skilled in carpentry and construction to participate in this exciting project.

Habitat Restoration: With the new Conservation Center nearing completion, site restoration will soon be underway. Rescued plants from the construction site and plants propagated from seeds gathered at Sam's Point will need to be planted. Help restore the Preserve entrance to a natural landscape.

Visitor Center: Assist our staff at the visitor center on weekends. Orient visitors to the Preserve and help with items for sale.

Shawangunk Ridge Biodiversity Partnership

The Shawangunk Ridge Biodiversity Partnership is a science-based consortium of landowners and managers along the ridge. Formed in 1994, the Partnership adopted the following vision:

"The Shawangunk Ridge Biodiversity Partnership will work together and with other interested organizations to maintain and, where necessary, restore natural communities and native species of the Shawangunk Mountains and the ecological processes on which they depend."

Through field research and scientific analysis, the Partnership has collected extensive information on the natural communities and rare species of the Northern Shawangunks. This information has made it possible to design biodiversity protection and management programs for the Shawangunks.

Conservation "targets" have been identified which include the dwarf pitch pine barrens, the chestnut oak forest, and cliff and talus. Threats to these natural communities, such as fire suppression, recreational use

and encroaching development have also been analyzed.

In January, 2003 the Biodiversity Partnership adopted the *Protection and Management Guidelines for the Shawangunk Mountains: Vision, Goals, Strategies and Actions for Conservation of the Shawangunk Mountains.* These guidelines were developed to effectively address these threats.

The Partnership is now implementing these actions, providing environmental education, and working with local communities to preserve open space on the slopes of the ridge.

The Partners:
Cragsmoor Association
Friends of the Shawangunks
Mohonk Preserve
The Nature Conservancy
New York Natural Heritage Program
NY State DEC's Division of Fish and Wildlife
New York State Museum
Open Space Institute
Palisades Interstate Park Commission and New York State Office of Parks, Recreation, And Historic Preservation

Meet Our New Interns

Sam's Point welcomes two new interns to our staff, filling five month Student Conservation Association (SCA) positions. Their work will encompass a variety of projects such as boundary posting, planting rescued plants from the construction site, and developing a nature trail in the vicinity of the old miniature golf area.

Danielle Dyer earned her degree in Wildlife Conservation from Unity College. She is interested in sharing her knowledge with others and informing people about the importance of conservation, especially in heavily impacted areas. Her goal is to someday teach high school Biology and Ecology.

Alisha Shumaker is a graduate of the Institute of Environmental Sciences program at Miami University in Ohio. She has experience in environmental studies of water resources and the application of GIS. Her studies have led her to Belize, Central America to study the ecological effects of logging on wildlife in a tropical rainforest.

Danielle Dyer (left) and Alisha Shumaker (right) are serving five month positions as Student Conservation Association interns at Sam's Point.

New Group Visit Policies Adopted

With stunning views, easy access from many metropolitan areas and an extensive trail system, Sam's Point Preserve is experiencing increased recreational use by camps and school groups.

To provide environmentally friendly recreational opportunities for citizens and

children of the region, TNC and OSI have adopted new policies regarding group visits.

Twelve or more visitors is considered a group. Groups cannot exceed 66 visitors. There must be one adult for every 10 children between 6 and 16 years old. Children under six require one adult for every six children.

The visiting organization must make a reservation, and provide the Preserve with a certificate of liability insurance, and a parking fee prior to the visit.

To schedule a group visit please contact the Preserve Manager, Heidi Wagner, at (845) 647-3123.

How to have a safe and respectful group visit :

- Bring along ample drinking water. Water found along the trails is not drinkable.
- Stay on designated trails.
- Pack a cell phone and first aid kit for emergencies.
- Fires and barbeques are not permitted due to the threat of wildfire.
- Swimming at Lake Maratanza is prohibited.
- Littering is strictly forbidden.

Summer 2004   Volume 1   Issue 1

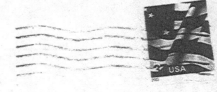

Sam's Point Preserve
PO Box 86
Cragsmoor, NY 12420
(845) 647-7989

Sam's Point Contacts

Preserve Manager:
Heidi Wagner, (845) 647-3123, E-mail: hwagner@tnc.org

Shawangunk Ridge Program of The Nature Conservancy:
Cara Lee, Director, 108 Main Street, New Paltz, NY 12561
(845) 255-9051, E-mail: clee@tnc.org

Open Space Institute:
Paul Elconin, Land Steward, (914) 276-2618.
E-mail: pastaelco@optonline.net

Sam's Point Advisory Council

The staff wishes to thank the volunteer members of SPAC for their continued support and advice.

Paul Elconin, Open Space Institute
Bob Anderberg, Open Space Institute
Hank Alicandri, Mohonk Preserve
Irwin Rosenthal, Village of Ellenville
Elliott Auerbach, Village of Ellenville
Paula Medley, The Cragsmoor Association
Rob Segal, NY/NJ Trail Conference
Thomas Cobb, Minnewaska State Park and Preserve
Jack Grifo, Hamlet of Cragsmoor
Wendy Harris, Register of Professional Archaeologists
Maureen Radl, Friends of the Shawangunks
Liana Hoodes, Town of Shawangunk

Mr. Harold Clark
4460 Grumm Road
Hamburg, NJ 07419

Sam's Point Preserve is owned by the Open Space Institute and managed by The Nature Conservancy.

Highlight on the Dwarf Pitch Pine

Jack Fagan

Pitch Pine was once a source of resin. Colonists produced turpentine and tar used for axle grease from this species. Pine knots were fastened to poles and used as torches at night. This high resin content of the dwarf pitch pine and the understory of huckleberry, low-bush blueberry and sheep laurel help to carry a fire along when it occurs at Sam's Point.

One of the few examples of the ridgetop dwarf pitch pine barrens in the world are found in the Northern Shawawngunks, with the greatest concentration existing at Sam's Point Preserve.

Pitch pines (*Pinus rigida*) are a slow growing type of evergreen tree adapted for extremely harsh growing conditions. Many pitch pines are between 200-300 years old and stand only 5 feet tall.

The size of pitch pines are limited by several factors including: genetics, soil, and environmental conditions such as wind, elevation and fire.

Pitch pines can grow on layers of soil as thin as a few centimeters by utilizing a broad root net that expands outward and takes advantage of vertical cracks in the rock.

Well adapted for fire, pitch pines have extremely thick bark, quick sprouting root systems, and needles able to sprout directly from the tree trunk.

Pitch pine are wind pollinated in May and produce two types of cones; *serotinous* cones which open only after being exposed to heat and *non-serotinous* cones which open spontaneously during the winter or spring following cone maturation. Cone serotiny is thought to be an adaptation to fire, giving serotinous pitch pines a better chance of survival when subjected to repeated burns. Research will soon be conducted to determine the level of cone serotiny at Sam's Point.

Courtesy of Hatti Langsford, Interpreter, Minnewaska State Park and Preserve

Issue #30   2005 May

Wawarsing.Net

Cover: New Sam's Point Conservation Center, Cragsmoor, Town of Wawarsing, Ulster County, New York, USA. Earth. The new eco-friendly site officially opens May 22nd but you can get a peek, starting on page 16. Then, read about the "Gunks" and what makes them so special, in Marion Dumond's feature article on page 18. Then join us at 1 PM May 22nd.

Published by the
Ellenville-Wawarsing
Chamber of Commerce
Also Online at
www.Wawarsing.Net

Open For Business

New Conservation Center to Open at Sam's Point Preserve

The Nature Conservancy and the Open Space Institute, Inc. have scheduled the opening of the **Sam's Point Conservation Center** at *Sam's Point Preserve* in Cragsmoor for May 22nd. The 3,000 square-foot building *(cover, and photo, right)* is a model of "green" building practices, and was designed by nationally-recognized architect Matthew Bialecki, AIA, to complement and reflect the dramatic setting at **Sam's Point**.

The Center, a project of The Nature Conservancy, will serve as a base for scientific research, land stewardship and education, and houses exhibits focusing on the unique geological, ecological, and cultural features of the *Preserve*.

"It tries to emulate the character of Sam's Point," says local architect Matthew Bialecki, who kept the preserve's geology, ecology, and botany in mind when designing the building. "It's a landscape with a roof on it," he adds. The center's design, which meets the standards of the National Green Building Council, was constructed using local, sustainable wood and has a passive solar design (meaning it regulates its own temperature with only a minimal amount of extra heat needed). The wallboard is made from recyclable materials and the insulation consists of cotton scraps from blue jeans.

Constructed of "Gunk-crete" – a locally-manufactured cement product that is a specially-formulated concrete and quartzite aggregate similar to the local Shawangunk conglomerate, evoking the bedrock of the **Shawangunks** – and sustainably-harvested hemlock timbers *(photo, right)*, the building is sheltered by a recycled steel roof, a unique "Umbrella Roof," named for its inherent shading qualities and designed to dissipate summer heat through a layered system of high-performance insulation with a radiant barrier under recycled metal roof panels. In combination, the special features of the building result in a 50% increase in energy-efficiency.

The Center demonstrates practical applications of energy-efficient, state-of-the-art sustainable building practices and passive solar design that will provide maximum comfort to *Preserve* visitors. The earth-bermed building was designed as an extension of the landscape; flooring, timbers, structural framing and lighting pass seamlessly from interior to exterior, dissolving the normal boundaries between the site and the structure.

For the outer walls, Bialecki tried to recreate the coarse white stones from the **Ridge** located above the center. Thus, the "Gunk-crete" that closely resembles the

Shawangunk conglomerate. A glass wall, outlined by long wooden beams, frames the towering ridge and leads visitors outside to the preserve's trails. "The overall intention of the center is to provide not only support for the land conservancy commission, but to also be an educational facility – an interpretive facility," explains Bialecki. *(photo of model of site, next page, top left)*

The landscaping, designed by Stefan Yarabek, ASLA, includes restoration of damaged areas, improved parking and signage, and features native plants collected at the *Preserve* by interns and volunteers.

A forty-foot mural on the back wall by noted artist Linda Thomas depicts the distinctive habitats of the *Preserve*, featuring the globally-rare ridgetop dwarf pine barrens and ice caves environs located at the *Preserve*. Visitors of all ages will delight in finding more than 90 species of plants, birds, mammals, and insects native to the *Preserve* within the expanse of the mural. A computer will make the mural interactive, helping visitors discover what may not be visible during a daylong visit. Displays featuring photos, stories, and activities that explain the geology and history of the area will also be on view.

According to Cara Lee, Director of the Conservancy's *Shawangunk Ridge Program*, "The new **Conservation Center** is designed to inspire and inform visitors about the extraordinary beauty and special ecology of **Sam's Point**." She added "**The Center** will welcome school groups, volunteers, hikers, and others who come to the *Preserve*, providing a place of discovery for all who visit." Further, "the building is in keeping with the historical and artistic element" of the area, which was an early art colony. The new **Center** replaces the old visitors' center *(photo, left)* which has been razed.

Lee explains that, although recycled materials often cost more than their counterparts, their benefits increase over time: "We feel like [the extra costs] are worth it in terms of what they're doing to educate the public, and in terms of how they're contributing to the environment."

The Open Space Conservancy, the land acquisition affiliate of the Open Space Institute (OSI), acquired the ⟋

Sam's Point Preserve in a series of transactions that culminated in 1997. According to OSI's president, Joe Martens, the two highest summits in the entire 245-mile **Shawangunk Range** are located at the *Sam's Point Preserve*.

The preserve is managed by The Nature Conservancy. In addition to developing the ***Conservation Center,*** The Conservancy provides public hikes, manages hunting on the *Preserve* and works with a corps of more than 60 local volunteers on trail maintenance and other aspects of stewardship. "Our conservation partnership has resulted in **Sam's Point** being managed both for recreation and protection, and the ***Conservation Center*** will provide a wonderful opportunity for people to gain better appreciation for the **Shawangunks**," said Martens. *(photo below, of tourists at Ice Caves entrance, about 100 years ago.)*

The **Northern Shawangunks** are widely-recognized as one of the most important sites for biodiversity conservation in the northeastern United States. The **Ridge** supports more than 35 natural communities, with five that are globally-rare. *Sam's Point Preserve* is home to the world's best example of a dwarf pine ridge community, where more than 30 rare plant and animal species can be found, leading The Nature Conservancy to designate the **Ridge** as one of Earth's "Last Great Places" for landscape-level biodiversity conservation.

"This new center will help people who visit the **Shawangunks** better understand this distinctive and fragile ecosystem and the importance of protecting it," said Carol Ash, Executive Director of the Palisades Interstate Park Commission, and manager of the neighboring *Minnewaska State Park Preserve.*

Funds for the project are from public and private sources, with a substantial grant from the Clean Water/ Clean Air Bond Act.

Sam's Point Preserve is open year round. For information on programs, call the *Preserve* at **845-647-7989**.

For more information on The Nature Conservancy and the work being done by the Eastern New York Chapter on the **Shawangunk Ridge** and beyond, please contact Sharon Pickett at **914-244-3271 ext. 27**, and visit the Nature Conservancy's web site at **www.nature.org**.

The Nature Conservancy is a leading international, nonprofit organization that preserves plants, animals and natural communities representing the diversity of life on Earth by protecting the lands and waters they need to survive. To date, the Conservancy and its more than one million members have been responsible for the protection of more than 14 million acres in the United States and have helped preserve more than 83 million acres in Latin America, the Caribbean, Asia and the Pacific.

Founded in 1963, the Open Space Institute, Inc. (**www.osiny.org**) is a nonprofit land conservation organization that has protected more than 18,000 acres in the **Shawangunks** and 90,000 acres throughout New York.

Through its Northern Forest Protection Fund, OSI has assisted in the protection of close to 600,000 acres in NY, Vermont, New Hampshire and Maine. OSI recently launched its New Jersey Conservation Loan Program to protect threatened landscapes in New Jersey.

Log on to **www.osiny.org** for more information about the *Sam's Point Preserve* and the *Open Space Institute Shawangunk Ridge Land Protection Program.*

25

Forward, into the Past

Shawangunk Mountain Treasures and Pleasures

by **Marion M. Dumond**
*Former Town of Wawarsing Historian
& Ellenville Public Library Director (Retired)*

Climbers call them the "Gunks," public relations types for area hotels mistakenly refer to them as part of the **Catskill Mountains**, visitors and area residents mispronounce their name more often than not, but the **Shawangunk Mountains** (pronounced "Shon-gum", an Indian word believed to mean "white rocks") are reputed to have stood for 450 million years. They are part of a ridge system 100 million years older than the **Catskills**.

According to The Nature Conservancy, the **Ridge** is characterized by shallow, acidic soils, hospitable to only the hardiest of plants. The distinctive cliffs and boulders are formed of white conglomerate – sedimentary rock consisting of rounded fragments (often quartz) cemented together. Shale underlies the entire **Ridge**, noticeable in quarries and roadways. It is a good source of fossils.

Translated into very simple terms for the non-geologist, the ice caves *(photo, right, from approx. 100 years ago)* were formed after layers of shale and quartz were molded from mud and sand pebbles millions of years ago. The soft shale underlay gave way for the heavy weight of brittle quartz, which eventually caused the cracks and crevices of the ice caves. Local geologists will find copies of far more scientific studies in the files of the *Ellenville Public Library & Museum.*

Geologist David Howell of the U.S. Geological Survey, who grew up in Cragsmoor, described the caves as being formed of Shawangunk conglomerate, millions of years old, a kind of quartz that is very acidic and low in calcium. The lack of nutrients, thin soil over bedrock and harsh climate contribute to the dwarfing of pine trees, creating another unique feature of the **Shawangunks**. The *Sam's Point Preserve* contains some 2,000 acres of dwarf pine barrens, part of the rare ecosystem that includes the ice caves. "The dwarf pines grow nowhere else in the world at this elevation," said Cara Lee, **Shawangunk Ridge** Program Director of The Nature Conservancy.

For centuries, Native Americans farmed the fertile valleys and hunted the **Ridge**. In the seventeenth century, European settlers developed the area along the **Ridge**, building stone houses and clearing valley fields for agriculture.

The combination of farming and intensive tree harvesting by charcoal burners, hoop makers, and tanners cleared much of the **Ridge** forest by the 19th century. In

that century, the beauty of the powerful landscape drew artists like Edward Lamson Henry, Charles C. Curran, and George Inness, Jr., to make the artist colony in Cragsmoor their summer home.

Until the middle of the twentieth century, huckleberry picking was an important summer occupation. *(See Wawarsing.Net #21, August 2004, pages 20-21)*

Today, over 600,000 rock climbers, naturalists, hikers, cross-country skiers, and other visitors travel to the **Ridge** each year to enjoy the spectacular landscape and history of the region.

Ellenville has its own unique part of the **Shawangunks**, called the **Ellenville Fault-Ice Caves**, which was designated a National Landmark in 1967 *(photo, above, Mayor Eugene Glusker, right, introduces Robert Rose)*. Although owned by the Village of Ellenville for almost 100 years, the **Ice Caves** are actually in Cragsmoor. National Park Service Chief Geologist Robert H. Rose, speaking at official ceremonies designating **Ice Caves Mountain** a Registered National Natural Landmark on September 28, 1968, said, "This very narrow belt of

26

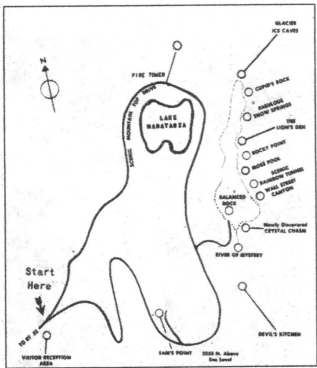

that the particular cave system described is an especially ecologically-sensitive area and the number of visitors is tightly monitored.

When the **Ice Caves** are mentioned, nearby **Sam's Point** and the legend concerning its name frequently become part of the conversation. Sam Gonzales (sometimes spelled "Gonsalus") was a trailblazing trapper in the **Shawangunks**. Local Indians disliked him because he would alert settlers when the Indians were near. One day a small band of Indians cornered Sam at a 200-foot cliff. Sam had to choose between the cliff and the uncertain hospitality of the Indians. He chose the cliff, leaping off into open space *(right, from model in Ellenville Museum)*. Fortunately for him, his fall was cushioned by shrubs and trees, leaving Sam unhurt and able to return to his home. In honor of that daring leap, the cliff was thereafter called **Sam's Point** *(photo, below)*.

The Ellenville Tract, consisting of approximately 4,623 acres on the **Shawangunk Ridge**, was acquired by the Village of Ellenville between the years 1899 and 1921 in five separate transactions for a little over $10,000.

Until the 1930s, the non-watershed part of the property was treated as park land and a substantial network of trails was created. During the 1930s, the Village began to explore the potential of the non-watershed land for potential revenue, from mineral exploration, an underground storage facility for gas, a glider port, and radio transmission sites. Fifty years later, the Village investigated the possibility of establishing a wind-power project in the interest of acquiring cheaper electric rates. The conflict between the financial gain and the unimpaired eco-system and panoramic view *(photo, next page, top right)* defeated that proposal.

The decision by the Village Board to lease the 4,081 acres that included the **Ice Caves** area, outside the Village corporate lines but an area where the Village owned its secondary water supply in the form of **Lake Maratanza**, was hotly debated in April of 1967. The pros and cons of the leasing agreement were so thoroughly debated that it took until 2:30 a.m. before the Village Board agreed to lease the specified area to *Ice Caves Mountain, Inc.*, composed of Clifford Forman of Cooperstown, NY, and Fred W. Grau of Walker Valley, NY. *(photo, next page, top left, with landmark plaque)*

The term of the lease was for 15 years (plus an option to renew for 10 more) at $3,000 per year rental, plus 10% additional on ticket admissions, plus 5% additional on future possible development. The 1970 audit reported $65,327 in admissions, resulting in income to the Village of $6,532.70 from their 10%, an increase of $997.51

plateau mountains extends from central Alabama to the upper Hudson River. Geologists characterize the fault and caves as a spectacular example of process called gravity tectonics... It is doubtful whether a finer example of gravity tectonics exists anywhere else in the United States."

The landmark area was cut back in 1977, excluding the "original" ice caves and a large fault known as Sunken Valley. The designation was limited to the immediate area of the **Ice Caves Mountain** loop road *(photo, above)* as a result of a boundary study report compiled by Paul Favour, park ranger for Natural Landmarks.

In a Kaatskill Life article (Summer 2003), author Bob McElroy described "yawning rock chasms, which are called 'ice caves' for the deposits of snow and ice that lie in their frigid depths through much of the summer. High above the **Rondout Valley**, violent forces have torn gaping wounds in the mountain's bedrock, rending a system of deep fissures *(photo, "Great Crevice" below)*. Geologists call these events fault-block fissures." He concluded his account: "There are ice caves at other locations in the northern Shawangunks. The **Shingle Gully** group or 'Greater Ice Caves' is the most spectacular." Heidi Wagner, Manager of the *Sam's Point Preserve*, cautioned

27

from 1969, according to Town Clerk Lillian Finkelstein.

Until December of 1996, *Ice Caves Mountain* continued to run its tourist concession on the mountain *(Old Visitor's Center and parking lot, bottom right; brochure, below)*. It was the purchase of this lease by the Open Space Institute (OSI) in 1996 that set the path for the subsequent sale of the full 4,621 acre **Ellenville Tract** by the Village of Ellenville to OSI in October 1997.

The renamed *Sam's Point Dwarf Pine Ridge Preserve* was described in the Fall 1997 "Shawangunk Watch" as "a landscape of superlatives. It protects the only dwarf pitch pine ridge community in the world that is located on bedrock." The Nature Conservancy (TNC) manages the new preserve under an agreement with OSI. The Conservancy considers the **Ellenville Tract** to be of global ecological

significance, primarily due to the extensive pine barrens habitat and the occurrence of a variety of rare and endangered species on the tract. TNC designated the **Shawangunk Ridge**, including the **Ellenville Tract**, as one of the 75 "Last Great Places" in the Eastern Hemisphere.

Information for this article was gleaned from the extensive files of the *Ellenville Public Library & Museum*, (as were photos and graphics reproduced with their permission and courtesy), including many issues of "Shawangunk Watch," published by *Friends of the Shawangunks* & the *Shawangunk Conservancy*. Newspaper clippings, brochures, publications of the New York State Museum, pictures, and related materials are included in the files that are available to the public during regular *Local History Museum* hours. For hours and additional information, call **845-647-5530**.

And remember: "SHON-gum!"

Roads/Schools/
Cragsmoor Named

YOU CAN'T HARDLY GET HERE FROM THERE

Only rugged Indian trails used by hunters, trappers and Indian scouts existed until Revolutionary times.

In the early 1800's a very rough road was built up the mountain and was abandoned by 1824 when the New Gully Road was constructed. E. L. Henry depicted travel on this road in his painting "On The Old Gully Road 1889-1891". Seven years prior, the painting he named "A Hard Road To Travel 1882", could well have been an earlier version.

Road improvements began a serious turn for the better when around 1851 the Plank Road was completed. It took two hours to travel from Ellenville to Cragsmoor. There are many stories written about the accidents which occurred while travelling the Plank Road, which is now Route 52. This is not difficult to believe after reading the following quote from "Wawarsing, Where The Streams Wind by Katherine T. Terwilliger, page 76". It reads, "The first part of the improvement program was at Evansville, the settlement at the top of the mountain (now a part of Cragsmoor). More than 500 people made their way down the "smooth" new plank road to the loveliest village in the valley. The road was made with rough planks eight feet long, fourteen inches wide and three inches deep; they were spiked to four' by four's. Shoulders were roughly graded. There were turn-outs for passing."

READIN', WRITIN' AND 'RITHMATIC

Education was not over-looked in these times and there were schools in the area prior to 1820. For approximately twenty years lessons were taught in a rustic log building in what was called Evansville. Ultimately, a new building was erected on Sam's Point Road to fill the needs of a growing population. By 1900 another new shingled school was built further down Sam's Point Road and was used until about 1945, at which time students of Cragsmoor attended Ellenville school. (See Cragsmoor -- an Historical Sketch)

In 1958, the Cragsmoor Inn, which was then owned by Mr. and Mrs. Kenneth Phillips became, for a while the home of the Mohonk-Cragsmoor School, a boarding school for boys. (This as stated by Katherine T. Terwilliger in Wawarsing, Where The Streams Wind.)

By 1971 the inn was purchased by a real estate developer who, due to its extremely poor condition was forced to raze the once beautiful building in 1972.

THE NAME GAME

"The Mountain" became Evansville after the people who first settled there and was ultimately named Cragsmoor. People began visiting Cragsmoor because of its abundance of fresh air and an awe-inspiring beauty. A summer colony began in the early 1870's when folks realized that boarding houses generated much more income than farming. About 1873 Thomas Botsford built his first hotel under the cliff at Sam's Point.

During this time, many changes took place on the mountain. The name "Cragsmoor" was chosen and a post office established.

Frederick Dellenbaugh in 1892 gave Cragsmoor its name. There had been an on-going "taffy-pull" between Dellenbaugh for Cragsmoor, and Mrs. E. L. Henry who politely and secretly petitioned for the name Baim-Wa-Wa, which in Lenape means "passing thunder".

Originally, Mr. Dellenbaugh petitioned for the name "Winahdin" to be given to the settlement, however, Washington felt there was too much similarity between it and Windham, further north in New York State, and so disqualified the name "Winahdin". We are oh, so-o-o happy that it became CRAGSMOOR! (Factual data from Cragsmoor -- A Brief History and http//www.kbart.com)

By the way. the area of Cragsmoor consists of approximately fifteen square miles.

Early Social Events

HIGH SOCIETY

The following several pages convey the elaborate, diversified and often elegant events that the early settlers of Cragsmoor enjoyed. Much of the same type of societal "Happenings" are part of life in the community today. It has, since very early times, been a hub of activity always having something for everyone to participate in. It is still inhabited by many artists of varied interests.

Social events had begun many years ago by the ladies of Cragsmoor, who gathered for afternoon teas which were held at different homes. The artists themselves would gather weekly, again meeting at each other's homes. Many musicians and music teachers were present "on the mountain" during the summers. Cragsmoorians craved the finest in literature, art, music and drama. Many contemporary actors and actresses appeared in Cragsmoor's live theater performances.

A library was established in 1912 and housed within various locations, including The Pines Casino which was built by Eliza Hartshorn in 1899. Let it be known that at that time there were two "Casinos" in Cragsmoor. One located on Schuyler and known as The Pines Casino. The second was within Cragsmoor Inn at the top of what is now Inn Road.

The Cragsmoor Inn held many of the mountain's social events, such as an annual costume party, dancing, dress balls, concerts, plays, bowling, golf (on a nine-hole course), etc. If an activity was to take place in the evening, folks often trekked up the extremely winding road to the Inn using candle or kerosene lanterns to light the way.

All ages enjoyed games such as Statuary, Blindman's Bluff, Pease Porridge Hot, or dancing to the Virginia Reel. And, there was always so much more to do!!

It would not have been unusual to see Charles Curran impersonating Uncle Remus or to hear E. L. Henry telling a story. The Henry's home also hosted weekly musicals. There were picnics, hayrides and many, many activities for young and old alike.

Gardening was a marvelous pasttime, not only resulting in a bounty of fresh fruits and vegetables but also the profusion of showy flowers to adorn the yards, brighten the entire area and provide blossoms for indoor enjoyment, as well.

September 27, 2002

Cragsmoor Playhouse II
T. E. Bolger, Producer

Present

Love Letters

by

A. R. Gurney

Directed by Joy Weber

The taking of pictures and the use of recording or video equipment in this theatre is strictly forbidden. **Kindly turn off all cell phones and pagers.**

✻ A note about the "stage". In keeping with the preservation of our landmark building, special construction was necessary to create a removable shell which protects the original walls and floor of this area, while the "set" is constructed. Cragsmoor Historical Society is dedicated to preservation.

Please observe the emergency exits located in the front right of the stage and two in the rear of the building.

Smoking is not permitted anywhere in this building.

Playbill

Cragsmoor Playhouse II

2002 Season

Cragsmoor, New York

914-647-2362

Theatre In Cragsmoor
...a brief history.

The first production of the Cragsmoor Players was the Broadway success *Springtime for Henry*, opening on July 5th, 1936 and was directed and produced by Hugh Nevill. It was given at the Barnstormers Theatre, formerly known as the Bleakley Barn, which had been converted into a little theatre by its owner, Frederick S. Dellenbaugh, and dedicated on August 16th, 1917. Mrs. Dellenbaugh thought of the name "Barnstormers." The theatre had a capacity of well over a hundred seats. The stage had sliding doors in the back which when open would allow the audience to see the actors perform in the field beyond. The stage was 24 feet and 13 feet deep. The remodeling work was done by Bert Goldsmith and Co.

Mr. Dellenbaugh had acquire this land from the Bleakley family in 1902 and subsequently gave it to his son, Frederick, Jr. in 1935 before the plays began.

Hugh Nevill inherited a great tradition in the performing arts. Dramatic performances were given in private homes, and the Casino and the Pavilion of the Inn, and ever since 1917 they mostly graced the stage of the Barnstormers.

Many Cragsmoor residents, both young and old, were in the plays or helped out in other ways. Designing and building the sets and arranging the lights was no easy job, and there was a deadline to meet. This was especially difficult for the first production, but always present in the plays to come.

The Cragsmoor Players even put on skits at the Nevelle, and one was never forgotten because there was a fire back stage in the middle of the show. It was not serious and was extinguished almost at once. The show went on just the same and somehow the actors incorporated the coughing from the smoke into their lines, and the audience never knew there was a fire.

Elaine Perry was one of the final directors of the Playhouse and she was the daughter of Antoinette Perry, in whose name the American Theatre Wing's Tony awards are given each year to this day.

On August 19, 1957, the final performance of *Janus* a comedy by Carol Green, brought down the final curtain never to rise again at the Barnstormers Theatre in Cragsmoor.   (from Recollections and Research by William R. Howell, C.H.S. archives)

Barnstormers Theatre

Interested in Theatre?

The Cragsmoor Playhouse II is a great place to exercise your theatre skills. We encourage you to bring to the "table" your on stage, back stage, front of the house, back of the house, whatever talents you have. Join the fun of theatre.
call 647-7937.

Who's Who...

Stephanie Kovacs-Originally from Illinois, Stephanie made her way to the big city where she received the Stella Adler Award and her degree in acting from Tisch at NYU. After graduating, she joined the Florida Studio Theatre as a company actor and the Assistant to the Director of Education. Upon her return to New York, she began working as the Casting Associate at Joy Weber Casting and as the Director of Education with the Play Group Theatre. Representative roles include: **"Juliet"** in Romeo and Juliet, **"The Woman"** in Scotland Road, **"Henriette"** in The Learned Ladies, **"Shelley"** in The God of Isaac, and **"Heather"** in the Off-Broadway premiere of Tibet Does Not Exist. She received additional training at Yale, A.C.T., The Minneapolis Children's Theatre, and the University of Illinois. We welcome her to the Cragsmoor Playhouse.

Gregg Shults – A native of this area, Gregg has appeared in a Shadowland's production of **A Few Good Men**, at Forestburg Playhouse in **Fiddler On The Roof**, as Sasha, at Hofstra University as the lead in **Othello**, and **Fabian** in Twelfth Night. Other credits include **Our Town, Arsenic and Old Lace and Luv.** As well as performances at the John Housman Theatre in New York City. He was the recipient of a full New York State Summer School of Arts Scholarship at Skidmore. Recent credits include **Nuts** at the Hand To Mouth Players in Bronxville, **A View From The Bridge, All My Sons, Present Laughter** with the Yorktown Community Players, and at the Garrison Phillipstown Players, **Do Your Own Thing.** Gregg made is debut at the Cragsmoor Playhouse as Mark in **Par For The Corpse.** His hobbies include hang gliding and mountain biking with his wife Marina. When not on stage, he can be seen locally being creative on many area roofs. His email address is Fiddleroofing.com

Joy Weber -(director) Joy's directing credits started at the tender age of 16 when she directed **"The Wizard Of Oz"** at camp in upstate New York. This production of **Love Letters** marks Joy first directorial endeavor at the Cragsmoor Playhouse. A graduate of the American Academy of Dramatic Arts, she welcome the chance to direct. Her other artistic interest are creative gardening and metal sculpting. A combination of these talents are on displayed in her gardens. A native of New York City, Joy enjoys life in the country and the chance to express her theatrical talents. At the top of her list of life long credits, she lists: **"HER BEST PRODUCTION WAS HER SON DR. ROBERT BUKA, ESQ."**

35

The Cragsmoor Association

What started as a neighborhood conversation on the lawn of Ruth DeTar's home on a summer day in 1978 evolved into the *Cragsmoor Association*, celebrating its twenty-fifth anniversary this year.

The purpose of the organization – the general preservation of the natural beauty of Cragsmoor and the revitalization of the community as an art and cultural center – was formalized at its first meeting on August 20th, 1978, at the home of Pete and Marie Stanger. Of immediate concern was the protection from development of an area known to Cragsmoor residents as "**Bear Hill**." Vincent P. (Pete) Stanger was elected president and the work began.

As with any newly-formed organization with a mission, the raising of funds to achieve their purpose consumed the *Cragsmoor Association* and created a flurry of activity which resulted in meeting their financial goal, aided by a generous donation from David Croyder. **Bear Hill**, sometimes called "**Bear Cliff**," was purchased from Halsey Sherwood of Gardiner, who had previously contemplated developing the parcel, and the area was declared "forever wild."

Achieving their immediate goal did not fully satisfy the members of the *Association* that has continued its endeavors in the preservation of Cragsmoor's natural beauty, including opposition to overflights and a battle against black fly infestation.

An offshoot of the determination that much of Cragsmoor should remain "forever wild" as an integral part of the preservation efforts led to the creation of a land conservancy in Cragsmoor.

The *Cragsmoor Association* does not "rest on its laurels" even today, continuing its community fundraising with such events as this past summer's highly successful silent auction at the firehouse, which benefited both the *Association* and the *Cragsmoor Fire Company*, equally. Continuing with its efforts to increase awareness and appreciation of Cragsmoor's natural beauty led the *Association* to cooperate with the New York-New Jersey Trail Conference in that organization's extension of its trail around **Bear Hill**, which is, of course, open to the public.

The *Association* holds its annual meeting the first Saturday in July and is currently served by James McKenney as president. Dues are a reasonable $10 per year for individual membership. Voting membership requires that the potential voter be a resident or homeowner in Cragsmoor.

The Cragsmoor Historical Society

The Cragsmoor Historical Society was founded in 1996 for the purpose of preserving and interpreting the history of Cragsmoor. At that same time, the few remaining members of the historic *Cragsmoor Federated Church* concluded they did not have the resources to sustain their building.

(See photo above, from the collection of Sally Matz; this picture shows the church before it was obtained and converted by the Historical Society.)

Rather than sell the building and see it converted to residential use, the congregation gave it to the newly formed *Society* in 1997 with the hope that the larger Cragsmoor community would invest in the deteriorated building and save it for future generations.

First and foremost, a new basement was constructed under the Community Room; this was necessary since the old dirt basement had three feet of water in it for many years. Next, the electrical system was improved and a smoke and fire alarm system was added, together with a telephone.

Prominently sited close to the road at the gateway to the *Cragsmoor National Register Historic District*, it is a familiar and cherished landmark to residents and visitors who come to Cragsmoor to see its architectural treasures, dramatic scenery, and the popular nature preserves at **Sam's Point** and **Bear Hill**.

Over the last five years, the *Society* has successfully raised money for, and has completed, some of the critical structural repairs necessary to keep the building standing. Currently, we are raising money to replace the roof and the interior ceiling. Donations in any amount are welcome and needed.

Please mail your tax-deductible donation to: *Cragsmoor Historical Society*, P. O. Box 354, Cragsmoor NY 12420. Issue 11 Page 11 Thank You.

"Save Me A Place at Forest Lawn" at Cragsmoor Playhouse

The Cragsmoor Playhouse will present "*Save Me A Place At Forest Lawn*," a play about two elderly and lonely widows as they lunch at a cafeteria and face the uncertainty of their remaining years. The play, held at the *Cragsmoor Playhouse*, will be presented on October 1st & 2nd and 15th & 16th.

The New York Times says, "Playwright Lorees Yerby creates dialogue that is both true and good… the women have a real and an appealing dimension. Miss Yerby appreciates the dignity of the human condition, and manages to avoid the grossly sentimental, even as the women blunder on with their somewhat simple ideas about life after death."

"It is written simply, touchingly and with considerable humor," said the New York Post.

Sheila Glenn plays Gertrude. This past summer, Sheila was in Forestburgh Playhouse's productions of "The Diary of Anne Frank" and "The Sound of Music" and played Fraulein Schneider in the Summerstar production of "Cabaret" in Middletown.

Sara Simas plays the part of Clara. She is life long resident of Orange County and is a classically-trained singer, voice teacher, and actress. Her roles have ranged from "Lucy" in Charlie Brown to Angelica in Puccini's opera "Suor Angelica."

She teaches voice at the Neighborhood School of Music in Goshen and in her own studio in Middletown.

The Cragsmoor Playhouse welcomes these two actresses to our stage bringing them together after a thirty-year absence of working on the same stage.

Producing the play is Tom Bolger, who finds bringing theater back to Cragsmoor after a 45-year absence both exciting and challenging. Tom's most recent production for the *Cragsmoor Playhouse* was "Mass Appeal." His involvement with the *Cragsmoor Playhouse* puts to good use the theatrical skills he developed in his many years as an actor, director, and set designer.

A graduate of the American Academy of Dramatic Arts, Tom is a life member of the Art Students League and is currently a freelance design consultant.

The Cragsmoor Playhouse is located between Pine Bush and Ellenville, on Cragsmoor Road, one mile north of Rte 52.

For information, call Tom Bolger at 647-7937 or Sally Matz at 647-6384. Proceeds benefit the restoration of the *Cragsmoor Historical Society* headquarters building.

About This Building..

Welcome to the *Cragsmoor Historical Society Headquarters* (the old Federated Church Building). The building was originally the Mountain Methodist Church established in 1880. It was erected on land contributed by J. D. and Marie Decker. Services were held when clergy came up from the villages below the mountain. With trips to Ellenville several hours in duration, a Cragsmoor church to serve the various religions affiliations was very desirable.

In 1906 a search for a religious society to meet these needs year round was initiated by Mr. and Mrs. George Inness, Jr. and Mr. and Mrs. Edward L. Henry. The two men traveled to New York City to meet with leaders of the Federated Church movement and for $250.00 the mountain chapel was acquired to serve Cragsmoor on a entirely non-denominational basis. No resident pastor served the church until the arrival of Rev. H.M. Cary in 1908.

In the winter of 1909-10 an extension was built to accommodate the larger summer congregation and to function as a social gathering place. This addition was provided by Mrs. George Inness, Jr. The last pastor to serve here was Rev. Fred Reustle. In 1996, the board of the Federated Church gave to the **Cragsmoor Historical Society** this building, and its restoration is in progress. We welcome you and hope your enjoy your visit to Cragsmoor.

On this stage...

Par For the Corpse

I Never Saw Another Butterfly

Voices I

Robert Frost

Jack London

- · · · -

37

Town of Wawarsing,

The Hamlet of Cragsmoor

Cragsmoor Historical Society
Former Federated Church Building

Cragsmoor Historical Society
P O Box 354
Cragsmoor NY 12420

*Dedicated to Preserving
Cragsmoor's History*

Cragsmoor Historical Society
*P.O. Box 35
Cragsmoor , N.Y. 12420*

845-647-6384

Membership includes :
A subscription to the Cragsmoor Historical Journal.

Invitation to special events.

Advance notices on exhibitons and workshops.
Special theatrical productions.

Be Part of History - Join

If you would like to share our preservation interests, please join us. Complete the bottom form. Yearly membership is $10 for an individual and $20 for a family.

Life memberships are $100 for an individual and family life it is $200. Donations are always welcome.
(make check payable to Cragsmoor Historical Society)

Name _____

Address _____

_____

Phone _____

E-mail _____

Amount enclsoed $ _____

Area of special interest _____

_____

Points of Interest:

Sam's Point Dwarf Pine Preserve

The Stone Church and its vista

Bear Hill Preserve

Cragsmoor Free Library

Many Cragsmoor homes, dating back to the 1800's are in our Historic District. These homes are on the National Register of Historic Buildings, they display various architectural design elements. A brief ride around our mountain will exhibit these features.

Organizations

Cragsmoor Historical Society

Cragsmoor Free Library

Cragsmoor Volunteer Fire Company

Cragsmoor Association

Cragsmoor Playhouse

Cragsmoor Conservency

Some of the historic past that no long exists in Cragsmoor due to fire or negelct:

The Old School House
Garrett's General Store
The Cragsmoor Inn
A Community Pool
A number of boarding houses.

Barnstormers Theater - 1925

About the Society...

Founded in 1996, the Society's objectives are to discover, procure and preserve whatever may relate to history in its several phases; economical, military, political, literary, artistic, etc., but particularly material regarding Cragsmoor and its environs, in the State of New York.

We encourage the writing of papers and the delivery of addresses on subjects of historical interest. Also we encourage the collection of objects of historical value and arrange for their preservation and exhibition.

Some background on this mountain and it's ridges...

Geogoloists tell us that the Shawangunk conglamerate, the caprock of the ridge, consisting of quartz sand and quartz pebbles, was laid down during the late Ordivician or early Silurian times, that is between 400 and 450 million years ago.

During the Appalachian revolution between 280 and 350 million years ago the ridge was formed by plate collision. If you know that most mountain ranges are formed by the collision of continental plates.

A bit of history... Cragsmoor was settled in the mid 1800's with a few farms and boarding houses for summer visitors.

Transportation via a Surrey or in winter by Sleigh from Ellenville. Some visitors came for their health recommended by city doctors. Artists found it to be a wonderful place with its scenic beauty. Therefore, many famous artists built homes here, including George Inness, Jr., E.L. Henry, Charles Curran, Helen Turner and Arthur I. Keller, to name a few.

Cragsmoor Historical Journal

Dedicated to Preserving Cragsmoor's History

Volume 5 Issue 1   Published by the Cragsmoor Historical Society, Inc.,   Post Office 354, Cragsmoor, N.Y. 12420   Winter, 2003

EVENTS-This past August the CHS was invited to participate in Ellenville's **Blueberry Festival**. We had a successful day in spite of the rain because of all the outstanding bakers who donated their culinary treats for us to sell. There was quite an interest in the pictures we had made from old post cards in our collections. A very big thank you to everyone who participated!

In December, we again had our **Holiday Bazaar**. We were "open" for two days, and what a success! We also had new participants, **Carolyn Peters Baker** and **Susan Clarke**, who sold beautiful wreaths they had made with the help and guidance of **Hilda Peters**. All of the greenery came from the fallen limbs and trees from the recent ice storms. Carolyn and Susan were also very successful selling their organic cat food and treats. Also featured at the Bazaar was maple syrup, which can still be mail ordered for any gift-giving occasion.

PROJECTS IN WORK...

Formation of the new Cragsmoor Artists Guild - an organization whose primary interest will be to acknowledge and record current-day working artists, produce an annual of present works, and sponsor a scholarship program for students. If you have an interest in this new idea, contact Tom Bolger, 647-7937 or Cragsmoor NY 12420-0070, tbolger70@cs.com.

PRESENT ARTIST
-PRESENT WORKS.

We begin a new feature with this issue, meet the current-day artists, get to know their art and visit with them in their ateliers.

CRAGSMOOR THEATER - We're planning a June to September season. Whatever your interest in theater is, you're welcome to participate. Watch for the casting call for performers and backstage crew to be posted at the post office. We are hoping for the formation of a repertory company.

EXHIBITIONS AND WORKSHOPS - We applied last November for grants from the Dutchess Council on The Arts and have been successful in obtaining two: For **Exhibitions**, we received $445 to promote a series of exhibits, including "Women Artists of Cragsmoor" and a 3-D show for mixed media sculpture. **Maureen Radl** is the coordinator
In addition, we received $350 for **Workshops For The Arts**, a hands-on program for pottery, quilting, painting, and preserving archival documents. **Sally Matz** is the coordinator.

JOIN / RENEW WITH PREMIUMS

Cragsmoor Federated Church - 1908 now the Historical Society's Headquarters

---

This Column is dedicated to the progress of restoration to the Society's Headquarters.

The Blue Roof

Despite what anyone thinks, IHOP (the International House of Pancakes) is not coming to Cragsmoor. Our headquarters' roof is covered in cerulean blue tarps to protect it from the elements.

We've been working very hard restoring this old landmark building. The importance of a new roof became evident when puddles were forming inside much too often. Don Moore is the contractor chosen to execute this phase of the restoration work.

We finally found a Canadian company willing to replicate the design of the old tin shingles. This is a very costly project, but must be done right if we are to be conscious of proper restoration.

Larry Gobrecht (new board member) climbed up and into the bell tower and found another piece of history. The bell was made by Melville Bell Company in West Troy, New York, September 1908. It is inscribed, "Young People's Society of 1904, who raised the money to get it erected, Cragsmoor Federated Church." Given the climbing around in the attic and through the dirt, grime and raccoon "guano," it was wonderful to find this bit of history.

The roof is now secure and the bowed center section of it has been repaired. The interior ceiling had to be removed so that support beams could be installed, together with additional braces, cleats, etc. The original tin ceiling was saved for possible reinstallation.

As with all old homes, our restoration campaign will continue as we begin 2003. The new foundation, new roof, new electric, etc., all add to our commitment of preservation.

The Cragsmoor Historical Society Headquarters building is available for services, talks, poetry readings, musicals, weddings and funerals.
Please book far in advance.

PRESIDENT'S MESSAGE

This message has been difficult to compose. I, my family, friends, and the whole mountain are still shocked by the sudden and unexpected death of my brother, Peter B. Howell, on Nov. 21, 2002. I am not sure that I have fully accepted the finality of his passing, either. Pete would come to Cragsmoor several times during the week and work on his many projects, then relax with us over one meal or another before he returned home. I keep thinking that perhaps he'll be over today, or when he does come I'll ask him how to fix or solve a perplexing problem. Pete was definitely on the side of solving problems. As a matter of fact, he relished the idea of having a situation that heretofore caused some kind of angst and he would research, if necessary, and then figure out the best solution. He enjoyed finishing the project with accuracy, cleverness, imagination, and style.

One day he brought his Hiking Club to the CHS for our monthly meeting. We presented a program for them and a pictorial display of old Cragsmoor. As a group was looking at the boards on which we had mounted the pictures, one board fell, then another. Instantly Pete went to his truck and brought in a cordless drill and reassembled the display. After the meeting, he shook his head and said that our "boards" had to go and he would make us a proper display unit. By the beginning of summer, Pete brought over two oak and cork bulletin boards. We can put them together or use them separately, make them zigzag or into a cube. They are in constant use. How could we have ever set up a display before?

Have you seen what he has done with the family home, The Pines? Pete remodeled the kitchen, moving all the plumbing that would freeze each winter because it was on the outside wall; made new cabinet doors; and corrected some archaic electrical problems. There were some leaks in the roof which have disappeared. He remodeled three bathrooms and the archway entering the house, including wallpapering, tiling, and I could go on and on. There was no job that he would not tackle because he loved to solve problems. Actually, Pete was energized by challenge.

His handiness can also be seen at Sam's Point, where he blazed trails, made bridges, and widened paths all for the hikers to enjoy their trek through and along the ridge.

Pete has left a beautiful legacy for us in many areas of our hamlet. He was a cheerful, quiet giver of himself. His absence will be felt, but the excellence of his works can be seen daily.

Sally Matz, Pres.

Pete Howell was an outstanding member of the Cragsmoor Historical Society. He not only gave his time to "help out" on numerous occasions, but also added to our archives, contributed to our finances and believed in our efforts. Donations in his honor are being made to the CHS building fund.   Ed..

NEW FEATURE - PRESENT DAY ARTISTS
Meet the Sigunicks

Bleakley Studios

Continuing in the Cragsmoor tradition of artists working together and inspiring each other, one extraordinary family of artists here works in a shared environment on a daily basis. The Sigunicks - Phil, Judy, and their daughter Ellen - share studio and living space at Bleakley Studios, a former boarding house for summer residents that was called Bleakley House. This imposing three-story structure was built in the 1890's and purchased by Phil in the 1970's. It dominates the hill at the eastern edge of the hamlet on Sam's Point Rd.

Now the great house is divided among the three Sigunicks, who describe their arrangement as equally inspiring, challenging, and frustrating. Phil states, "Whether subliminally or consciously, we all benefit from each other's creative energies and perceptions. There's nothing like seeing someone else working intensely when your own energies flag...or having someone to bounce your efforts off, from time to time, who understands the process." On the flip side, frustrations develop around conflicts of habit. Ellen explains that while one needs music and a dust-free environment, the person in the next room may require silence and works in a medium that creates dust. However they have worked it out, each of these artists has found a way to consistently produce outstanding works of art.

Phil immortalized some of Cragsmoor's more notable women, including Judy in a series of nudes during her pregnancy with Ellen. Over time, his focus was drawn more to the landscape. Working in pastels, he captured the shifting light on mountains, and clouds, ponds, and streams.

Starting out as a fiber artist, Judy came to Cragsmoor in the 70's, she, too, found clay to be an excellent medium of expression, Judy describes her work as a "query into life of animals, including humans,...about both the the disstinctions and likenesses amoung species." Her latest work in progress is a celebration of completing her fifty-nine year. It reveals her connection to the planet through animals in incremental transitions in her life. She has always tried to introduce a bigger sense of the enviornment and develop the concept by using other materials such as clay, cement, metal, etc.

Ellen is the product of the creative genious of both her parents. Studying art in Italy, where she began to hone her darkroom skills. In 1997, she went to Kenya for three months and lived with a Kikuyu family volunteering at a local primary shcool. Upon her return to the states, she attended the School of Visual Arts in N.Y.C., where she studied photography and worked as a photographer's assistant. Ellen returned to Kenya in 1999 to photograph, videotape, and record the voices of street children in Nairobi. And so the tradition continues withing this community and within this family. It is transferred from parents to child, and through her out into the world, each capturing the essence of life around him or her

with power and sensitivity, so that those who view their art are moved deeply and enriched.

Phil's work can be seen locally at the Cragsmoor Free Library. One of Judy's installations is at the Ellenville Library. Ellen is currently working making education a reality for children in Nairobi. *Mareen Radl*

❧❧

ON THE NATIONAL REGISTER OF HISTORIC BUILDINGS
Cragsmoor Historic District
"Bleakley House" ca 1890

The building is located on the west side of Sam's Point Rd., with a view of the north and west obscured by evergreen trees. The view to the southwest over Bear Cliff along the ridge to Highpoint Monument in New Jersey.

This house is a three story, five bay shingled dwelling with gable roof that was originally built in 1890 by two partners Merrill and Bryce as a rooming house for summer residents and visiting artists during the late 19th/early 20th centuries and again from the 1940's through the 1960's. On the 1899 map the house is called "Grand View boarding House" with Hornbeck and Deyo as owners. *(source: Ella Stedner, C. Sharp, K.T. Terwilliger).*

Since Bleakley House was situated in the Shawangunk mountains, 90 miles from New York City at an elevation of 2,000 feet, it offered delightful surroundings and many opportunities for outdoor life, including swimming, walking, tennis, golf was available and summer theatre.

The rooms were well appointed and attractive, each with running water. The interior contained, modern bathrooms; for recreations, an excellent library, a cozy little lounge ideal for bridge and cocktail parties. Area churches include: Catholic, Episcopal and Federated. Daily rates were $7.00 and weekly $40. Food: carefully planned meals served in a delightful dining room with beautiful views. Telephone Ellenville 63M. P O and telegraph: Bleakley Field, Cragsmoor via Ellenvile, Ulster County, New York In 1946 the manager was Arthur Holt. *(source- Cragsmoor Free Library)*

The second and third floors are visually divided by a flared belt course with a slight overhang and ball pendants at the corners. The house has a one story enclosed porch and shed roof on three sides and a square, central, two story addition on the norhteast facade with a flat roof and balustrade. The south gable end includes a wooden fire escape from the third floor to the porch roof.

The interior contains several staircases, as well as a mahongany and brass elevator serving all floors: the main entrance has classical details including a fanlight and sidelights. The stonework was done by John Keir.

The property also contains a shop. spring house, a large garden, stone well and a stone marker inscribed "BLEAKLEY HOUSE". A former swimming pool was filled in 1990.

(source- National Registar Historic Buildings)

ROCK SLIDE SHUTS DOWN RT 52 TO ELLENVILLE.
January 02, 2003
By Jessica Gardner, Times Herald-Record

Cragsmoor - The biggest rockslide in decades has shut Route 52 in Cragsmoor.

Authorities are unsure when the main road between Ellenville and Pine Bush will reopen.

An estimated 1,000 cubic yards of rock and dirt came down from the Shawangunk Ridge shortly after 6:30 p.m. Tuesday, filling about 85 feet of road with debris, said Peter Teliska, a resident engineer for the state Dept. of Transportation. No injuries were reported, nor any damage to nearby vehicles. The cause of the slide is unknown.

Some rocks were as small as a pebble; others were as big as a car and the large slab that's still against the rock face is the size of a three-car garage. said Chris Reister, safety officer for the Cragsmoor Fire Department.

"There are rocks that do come down once in a while, but nothing bigger than a wheelbarrow," said Reister, who's lived in the area for 15 years.

Work had to be stopped when other debris fell on the road and it looks like more could come tumbling down. That means drivers will have to stick to the detours until further notice. Route 52 is the main road between Ellenville and Pine Bush and takes travelers across the Shawangunk Ridge Because of its spectacular views of Rondout Valley, the road is a popular way to go.

Ironically, the rock wall was secured with pins by the D.O.T less than a decade ago in hopes of avoiding an incident, Reister said.

❧

(E-mail from Al Zalenski in Hawiai)

The last time I recall a dramatic rock slide on Route 52 was back about 1948. I had to walk as always to the old Post Office near the library, which was old man Garrett's house, and he also had the job of driving the school bus to Ellenville. It could have been in November; we went down about one-third the hill on Route 52 and had to stop because a tremendous slab of rock blocked the road completely. It had to be at least 10 feet thick and about 50 feet long. They said that it just came down just before we got there, thank God! No one was hurt. It took days before they could get one lane open.

I have an engineering mind and my theory is, water gets into the cracks of the slabs and then freezes in the winter and acts like a tremendous wedge of force. It freezes and melts repeatedly over the years until gravity dislodges the dislocated slabs.

Also by having to use the Gully Road, covered with dirt for safety, it give one a feeling of just how it was to travel up and down this road to Ellenville during winter ice and snow storms in the 1800's, prior to using route. 52.

JOIN / RENEW WITH PREMIUMS

CH

Some new additions to our archives...

1892 Austa Densmore Sturdevant.

This photo of one of her skectces is entitled *The Hospitalbe Door,* dated 1908. We became the recipient of serveral pieces of memobelia of this past Cragsmoor artist through the genorsity of Virginia Pinnick of Harrison, AR.

The gift includes some of Ms. Sturdevant linens, flatware from the Cragsmoor Inn, a letter opener. sissors, a bound copy of "Bear Cliff House", many original sketches of both Cragsmoor and Europe, also many letters and photographs. A exhibition catalog of her work and copies of her obituary. Sometime in the future the Society intends to exhibit a display of archives of past residents artists, along with examples of their works and these archives.

The Society is extremely grateful of this donation and our sincere thanks to Virginia Pinnick for her gifts. They have been cataloged and added to our collection of historic memorabilia.

❧

MARL BOYS LED BIG CATTLE ROUNDUP (Ellenville Journal December 29, 1953)

Cragsmoor - One of the most exciting cattle roundups in the annals of the Shawangunk Mountains - one that may well be woven into the legend and lore of the region - came to an end Tuesday evening when the Marl boys rounded up the last of five Black Angus cattle that had broken out of a pasture fence on the farm of Clyde Marl just before Christmas. The cattle took off with a speed and determination that convinced Mr. Marl they were intent on going places.

Mounted Pursuers - all the Marl boys and their friends - a total of 14 men on horseback - rode out on the roundup of the strays. They hunted day and night and high and low and aided by a low-flying airplane piloted by Hank Sylverson, a friend from Pine Bush.

The Charging Herd- Sunday, the posse cornered four of the mavericks near the Quannacut Camp in Walker Valley area and surrounded them carefully. The cattle were in no mood to be taken without a fight, and, heads lowered, they charged the horsemen. Discretion was the better part of valor for a few minutes as the men took refuge behind trees. Eventually they succeeded in capturing all four animals.

The Last Holdout - The last one was caught Tuesday night between Ira Jones' Road's End farm and Mountain Lodge in the Crawford area.

During the chase. Clyde Marl's horse suffered a severe cut in a hind leg while crossing a brook, and a veterinarian had to be summoned to aid the steed.

The Marl boys who took part in the chase included Clyde, Claude, Cliff, Ernest. Ott. Ike and Henry. *(Thank you Nancy Krom, daughter of the late Clyde Marl, for sharing this article.)*

JOIN / RENEW WITH PREMIUMS

From the archives...
The Cragsmoor Journal July, 15, 1912
Editorial

Has anybody noticed the air of dark mystery which has enveloped certain personages on the Mountain for the past week or two? You must have - it's fairly permeated the surrounding atmosphere - blurred the landscape. What solemn conferences have been held! How numerous have been the hurried visits to The House of the Four Winds and The Porches - not a strange state of affairs in itself, but made so by the suppressed excitement which emanated from the callers.

A crisis was reached shortly after the arrival of Miss Hazel Mackeye at Dr. and Mrs. Northrop's. The ether was charged with a sense of something about to happen; the trips and conferences were reboubled, and soon the mysterious ones were stalking about, hastily turning over and skimming through the pages of small paper-covered volume.

Now, what is the meaning of those dread symptoms? Simply this: they all have bad cases of - not hay fever, but play fever. Yes, they are going to produce a play which will so utterly eclipse those of last summer that the finished shrieks of the damsels in "The Mouse Trap," and the heart rending farewells of the "Parting Friends," will fade into the dim glories of the past. The Productions will be given for the benefit of C.I.A. (if there is anyone who doesn't know what that means, let him ask Mr. Curran), and we feel confident that that statement is all that will be needed to open the hearts, hands and purses of all Cragsmoorians. In other words, we expect that all of you will be ready to help struggling actors with their parts, lend your thousand-dollar tra-la-las for stage properties, and above all, attend the performances in large numbers and applaud vigorously and enthusiastically.

❧

THE LITTLE BROWN CHURCH
Memories by Art Liang

To the left of the library is the little brown church. This is where Grandpa Curran went. Each summer he supplied all the flowers for the altar. Even though all those flowers came from his garden, one not excessively large, it never showed. It must have been God's way of compensating him for his generosity.

Just inside the front door hung a rope that disappeared through a hole in the ceiling. It was great fun to get to ring the bell on Sunday. The rope would cycle up and down through the hole. The first several times only a faint rumble of the rope going through the hole would be heard, then the familiar ring of the bell. The small weight of us youngsters against the combined weight of the bell and rope would lift us from the floor if we held tight.

I faintly remember being baptized in this small, friendly church. Many of us kids were to attend Sunday school here. As I remember, the classes were quite boring, and we, overly energetic youngsters, would plot and scheme as to how we would distract the teacher while we escaped through the open window, in order to go play. Grandpa was so dedicated to this church that after his death our family brought the first electricity to the building and had a fluorescent light installed in his memory. All my life. whenever I hear the song

---

"The Little Brown Church in The Dell".I think of the little brown church beside [🔲 Art] the library.

❧

FROM OUR POST CARDS ARCHIVES dated Apr. 7th,1909. *"Just a line to let you know we're on this beautiful mountain and having a good time. Best regards, M.Q.*

The Cragsmoor Journal
August 11,1911

The eleventh series of Mrs. Dellenbaugh's Dramatic Mornings on the Mountain began with the comedy by Oscar Wilde, "A Woman of No Importance."

Is it eleven times that all the joy and friendliness of the mountain have come to listne to her magic voice, while the white choulds life themselves in the east? With these things of comedy, her vice and the subtle changes of her contenance filled all the studio and wide loggia of endridge, where Cragsmoor had gathered. M. F. Gay

❧

THE CRAGSMOOR CLARION
FIRST EDITION JUNE 17ᵀᴴ,1940
We recently found in our archives original copies of this news paper dedicated to theater in Cragsmoor)
Professors Browne and Peters Colorful As Ever

Once again the 1940 Season finds those hardy annuals, Profs. Browne and Peters in charge of the Art Department of The Cragsmoor Players.

Bob Browne is still at Trinity College. Hartford, and it may be that he will only be with us for a part of the season if his plans for a sailing trip up the coast of Maine matrialize. He has been doing a number of drawings this past winter for the Trinity Magazine  and is also responsible for new "map". Charlie Peters took advantage of the heavy snow at Cragsmoor this year to paint a number of very interesting winter scenes-especially one of a panaorama of clouds as seen from Bear Cliff.

"Theatre in the Clouds"

Cragsmoor Historical Soceity
P O Box 354
Cragsmoor New York 12420

U.S. Postage Paid
Non-profit Org.
Permit #42006
Newburgh NY
12552

**Annual Membership
2003 Drive
Join/Renew**

CONGRATULATIONS

Mary Gunderman Marl celebrated her 90th birthday on September 18th. A long time resident, she married Clyde Marl in 1932 and shortly there after they moved to Cragsmoor. She has lived in her present home for the past 63 years.

Vincent "Pete" Stanger celebrated his 95th birthday on February 10th, We all send all kinds of love, hugs and best wishes to our dear friend and former board member, along with our thanks for all his contributions to our hamlet.

Jennifer Garolfalini reently became the Executive Director of the Neversink Valley Area Museum. She hold an Honors BA in Anthropology from the Univ.of Toronto and an MSC in Archaeological Computing from the University of Southhampton, UK. Jennifer and her husband are renovating an 1850's house located on Henry Road here in Cragsmoor.

Condonlences

To the family **Peter B. Howell**, who suddenly and unexpectedly died on November 21, 2002, we add our name to the long list of expressions of sympathy and hope this will help ease the aching hearts of his family.

(see Presidnet's message p.1)

HAROLD HARRIS - an accomplished sculptor, local historian, entrepreneur and long-time area resident, died Friday, March 7, 2003, at 80 years old. C.H.S. morns the lost of one of our outstanding memebers.

Thank you to:

Marie Stanger for starting and maintaining a catalog of the Cragsmoor Historical Journal from its inception.What a wonderful gift to our community.

Also to **John Stanger** for his continued support and interest in the Historical Society. Without even a call John had our driveway plowed after the many snowfalls during this rough winter.

During the summer he donated and delivered a truckload of gold, (manure) for **Caroline Peters Baker** who volunteered her green thumb and expertise to create and beautify the entrance to our property with herbs - deer proof plants so they will return this spring.

We are very grateful to the **VOLUNTEERS** for their help and for their interest and concerns about the well being of the building and purpose of the Historical Society.

CRAGSMOOR CONSERVANCY

The newly formed organization's aim is to preserve and protect the natural ecology of land in Cragsmoor and its neighboring regions, and to promote, by way of educating the public and otherwise, as to the protection, conversation and preservation of land and the scientific study of environmental stewardship

To acquire, by gift, purchase or otherwise, interests in real or personal property, both tangible and intangible, for such use as will further these purposes.

Also to enter into management agreements and such other arrangements for undeveloped property as will further these purposes.

Board members include, Jeff Slade, Jim McKenney, Joy Weber, John Losk, Paul Campbell and Mike Medley. For more information contact:Jeff Slade, Cragsmoor,N.Y.,12420 or www.jslade@sladelaw.com

CHS

Cragsmoor Historical Journal
P O Box 354, Cragsmoor, New York 12420
Founded in 1996
Thomas E. Bolger, Publisher 1996 -
Publishing @ Rockledge, Cragsmoor, N.Y. 12420-0070

Cragsmoor Historical Journal

Dedicated to Preserving Cragsmoor's History

Volume 5 Issue 2   Published by the Cragsmoor Historical Society, Inc.,   Post Office 354, Cragsmoor, N.Y. 12420   Winter - 2004

EVENTS:

May 9 - Early History of Cragsmoor a presentation at **Bard College** by **Sally Matz** and **Eileen Kolaitis**.

May 16 - Visitors from **Bard College** were welcomed to Cragsmoor . **Beryle Driscoll** lead a hike at Bear Hill and **Sally Matz** and **Della Sue Kass**, guided a tour of the Library and old Cragsmoor homes.

June 1- Walker Valley's Old Fashion Day, we were there participating.

June 15- CHS fund raiser theater party at Shadowland- the play, *Steel Magnolias*.

July 12 - Preserving Your Family Archives -with **Gary McGowan**, a Cultural Preservation and Restoration Specialist.

August 19 - Library Day - CHS headquarters used for the Art Show and rummage sale.

August 23- We participated in Ellenville's Annual Blueberry Festival

August 23 - Hosted the 1st. Annual Quilter's Quest. On display were quilts from the 1850's to the present time. Morning lectures on Judging a Quilt and Knowledge for the Quilter. In the evening, a lecture and demonstration about The Freedom Quilt and the Underground RR

August 29 - Sept. 7 -New Art Space- Art Exhibit "All in the Family " (see page 3.)

August and September - Exercise classes.

September 27 - Art Exhibit - "Out From Under" **Joan Lesikin**.(exhibit was moved to the artist studio due to bad storm conditions and our present roof, which is now under repair.)

October 9 - Sam's Point Conservation Center - ground-breaking ceremony.

November - Friends of the Shawangunks used the Headquarters for their meeting.

December 6-7 Best ever Holiday Bazaar!

Saturday mornings through out the year at the Post Office - **Vickie Batrus** and **Beverly Simonelli** conducted bake sales of all kinds of cookies, pies, cupcakes, candies and maple syrup. These are a very helpful fund raising events enjoyed by the whole community.

'Neither wind nor rain'…..) but, better said, "Even with wind, and rain, and snow, sleet and hail, we were able to have very exciting events take place at the Historical Headquarters this year. We also were invited to participate in "off campus" activities as well. We are getting a wonderful reputation of being "doers", "creative thinkers", and "go-getters".

The Cragsmoor Historical Society Headquarters building is available for services, talks, poetry readings, musicals, weddings and funerals.
Please book far in advance.

Cragsmoor Federated Church - 1906 now the Historical Society's Headquarters

This Column is dedicated to the progress of restoration to the Society's Headquarters.

During the month of June a grant writing committee was formed to gather informaton and prepare documents to apply for a 2003 Environmental Protection Fund Grant for the Historic Preservation of the former Cragsmoor Federated Church Building.

This committe consited of board members, Sally Matz, Lynn Garofalini, Larry Gobrecht, Maureeen Rahl and Tom Bolger. In order to meet the dead line of June 20, many long evening hours were spent working on this project. Pictures of the existing conditions were taken both inside and out. A project narative was formulated together with the scope of work.

We hired the firm of Crawford & Sterns to compile the recommendations and to create a Conditons Survey of this landmark building.

The committee's aim is to return this building to its former state as it was in the early 1900's. We started this project on our own by first stablizing the basement which is now always dry. Next the electrical system was repaired, the stone work on the exterior of the foundation was completed and something really modern and important a telephone was added.

The budget summary, part of this grant request totals $202,000. The grant request is for $101,000, our share, this is a matching type of grant. Hopefully we will be awarded the full amount and be able to complete this historic restoration project. We anxiously await some news on this grant it's on the Governers desk... *2/25/04 -We have just heard - NO , but we can reapply this coming Spring.*

As this journal goes to press, some good news - State Senator John J. Bonacic called to say that he has approved a Senate Legislative Initative of $10,000 to help bring us closer to our goal. A special thank you to Senator Bonacic for his efforts, we are most appreciatvie. *Ed.*

President's Message

"Patience is golden" I guess I really don't know what that means, or perhaps I'm impatient. If it were true and taken at face value, we would be squinting from the reflection of the CHS Headquarters.

We have written several Grants, not an easy task, which would really help raise the needed funds to make our Headquarters safe, sound, and secure. (To say nothing about being a pleasure to be in.) We are still anxiously waiting for a response – any words, one way or another about our applications. Believe me, you will hear, in a special letter, the moment we learn of our success.

In the meantime we're planning our Events for the 2004 Season keeping in mind that the largest Grant we've applied for is a matching Grant. That means that we must have the same amount of money that is being awarded to us. We really will concentrate to have activities that will bring in the most revenues.

Everyone has been so supportive of the Historical Society and we hope that you continue to help with your donations.

Let's get this building restored so that we can concentrate on being a Historical Society!

Sally Matz, Pres.

We Found Our House Through the New York Times

In 1961, my husband Henry and I read a sales ad in the Sunday Times for a house in Cragsmoor, and then went to see the place. Built at the end of the 19th century by Frederick Ketcham Clark, who called it "Pine Top Hill," it now lacked even the most basic amenities: Never electrified, and its gravity-water system-complete with fountains ¾ destroyed in a fight with a neighbor, the grounds were littered with construction debris and fresh stumps from logging.

However, the sliver of a view toward the Hudson, and the house itself: on a promontory, with tall white pines, hemlocks and oaks, struck a chord. Immediately we knew this was the house.

The following week we closed the deal in Ellenville at the law offices of Kaiser and Murray.

(continued on page two.)

England has its crop art circles , and we have Roger Baker Above his latest master piece.

CNN LIVE AT DAYBREAK
Look at Some Crop Art
Aired July 11, 2003 - 05:57 ET
THIS IS A RUSH TRANSCRIPT. THIS COPY MAY NOT BE IN ITS FINAL FORM AND MAY BE UPDATED.
FREDRICKA WHITFIELD, CNN ANCHOR: Well, you've probably heard of pop art. But what about crop art?CNN's Jeanne Moos takes us to a hayfield in New York that has immortalized the lives of Elvis and now Einstein.
(BEGIN VIDEOTAPE)
JEANNE MOOS, CNN CORRESPONDENT (voice-over): It's the next best thing to getting inside the mind of Albert Einstein.
(on camera): What is this?
ROGERBAKER, ARTIST: Einstein's hair.
MOOS: It's where you mowed him.
(BEGIN VIDEO CLIP)
UNIDENTIFIED MALE: Albert Einstein, genius.(END VIDEO CLIP)
MOOS (voice-over): Albert Einstein, crop art.
BAKER: These protrusions in the grass here are the wrinkles in his forehead.
MOOS: Einstein was tops in many fields and now a hayfield in the Catskill Mountains.
BAKER: We are now in his right eye.
MOOS: A 35 foot eye. But from the ground, you'd never know you'd stumbled on the glint in Albert Einstein's pupil.
Starting from a sketch, artist Roger Baker used lawn mower tractors to carve Einstein's portrait.
BAKER: He's got great hair. It's a great image to do. I've always been fascinated with the guy. His mustache is really cool.
MOOS (on camera): Oh, let's go to his mustache.
BAKER: Let's go to his mustache.
MOOS (voice-over): The crop portrait coincides with an exhibit on Einstein at New York's American Museum of Natural History. But the E in this E equals Mc squared is 120 feet tall.
BAKER: Oh, look at the deer.
MOOS (on camera): Do they eat Einstein?
BAKER: Yes, they've grazed on Albert.
MOOS (voice-over): Nibbled on and landed on.
(on camera): So hang gliders land here?
BAKER: Hang gliders land here.

MOOS (voice-over): Some of these pictures were taken by a parasail pilot as he drifted back to earth. You can even see the shadow of an ultra light plane piloted by another photographer. Sure, there have been other crop portraits, from Larry King to Babe Ruth, but not with the fine lines of Einstein. This is not Roger's first.
(on camera): So Elvis was here and down there?
BAKER: It covered as far as you could see.
MOOS (voice-over): Last year, Elvis was cut into the very same field. The high point was mowing Elvis' sideburns.
From a hang glider's point of view...
UNIDENTIFIED MALE: When you really see it nice is when you're coming in to land.
MOOS: More than once Albert Einstein has had to take it on the chin, but this is one straw man who never had to say if I only had a brain.
Jeanne Moos, CNN, Ellenville, New York.
(END VIDEOTAPE
So what does Roger call his latest art form? "Field Art,"if you want to put a name to it."
"If I had a company, I'd call it Bakersfield." he said. *(Our thanks to CNN.NET for the transcript)*

❧❧❧

FROM OUR POST CARDS ARCHIVES

Winter Scene - Cragsmoor N.Y. early 1900's

❧❧❧

CRAGSMOOR, NEW YORK
From Wikipedia, the free encyclopedia.
Cragsmoor is a town located in Ulster County, New York. As of the 2000 census, the town had a total population of 474.
Geography - Cragsmoor is located at 41°40'6" North, 74°23'17" West (41.668298, -74.387962)1. According to the United States Census Bureau, the town has a total area of 11.3 km² (4.4 mi²). 11.3 km² (4.4 mi²) of it is land and none of the area is covered with water.
Demographics - As of the census of 2000, there are 474 people, 189 households, and 137 families residing in the town. The population density is 41.9/km² (108.5/mi²). There are 257 housing units at an average density of 22.7/km² (58.8/mi²).Racial makeup of thetown is 94.09% White, 0.00% African American, 0.84% Native American, 0.00% Asian, 0.00% Pacific Islander, 1.48% from other races, and 3.59% from two or more races. 4.85% of the population are Hispanic or Latino of any race.

There are 189 households out of which 29.6% have children under age18 living with them, 59.3% are married couples living together, 8.5% have a female householder with no husband present, and 27.5% are non-families. 20.1% of all households are made up of individuals and 9.0% have someone living alone who is 65 years of age or older. The average household size is 2.51 and the average family size is 2.92.

In the town the population is spread out with 23.2% under the age of 18, 5.5% from 18 to 24, 27.2% from 25 to 44, 31.6% from 45 to 64, and 12.4% who are 65 years of age or older. The median age is 40 years. For every 100 females there are 100.8 males. For every 100 females age 18 and over, there are 96.8 males.

The median income for a household in the town is $64,500, and the median income for a family is $56,250. Males have a median income of $42,250 versus $55,556 for females. The per capita income for the town is $22,712. 11.1% of the population and 9.4% of families are below the poverty line. Out of the total people living in poverty, 19.1% are under the age of 18 and 0.0% are 65 or older.

❧❧❧

We found our house.... (con't from page one.)
The seller was Ernie Muller, who had bought the property from Ferdinand and Doris Decker, Clark's heirs.

That summer, at seven each morning I drove to the phone booth at "Ridge Runners Roost" on Route 52 to prod the Ellenville Electric Company into bringing us power. First they demanded $5000 a pole, but then agreed to do it free, conceding that other houses might be built someday. Earl Tice and his young nephew Earl Thornton did the wiring and Kenneth Clark installed the plumbing, aided by Claude Marl on backhoe. When Clyde Gresham, our first handyman, proved inefficient, we engaged the first of many carpenters: Irving Baxter. With "electric" came a telephone (Ellenville 205R1). The operator would inquire, "number, please," when one picked up the receiver.

We hired Francis Schwab to build a retaining wall. Henry wanted a dry-laid stonewall, and Francis was one of the few who remembered that then-dying art. Later, he helped Henry with other projects, including a terrace of architectural stone samples from Henry's office, Emery Roth and Sons. Many of these stones can be found in New York's high-rise buildings of the sixties and seventies. We imported topsoil for flowers and even succeeded in growing a lawn over our gravel surface.

Marie Stanger was the first to welcome us, bringing a small gift. *Leni Kroul*

Cragsmoor Heritage **CHS 2**

New Art Space at CHS

Ellie Hollinshead, Ellie Brown Croyder and Hattie Croyder Buchholz are present day Cragsmoor artists in the "All in the Family" tradition. They are niece, mother and daughter, and they trace their roots to an earlier family artist, Hannah Carpenter Gaskin. Hannah Carpenter Gaskin (1835-1911) was Ellie Croyder's great grandmother, the mother of Judge Brown's wife, Helen. It was, in fact, Hannah Carpenter who first introduced Judge Brown to Cragsmoor. She was a teacher, an artist, and an inspiration to the single mothers and struggling artists of today! After the death of their young son, Ralph,from scarlet fever, Hannah's husband walked out, and she was left to support little Helen on her own. She managed with style - teaching painting in New York City and at Rutgers University, and finally opening her own art school in Poughkeepsie - quite a feat for a woman of her day. Her great, great granddaughter, Ellie Hollinshead, is proud to own Hannah Carpenter's palette and easel. Ellie Hollinshead began drawing and painting at a very early age and Cragsmoor has been an important influence on her art. This can be noted in her use of animal imagery and vivid representation of plant life. Cragsmoor memories are reflected in Ellie's later landscapes too. Some of her paintings evoke the fleeting passage of childhood; some are studded with collage keepsakes, writings and bits of nature. Some recall classical or mythological themes. All show a close bond with nature.
Hollinshead received her MFA from Indiana University after studying art and art history at Oxford University and obtaining her BA with distinction in Art from Yale University. She has been a faculty member at the Rhode Island School of Design since 1982 and is presently an Associate Professor of Art. Her work has been featured in over 40 exhibitions including solo shows at the Greenberg /Wilson Gallery, the Nancy Moore Gallery, and in a group show at The Drawing Center. She will be exhibiting new work in a two-person show at The Painting Center in New York City this coming fall. Her work has been favorably reviewed by The New York Times, Artforum, Cover, Artspeak, and The Providence Journal.

Ellie Croyder, Ellie Hollinshead's aunt, has also been influenced by Cragsmoor and its artistic tradition. As a child, she ranged the mountaintop with Sally and Peter Howell and Arthur Liang - enjoying the freedom and relaxed pace of a by gone era. She recalls watching Charles Curran, Arthur's grandfather, complete oil paintings in his garage-studio. She remembers Judy Hunsicker too, who always allowed a younger generation watch her work. Ellie was also privileged to attend the Kinaloha classes of Cragsmoor artists, Rachel Taylor and Ruth Garrigues.
Ellie graduated from Vassar in 1956 and resumed painting some years later when her five children were half grown. She studied portraiture and landscape painting with Elisabeth Boyd in the Washington DC area where she has sold and exhibited. Cragsmoor remains a primary inspiration for Ellie. She enjoys photographing favorite views and vistas in the summer and painting them in the less harried winter months. Ellie enjoys painting figures in outdoor settings and also specializes in pet portraits and miniatures.
She is the proud grandmother of six. Like her mother, Ellie, and her cousin, Ellie, Hattie Croyder Buchhold loved childhood summers in Cragsmoor. She admired her cousin's paintings, and with her twin sister, Polly, sometimes modeled for Ellie Hollinshead. Hattie is a keen observer of nature and her favorite subjects are trees, animals and water creatures. Hattie works in several media and her art ranges from the whimsical to the realistic to the abstract. Hattie graduated in 1989 from Washington University in St. Louis with a BFA in printmaking.

She is versed in collographs, lithographs, woodcuts, and etching. Before college, Hattie attended a Rhode Island School of Design summer art program and later, spent four months in Florence, Italy studying printmaking and Batik. She has exhibited with The National Wildlife Federation and shown and sold work in Virginia and Maryland. Hattie's fanciful illustrations of fruits, vegetables and animals appeared in a published cookbook. At present, Hattie is working with her mother on three children's stories; two are dinosaur tales and the third is about a little girl with a magic seashell. Hattie is the mother of two toddlers and also holds a Masters Degree and license in social work. *Ellie Brown Croyder*

The Cragsmoor Historical Society hosted an exhibition of works by these three women of the Brown family at the Historical Society headquarters August to September.

❧❧

FIREMATICS - ANNUAL SERVICE
August 10th,2003
Welcome, by Pres. Bill Ruston
Good Morning. On behalf of the Officers and Members of The Cragsmoor Volunteer Fire Company it is my pleasure to welcome you to our fourth annual Firematic Service. The theme of today's service is heroes: both at home and overseas.
As in the past, it is particularly wonderful that we can look forward to a morning of excellent music.

The music will stir the soul and lift the spirit. Playing trumpet today will be Katrina Kass, the daughter of one of our members, and Dr. Ambrose Jackson, a music teacher in the Ellenville Schools. Dr. Jackson is also Katrina's teacher. Singing this morning will be members of the New Amsterdam Singers. And, of course, we are pleased that our Chaplain, Chuck Matz, will be leading us on the piano. We welcome all of you and appreciate your efforts on this congregation's behalf.
We especially welcome to this service Chaplain Franklin Knower, who will be officiating and giving us his thoughts on the Scripture. Chaplain Knower has been a firefighter for 35 years and has served as a Chaplain for 29 years, working with FASNY and the Nyack Hospital.
Finally, we will remember that great hero, Bob Hope, who took care of our fighting men and women around the world for the past 50 years. As USA Today wrote "Particularly worth remembering ... are [Bob] Hope's deepheld beliefs about the debt the nation owes its young men and women it sends to fight its wars. While that debt can never be repaid, Hope showed us how it can be recognized."
Once again, I am pleased to welcome all of you to this service.

The first of this annual service was held on August 6th,2000, in honor of the Fire Company's 50 Anniversary.

❧❧

Stalagmites, Stalicties or Cragssickels?, Jan.'04
❧❧

TURN OFF
From dawn to dusk chores to do
and problems to solve.
Now it's time to slow down and
turn your head off.
Dinner is done and lights are dim.
Please head turn off.
Hot shower taken warm walk too.
Please head turn off.
The clock has both hands up.
Head it's time to turn off.
Nothing but boredom on TV.
Head won't you turn off.
It's three AM and all is quiet.
Head Please turn off.
Now it's four. Damn it head I
said turn of-zzzzz.

Art Liang

Cragsmoor Historical Soceity
P O Box 354
Cragsmoor New York 12420

U.S. Postage Paid
Non-profit Org.
Permit #42006
Newburgh NY
12552

Join - Renew

MILESTONES

CONGRATULATIONS

Vincent "Pete" Stanger - is the only person known who gets younger with each Birthday! February 10th he was 91 years young. (Sorry about the misprint in the past issue.)

Major Jack J. Jensen -was promoted to LT. Col Jensen. He is now in Afghanistan for the second time. (Jack is the son-in-law of Sally and Chuck Matz.)

Margaret Louise Matz -born Nov. 9th, 2003, in Boston. She is the third daughter of Bridget and David Matz.

CONDOLANCES

Albert W. Rode
Grace R. Carlew
Margaret Noell Kindberg

We all express our deepest sympathy to the families of our departed friends.

Autumn in Cragsmoor

My favorite time of year. Orchards filled of beautiful ripe apples, leaves turning color, geese flying south for the winter. The monarch butterfly on his way to Mexico. These things happen every year.

Election day - now with over 300 registered voters in Cragsmoor can be very busy. Veteran's Day in Cragsmoor is rather a quiet time. Halloween, a time for Jack O'Lanters, masks, costumes and trick or treat. Noticing the Halloween decorations more prolefic every year.

The annual Historic House Tour is one of the special autumn happenings in Cragsmoor.

It is also a wonderful time for hikers at Sam's Point. Thanksgiving is that special time for families to gather and celebrate the harvest with exceptional feasts and a time to be thankful for all God's gifts.

Now is the time to look forward to the first snow fall and the long winter ahead.
V. Pete Stanger

Thanks you to **David Howell** for adding to our archives by donating two original paintings by former artist **Edward J. Gay**.

We are the recipient of a grant from the Dutchess Counel on the Arts. This grant will help our Theater Productions this Spring. We very much appreciate this award. **Tom Bolger** will be organizing this years *"Theater in The Clouds."* Anyone interested in theater arts can contact him at 647-7937 or tbolger70@cs.com This season we will be working on a Readers's Theater to be held on *Saturday Nights.* and two major productions.

A very special ***Thank you*** to our postmaster, **Rudy Travali**. He's always very helpful and extends himself to be a part of our community. Rudy goes beyond his call of duty as a postmaster, to be a good citizen and neighbor.

Once again the **Holiday Tree** at the Post Office was lighted on December 8th. This tree honors all the community volunteers who give of themselves continiously. A lovely holiday party followed at the Firehouse.

CHS
Cragsmoor Historical Journal
P O Box 354, Cragsmoor, New York 12420
Founded in 1996
Thomas E. Bolger, Publisher 1996 -
Publishing @ Rockledge, Cragsmoor, N.Y. 12420-0070

Cragsmoor Historical Journal

Dedicated to Preserving Cragsmoor's History

| Volume 5 Issue 3   Published by the Cragsmoor Historical Society, Inc.,   Post Office 354, Cragsmoor, N.Y. 12420 | Winter - 2005 |

EVENTS: 2004

FEBRUARY - We hosted the Friends of the Stone Church for their Sunday Service. The chapel was still in the process of having the inside archway cleaned and repointed. One hundred years of dripping water left a thick layer of mineral deposits, including the formation of several stalactites. Be sure to notice the excellent cleaning job that was done.

MAY 29-31 - WE PARTICIPATED IN THE MOUNTAIN TOP YARD SALE.

JUNE 6 - We hosted a Theatre/Reception Party. Those who attended were entertained by a wonderful production at the Shadowland Theatre in Ellenville then returned for a lovely reception at The Pines in Cragsmoor. The theatre personnel and actors also joined us at the reception.

JUNE 6 - Old Fashion Day in Walker Valley

JUNE - MASS APPEAL at the Playhouse

JUNE 26 - The Library held their Annual Meeting in the Event Room

July 10 - Archival Day with Archivist Gary McGowan.   Gary was very helpful in sharing recipes and Do and Don'ts for cleaning metal items (silver, copper, brass, and pewter) and storing paper and material artifacts.

JULY 15 - The Director of Sam's Point held a Staff Meeting at the CHS Headquarters.

AUGUST 15 - Library Festival

AUGUST 20 - Blueberry Festival was held in Ellenville; we had a table and sold items made by a group of Creative Ladies from our Society.

AUGUST - Save Me a Place at Forest Lawn.

AUGUST 2 The Shawangunk Garden Club held their monthly meeting at the Headquarters.

OCTOBER - Save Me A Place at Forest Lawn at the Playhouse.

DECEMBER 9-11 - The Holiday Bazaar This was the most successful **Bazaar** thus far.

A charming corner of the 2004 Bazaar

We're working on the 2005 event aleady to make it even more unique.

Cragsmoor Federated Church - 1906 now the Historical Society's Headquarters

---

This Column is dedicated to the progress of restoration to the Society's Headquarters.

The Green Roof!

This is probably a more appropriate color. The old roof consisted of green tin shingles and the new one will be also.

Currently the 2004 Environmental Protection Fund-Historic Preservation Grant that we applied again for is on the Governer's desk. We are anxiously waiting to hear. This is a matching grant which will involve our community in saving the Old Federated Church building.

We are awaiting on pins and needles, with bated breath and verklempt (can't speak) for word on our grant application.

We were rejected last time we applied in 2003. There is only so much money and a lot of applicants. Awards are given by a panel of judges who decide which project is the neediest. This grant is statewide, so many counties apply. In 2003 only two projects were awared grants in Ulster County.

Our Historic Society grant-writing panel is doing its best to accomplish this task of receiving a 2004 grant.

In Sally Matz's Presidents Message, we applied for, and will receive some monies to work on another project, an Archival Room in the basement of the building. Work on this project will begin some time in the near future.

Restoration to historic building is expensive and time consuming. However, there is no other way to achieve success. We are trying every way we know to get the help and money needed to preserve this building.

Our concern for the community and its heritage is important to the Society. Preserving our history both past and present is part of our mission. We've started with the green roof.

The age of computors strives for the fastest way to communicate. In 1911 for a connection just pick up the telephone and say **CRAGSMOOR**, that may have been the original road-runner.

PRESIDENT'S MESSAGE

"Obstacles are things we see when we take our eyes off the goal." This belief is alive and well in the thinking of the Board Members of the Historical Society!

We certainly have had our share of imposing obstacles, but finally the tide (even on the mountain) is beginning to turn. We received a very generous grant of $10,000 from our Legislator John J. Bonacic which will enable us to move ahead with one of our goals. We have proven that the basement is dry, the walls and floor are secure, and now we can make this space into an **ARCHIVAL ROOM.** We have collected thus far an impressive amount of Cragsmoor History - family histories, anecdotal stories, pictures, postcards, photos and artifacts. We will have a secured space to properly store and then share the collection with the community. With this room we will be able to continue to collect archival materials and preserve our history so that it does not get lost and forgotten but preserved for future generations.

These collections will be properly stored in fire resistant cabinets and in a moisture controlled atmosphere. Also, the Cragsmoor Association has a sizeable number of files which are presently being stored in our basement. The completed **ARCHIVAL ROOM** will insure the preservation of these materials, as well.

Part of our Mission Statement is to preserve and protect. It is gratifying to know that this is being done in the proper way.

We are extremely grateful to Senator Bonacic for his financial help. This room will become a reality because of his help. There also have been many other people and organizations within our community and from neighboring communities who have been supporting our efforts. We are so invigorated and strengthened by this support. Let's keep this inertia moving forward!

Sally Matz, Pres.

Ever Wonder Where "That" Came From? Now you Know!

In the late 1700's many houses consisted of a large room with only one chair. Commonly, a long wide board was folded down from the wall and used for dining. The "head of the household" always sat in the chair while everyone else ate standing or sitting on the floor. (continued on page 4.)

Mahamudra Hermitage

A Buddhist Retreat Center planned for 89 acres on Cragsmoor Road.

Darmakaya, a tax-exempt Buddhist group, recently submitted a sketch plan to the Town Planning Board for a retreat center that they plan to build. A meeting was held on Sunday January 16th at the Firehouse so the Community would have a chance to discuss the project.

The proposal is of such a large scale that it will have a major impact on Cragsmoor and Warwarsing. Representative of Dharmakya, the group planning the retreat were invited to attend, but could not be present.

To learn more about this project and for a copy of questions concerning the Mahamudra Buddhist Hermitage, please contact Jim McKenney, Pres. of the Cragsmoor Association. (jim@jhmck.com or 647-8291)

The 2004 season included two, each with two character, plays. First, **Mass Appeal** by **Bill Davis.** We were very pleased to have the author of the play with us at the final performance.

This play dealt with the relationship of a older, wiser priest and a younger student in training. We were fortunate to have two talented award winning actors came to Cragsmoor to play these roles, **R. David Townley and Christopher Weber.** The production was met with excellent reviews. **James F. Cotter** for The Times, Herald Record wrote... "Scenic Artist **Roger Baker**, created an imaginative gothclike parish office,"featuring "stain glass" windows, created with sidewalk chalk. **April Mari's** costumes also helped capture the liturgical setting. **Tom Bolger** deserves credit for producing this play with a fine cast in a churchlike setting."

In October we presented **Save Me A Place at Forest Lawn** by Lorees Yerby. The story of two elderly women, dear friends, who plan their demise. This play also won critical aclaim by the drama critic for the The Associated Press. "The two actors performed with and against each other with believability and conviction, they seem to be soul mates on stage. **Shiela Glenn and Sara Simas** graced our stage for a reunion performance after 30 years of not working together. The setting was a lunch room in Hollywood,Calfornia, the set decoration was achieved by residents drawning with sidewalk chalk on the black walls.

We were fortunate to have the **Dutchess County Arts Council** help with a grant. The 2004 season was our second grant award. This year we applied again to the Arts Council and were awarded $1,375 at a grants cermoney held at the Cunnen-Hacket House in Poughkeepsie. We were also awarded a *Certificate of Merit* from Senator John J. Bonacic.

This season a *Second Stage -A Reader's Theater,* is planned, perhaps on Saturday nights with a light dinner. Interested? call Tom Bolger at 647-7937 or tbolger70@cs.com.

The Critters of Cragsmoor Chapel

I was given the great privilege of being taken to Cragsmoor in the summer of 1944. I was six months old and like my mother before me, grew up in that most beautiful mountain community. My eyes probably first focused on the blue Catskills to the north and the white cliffs of Sam's Point to the east. As I grew up I was taken to the stone church or as it is properly called, The Chapel of the Holy Name, every summer Sunday for services. The church is built on the style of English country churches and sits on the edge of the mountain. The ladies took great care cleaning the floors and pews and arranging flowers from their gardens each week. A priest from Ellenville or in the early days, from Cragsmoor itself, conducted the service which was of the Anglican persuasion.

We all loved animals, but we didn't take them to church. At least we didn't plan to take them.

Everyone I knew had a dog or two and a cat. Some even had horses. My mother, for several summers, rented a horse for us and returned her in September. One summer we had an especially smart mare named Maud. It didn't take long for Maud to figure out her door latch and opened it with her lips. One Sunday morning, before we realized what Maud was doing, we got an angry phone call from Mrs. Lewis, who was the church's most ardent caretaker.
All I heard was my mother say,"Oh I am sorry. We'll go get her right away and clean it up." Maud had moseyed over to the church, ate her fill of grass, left foot prints on the lawn and a large gift on the steps. That was only one animal incident at the stone church.

One very, humid lazy August Sunday as we sat in the chapel listening to the rector, a small snake emerged from the stones behind the minister's head. We all sat up straight and stared. The snake wavered around and the priest kept speaking and then the snake disappeared back into the wall.

After service we told the priest what happened and he laughed and said that he wondered what was so especially compelling about his sermon. Many times a dog would follow his family to church and you would hear barking or tag jingling until the dog found his family. If he or she was good she could stay, if noisy you would hear someone taking the pet out.

There were weddings in the church and garden parties on the lawn and we loved hearing the bell toll when someone pulled the big, thick rope. We all took turns on the rope.

The chapel is still there today thanks to those who work to keep it going and I hope it always will be. I learned the most important things in life, manners, friendship, kindness, laughter and doing one's share, within its warm and friendly walls. *By Lucy (Hunsicker) Muller*

Happenings in 2004:
Cragsmoor Association: (see column one)

Stone Church:
New stainglass window installed in June, honoring the memory of Afton Audree Johnson Slade, Jeff Slade's mother. The Interfaith Window includes symbols of eight major religions. "For my house shall be called a house of prayer for all people."

Isaiah 56:7

Peace Pole

May Peace Prevail on Earth
This message is in eight corresponding languages. Peace Poles Around the World: Over 250,000 planted in extraordinary locations: Magnetic North Pole, Pyramids of El Giza, Egypt, Gorky Park, Russia, Atomic Bomb Dome, Hiroshima, The Hague, Netherlands and Cragsmoor, New York.

Sam's Point: A new visitors center has been built and will be dedicated in May.

Cragsmoor Free Library:January 2004 events started off with, Origami with Della Sue, February the annual Valentine's Day Party .Mother's Day Flower Sale, the annual Bird Cage Party was held July 17th The annual Festival Day was held on the 14th of August., annual Walking Tour days in September, the RAKE IT IN RAFFLE tickets sold out.

"**Game Night**", for the Youth Group is very popular. **Book signing** - Sue Sternberg- Successful Dog Adoption, John E. Winkler- An Enchanted Land: The Shawangunk Mountains, Charles Davidson and Lincoln Diamant. Cowrote - Stamping Our History. "Is Your Mind Playing Trick or Treat?" -a presentation by Dr. Kathleen Covalt., Dr. Irene Seeland- The View from My Window - Poems and Prayers - the Songs of my Life.

A **surprise farewell party** was given for departing Director, Eileen Kolaitis. The new director of the Library is Hattie Grifo.

Cragsmoor Volunteer Fire Company - held their annual Ecumenical Sevice. Semiannual Pancake Breakfasts which we alwys look forward too. Remember to test your smoke detetors and dial 911 for all emergency calls.

Once again the Holiday Tree at the Post Office was lighted This tree was errected to honor all the community volunteers who give of themselves continiously.

Cragsmoor Heritage   **CHS 2**

Landmark Status

Over 78,000 properties have been added to the National Register of Historic Places since the roster was created in 1966. This status for your house can mean money in your pocket, but it may come with strings attached.

The best-known historic house designation is a listing on the National Register of Historic Places, a roster of properties administered by the National Park Service. While such a listing validates a house's period architectural character-and offers prestige that may lead to a modest resale boost--it is considered "honorary" and carries no restrictions on what the owner can do to the property. That means it offers no protections, either.

So why bother being on this National Register listing? The answer is simple: tax breaks. If your house is at least 50 years old and is a good example of a period architectural style, getting it listed can open the door to significant financial benefit--state income-tax credits and/or municipal property-tax reductions--that can offset the cost of fixing the place up. (For more information go to www.cr.nps.gov/nr/listing.htm).

The Ultimate Preservation Strategy: Giving it Away.

If you're really serious about preserving your old house, take matters into your own hands by granting a preservation easement to a nonprofit organization, such as a local historical society. Not only will you save your house, you'll be making a charitable donation that you can write off on our income taxes. An easement is basically an attachment to the deed that grants the recipient legal rights to a portion of the property, whether the entire structure, just the facade, or a single room. Once recorded, a preservation easement becomes part of the property's chain of title, binding not only the homeowner who grants it but future owners as well and as a result you'll pay less in property taxes. While it may reduce the appraised market value, because you no longer own all of it, the "Listing" can also have significantly higher resale value. To get the tax write-off, the house must be listed on the National Register of Historic Places and the easement must go to an approved non-profit.

For more information, go to http://www2.cr.nps.gov/tps/tax/easement.htm.

Preservation restrictions might impinge on your right to redesign your porch, but they can also prevent your neighbor from erecting a vinyl-sided McMansion in place of the clapboard salbox next door.

Many houses here in Cragsmoor are in the Historic District. To learn more about historic conservation, there are federal standards known as *"The Secretary of the Interior's Standards For the Treatment of Historic Properties."* These federal standards will help in preservation, rehabilitation, restoration and reconstruction. Rebuilding a historic home requires a special contractor or developer who is licensed and experienced in the work, both hands-on experience and experience working with your local planning, building and permits offices.

Ask friends, family, co-workers and others you trust for referrals for experienced contractor in historic properties, then check him or her out as you would any contractor.

(information for this artical gathered from This Old House-March, '05 article by D.Akst and RealtyTimes, article by B.Perkins)

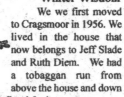

Pete's Words of Winter Wisdom

We we first moved to Cragsmoor in 1956. We lived in the house that now belongs to Jeff Slade and Ruth Diem. We had a tobaggan run from above the house and down around the driveway. Good fun!

One winter we had so much snow it took 3 days for the bulldozer (it was fairly common for bulldozers to do the plowing) to clear the road to Sam's Point. You could walk up the middle of the road on packed snow 3 feet high -drifts were left. We had to park our car at the firehouse and bring our groceries home by toboggan.

On weekends we would take the toboggan over on the golf course between the Beverage cottage and the Munsen house - whizz - walk a mile!! Then stop at Munsens for hot chocolate and brownies or come home for the same with the Stanger and Houghtaling children.

We would put on our skies at the front door and go back thru the woods and around Bear Cliff and back thru the Cragsmoor Inn property looking for animal tracks.

One year the plow piled up snow in our yard and John, our son, made an igloo with an electric light, radio and rug. Another year John made an Easter Bunny 10 feet tall on the front lawn when we had a late winter storm and an early Easter.

Since they didn't plow the Gully Road, one Sunday, John, our son and Cecilia, our daughter rode down the Gully on their sleds to church in Ellenvile.

Another winter when there wasn't much snow we went ice skating on Horn's pond. It was quiet popular back then.

One Christmas eve when our daughter, Mary was here with family, we woke up and it was 25° below zero! Our son-in-law, who was from the Dakotas, didn't know it got that in New York.

We didn't have a snowmobile and a lot of TV, so we played pinochole, poker and other games inside and tried to keep warm when it was super cold. Layering of clothes is still the best way to keep warm outside. *Pete Stanger- age 92*

❧

FROM OUR POST CARD ARCHIVES

Postmarked July 27, 1905, this postcard depicts the original church and steeple before the addition of the community room.

Inscription Found on Rock

One bright, colorful audumn day last year, when the call of mountain trails was irresistible, Ken and Lucille Phillips drove over to Sam's Point near Cragsmoor and hiked across the backbone of the Shawangunks to Awosting Lake. This seven-mile hike through uninhabited wildness, with views of river valley on both sides of the mountain, is an exhilarating tonic at anytime, but this day it was golden! The Verkeerderkill Falls, about half way to Awosting, were a sparkling mist in the sun, dancing and tumbling in cascades to the foaming stream far below. A mile or so beyond at Haseco Lake a brisk breese blew and wild ducks were bobbing up and down.

Before reaching Haseco, however, they stopped to admire an unusual extensive view from a broad, flat slab of glacier-polished rock on one of the highest points of the ridge. Glancing down at their feet, they were puzzled to see letters cut in the rock, partly obliterated by time and lichen. A few words were legible and intriguing, but time was slipping by so it was necessary to wait for another day to satisfy their curiosity. A number of people were questioned, but on one seemed to have any knowledge of an inscription there.

At the first opportunity after their house was closed for the season, Lucille and Ken hiked there again, with Suzy and Kevin this time, taking a roll of while paper and pencils to make a "rubbing." Finally deciphered, it read "Who amoung us shall dwell with everlasting burnings."

When Dominie and Mrs. Wullschleger of New Paltz heard the story, they quickly traced the quotation to Isaish 33.14. Reading that chapter in the Bibile, and then reading "Legends of the Shwangunk" by Philip H. Smith, published in 1887, with its hair-raising tales of Indian massacres, scalpings, burning of homes and crops, kidnapping and forced marches, captured prisoners, Tories and Revolutionists - it is easy to imagine a religious man, perhaps having lost home and family in an Indian uprising or Colonial war, seeking sanctuary high on the mountain, looking over the vast expanse of then undeveloped land toward the Hudson River, searching his soul for God's answer.

If any reader knows about the origin of this inscription the information will be much appreciated.

The above appeared in the Minnewaska News in the Spring of !960. The article was sent to Bill Howell in 1979 by Lucille Philip, in her notes she added "I have also hear mention of inscriptions at the base of Verkeerderkill Falls, which include the word "devil" or "devils."

Sam's Point Ledge 2,342 a.s.l.

Cragsmoor Heritage   **CHS 3**

Cragsmoor Historical Soceity
P O Box 354
Cragsmoor New York 12420

Permit #42006
Newburgh NY
12552

Join - Renew

Grants Awarded

$1.14 million in grants were awarded for 10 projects as part of a program to help Hudson Valley communities redevelop waterfront areas, create outdoor recreational opportunities, and protect local landmarks.

Ulster County projects include $100,000 to restore the **Cragsmoor Federated Church** in the **Cragsmoor Historic District** and $25,374 for the Village of Ellenville to improve **Berme Road Park**.

Wawarsing.Net Magazine • 2005 August
Issue 33   Page 6

CONGRATULATIONS

David L. Howell's new book *Geographies of Identity In Nineteenth-Century Japan* has just been publised. David is a former resident of Cragsmoor and currently is Professor of East Asian Studes and History at Princeton University. (He is also the brother of Sally Matz.)

❧

Eileen Kolaitis former Librarian of the Cragsmoor Free Library is off to new adventures in teaching. Eileen was the first secretary of the Cragsmoor Historical Society. We wish her well it was a pleasure to have her be part of our community. *Good Luck Eileen!*

❧

Opportunities

C.H.S. receives monthly notices from the *Dutchess County Arts Council*, regarding grants in the Arts. They include Art Projects, Fellowship Programs, mini grants, Curotorial Opportunities, Virtual Projects, Literary Arts, Media Arts, Theater Arts, Puppet Theater, Photography, Pottery, Sculpture, Ceramics, and more. Grants range from $250. to $10.000. For a copy of the latest bulletin, e mail Tom Bolger at tbolger70@cs.com.

❧

Continued page 1. Ever Wondered....

Once in a while an invited guest would be offered to sit in this chair during a meal (who was almost always a man.) To sit in the chair meant you were important and in charge. Sitting in the chair, one was called the "chair man." Today in business we use the expression/title "Chairman of the Board."

❧

CONDOLANCES

Our sincerest sympathies are extended to the families of these members of the Historical Society and friends to Cragsmoor who have passed this year. Their energies, kindnesses and good deeds will be missed.

Mary Frances Butterfield
George Christie
Michael Mc Combs
Dorothy Mc Combs
Arthur K. Holden
Andrew L. Jackson
Edward Keefer
Margaret Noel Kindberg
Sara Levy
Milton Resnick
Dorothy Reustle
Iven Veit
Lewis Hays Waugh, Jr.
Barbara Weber

Announcement

The CHS is proud and very pleased to announced that **Carolyn Peters Baker** has joined our Board. Carolyn, the daughter of C.Ralph Peters and Hilda, is very well known for her gardening skills and enthusiam for anything that she does. She has been a resident of Cragsmoor most of her life and has many friends and relatives who are quite knowledgeable of Cragsmoor's past. Carolyn contributed greatly to the success of the Christmas Bazaar.

We are also very pleased to announce that **Alicia von Rhein** has become a member of the Board and also has taken over the job of Secretary. Alicia is a 25 year resident of Cragsmoor who formerly worked in New York City.

We are so fortunate to have both Carolyn and Alicia as memebers of the Society and on our Board .

CHS
Cragsmoor Historical Journal
P O Box 354, Cragsmoor, New York 12420
Founded in 1996
Thomas E. Bolger, Publisher 1996 -
Publishing @ Rock Ledge, Cragsmoor, N.Y. 12420-0070

51

Cragsmoor Holiday Bazaar, A Real Roof Raiser

by Thomas E. Bolger

The *Cragsmoor Historical Society* will be holding their annual holiday bazaar on **December 6th & 7th** from **10: 00 AM to 5:00 PM** on the **Cragsmoor Road**. This annual event again will be for two days, due to popular demand! And, we're literally raising our roof!

Well-known Cragsmoor artists, craftspersons, and local entrepreneurs are making one-of-a-kind items for this event. Our gourmet cooks will be serving homemade soups to keep you warm. Our resident bakers will have a variety of homemade goodies for your holiday table. There will be a special table for animal lovers, with items your pets will enjoy. Nature lovers are not to be forgotten either. Wreaths made from our own mountain greenery and live plants for the season will be available for you to purchase. There are just too many gift-giving possibilities available to mention here.

The *Cragsmoor Historical Society* was founded in 1996 for the purpose of preserving and sharing the history of Cragsmoor. In the year 1997, the Board of *the Federated Church* gave the building to the *Society*. Since that very first day, the *Society* has been making a conscientious effort to restore the building so that it would appropriately house the history of the mountain and the area and be able to display the history for others. *(See Issue #11, page 11 of Wawarsing.Net for details.)*

Then, the big blow of needing a new roof for the 124-year-old building became apparent; the weight of the snows would definitely have collapsed the building. However, we ran out of money and are currently awaiting a building restoration grant. The building is ready to receive the metal shingles similar in design to the rusty old ones that had to be removed. The interior ceiling will also be restored. As you can imagine restoration is much more costly than repairing. We're getting there, but still have a long way to go.

Please help us "raise the roof" in Cragsmoor! For more information call **647-6384** or **647-8378**.

Forward, into the Past

Revisiting The "Lost" Cragsmoor Country Club

by Geoff Walsh, *PGA*

Rising majestically from a mountain plateau 1,857 feet above the valley, *The Cragsmoor Inn* opened in 1904. Under the guidance of Austa Densmore Sturdevant, a remarkable visionary, artist, and renaissance woman, the Inn flourished for decades. With the promise of clean, cool, invigorating air, the 105-room Cragsmoor Inn became a getaway destination for many a harried guest. Vistas of unparalleled beauty were visible; ever changing, yet ever remaining the same. The profile of the Shawangunk Mountain Range to the east remains constant. The promontory today known as **Sam's Point** juts out notably from the ridge. The rolling hills to the west and the Catskills to the north provide Cragsmoorians and visitors a comfort and promise that suggests this view will remain forever undisturbed.

In 1924, on land leased from, and adjacent to, the Cragsmoor Inn, a nine-hole golf course, reputed to be one of the best in the east, had its beginning.

The firm of Wayne E. Stiles, Golf Architect, was hired and construction began in the autumn of 1924. Mr. Stiles had an office in Boston and partnered with John Van Kleek, who ran a branch of the company in St. Petersburg, Florida. Mr. Stiles built more than sixty courses between 1924 and 1932, mainly in New England. The 1920s are widely recognized as the Golden Age of course design, and Mr. Stiles's designs placed him in direct competition with the most prolific and preeminent golf architect of the twentieth century, Donald Ross. Mr. Ross worked out of a Rhode Island location, and the two vied for many course designs in the northeast. Many compare the works of

Continued –

Cragsmoor Historical Society
P O Box 354
Cragsmoor NY 12420

52

Wayne E. Stiles with Donald Ross's, certainly a compliment to Mr. Stiles's abilities. His courses remain highly respected to this day.

Under the direction of Mr. Stiles and his site foreman Leonard Marl – a native Cragsmoorian – six holes were ready for play in the spring of 1925… and the game was on. With the addition of three holes, the nine officially opened in August 1928. Soon, plans for another nine holes on adjacent land owned by Mr. Inness received consideration. In keeping with the conditions of ownership, Mr. Inness agreed to deed the tract of land to the *Cragsmoor Company, Inc.* at a cost of two shares of preferred stock per acre. Those nine, never built, apparently became a casualty of the economic crises of the 1930s.

The course measured a substantial 2,900 yards. It possessed challenging green complexes, wide fairways, and deep bunkers. The fifth green was located directly in front of the Inn. Many players stopped briefly for refreshments or lunch, and continued. This unusual routing is hauntingly similar to the famed Pine Valley Golf Club, which is widely recognized as the greatest golf course in the world. The fourth green is located so near the clubhouse that many members either play the four holes as a warm-up or stop for a quick bowl of Pine Valley's world-famous turtle soup before tackling the devilish par-three fifth hole.

Records indicate the *Cragsmoor Country Club* gained corporate status in 1926. Annual memberships required the purchase of not fewer than five shares of preferred stock or twenty-five shares of common stock in the *Cragsmoor Company, Inc.* Guests of members were allowed a once-a-year privilege to play, but only if residing within three miles of the *Cragsmoor Golf Club*. Guests of the Inn would pay a greens fee of $2.50 on Saturday, Sunday, and holidays; $2 on weekdays; $12 weekly; $40 monthly; and $85 for an annual pass.

Karl Collings of Landsdowne, Pa., served on the Golf Committee as the Club's first Chairman, along with four other members appointed by the Board of Governors.

According to the club's bylaws: *The Golf Committee is in charge of the club links, the water supply and all building and equipment pertaining to the management and upkeep of said water supply, and make and enforce rules for their use. It shall engage and control the club professional, such professional greenskeepers, their workmen and other employees as may be necessary, and subject to the provisions of Article X (Finance Committee) hereof, incur such expenses relating to the club links as may be necessary. It shall also have charge of all golf tournaments and matches and prizes to be awarded therefore.*

With information gathered from the *Cragsmoor Free Library* (many thanks to the Cragsmoor Free Library for their assistance), I arrived at **Old Inn Road** and proceeded up the long drive. I have done this before but, unable to find any remnants of the long-abandoned golf course, I left, wondering if it ever really did exist. I reached the top of the hill and looked to the southwest. From pictures and postcards I have studied, I knew that, without question, I was looking down the sixth hole of the *Cragsmoor Country Club*.

Continued –

I let my imagination take me back to the halcyon days of the *Cragsmoor Inn*:

"Young man, would you fetch my clubs? I'll be playing a round this morning." The man is a frequent guest of the Inn.

"Certainly, sir. Will you be playing eighteen holes?"

"I think I shall play fourteen, have lunch, and play the inward four after."

"Very well, sir."

The putting clock is located off the porte-cochere of the Inn. A covered rustic walkway connects the ninth hole to the Inn. The man strikes a few putts, and is off to the first tee. He plays the first five holes briskly and stops briefly for a refreshment, and continues.

He draws a handful of sand from the box on the sixth tee and makes a small mound on the ground. He gently places his Haskell ball on the sand tee and methodically goes about his address routine. (The Haskell ball replaced the gutta percha ball at the turn of the century, and added twenty to forty yards of carry to the average golfer.) He makes a good strike, but misses the green to the right, and strides down the expansive fairway carrying the mashie (the predecessor of today's 5-iron) he has just struck from the tee.

It is mid-July. As a frequent guest, he had paid his annual fee of $85 to the club professional in the spring. (The links opened May 1st and will close October 30th.) A local young boy, serving as his caddie, accompanies him. They engage in small talk as they reach the man's ball. The boy is tough and sinewy from carrying the canvas and leather bags of the many guests who have traversed over the rolling links this season.

The stately man is dressed in tattersall knickers, a white, long-sleeved shirt with a double-knotted Windsor tie, and sports a tam atop his balding head. Adjacent to the sixth hole, the boy sees two elegant women walking side-by-side towards the seventh green. They wear long white dresses; one dons a bonnet, and the other carries an open umbrella that provides welcome shade from the summer sun. A boy he knows is toting doubles (both bags) for the distaff golfers. The boys wave to each other. A church stands like a small cathedral beyond the seventh green. The boy will attend morning services tomorrow, with his tip – a gleaming new silver dollar – safely tucked in his pocket.

The lie is inspected; the ball has nestled down in the lush native grass adjacent to the 133-yard par three – a poor lie – (in 1931, changes in the club rules allow for play of preferred lies on the sixth and eighth fairways) and the man opts for a niblick (a 9-iron). The eager caddie hands him the club. The man addresses the ball and, after a couple of waggles, a shifting of the feet, the ball is arcing towards the flagstick. It lands softly on the green, takes two hops, and rolls to a stop eight feet from the hole. As they rise to the green the man turns to the boy and asks, "So, what will you be when you grow up?" "I don't know yet, sir. For me, it will be hard to leave this place."

The man gazes at the surroundings. "I can understand why, son."

In December 1936, Austa Densmore Sturdevant passed away at the age of eighty-one. Three years later, the *Cragsmoor Company, Inc.* purchased the property. In July 1958, the Inn became a boy's school, but heating the building in the winter proved too costly, and the school relocated.

The *Cragsmoor Country Club* closed in 1967.

Razing the *Cragsmoor Inn*, as part of a controlled fire drill, took place in the early 1970s.

- Special Edition -

Cragsmoor Historical Journal

Volume 6, Issue 1   Published by the Cragsmoor Historical Society, Inc.   Post Office Box 354, Cragsmoor, NY 12420   Winter 2006

Cragsmoor Federated Church as it appeared in an undated early 20th century photograph.

Restoration Project Now Underway!

It was with words of joy, jubilation, excitement, pride, and exaltation that we announced receiving approval for a matching grant of $100,000 in July from the NYS Environmental Protection Fund for the stabilization and restoration of the former Cragsmoor Federated Church building, now the headquarters of the Cragsmoor Historical Society.

Since we obtained title in 1997, we have been diligently working just trying to keep the building standing. Many of you are familiar with our endeavors, such as the new foundation, sills, walls, and roof stabilization, because you have graciously been a part of these projects with your helpful suggestions, generous donations, and above all patience. When restoration is the goal, more time, careful planning, and certainly more money are involved. The planning and fundraising tasks have begun in earnest. This grant and the funds raised to match it will at last make it possible for us to restore this significant National Register listed building to its pre WW I appearance.

This building holds a very prominent position in our hamlet at the entrance to the historic district, and residents as well as the increasing numbers of visitors will be able to observe the progress of its restoration.

The grant application process was arduous and extremely competitive. I believe our fully-funded request was successful because the past performance of the Board and strong community support gave convincing evidence of our ability to carry out the project. We are very proud to be recognized and generously supported by the State's Office of Parks, Recreation and Historic Preservation for this community-wide undertaking. This is our biggest challenge yet!

Sally Matz, President

The original church building prior to addition, undated view.

Original decorative crests will be conserved and reinstalled

Sanctuary, interior view

Past and Future

The original church building, built in 1879 to serve the Mountain Methodist Church, is the oldest public building in the historic Cragsmoor community and served the Methodists for over twenty-five years. In the last two decades of the 19th century, however, the remote mountaintop community saw its economy transformed from timber harvesting, small farms, and huckleberry picking to one that depended on summer visitors and a community of artists drawn to the clear, cool air and dramatic scenery of the Shawangunk Ridge.

In 1906, the congregation applied for and received a new charter establishing the Cragsmoor Federated Church. To accommodate the growing interdenominational community, the building was enlarged and architecturally transformed into the more picturesque and fashionable Shingle Style. The building has served as a place of worship and for community gatherings for most of the 20th century. But, even as membership dwindled, this small but stylish period building had continued to function as a conspicuous and important architectural landmark nestled next to the equally distinctive Cragsmoor Free Library – together helping to define the character of the Cragsmoor community.

As Cragsmoor grows, it seems wise to reestablish the former church's historic function in the community as a convenient and attractive location for cultural and social activities. It survives today with a remarkable degree of architectural integrity, both inside and out, with natural wood finishes, decorative metal sheathing, and period furnishing. We are confident that the work funded by private contributions, combined with matching funds from New York State, will encourage the larger community to join our success and help sustain the building over time. When work is completed, we will have much more than an attractive landmark associated with one of the earliest art colonies in the country. Cragsmoor will also have a safe repository for its local history archive, exhibition spaces, meeting hall, and cultural center.

Restoration Project
by Larry Gobrecht

The Beginning
The Cragsmoor Historical Society was established in 1996 for the purpose of preserving Cragsmoor history. At the same time, the Cragsmoor Federated Church building had suffered heavily from years of deferred maintenance. In 1997, the congregation gave the building to the newly-formed Historical Society with the hope that the larger Cragsmoor community would invest in the deteriorated building and save it for future generations.

At that point, the stability of the building was seriously threatened. For example, portions of the foundation had failed, as had the original decorative sheet metal shingled roof. Trim boards and soffits were missing or rotted in places. Poor site drainage had created moisture problems in the building. Structural failure in the roof supports over the front meeting room had caused the north and south walls to bow and water penetration to damage many of the interior metal ceiling panels. The original wood shingle siding on the east and south elevations had been replaced with asbestos shingles.

Since then, the Society has received remarkable local support in raising enough money to allow it to complete some of the critical structural repairs necessary to keep the building standing. The failed portions of the foundation were rebuilt and foundation drains were installed. The roof structure over the front meeting room was stabilized by pulling the walls back at the plate and reattaching the rafters. We also installed a forced hot air heating system, a new electrical panel, and smoke and fire alarms. In 2001, the Society was able to purchase an adjoining six acre parcel to the south that will prevent the encroachment of incompatible new construction while at the same time allow for the installation of a leach field.

The Next Step
Despite these accomplishments, there is much critical work remaining. Perhaps the building's most distinctive and conspicuous architectural feature was the patterned metal shingle roof that, unfortunately, was rusted beyond repair and had to be removed in order to make structural repairs. Water continues to enter the building during heavy driving rain as it is only protected by an unflashed, temporary, blue tarp roof.

Without gutters, the foundation drains are only marginally effective and rising damp from pooling water is damaging the historic shingles on the north elevation. Interior stamped sheet tin ceilings were removed in the meeting room in order to stabilize the roof structure, leaving the framing system exposed above the plate. The windows, cornice moldings, frames and doors all need restoration. New paint is needed both inside and out. Although the original natural finish interior woodwork is remarkably intact, finishes need to be restored where water damage has taken its toll.

The Cragsmoor Historical Society recognizes that the success of the project depends on careful planning, technical advice from professional individuals familiar with the Secretary of the Interior's Standards for the Treatment of Historic Buildings, and coordination with a wide range of governmental and non-governmental organizations. With a small grant from the NYS Council on the Arts, we retained the services of Crawford and Stearns Associates of Syracuse to prepare an existing conditions survey and to make prioritized recommendations for treatment.

Several members of the Society and its Board have diligently researched the availability and suitability of the various materials and products needed for repair and replication of significant decorative features, especially patterned sheet metal shingles and wall/ceiling sheathing.

Wendy Harris has already completed the archeological survey. Paint analysis and a review of code and safety requirements will be completed before work is commenced. Additional plans include handicap accessibility, creating a climatically controlled archival room in the basement, and an easily accessible bathroom.

Recent view with roof tarp

Existing basement stairs

Open ceiling awaits new decorative tin panels

Resisting the Ravages of Time

Time takes its toll on all living things, as well as on those objects and structures designed by humankind with the hope of being indestructible. In Cragsmoor, which once boasted seventeen boarding houses, inns and/or hotels along with private residences, some buildings were razed because advanced deterioration was too costly to repair, or they met their fate in an unexpected fire. Since the mountain has been blessed with a courageous volunteer fire department, few buildings have been totally lost. Wooden buildings may be the least durable over time, but even those of stone are susceptible to cracking and crumbling masonry if not maintained. The decaying foundations of long-lost buildings, such as the Peter Brown house that stood on the corner of Henry and Schuyler Roads from 1849 to the early 1900's, are frequent reminders of their fate.

It is not unreasonable to expect that someday, if unchecked, nature will have its way and reclaim all that humans have created. It has, for example, successfully ravaged the berry pickers' shacks at Sam's Point. Left unattended, their basic elements of wood, tin, and glass have rapidly returned to the earth from which they came, encouraged by the force of gravity and the weight of many snowy winters.

Those surviving buildings which haven't met their demise by fire or demolition stand as testaments to the pride this community takes in protecting its past. Fortunately, most of the older residences in Cragsmoor have passed into the hands of caring stewards. Many generations have found warmth, protection and peace in houses that were built 100 or more years ago. Some buildings may have suffered from neglect from time to time over their long histories, but if they were lucky, caring owners eventually came along with willing and loving hands to bring them back to life. Many such restoration projects are unending, with some do-it-yourselfers dedicating countless hours of their free time over many years to conserve historic

homes that will long outlive them but provide shelter for generations to come.

Cragsmoor has made a name for itself as a community with a great respect for its architectural heritage. Not only do many of the residents dedicate time and money to their own homes, but they have also shared their resources to conserve historic public buildings such as the Library, and the Stone Church. Most recently the Gatehouse at Sam's Point can be added to that list. Dating back more than a century, the building once used by the Stedner Family when they managed the gate to Sam's Point, has been restored by The Nature Conservancy to its original simple beauty.

It is this outstanding record of preserving its older buildings that qualified Cragsmoor to be listed on The National Register of Historic Places. The Historic District is composed of a unique grouping of 19th and early 20th century residences with three public buildings as its cornerstones: the Cragsmoor Free Library, the Stone Church, and what is now the Cragsmoor Historical Society building. Fortunately, the Library has been faithfully maintained by the community over the course of its life, and the Stone Church has undergone major restoration over the past ten years.

Now, however, it is the Historical Society building that needs our urgent attention to be elevated to the high standards of the other two. Although the foundation under community room has been rebuilt, the upper part of the building is in danger of being lost if immediate action is not taken. Its prominent position at the entrance to the Historic District, and its long history from the 1870's as the first church in Cragsmoor, certainly make it deserving of our attention. By joining the effort to match the generous state grant for $100,000, we can all help to save this venerable old building from the ravages of time.

Maureen Radl

Keeping the Memories

"As we grow older some memories are gone but preservation will bring back memories of many events from the past so they can be passed on to our children, grandchildren, and great-grandchildren.

With the restoration of the Chapel, these memories will remain for many years.

As people are becoming more and more interested in genealogy, archeology, and restoration, preservation becomes more important.

We would hate to think some of these precious historic places would be lost due to neglect and/or fire.

More people become interested in Historical events and sites; Cragsmoor is actually a living museum as are many communities, especially along the eastern seaboard. Therefore, it behooves us to increase our effort to preserve what evidence we have of how those who came before us lived and died."

Vincent P. Stanger, age 92

 CHS

The grant (described on page 1) from the New York State Office of Parks, Recreation, and Historic Preservation's Environmental Protection Fund is a matching grant: Each dollar you contribute will be matched by this grant. In order to receive the full $100,000 from the State, we must raise a matching $100,000.

Contributions to the Cragsmoor Historical Society are tax-deductible to the fullest extent permitted by law.

THANK YOU FOR YOUR GENEROUS SUPPORT

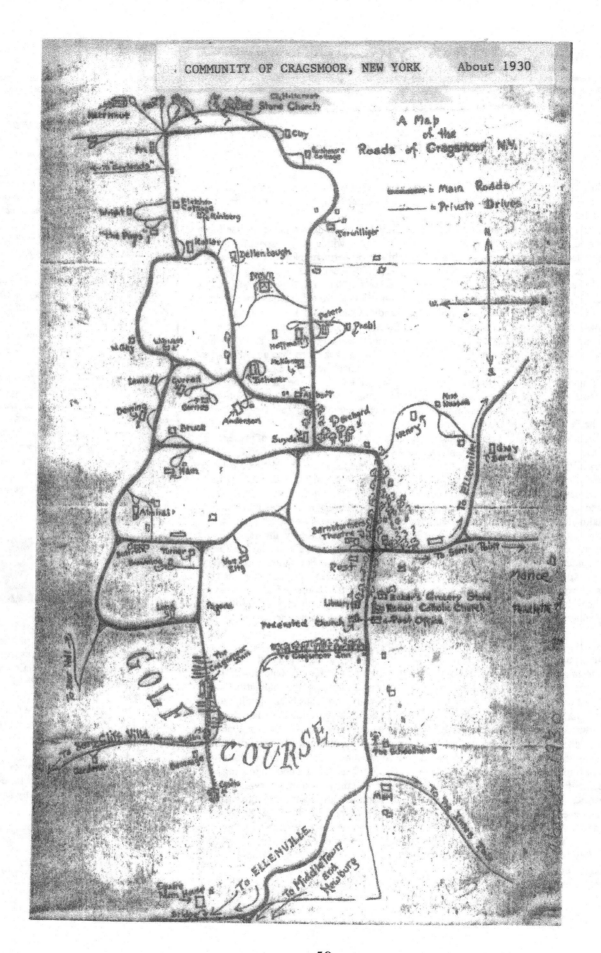

Religion

GIMME THAT OL' TIME RELIGION

The very first church in Cragsmoor began in 1880 and was originally known as the Mountain Church, which later became the Cragsmoor Federated Church. Visiting clergy from nearby towns led the services. The land on which the church was built was donated by the Decker family and strictly stipulated that it was to be used for church services only. Today it is the home of the Cragsmoor Historical Society.

The Chapel of the Holy Name, known as the Stone Church, was built in 1895 from local fieldstone and was donated by Eliza G. Hartshorn, in memory of her husband, Dr. Isaac Hartshorn. Mrs. Hartshorn was one of the founders of Cragsmoor. Today the Stone Church (Episcopal) still holds services, and many very beautiful wedding ceremonies are performed there -- both indoors and out. The view from the stone arch is spectacular.

Sacred Heart Chapel, built in 1898, was originally a Catholic Church. It is today the private residence of Joy Weber. It looks much the same on the exterior except for additions. The altar and decorative painting inside the home are original to the church and remain as they were. The chapel was moved in 1914 to a site across the street from the Cragsmoor Library. Again, in the 1940's the chapel was moved to its present location on Meadow Lane. (Information gathered from Cragsmoor -- an Historical Sketch.)

Joy, very graciously, invited us into her wonderful home and allowed pictures to be taken, some of which appear on the following page.

CHAPEL OF THE SACRED HEART Built 1898 (Photo taken 2004)

Interior of the home of Joy Weber – Formerly Catholic Church
This is a guest room which faces the front of the former chapel.
The altar area is opposite where the archway is located.

Joy Weber added this lovely interior sign.

Before Today's Headlines

BY KATHARINE T. TERWILLIGER
HISTORIAN OF THE TOWN OF WAWARSING

It is hoped this column may enrich our contemporary life as it tells something of the roots from which our community has grown.

000

The greatest changes were in Cragsmoor, the name given in 1892 to the settlement on the Top of the Mountain.

It was fast becoming one of the most famous summer colonies in this part of the country. There was an interesting development in the houses of worship.

The picturesque and dignified Chapel of the Holy Name, erected by Mrs. Eliza G. Hartshorn, one of the founders of the summer colony, held its first services

in 1897. (See an early picture of this lovely Chapel elsewhere in today's Journal.) In 1914 Mrs. Edward Clay

gave to St. Mary's in Ellenville the private oratory she had erected on her own property twelve years before. This is known as the Chapel of the Sacred Heart.

To take care of all who were neither Episcopalians nor Catholics, other residents formed the Federated Church in 1906. They acquired the Methodist Chapel and by 1908 had considerably enlarged it.

The Chapel of the Holy Name in Cragsmoor was completed in 1897. It was designed by F. S. Dellenbaugh for Mrs. Eliza G. Hartshorn who erected it in memory of her husband. The dwellings also were built by Mrs. Hartshorn — Ruhberg on the left, completed in the late 1880s, was for many years a convalescent home for the Brothers of Nazarath; Hillcrest on the right was built in 1897 for Father Odell, vicar of the chapel. This picture — courtesy of Gladys Clay Bitting — was taken by LeGrand Botsford, probably about 1900.

ELVL
JOURNAL
6-24-1971

63

Chapel of the Holy Name   Cragsmoor, N. Y.

COPIED FROM OLD POSTCARDS

Memorial Arch at Chapel of the Holy Name   Cragsmoor, N. Y.

The Chapel of the Holy Name
Dedicated 1897   Rededicated 1997
STONE CHURCH
EPISCOPAL
SUNDAY WORSHIP 11 AM

SIGN PAINTED BY LOCAL ARTIST, ROGER BAKER

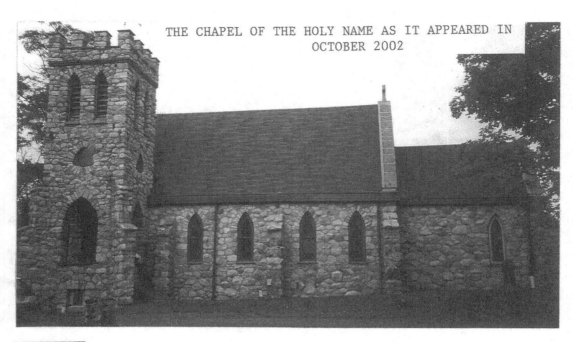

THE CHAPEL OF THE HOLY NAME AS IT APPEARED IN OCTOBER 2002

THE ALTAR

Inscription Reads:
ISAAC HARTSHORN
Born July 6, 1804 Died Jan. 29, 1877

LOOKING UP AT THE BEAUTIFUL
ROSE WINDOW LOCATED ON THE
FRONT WALL OPPOSITE THE ALTAR

Inscription Reads:

EDWARD GARDINER HARTSHORN
Born Mar. 9 1857 Died Aug. 29 1858
IN HEAVEN THEIR ANGELS DO
ALWAYS BEHOLD THE FACE OF
MY FATHER WHICH IS IN HEAVEN

Chapel of the Holy Name
Cragsmoor, New York

Chapel of the Holy Name
"The Stone Church"
PO Box 151
Cragsmoor, New York 12420

Construction on Cragsmoor's landmark Stone Church was begun in 1895 under the supervision of John Keir, a Cragsmoor resident. The cornerstone was consecrated on August 29th that year. Nearly two years later, on June 19th, 1897, the 900-pound bell in the tower was finally raised. A Latin inscription on its side reads, "In Honor of the Blessed Trinity and All Saints, 1897." The first service was held the next day, Sunday the 20th.

The chapel, built of stone from the mountain, was designed by Frederick S. Dellenbaugh, an architect and prominent Cragsmoor resident. He also helped in the design of the rose window, given in memory of his wife, and was executed by Lamb Studios in 1932. (An earlier window had been blown out in a storm in 1909.) The inscription around the window reads, "Her Smile Was Like a Benediction."

Eliza G. Hartshorn of Newport, Rhode Island and a summer resident of Cragsmoor, built the chapel as a memorial to her husband, Dr. Isaac Hartshorn. She had given the land and funds for building the chapel in the hope that it would be taken over by the Brothers of Nazareth of the Order of the Holy Name. Father Daniel I. Odell, a close friend and recipient of Mrs. Hartshorn's munificence, was to lead the religious order and establish an "ecclesiastical community." This plan did not materialize, however, as the Brothers were given land elsewhere and left the mountain before the chapel was completed.

Father Odell owned the chapel until about 1922, when he transferred ownership of the chapel, altar, pews, organ and accessories of worship to the New York Altar Guild of the Protestant Episcopal Church. In 1945, the chapel became the property of the Episcopal Diocese of New York.

The Chapel of the Holy Name is not a parish church. It does not have a membership or ongoing ministry of pastoral care. It is maintained and operated by the Friends of the Stone Church, a non-sectarian group of volunteers who arrange services and concerts, handle the many weddings, and raise funds for the extensive improvements, restoration, and maintenance of the building. Any contributions towards the betterment of the chapel are appreciated.

Our Prayer

Almighty Being, Creator and Parent,
Present among us.

Your holy spirit is our strength and salvation.

Let us be instruments of your will
And create the world of love and peace
you intended for us.

Nourish our bodies and our souls.

Keep us ever in your grace
And lead us toward insight and compassion.

Help us forgive ourselves,
So that we can forgive others.

For it is only through you that
we will find peace and fulfillment.

AMEN

Created by The Stone Church Community
2001-2002 (transcribed May 12, 2002)

Cragsmoor Peace Celebration

Speakers representing four of the major world spiritual traditions will lead an interfaith peace service at the **Stone Church** in Cragsmoor, **11 AM, Sunday, September 7th**.

"A Celebration of Peace, Hope, and Compassion" will mark the second anniversary of the events of September 11, 2001. Presenters will offer prayers for the peaceful evolution of the human family by drawing upon some aspect of their own beliefs, which will lead to a greater understanding of the common elements in all of these traditions. The Islamic presentation will be made by David-Iman Adler. He is a frequent speaker on Islam and is affiliated with the *Abode of the Message* in Lebanon, New York. Together with his wife, he has presented workshops for Muslims and others to understand the inner spiritual meaning of the Islamic prayers. He is the Imam for Berkshire Medical Center and has also served several other communities in eastern New York and western Massachusetts.

Christian prayers will be offered by the Reverend Doctor Joan Campbell, Director of Religion at the Chatauqua Institution. Last year, she organized a lecture program called "Paths of Transformation" which explored the three Abrahamic faiths – Judaism, Christianity, and Islam – as a source of transformation and hope for peace. Up until 1999, she served as General Secretary of the National Council of Churches for ten years. During that time she worked closely with such luminaries as the last four US presidents, Nelson Mandela, and Desmond Tutu. She was responsible for the rescue of three American soldiers from Belgrade during the bombing there in 1998, and is perhaps best known as the American most responsible for helping reunite Cuban child Elian Gonzalas with his family in the spring of 2000.

Another speaker will be the Venerable Guo Yuan, vice president of the Dharma Drum Mountain Buddhist Association of the United States. He is also head monk at the Chan Meditation Center in New York City and the *Dharma Drum Retreat Center* in Pine Bush. He has assisted at intensive retreats in Russia, England, Germany, and Mexico. He also lectures and guides meditative practice in the United States and Canada, and has participated in numerous interfaith dialogues.

Rabbi Tsurah August will also make a presentation. She is the New York site director for Transitional Keys, a program for improving the quality of life for elders living in communal settings through ritual and the arts. She has also worked in acute and long-term healthcare facilities and in her home community of Woodstock and served as the advisor to the Jewish students at Vassar.

The program will include prayers and comments from the congregation, candle lighting, and music by Helga Koenig on the Indian Flute and Charles Matz on the organ. This event is in keeping with the mission of the *Friends of the Stone Church* to share this sacred space with believers of other spiritual traditions, in order to find the common ground that unites them all. All are welcome at this event, which will take place in this hundred-year-old church set on the edge of the Shawangunk Ridge in the historic district of the Cragsmoor art colony, It commands inspiring views of the Catskills and the Rondout Valley and is proximate to the famous hiking trails on the 5,000-acre **Sam's Point Preserve**. Cragsmoor is off **Rte. 52**, between Ellenville and Pine Bush. Take **Cragsmoor Road** for two miles to the Post Office. Continue straight and follow signs to the **Stone Church**.

Call **647-6384** for additional information.

Music Benefit at Stone Church

On **Sunday, September 7th**, at **3:00 PM** Zoe B. Zak (*above, left*) and Steve Gorn (*above, right*) will be performing their special brand of music at the **Stone Church** in Cragsmoor. The *Chapel of the Holy Name*, most commonly called the **Stone Church**, is a welcoming, century-old, community-oriented, Episcopal church that hosts a wide variety of musical concerts in an intimate, beautiful, and acoustically-excellent space.

Zoe B. Zak is an accomplished singer, keyboard player, accordionist, composer, producer, arranger, and bandleader. Steve Gorn is a master on the bansuri bamboo flute and soprano saxophone and has played in concerts and festivals throughout the world. Together with Dean Sharp, Zak and Gorn recorded the CD "Conference of the Birds" in 2002. Zak has been intimately involved in the creation of over a dozen CDs (singing, playing keyboards and accordion, producing, and composing). Zak has led her ensemble in many concerts in the area, combining avant-garde piano improvisations with folk-rock, mixing elements of Zydeco with texts and melodies of three thousand-year-old religious traditional music. Gorn has been featured on several recordings with such greats as Paul Simon, Krishna Das, Karsh Kale, Richie Havens, and Anant Jesse. Gorn has composed numerous works for theater, dance, and television. Zak and Gorn have appeared on WAMC's Dancing on the Air (Jay Unger and Molly Mason). This is Gorn's second musical visit to the **Stone Church** – his first was a very beautiful and well received solo concert.

A $10 donation for admission is suggested. Proceeds will go to the restoration of the **Stone Church**. For info about the concert, call **647-6384**.

*Browsers peruse the bargains at the **Cragsmoor Book Fair**, held August 9th at the Cragsmoor Historical Society. Food, crafts, art, and second-hand items were also available.*

Issue #11   2003 October

Wawarsing.Net

Published by the Ellenville-Wawarsing Chamber of Commerce
Also Online at www.Wawarsing.Net

Town & County Election Special!

Forward, into the Past

Cragsmoor's Stone Church

by Marion M. Dumond
*Former Town of Wawarsing Historian
and Ellenville Public Library Director (Retired)*

A variety of hamlets and one village comprise the Town of Wawarsing, each distinct and unique. The settlement at the "top of the mountain" may predate Ellenville, since deeds of the period before 1800 mention some residents' names as owning boundary lands. According to Katharine T. Terwilliger, settlement on the mountain in the area we know today as Cragsmoor began before Ellenville had its first few houses. Early family names included Goldsmith, Fisher, Terwilliger, Farr, and Wilhelm, among others.

As communities came into existence, the need for improved transportation grew. When the plank road connecting Ellenville and Newburgh was dedicated on December 22, 1851, the first part of the program was held at Evensville, the settlement at the "top of the mountain," now part of Cragsmoor. More than 500 people made their way down the "...smooth new plank road to the loveliest village in the valley."

When the railroad reached Ellenville in 1871, the beautiful scenery of the Town of Wawarsing, its good air, and pure water attracted vacationers, many of whom returned to make this area their home, even if only for the summer months. A leading summer colony developed at the "top of the mountain," later to be named Cragsmoor.

Boarding houses flourished, summer homes were built. The 1901 issue of "Summer Homes," a promotional booklet published by the railroad, said that Cragsmoor abounded "in most delightful and romantic walks and drives." *Mount Meenahga* on the **Shawangunk Mountains** (see the August 2003 issue of *Wawarsing.Net*) was the first summer resort of prominence in the Town of Wawarsing. *Mount Mongola* (early 1890s) grew from the Farr homestead into a popular and successful resort; the *Cragsmoor Inn* followed in 1904 *(see photo below; the buildings no longer exist)*. Many smaller and less well-known boarding houses abounded.

Cragsmoor Inn, Cragsmoor, N. Y.

Cragsmoor's breathtaking views, natural beauty, and magnificent sunsets drew artists from far and wide. One of the leaders in the development of Cragsmoor as a summer colony was Frederick S. Dellenbaugh, an artist, author and explorer. The noted genre artist, E.L. Henry (much more about him in a future column), and Mrs. Eliza G. Hartshorn, often called a founder of the summer community, collaborated with Dellenbaugh in a variety of projects.

Dellenbaugh was part of Major John Wesley Powell's

second expedition through the Grand Canyon, serving as historian, mapmaker, and artist. His talents and interests were many, and Cragsmoor benefited. In 1885 he married an Ellenville girl, Harriet Otis, in a home ceremony at which Rev. Henry Ward Beecher officiated. He designed and built their home on the mountain in 1891, the year before he recommended the name Cragsmoor for the community which was to receive a post office.

Mr. Dellenbaugh was a frequent contributor to the *Ellenville Journal*, supplying articles about local history or his many expeditions and many letters of commentary. His design of the *Chapel of the Holy Name* (the **Stone Church**) for Mrs. Eliza G. Hartshorn may be his most significant contribution to this area, which he loved so much. He also donated the land and designed the building for the *Cragsmoor Free Library*, completed in 1925. The building, somewhat modified and expanded, still serves its community as an association library, guided by local residents as trustees.

Mrs. Hartshorn of Newport, Rhode Island, was a summer resident of Cragsmoor and a friend of Dellenbaugh. She built the *Chapel of the Holy Name* as a memorial to her husband, Dr. Isaac Hartshorn. Construction of the chapel, using local stone from the mountain, began in 1895 under the supervision of John Keir, a Cragsmoor resident. The bell in the tower was put in place two years later and the first service was held the next day, August 20, 1897.

Dellenbaugh not only designed the Chapel; he assisted in the design of the rose window that he gave in memory of his wife. The inscription around the window reads, "Her Smile Was Like a Benediction."

Mrs. Hartshorn had given the land and construction funds in the hope that the chapel would be taken over by the Brothers of Nazareth of the Order of the Holy Name and be part of an "ecclesiastical community."

Unfortunately, the Brothers left the Cragsmoor area before the chapel was completed. Father Daniel Odell, who was to have been the leader of the community, owned the Chapel until about 1922, when he transferred it and its contents to the New York Altar Guild of the Protestant Episcopal Church. The Chapel became the property of the Episcopal Diocese of New York.

For many years the Chapel was open only during the summer months, if then, with services conducted by clergy from nearby Episcopal churches or guest clergy.

The Chapel of the Holy Name, more popularly called "the Stone Church," is not a parish church. It does not have a membership or ongoing ministry of pastoral care. What it does have is a dedicated nonsectarian group of volunteers operating as the *Friends of the Stone Church* who arrange services and concerts, handle the many weddings held in this picturesque house of worship, and raise funds for the extensive improvements, restoration and maintenance of the building.

Worship services are now conducted **every Sunday from Memorial Day to Labor Day** and on **the first Sunday of every month** from Labor Day to Memorial Day, all at **11:00 AM**.

The most recent issue of the *Stone Church Newsletter* (No. 7, Summer 2003) details the renovation of this architectural masterpiece during the nine years since the *Friends of the Stone Church* assumed control of the Chapel. The ten-year restoration project envisioned by Cragsmoor architect Ken Bovo is on schedule and has included a new concrete basement, the installation of a new furnace, roof repair, replacement of mortar and re-pointing the stone work, new lighting, the installation of an indoor bathroom, and restoration of two of the stained glass windows, at an expense of approximately $185,000 to date. A magnificent new Church sign has been installed, the work of gifted Cragsmoor artist Roger Baker. The sign is mounted on two pillars made from local stones and recites both the Chapel's 1897 dedication and its 1997 rededication. *(See photo below. All images in this article are from the collection of Sally Matz; other than the below recent photo, they are from early 20th century postcards.)*

The work continues, funded principally by donations and weddings. Couples of all faiths and orientations may be wed at **the Stone Church**. The fee is $500, which covers cleaning before and after the wedding as well as candles for the ceremony, which may be held inside or outside, weather permitting. Couples receive a certificate designed by John Duncan with beautiful individualized calligraphy by Della Sue, as well as a memento of **the Stone Church**. Reservations and additional information can be made by calling Sally Matz at 845-647-6384.

Thirty-five weddings have been scheduled at the Chapel for 2003, with October being the most popular month (two weddings each and every weekend during the month). Six reservations are already on the books for 2004. Sally Matz has been analyzing where the wedding parties live and how they came to know of the Chapel's availability. Geographically, the largest number come from Orange County and many learned of the Chapel from hiking at **Sam's Point**. There is no doubt that **the Stone Church** is one of the most beautiful churches in the area and that the surroundings afford multiple "photo ops."

All funds from church rentals (weddings) and donations go directly to the restoration project and maintenance of the Chapel. Much still needs to be accomplished.

Stone Church Day has been scheduled for November 2, 2003, at which the artisans who have worked on the Chapel will talk about their discoveries and their challenges in restoring the 106-year-old building. The time of the program is still tentative, but the community is invited to save the date and watch for further details. For those who want to learn more, copies of the newsletter are available at **the Stone Church**. Additional information came from an informational sheet published by the Friends, plus Katharine Terwilliger's historical writings and conversations with Sally Matz.

The Friends of the Stone Church deserve the area's gratitude for their selfless dedication to the preservation and restoration of this architectural and historic treasure.

Well done!

Note that the *Town of Wawarsing Bicentennial* ornament project chose **the Stone Church** as one of the first two ornaments to be released in 2003. Additional copies have been ordered and will be available again in late October, just in time for holiday giving.

STONE CHURCH NEWSLETTER

Episcopal Chapel of the Holy Name
No. 7, Summer 2003
Published from time to time by Friends of the Stone Church,
PO Box 151, Cragsmoor, New York 12420

The Chapel Is Warm!

When this newsletter was last published (Spring 1999, see page 6), the Chapel was in the midst of a major overhaul. The rotting floor had been removed and the sub-floor dug out to a depth of four feet. A new concrete basement was then poured, concrete pillars were erected and steel beams were brought in to support a brand new floor of Douglas fir. Although this new floor is so authentic that no one thinks it's new, it has made a huge difference to the Chapel. A waterproof basement made it possible to install new heating ducts and a new furnace, paid for by the Episcopal Diocese of New York, which holds title to the Chapel. The Chapel became both dry and warm, and the continuous seepage of moisture and dirt from the old mud basement became a thing of the past. Sally Matz, who has reason to know, says that the amount of dust in the Chapel has been reduced to almost nothing.

The addition of heating has given the Chapel a new all-year-round existence. Whereas weddings previously had to be limited to the warm-weather months, they can now be scheduled in any season, resulting in an increase in the revenue vitally needed to renovate, repair and then maintain this historic 108-year-old building.

With heat, we are also able to conduct year-round worship services, and a vibrant series of Fall-Winter-Spring services began two years ago, as you can read elsewhere in this Newsletter.

Finally, heat (and the roof repairs of Michael Hughes) have virtually banished the moisture that haunted the Church from the time it was built. The stone walls have stopped oozing, and water no longer drips from the arches onto the communion rail. Soon, we should be able to clean the interior stone and return it to its original condition.

Renovation Report

When Friends of the Stone Church assumed control of the Chapel in 1994, we commissioned a Master Plan describing the renovations that had to be accomplished to preserve this architectural masterpiece for the next 100 years. That Plan, by Cragsmoor architect Ken Bovo, envisioned a 10-year restoration project that would cost approximately $225,000.

Ken was right — on the money as well as on the time necessary to do the work. To date, the Friends of the Stone Church have spent approximately $185,000 on the renovations, and much of the required work will be completed within the ten-year time period.

A good deal of our resources (almost $40,000) have been spent on the roof. We experienced a bit of grace when master mason Michael Hughes appeared on the scene a few years ago to offer his considerable skills to repair the roof and the stone work. Since then, Michael has spent hundreds of hours replacing mortar, installing flashing and other roofing schemes and repointing the stone work to his exacting standards, which may exceed those of the considerably-talented masons who built the Church in 1895-97. The results are apparent: the leaks that even architect Frederick Dellenbaugh decried are virtually gone.

We were equally lucky to be able to employ the services of master woodworker Brad Venditti and his staff. Brad's work on the interior was detailed in the last newsletter. Since then, Brad has painstakingly copied the Gothic molding of the original doors and recreated them in solid mahogany, a work which rivals the gates of heaven in beauty and craftsmanship. The hardware came from Baltica, a Lithuanian company with old-world standards. As with his work on the floor, Brad's craftsmanship is so authentic that most people do not realize that the doors are completely new. Brad also recreated the chancel's wainscoting, which had long ago disappeared.

The beauty of the ceiling of the Church, which some have likened to the inside of the hull of a sailing ship, has been tremendously enhanced by new lighting designed by Tom Bolger. People ask what we have done to "fix up" the beams and other woodwork, and the answer is, "Nothing except new lighting." What we did have refinished, however, are the beautiful chestnut pews. We discovered that our local community is home to Keck Industries of Middletown, a nationally known church-pew refurbisher. Now, our old pews glow warmly, and they have been unscrewed from the floor so they can be moved to create new seating arrangements for worship services and concerts.

Finally (and perhaps most importantly), the Chapel now has an indoor bathroom, for the first time in its existence. No more "Jonny on the Spot." The cost to date of all this interior work (including the doors) is $92,500.

The third remarkable craftsman who has worked on the Chapel is Phillip Godenschwager of Randolph, Vermont, who restored two of the stained-glass windows ($6,100). A friend of local artist Roger Baker (see article on the new Church sign), Phil removed the two most damaged windows from the chancel, took them to his Vermont studio, removed all the lead and painstakingly recreated the windows as if brand-new. The results are striking, and you should walk up into the chancel to admire them the next time you come to the Stone Church. Phil is not done, however. The other stained glass windows still require extensive work, which we hope to complete soon.

Save the Date: STONE CHURCH DAY – NOVEMBER 2, 2003

Church Depends Principally on Donors and Weddings

As we pointed out on the first page, the renovations to date have cost approximately $185,000, and that is only part of the cost of operating the Church. Although the Episcopal Diocese of New York, which owns the Chapel but allows the Friends of the Stone Church to operate it and to direct the restoration, pays for the insurance and the electricity, the Friends of the Stone Church are responsible for the rest. In addition to the restoration costs, there are expenses for heat, furnace maintenance, various supplies and stationery and the costs of the fund-raising events and worship services. When these expenses are added to the restoration costs, the total spent over the past nine years has been closer to $250,000.

Where have these funds come from? The principal source has been direct gifts from literally hundreds of donors, including one family which has contributed approximately $80,000 of the $110,000 raised from gifts, most of which were given during the heavy construction period of 1999-2000. Since then, the level of giving has dropped to about $1,000 a year.

The second most significant source of funds has been the rental fees for weddings held at the Chapel. In future years, this will be the principal source of income to finance the renovations and repairs that are still needed. The total income from weddings from 1994 to date was approximately $75,000. Last year (2002), weddings contributed approximately $18,000 of the $28,000 spent on the Chapel. The Friends of the Stone Church have increased the wedding rental fee to $500 (it was $75 before the Friends became involved), and there are 30 weddings on the calendar for 2003 and three for 2004.

The third source of funds has been offerings taken during worship services. Over the past nine years, about $25,000 has been raised this way, and the total last year was almost $5,000. Since most of the worship services are conducted by volunteers, virtually all of this income can be used to restore and maintain the Chapel.

The Friends of the Stone Church sponsor a number of concerts and other community events, but, for the most part, those functions do not contribute substantially to the Chapel's income. There is a limit to the number of people who can attend (a maximum of about 140), and there are many expenses associated with these events, such as performer fees, instrument rentals and publicity.

For the future, the Friends of the Stone Church believe that income and expenses (principally for the many restoration projects that remain, see article below) will average about $25,000 a year.

The Renovation Road Ahead

While much work has been accomplished, much still remains. Foremost on the list, virtually every one of the stained glass windows is in need of some repair. And after those repairs, each window will need to be protected against future wear by installing an exterior protective window. There are 21 windows in all, so at $500 per window, this improvement alone will cost more than $10,000.

There are also nine windows that do not contain stained glass. The Friends of the Stone Church are encouraging members of the community to donate new stained glass windows for these locations. The costs will range upward from $6,000 per window. There are many craftspeople available to create new windows, including the Lamb Studio, which designed and constructed the rose window some 70 years ago and recently expressed interest in creating new windows. Contact Sally Matz at 845-647-6384 if you are interested in donating a window.

Beyond the stained glass, work remains to be done on the woodwork in the Church. This summer, the Friends of the Stone Church hope to complete the restoration or replacement of the wainscoting, and the door and window frames need work as well as the floor in the chancel, which may have to be replaced.

There is also a considerable amount of stone work needed. Most pressing is the need to restore the arch overlooking Mt. Meenhaga and the Rondout Valley, which is perilously close to collapse. And the stone inside the Chapel is stained and caked with deposits from more than 100 years of constant dripping from a leaky roof. Now that those leaks have been virtually eliminated, it is time to clean that stone.

The time has also come to replace the existing remnant rugs — gifts from a couple whose family owned a rug store — with something more permanent.

As you can see, keeping the Chapel in shape is a never-ending responsibility.

Memorial Garden Established

In the summer of 2000, donations from the family of Marie Buckman established a Memorial Garden at the Stone Church. At a service on July 7, 2000, Marie's ashes were placed in the Garden, located immediately south of the Chapel. In attendance were Marie's husband, Robert, her son, Peter Veruki, her daughter, Andrea Swift, and a number of stepchildren and grandchildren. A beautiful granite stone identifying the Garden's purpose has been installed in the Garden, and there is a wall plaque just inside the main door of the Church listing those whose ashes have been spread in the Garden.

If you are interested in spreading the ashes of a loved one in the Garden and/or holding a memorial service in the Stone Church, contact Sally Matz (845-647-6384).

Make a Donation Today!

As you can see in this Newsletter, the Stone Church is alive with services, concerts, weddings and memorial events. This active life has been made possible by the reconstruction efforts of the Friends of the Stone Church. But, as you can also see, none of this would be possible without substantial donations from all segments of our community.

Please help us keep this work going. There is still a lot to do. Enclosed with this Newsletter is an envelope addressed to Friends of the Stone Church. Please take a moment to write out a check to "Friends of the Stone Church" for as generous a sum as you can give. All gifts are fully tax-deductible donations to a church.

New Church Sign

A magnificent new Church sign has been installed, the work of gifted Cragsmoor artist Roger Baker. Among his other accomplishments, Roger is the artist who designed and then mowed the incredible portraits of the Statue of Liberty, Elvis Presley and Albert Einstein into the fields where the hang-gliders land in the Rondout Valley just south of Ellenville.

The Chapel's new sign is mounted on two pillars made from local stones selected by Roger. It recites both the Chapel's 1897 dedication and its 1997  rededication, presided over by Episcopal Bishop Catherine Roskam. A separate sign, which is removable, announces upcoming worship services.

Three+ Years of Summer Worship

The Stone Church has continued its rich spiritual life over the past three years with weekly Sunday worship services from Memorial Day to Labor Day. In keeping with its openness and ecumenicity, the Chapel has been host to a wide range of faiths and styles. In 2000, services were led by lay leaders Elinor Barnes, Jeffrey Slade and Linda Duval and by ministers Gregg Wood, Jay Vogelar and Ralph Thompson. The traditional Blue Grass service, led by the Kerr family, took place on August 13, featuring that foot-stomping favorite, "Jesus Makes House Calls, 24 Hours a Day!"

In 2001, the Chapel was again blessed by the leadership of Rev. Gregg Wood and local pastors Robert Hewitt (Pine Bush Methodist), Walter Steinhard (Ellenville Methodist) and Ralph Thompson (Thompson Ridge Presbyterian), A highlight of the summer was a service led by The Venerable Guo Yuan, Abbot of the Buddhist Chan Meditation and Dharma Drum Retreat Center in Pine Bush, who explained the basic tenets of Buddhism on July 1. Earlier in the year, Rabbi Andrea Weiss led a Bible study on May 6.

2001 Services were also led by lay leaders Herb Trempe, Don Lee, Tony Mitchell, Jeffrey Slade, Walter Alvarez and James Alley. Tradition continued in August with the Blue Grass service and the annual Firematic service, honoring the service of the volunteer fire companies in the area. On July 22, a service was led by members of the Bruderhof Community, featuring the children's choir, Dove 2000.

Of course, the world changed sharply on September 11, 2001, and the community joined in a moving service of prayer and remembrance on September 16, led beautifully by Maureen Radl. One year later, on September 15, 2002, Maureen organized an ecumenical Celebration of Peace, Hope and Compassion, led by Rev. Dr. Joan Brown Campbell, former General Secretary of the National Council of Churches, Rabbi Tsurah August, Jewish Chaplain of Vassar College, Buddhist Abbot the Venerable Guo Yuan and Dr. Sadr, an Islamic scholar.

During the summer of 2002, services were led by lay leaders Herb Trempe, Jeffrey Slade, Dr. Joy Carol and Don Lee and by Rev. Gregg Wood, Rev. Robert Hewitt, Rev. Kent Jackson, Rev. William Scafidi and Father John Ryan. A group from a local Quaker meeting led a traditional Quaker service in June, and the Blue Grass and Firematic services were highlights in August.

This summer (2003), services have been led by Jeffrey Slade, Elinor Barnes and by five clergy attending a Union Seminary retreat, including Episcopal Bishop Jeffery Rowthorn. During the summer, the Chapel will continue with its mix of lay and clergy-led services, including the Blue Grass and Firematic services in August. All are welcome.

New Electric Piano Enlivens Stone Church

Our electric organ is growing old; parts of it do not work, and its days and usefulness are both limited. Therefore, Mr. Matz, our marvelous musician, located a new electric "piano" which has been installed next to the organ and will greatly enhance the musical options at the Stone Church. "Piano" is in quotation marks because this instrument is much more than a piano. In fact, it can replicate the sound of an organ, a harpsichord, a bell choir and a variety of other musical instruments. And a performer can even pre-record a performance, which can then be played back at a later time! The instrument is particularly useful during weddings, where it has been much appreciated.

Fall/Winter/Spring Series

With the installation of the new heating system in the Winter of 1999, it became possible for the first time in many years to hold Stone Church worship services in the colder months. Accordingly, services are now held on the first Sunday of each month from October to May, designed to bring members of the community together in dialogue about important issues of faith.

These services began in November 2001 with a series devoted to the Lord's Prayer. Study sessions were led by Jeffrey Slade, Walter Alvarez, Paul Campbell and Wendy Harris, Ruth De-Tar and Kathleen Muldoon and John Duncan. In May, our study culminated with a group creation of a new prayer, embodying what we believed to be the essence of the Lord's Prayer, interpreted for the 21st Century. The prayer was taken down by Calligrapher Barbara Bash and is now hanging in the chancel. Here it is:

Almighty Being, Creator
and Parent,
Present among us.
Your holy spirit is our strength and
salvation.
Let us be instruments of your will
And create the world of love and
peace you intended for us.
Nourish our bodies and our souls.
Keep us ever in your grace
And lead us toward insight
and compassion.
Help us forgive ourselves,
So that we can forgive others.
For it is only through you that
we will find peace and fulfillment.
AMEN

A new series ran from October 2002 through May 2003, focusing on The Beatitudes. Study sessions were led by Jeffrey Slade, Ruth Diem, John Duncan, Paul Campbell and Wendy Harris, Maureen Radl and Charles Matz.

Stone Church Day – November 2, 2003

On November 2, 2003, the entire community is invited to attend a day-long celebration of the history, art and reconstruction of the Stone Church. In attendance will be the remarkable artisans who have been rebuilding the Stone Church. They will discuss their work with us as well as the remarkable structure, from its stained-glass windows to its elaborate stone work.

The day will begin at 10:30 a.m. with a worship service, followed by a light lunch at noon. Starting at 1:00, we will present a program devoted to the history and construction of the Chapel. A donation of $10 will be welcomed to cover the cost of the event.

More details will be made available in September. But save the date on your calendar!

The Hills Are Alive With the Sound of Music

Led by our own Maestro Charles Matz, the Stone Church has continued its rich tradition of summer concerts. The highlight of 2000 was an extraordinary performance by pianist Ignat Solzhenitsyn, son of Nobel Prize-winning author Aleksandr Solzhenitsyn, who filled the Church to overflowing with more than 140 enraptured guests listening to pieces by Schubert and Prokofiev. In August, the style shifted dramatically, as the 21st Century "Jass" band performed. The summer also featured a memorable performance by Tony Trischka, one of the best banjo players in the world and a resident of the Hudson Valley. In December, Rev. Gregg Wood led a Celebration of Lessons and Carols.

In 2001, the brilliant students of Pianist Yuri Kim entertained the community, and the Saints of Swing offered an upbeat jazz performance on Labor Day weekend.

2002 featured a performance on May 26 by harpist Victoria Drake, whose selections ranged from classical (Scarlatti and Bach) to modern jazz (Brubeck). At the end of the summer, Steve Gorn, a bamboo flutist (and the husband of Calligrapher Barbara Bash, who transcribed the Prayer hanging in the Chapel), entranced a large audience with music from the Indian traditions.

Concerts will continue this summer, so watch for announcements. And if you would like to offer a concert or know of someone who would, contact Chuck Matz at 845-647-6384.

If You Want To Make God Laugh, . . .

Here are some traditional Bible stories, as reinterpreted by children:

-Lot's wife was a pillar of salt by day, but a ball of fire by night!

- The Jews were a proud people and throughout history they had trouble with unsympathetic Genitals.

- The Egyptians were all drowned in the dessert. Afterwards, Moses went up on Mount Cyanide to get the ten ammendments.

- The first commandment was when Eve told Adam to eat the apple.

- The seventh is "Thou shalt not admit adultery."

- Moses died before he ever reached Canada.

- Then Joshua led the Hebrews in the battle of Geritol.

- David was a Hebrew king skilled at playing the liar. He fought with the Finklesteins, a race of people who lived in Biblical times.

- Solomon, one of David's sons, had 300 wives and 700 porcupines.

- Jesus was born because Mary had an immaculate contraption.

- Jesus enunciated the Golden Rule, which says to do one to others before they do one to you.

- St. Paul cavorted to Christianity. He preach holy acrimony, which is another word for marriage.

- A Christian should have only one spouse. This is called monotony.

Four Years of Weddings at The Stone Church

As we discussed elsewhere in this newsletter, weddings are very important to the Stone Church, and not just for their financial contribution to the restoration of the Chapel. Weddings help fulfill the mission of the Church by offering a spiritually rich environment for a very important moment in the lives of the participants. Weddings also give the wider community an opportunity to learn about the Stone Church, its history and its current vibrant life.

Couples who have been married in the Stone Church have contributed in other ways as well. For example, one couple came up The Mountain in advance of their wedding dressed in jeans and cleared brush from the mountainside that was obstructing the glorious view from the arch. Another couple planted a tree to commemorate their wedding.

In recognition of the importance of weddings, therefore, we are attempting to publish the names of all couples wed in the Stone Church. We have some catching up to do, so here are four years of brides and grooms. If your name is missing or incorrect, please let us know. We regard all couples as part of the extended family of the Stone Church, and we want to keep in touch with each of you. Send us news or reminiscences for future newsletters.

1999 (18): Nancy Coyne and Gregory Chase; Heather Dixon and Kevin Kraham; Eyonne M. DuBois and Christopher G. Benson; Sylvia Gale and Alistair Jones; Kristina Gantz and Lon Skidds; Deborah A. Gibson and Paul Dwyer; Sarah K. Hanssen and Aaron M. Nye; Elyse A. Kowalik and Gary A. Clearwater, Jr.; Rebecca Lehde and Gary Egger; Brenda Masterson and Mark Shaw; Laura L. Scherrieble and James Michael Bober; Jana Rearich and Nathan Raven; Erika Lynne Weber and Steven Carl Baranowski; Andrea Wickham and Ryan W. Bussard; Mary Beth Wilhelm and Christopher Lutz; Lorraine M. Wood and Dale R. Deidorn; Jana Woodland and Jon Harbison; Abigail Zettowch and Adam Mance.

2000 (27): Michelle Ahart and Robert Bosland; Irene E. Bach and Justin Samberts; Leanne Bakke and Michael Myers; Frances Carmona and Michael A. Ledesma; Candis DeBetta and Stuart Parsons; Tara DiGiovanni and Patrick Mickelson; Aimee Dillon and Eric Tamweber; Kimberly A. Elwood and Dale McIntosh; Vira Feliciano and Alex Berkobein; Dawn Grote and David Smith; Julia Hill and John Fraino; Dale Hlavacek and Daniel Mance; Lanette K. Hunt and Nando A. Plate; Susan L. King and Mike Erickson; Julia Lundell and Patrick Kinbrell; Kathleen McCarvill and Thomas P. Burns; Diane Marie Miller and Edward Arthur Marl; Amy Mousley and Scott Carr; Kathleen Painter and Robert Poitras; Deborah A. Pinkerous and Marc G. Laclaverie; Alicia Pratt and David Herman; Maureen Rockwell and Timothy Scheels; Susan F. Rose and James J.Burns; Pirkko Salminen and Lindy Marryshow; Rachel J. Squires and George R. Countryman; Kimberly A. Warren and Robert M. Flynn; Miriam Williams and Edward Weig

2001 (17): Cassie Crisano and Ryan Chan; Tina M. Carlile and Thomas A. Young; Laurel Decker and Brian Humphrey; Stephanie M. Grant and Steven K. Dye; Carmen P. Guerra and Carlos Cuellar; Angela J. Grasso and Jan F. Towne; Stephanie Marshall and Matthew Borzio; Lynnette M. Ritoch and Roger A. Wright, Jr.; Susan A. Knight and Edward H. Shafer; Allison Wilson and Donald McKay; Rene Terwilliger and Phillip Pereira; Pamela Denull and Steven Cox; Debbie Foster and Rocco Surace; Erin L. Nelke and Dino R. Anello; Joyce Van Blarcom and Louis Turnbull, Jr.; Melissa Wilhelm and Jason VanHorn; Megan K. Hnath and Michael P. Straube

2002 (31): Rachel J. Beiling and Shane L. LaForge; Hillery Bosworth and John Apter; Eileen Particia Boyle and Joseph Raymond Gardocki; Nancy D. Carbone and William H. Lobb, III; Barbara Canzoneri and Kevin McGrath; Andrea Claire and John Allen; Andrea Coppola and Vinnie Greco; Patricia Delessio and Philip DeMarco; Mauareen Diehl and Nicholas Brown; Paula Dunn and James Montanya; Basia Dybicki and David Fabian; Haley Flynn and Gregory Bowman; Kathleen S. Fowler and Sean M. Morgan; Sonja C. Frederick and Nicholas E. Cannistra,Jr.; Christine Gould and Justin Rodriquez; Jeane Graziano ands Edwards R. Tamburo; Cathy Henry and John M. Wilhelm; Christina Horton and Ignacio Lara; Lauren Kulesa and Jason St. Germain; Kerry McGrath and Matthew Courtney; Ines McQuillan and Richard Sherman; Sera L. Moore and Samuel L. Mance; Rachel Muniz and John Caviano; Kathleen M. Petrillo and James A. Bair III; Deborah Peters and Daniel Lewis; Desha Rajcoomar and Brian Staigis; Abgela M. Rincon and Scott R. Smith; Eleni K. Rodriquez and Shannon Countryman; Jamie Russell and Daniel Gallo; Paige Sheard and Steven Pinto; Jean Uhl and Jason Lazio.

Wedding Policy and Practice

Couples of all faiths and orientations may be wed at the Stone Church. The fee is $500, which covers cleaning before and after the wedding as well as candles for the ceremony. (The proceeds go only toward the direct expenses of the wedding and to restoring the Chapel.) Weddings may be held inside or outside, weather permitting, and the grounds are available for receptions, for an additional fee. Couples receive a certificate designed by John Duncan with beautiful individualized calligraphy by Della Sue, as well as wooden replicas of the Stone Church and the arch.

Reservations can be made by calling Sally Matz at 845-647-6384. While the Stone Church does not provide someone to officiate at the service, Sally can suggest a wide range of local services, from officiants to caterers, florists, musicians and photographers.

Thanks!

The Friends of the Stone Church are very much of a volunteer organization, and we depend heavily on many helping hands to keep the Chapel going. Our special thanks go to John Stanger, who faithfully plowed the Church grounds during the recent heavy winter (replacing our late friend George Stedner), and to Dick and Pat Peters, who cared for the grounds in the warmer weather and planted flowers and bushes around the new sign.

We are also thankful for the flowers donated by Scott Stedner of the Eastern Correctional Facility.

Of course, the Church could not function without the tireless efforts of Chuck and Sally Matz, who clean the Church before and after weddings and services and are available at all hours to do whatever needs to be done.

But they cannot do it all. Therefore, the Friends of the Stone Church are soliciting the involvement of other members of the community, in particular to be present during weddings and rehearsals, to supervise the use of the chapel and to direct parking. A portion of the fee for the rental of the Church will be used to compensate these efforts, so if you are interested in earning a little extra cash, contact Sally Matz at 845-647-6384.

Newsletter Delay Explained

Four years have passed since the last newsletter. Since then, the Millennium has come and gone, more than 100 people have been married at the Stone Church, and year-round services have been under way for several years — all without a newsletter.

Unfortunately, during the very same period, the Editor started a new law practice, founded the Cragsmoor Conservancy and got elected President of his co-op board and Chair of the Riverside Church Ordination Committee. There is only so much one can do. Hopefully, the next in this series of "occasional" newsletters will not require a gestation period of 48 months.

Summer 2003 at the Stone Church

Sunday Services continue at the *Stone Church* (*Chapel of the Holy Name*) in Cragsmoor during the 2003 summer. During the month of July, worship services will be conducted by: Victoria Moss, Director of Spiritual and Religious Life at Davis-Elkins College in Elkins, VA; Rev. Robert Hewitt, Pastor of Pine Bush United Methodist Church; and Dr. Joy Carol, Spiritual and Healing Leader at St. John the Divine Cathedral in New York City.

For more information call **647-6384**.

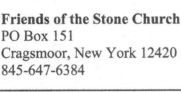

Friends of the Stone Church
PO Box 151
Cragsmoor, New York 12420
845-647-6384

Friends of the Stone Church is a non-sectarian organization dedicated to the restoration, preservation and operation of the Episcopal Chapel of the Holy Name in Cragsmoor, New York, a property of the Episcopal Diocese of New York. Worship services are conducted every Sunday from Memorial Day to Labor Day and on the first Sunday of every month from Labor Day to Memorial Day, all at 11:00 a.m. Other events are scheduled from time to time, and weddings, memorial services and other appropriate gatherings may be scheduled by making a request to Friends of the Stone Church, who also gratefully accept donations for the preservation and programs of the Stone Church. All checks should be made payable to "Friends of the Stone Church" and are tax-deductible donations to a religious organization.

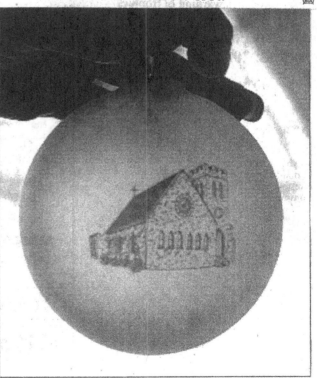

The Cragsmoor Stone Church, as seen on one of the Bicentennial Committee's new memento ornaments, first available at Terwilliger House July 12th. See the article on Page 17 for more details!

Peace Pole Dedication at Cragsmoor Celebration

The dedication of a peace pole will be the highlight of the annual Celebration of Peace and Hope at the *Stone Church* in Cragsmoor Sunday, September 12th at 11 AM. The pole carries the message, "May Peace Prevail on Earth" in eight languages and will be one of more than 250,000 similar monuments erected in 180 countries, expressing the universal longing for peace among all people.

During the dedication, Deborah Moldow, Director of the World Peace Prayer Society will lead a World Peace Flag Ceremony. Participants will carry flags of different countries while everyone sends a prayer for peace to each country whose flag is displayed. Birds of a Feather, a Woodstock community drum group led by drum teacher, Fre Atlast, and accompanied by vocalists Rev. Lynn Keller and Davida, will perform the chant "Om Shanti" at the edge of the cliff.

The dedication will be preceded by an interfaith service of prayers for peace led by representatives of several spiritual traditions. Music during the service will be led by Matthew Cantello, a Music Healing Practitioner.

The first presenter will be Reverend James C. Davis, an interfaith minister, teacher, earth activist, and visionary. He is Environmental Director of the Wittenberg Center for Alternative Resources, where he designed and supervised the construction of the Center's World Peace Chamber.

Sister Dorothy Steinfeld will represent the Brahma Kumaris World Spiritual Organization. Sister Dorothy is Programs Director and one of the main coordinators of the Peace Village Learning and Retreat Center.

The Buddhist presentation will be made by His Eminence, the Fourth Trungram Gyaltrul Rimpoche, the founder and spiritual director of the United Trungram Buddhist Fellowship. He is also leading the development of a retreat center in Cragsmoor, the sole purpose of which is contemplative practice and instruction in the Buddhist skills of meditation.

Everyone is welcome to this event. Cragsmoor is off **Rte. 52**, between Ellenville and Pine Bush. Take **Cragsmoor Road** for two miles to the **Post Office**. Continue straight and follow signs to the *Stone Church*. Call 647-6384 for info. ⌂

From the Editor

"There is no way to Peace... Peace IS the way." – A.J. Muste

On a gorgeous, bright September 12th, dozens of persons, including guests representing foreign lands and faiths, gathered at the **Stone Church** in Cragsmoor to plant a Peace Pole and partake in an interfaith Celebration of Peace and Hope. *(See the September 2004, Wawarsing.Net #22, for details. Above, Reverend James C. Davis prepares to bury a Mohawk war hatchet at the base of the pole, honoring the Iroquois tradition of placing weapons under treaty trees.)* Following are edited remarks by event organizer Maureen Radl of Cragsmoor, speaking at the ceremonies:

"It is with a joyous heart that I welcome you all here today on behalf of the *Friends of the Stone Church*. The shining faces of so many who have celebrated peace and hope with us in the past, is a testament to the need for this event to continue. But the sight of so many new faces shows that our ranks are growing, and that is important. For we are part of the armies of peace that are rising up in every country to pray and sing and drum our message of love into every corner of this troubled planet. We must never lose faith that peace is achievable. For no matter how dark the future may look, as long as we persist, as long as we hold on to the vision, someday, perhaps even in our lifetimes, peace *will* prevail on earth.

"Some of you are familiar with how this event first came into being, but for those of you who don't know, it bears repeating. On the first Sunday after 9/11, we held an impromptu memorial service for the victims of that tragedy. We had been unable to reach many of our friends in the city all week, but at that service we were all united, a group of sorrowful and distressed but none the less enlightened people. Many of you spoke with great eloquence and deep emotion about your experiences near the site and your reactions to what had happened. If my memory serves me well, there was not one who did not pray that those events would not lead to even greater acts of violence worldwide.

"I guess you all know the rest of the story. Our prayers have not yet been answered because as part of the human race we have not yet found a way to resolve differences peacefully. So each year on the Sunday closest to 9/11, we convene again, to search for a way to restore peace in our lives and in the world. Our interfaith service has drawn upon the wisdom of diverse spiritual traditions to pray for the peaceful evolution of humankind.

"When we come together for this celebration we recognize the bond we have as people. If we could dissolve colors, shapes, forms, and languages, then we could see all of ourselves as creatures, sharing the extraordinary universe that the Creator has designed for us. During the past few years there has been much pain, sadness, suffering, and loss among people everywhere, even in our country, in our community, and in our personal lives. But in a spiritual gathering like this, we hope to find peace and joy for the souls that have been burned in the fire of the world. And when we access the peace in our own hearts and acknowledge that there is peace in everyone, then we can share that peace in other places.

"Let us work toward world peace by honoring the earth, honoring its people, and celebrating the unity of the human spirit."

Cover: Peace Pole, The Stone Church, Cragsmoor, Town of Wawarsing, Ulster County, New York, USA. A new, beautifully-carved wooden Peace Pole was planted in Cragsmoor, joining over 250,000 worldwide. The prayer "May Peace Prevail on Earth" is inscribed in eight living languages (English, Hindi, Hebrew, Punjabi, Tibetan, Chinese, Arabic, and Delaware) representing eight of the major faiths. (www.worldpeace.org)

Issue #23   2004 October

Wawarsing.Net

Published by the
Ellenville-Wawarsing
Chamber of Commerce
Also Online at
www.Wawarsing.Net

79

9/11 Celebration of Peace and Hope at Cragsmoor's Stone Church

Since the tragedy of September 11, 2001, a *Celebration of Peace and Hope* at the hundred-year-old **Stone Church** has brought meaningful expression of the universal longing for peace among the world's people. With the dedication last year of a peace pole *(photo, top right)*, inscribed with the message, "May Peace Prevail on Earth" in the languages of the eight major religions of the world, the *Peace Celebration* continues to bring together children and adults from all walks of life to pray for peace and understanding in our world.

The interfaith ceremony will be held on **Sunday, September 11**, beginning at **11 AM**, followed by a pot luck lunch on the mountaintop churchyard. A concert of Celtic music will be presented at **2 PM**. Speakers will represent a broad spectrum of spiritual beliefs, offering perspectives on the journey to a more harmonious existence.

Miriam MacGillis, OP, a former coordinator of Peace and Justice Education, is a co-founder of Genesis Farm, a center for Earth studies, rooted in spirituality. She has worked there since 1980, developing the farm as an ecological learning center which practices biodynamic methods of agriculture in tune with the natural rhythms of Earth. The goal of the center is to find a new vision of how to live on the planet in harmony with the natural world and with each other in a bioregional context. The programs draw upon the wisdom of many cultural groups, all of which she feels we need, to meet the critical problems before us. She also coordinates programs exploring the work of Thomas Berry as he has interpreted the New Cosmology, and she has lectured extensively and offered workshops worldwide.

Swami Srinivasananda has dedicated his life to the oath of Inner Peace and Unity in Diversity as taught and lived by Swami Sivananda and Swami Vishnu-devananda, who demonstrated that the greatest offering to world peace and brotherhood is a total commitment to service and mediation. Swami Srinivasananda served as the director of the Paris Center from 1980 to 1983 and the Los Angeles Center from 1983 to 1986. He has also served as the director of the Val-Morin ashram from 1992 to 1994. Since 1994, he has served as the Acharya for the Sivananda Ashram Yoga Ranch, the New York and Chicago centers and affiliated Sivananda centers of the eastern region of the US, and is the American editor of the Yoga Life Magazine.

Bonnie Myotai Treace, Sensei is a Zen Buddhist teacher and poet. She is the founder of Hermitage Heart, a form of Zen training that supports solitary practice, deep study in community, and commitment to the environment. Sensei was for many years Vice-Abbess of Zen Mountain Monastery in Mount Tremper, NY, and the teacher and Abbess of the Zen Center in New York City. In her Dharma talks and retreats, she is both calming and engaging. According to the Garrison Center, where she recently led a summer session, her "style of full-immersion creates an opportunity for whole-hearted engagement that can open up what may have felt closed or contrived. She works with students on easing the mind's constrictions and sense of suffering."

Rev. Kari Schreiber, will offer prayers for peace from

the Beloved Community, a spiritual and educational group that strives to align with the teachings of inner peace at the center of every religion. It has organized peace vigils in Iraq, Afghanistan, Bosnia, Israel, and many other locations worldwide.

The *Celebration* will also be enriched by the music of two outstanding performers. Musician and hypnotherapist, Peter Blum, will play the Himalayan singing bowls. He has been working with the mysterious sounds of these ancient instruments for the past fifteen years and is involved in the extensive observation of the effects of sound and music on body and mind for healing and creativity. Singer and songwriter, Victor Roland Mousaa, will share songs written for the Native American Cultural Alliance. Some of his music has also been inspired by his work in the civil rights, anti-nuclear, and peace movements.

If time permits, members of the congregation will be invited to share brief prayers, poems, or comments. There is no admission for this morning event.

Cragsmoor, an historic art colony in the **Shawangunk Mountains**, is located off **Rte. 52**, between Ellenville and Pine Bush, five minutes from the *Sam's Point Preserve*. Follow **Cragsmoor Road** to the Post Office and continue straight, following signs to the **Stone Church**. ⬠

9/11 Peace Concert in Cragsmoor

As part of the annual *Celebration of Peace and Hope* held on **Sunday, September 11** at the **Stone Church** in Cragsmoor, a concert by *Capall, a Celtic Cross* will be held at 2 PM.

With singer Maura Ellyn, bansuri flutist Steve Gorn, guitarist Peter Einhorn, and percussionist John Wieczorek, Capall offers haunting invocations of love, loss, and memory in shimmering arrangements crossing far-flung musical cultures. In clubs, concerts and festivals, Capall explores the music and poetry of Yeats, Burns, Mirabai, patriots, exiles, contemporary artists and those whose names have been lost. In the echoes, whispers, textures and rhythms of many cultures, Capall discovers a new sonic universe.

Capall, travels over time as well as the globe, weaving past, present and future like the language of dreams. An ancient Indian raga finds echoes in an old Irish air recast with words in the spirit of Mirabai twined by a Krishna melody for the bansuri.

Steve Gorn, bansuri flutist and multi-reed player *(photo, left)*, has performed Indian classical music and new American music in concerts and festivals throughout the world. Composing and playing for theater and dance, he has worked with Jerome Robbins, Julie Taymor, and others. The New York Times has called his music exquisite and evocative, and Paul Winter has said he plays with "liquid grace...a master of sound-magic."

Maura Ellyn, whose voice the New York Times has described as "strong, lyrical and subtly expressive," has performed on many stages, from the ancient theater at the foot of the Parthenon to the plaza of the late World Trade Center, in festivals, concert halls, theaters and clubs. Singing experimental, theater, jazz, Latin, and world music, she has played and recorded with many great composers and musicians, among them, Lou Harrison, Teiji Ito, Gary Peacock, Billy Hart and Cyro Baptiste.

Peter Einhorn, guitarist, composer, teacher and regular member of the Metropolitan Opera Orchestra is also an award-winning composer, having scored dozens of films and written music for radio, television and multimedia format. Besides leading and recording with his own groups, Peter has worked with Jim Hall, Steve Swallow, John Scholfield, Karl Berger, and many others.

John Wieczorek, multifaceted musician and percussionist, has studied contemporary, ethnic and electronic percussion for over twenty-five years. He has played and recorded with jazz, Indian, pop, and world musicians, such as Mark Dresser, John McPhee, Pandit Samir Chatterjee, Glen Velez and has toured with Bet Williams and John Hodian's "Epiphany Project."

The concert will be held as the closing of the annual *Celebration of Peace and Hope*, which starts at 11 AM. Speakers representing some of the world's religions will offer their perspectives for achieving peace and harmony among all people. It will be followed by a potluck lunch on the lawn before the concert. Tickets for the concert at **2 PM** are $15 for adults, $8 for seniors. Children under 5 are free. The **Stone Church** is located at the edge of the **Shawangunk Ridge** off **Rte. 52** between Ellenville and Pine Bush. Take **Cragsmoor Road** to the Post Office and follow signs to the **Stone Church**. For more information, call **845-647-6487**.

About Cragsmoor

Cragsmoor - A Brief History

Located in Ulster County, N.Y., Cragsmoor first came into existence in the early 1870's when Edward Lamson Henry, William H. Beard, J.G. Brown, Mrs. Eliza Pratt Greatorex and her two artist daughters, Kathleen Honora Greatorex and Eleanor Gretorex, discovered the enchantments held by the plateau in the Shawangunk Mountains. E.L. Henry was the first artist to build a summer home here, and Mrs. Henry christened the house NA-PEE-NIA, a name from the Lenape Indians. Word quickly spread to other artists about Cragsmoor and its wonders, though the colony did not attract the traditional struggling artist with little or no recognition. On the contrary, artists of note who were already prosperous sought to make their homes among the splendor.

The sweeping vistas painted by the Hudson River school were not as popular at the time as settings where people were more predominant. Cragsmoor's artists specialized in the latter. Their mountain getaway was a wonderful source of scenic beauty and local characters. For example, the September 1, 1912 edition of the local paper, the *Journal*, noted, "Peter Brown died....a great loss to Mr. [E.L.] Henry, for he had utilized him as a model in some of his most striking pictures." Mr. Henry also used a local carpenter, Joseph E. Mance, for some of his paintings while Frederick Dellenbaugh often captured "Grandpa" Coddington (a local farmer) in his works. Of course, the painters used themselves and each other as subjects as well.

Eliza Hartshorn, a wealthy lady from Newport, was a primary figure in the development of Cragsmoor. She was related to both Mrs. E.L. Henry and Mrs. Frederick Dellenbaugh. During her first visit to the Henrys in 1886, she immediately purchased some land in the colony. Houses, barns, public buildings and roads were constructed at her impetus, with Frederick Dellenbaugh as the architect.

Although Dellenbaugh was a man of many interests and accomplishments, he never had formal architectural training. As a result, his houses were unique, innovative and eccentric. Closets would be placed in what would otherwise be wasted space, but he seemed to care very little for the dimensions of stairs. Very few of his staircases allowed for the passage of large furniture and some were even rebuilt so they could be utilized for that purpose. A Dellenbaugh house often had no two windows alike, for he enjoyed salvaging windows from houses scheduled for demolition in the city and working them into his designs on the mountain. (Note: The Barnacle is a Dellenbaugh house)

Dellenbaugh also gave Cragsmoor its name, despite stiff competition from Mrs. Henry. When the residents petitioned for a post office, Dellenbaugh offered "Winahdin", but was rejected on the grounds that it sounded too much like another upstate New York community, Windham. He then created "Cragsmoor." Mrs. Henry suggested the name "Baim-Wa-Wa" for the community. She maintained that it was the Lanape name for "passing thunder" and secretly circulated a petition against the adoption of "Cragsmoor." Dellenbaugh found out about Mrs. Henry's endeavors accidentally, and declared that he would leave rather than live in a community with such a silly name. He then got together with the local postmaster and wrote a letter to the Post Office Department, wherein he claimed that the bulk of the citizens favored his invention over Mrs. Henry's. Since the Post Office Department desired brevity, the name was immediately accepted.

During the summers at Cragsmoor, the *Journal* reported the presence of a number of musicians and music teachers. The best known was Maud Powell (1868-1920), the greatest female violinist of her day and a close friend of the Henrys. Theater people were attracted by Barnstormers Theater, an outgrowth of the readings, amateur theatricals and tableaux that were popular at Cragsmoor from its earliest days as a summer colony. It is rumored that Thornton Wilder wrote "The Skin of Our Teeth" while staying with Jessica Bruce in Cragsmoor.

Cragsmoor's summer residents were very civic minded. The Cragsmoor Free Library was first established in the Pines Casino, built by Eliza Hartshorn in 1899 for use by the young people. Around 1912 a library was inaugurated for both summer and permanent residents and was housed at various locations until 1923. In 1923, the trustees built a permanent library designed by Dellenbaugh and constructed on land he donated.

The summer denizens also ensured their spiritual needs were met. In 1895 and 1896, Dellenbaugh designed and constructed the Episcopalian Chapel of the Holy Name with money supplied by Eliza Hartshorn. The Federated Church was built in 1903, a venture heavily funded by the Innesses. Charles Curran served as deacon.

Describing the Cragsmoor summer colony in 1906, the *Journal* found "a harmonious community… active-minded and deeply interested in the best art, literature, drama and music: so that mingled with the atmosphere of relaxation is also one of pleasant mental activity. These people have seen the world far and wide, yet they find the charms of Cragsmoor undimmed by comparison." In spite of the fact that six years later the same paper complained that life on the mountain was becoming "too formal" very little changed there during the war years and beyond.

However, by 1928 Edward Gay, Eliza Greatorex, E.L. Henry and Arthur Keller were dead. Carroll Brown and Dellenbaugh only survived them by a few years. By the time Charles Curran died in 1942, the glory days of the art colony had long been over. Gone are the days when Mrs. Hartshorn was thrown from her buggy while going down the gully road. No one walks past Curran's house, singing, "steer clear of that man, for to get you to pose is his plan" anymore. However, the magic still prevails, and the views are just as inspiring.

Help us with the Curran catalogue raisonne

Home

Cragsmoor

TO DISCOVER : CRAGSMOOR BY A GLIMPSE

" From this spot,

as if like birds,

women and men rise

in the lifting wind"

(semi-anonymous, inscribed into windsock pole, hang gliding launch site, Cragsmoor,NY)

	ragsmoor *is* nestled on a high plateau at the southernmost tip of the Shawangunk Mountains, overlooking the lower Hudson Valley and ultimately Manhattan (at 75 miles distant) to the East and South, with Ellenville, its Roundout Valley and the Catskills providing the view to the West and North. Its one of those special places that came into being not through commerce or convenience, but rather through its' tendency, be it geographic, cultural, or just the way the light bounces off of things, to instill in its visitors a mild sense of wonder and ease.
	idge soaring may not be part of most peoples' normal vocabulary, but the ridge on which Cragsmoor is perched lies perpendicular to the prevailing Northwest breeze – this peculiar arrangement provides hundreds of hours of sustained motorless flight per year... just ask the birds – or the sailplane pilots from nearby Wurtsburo airport, or the dozens of hang glider pilots who have made Cragsmoor and the surrounding area their home. This free-flight phenomena frequently fascinates families and friends. See www.ushga.org
	rtist colony: In 1879, a Manhattan-based painter, Edward Lamson Henry, (elected to the National Academy of Design in 1867) first visited Cragsmoor, staying at what was then called the Mountain Hotel (now a private residence). Evidently he enjoyed his stay; he and his wife Frances subsequently returned, bought property, designed and built his studio/home and two guest cottages. His arrival marks the start of a very productive artist colony that bustled every summer for his next 40 years. See www.kbart.com
	reat hiking: Impressive vistas flank this little hamlet - two nature preserves are open to residents and tourists alike. Bear cliff to the southwest is an easy walk with sunset views that make you wish you brought your picnic basket. Open Space Institute has secured 4,600 pristine acres on the other side of Cragsmoor, known as Sams Point, which abuts Minnewaska State Park, which in turn abuts the historic and impressive Mohonk Mountain House. See www.mohonkpreserve.org
	tatue of Liberty ? Yes that's right, the Statue of God-Blessed Liberty, in where else but Cragsmoor... In 1963 , pilot and resident Tony Covelli experienced the Statue in a way that millions of other immigrants can strongly relate to – "...I could never forget the view of the Statue of Liberty I still have in my mind and my heart, from when I was 18 ...seeing her from the boat, her beauty and all it represents, it just stays with you..." In 1990 he acquired the 30 acre hang gliding landing field in the

valley below. During the summer of 2000, resident, pilot, and artist Roger Baker wanted to use this field as a GIGANTIC canvas – and decided to use Tonys' suggestion. Along with Tom Mackey, the three pilots then mowed an image TEN times the size of the actual statue. The execution of the idea was perfect, the result is magical... PHOTOS

 usic at the Stone Church: Summer concert series – striking architecture, inspired performaces, and great acoustics... a pleasant way to enjoy the enchantments of the place – very pleasant indeed, and don't forget to take in the sweeping view from the church's memorial archway. See photos

 ur Historical Society: Responsible for Cragsmoor being designated a National Historic District, the group has recently taken on the herculean task of renovating some key structures, notably the Federated Church building on Cragsmoor Road. A noble objective in progress...See photos

 ur lovely Free Library: Subtly rustic in its use of peeled chestnut columns, fieldstone fireplace, and painting collection, the library has a cozy ambiance. It plays an important role in the local history and cultural events, and is also a living place were the kids of the community enjoy workshops as well as adults enjoy the resources. See photos and Library site http://www.zelacom.com/~cragsmoor/

 ustic Furniture: Don't forget, there is high-tech rustic furniture being built right here in Cragsmoor, since 1995 in fact... to see some, check out the rest of the site – enjoy, and thank you

Flying over Cragsmoor   Cragsmoor by photos

BIBLIOGRAPHY

HAKAM, Margaret and HOUGHTALING, Susan. *Cragsmoor An Historical Sketch.* Cragsmoor Free Library, 1983.

HILL, May Brawley. *Grandmother's Garden. The Old-Fashioned American Garden 1865-1915.* Harry.N.Adam, New York 1995.

TERWILLIGER, Katharine. *Wawarshing. Where The Streams Wind.* The Rondout Valley Publishing Company. Ellenville, N.Y.1977.

All these documents are available at Cragsmoor Free Library.

Histories and Mysteries of Cragsmoor

by Lucy Muller

Most of these stories are hearsay, but, in my 61 years in Cragsmoor, I can tell you that I experienced many first hand.

Let me start way back at the turn of the of the 19ᵗʰ century into the 20ᵗʰ. In 1901, my grandparents, Christine and Anderson Polk, lived in New York City. They had one baby and wanted him to have cool, fresh air in the summer. My grandmother knew of the summer retreat and artist colony called Cragsmoor. She had stayed at the *Inn* or the *Blakeley House* a few times. So my grandparents looked around and bought a farmhouse located at the corner of **Henry Rd. & Schulyer Ave.** at the north end of the mountain. They had the house put on wheels, not that uncommon, and moved to the edge of the mountain facing the Catskills. The house was the fourth to the left of the **Stone Church,** if you're looking at the view *(photo above).* They added a porch, but had an outhouse and a dug well in those days. The only heat was a fireplace, so the house was only open in the summer.

In 1906, my mother came along and by this time the family had to travel by train all the way from Baltimore. My grandmother would pack up in May, take the train to Ellenville and then wagon up the **Gully Road** to Cragsmoor. It took two hours with two stops to water the horses. My mother told me that they would be black with soot at the end of the journey.

Cragsmoor was ideal for children to explore and yet be safe. There was a swamp, which we would now call wetlands. At the end of the driveway one could hear the bullfrogs and catch tadpoles. There were huge pine trees to climb and **Diana's Bath** between Cragsmoor and Mt. Monagha to swim in. There were blueberries to eat off the bush and patches of blackberry to chomp on.

Every Sunday, the family would attend services at the *Chapel of the Holy Name* and the priest lived in the rectory all summer. I bet the clergy scrambled for that cushy job every year.

After Labor Day, the family would close up Treetops (the name of the house then) and take the train back to the city. It makes me so happy to think that the house, now called Katzview, is on the National Historic Register.

My mother was a model for many of the famous Hudson River School of artists. She sat for Helen Turner, Charles Curran, Charles Gay, and E. L. Henry. She is the young girl in blue in a landscape by Charles Curran hanging in the *Cragsmoor Library* and she is the *Young Woman with a Lantern* by Helen Turner. She took art lessons herself and attended the Academy of Fine Arts in Philadelphia. My mother's specialty was pastel portraits. It is quite amazing, as she is the great, great, great, great niece of the painter Charles Wilson Peale.

Now when my mother was born, her uncle married a young woman and they went on their honeymoon to New Orleans. The girl ate oysters, came down with typhoid fever and died. My mother was to be named Alethea, but when Julia Neal died, my grandparents changed her name to Julia Neal. It was so sad and each summer my grandma would have a special church service in memory of her sister-in-law.

The summer my mother turned four, she and her brother were taking naps and my grandmother was lying down in her downstairs bedroom. That's when she heard the footsteps in the dining room. Nana called out, but no one answered. She heard the steps again and this time she got up and looked – no one. And then she realized the steps were those of someone in slippers. She had forgotten to have the service for Julia Neal and, since Julia was tall, she had worn slippers at her wedding. My grandmother ran over to the rectory and got the priest to have the memorial service right away.

Fast forward to the 1940s. My mother is grown up, married, with two daughters. My sister, Nina, born in 1939, and me, born the winter of 1943. We lived outside Philadelphia, but when I was six-months-old, they hauled me up to Cragsmoor and my personal relationship with the place began.

We still had the outhouse and the dug well and the pitcher pump. What fun that was to pump and pump until the cold, delicious water would come pouring out. My bedroom was in a top left-hand side and every night before I fell asleep I could see the lights of Ellenville twinkling down in the valley.

We had such a great time. We went swimming at Haberman's pool by this time, but still went down the mountain to Diana's Bath when it was really hot. I had lots of cousins to play with and the same wetland and blueberry bushes of my mother's day. At that time we could walk or drive up to **Sam's Point** for picnics. That meant we could go up there at night; how I miss being able to do that now. No one damaged the pinelands then, but off-road vehicles weren't around either.

Lake Maratanza on top of **Sam's Point** was now a reservoir, and no one could swim in it. We also had **Bear Hill** to climb around and so much freedom. I especially remember walking barefoot everywhere. I liked to pop the tar bubbles on the road with my feet.

There was an old, old woman named Mrs. Wright up there when I was a kid. She walked with two canes and had a dagger in her sock. She looked just like the witch in *Hansel and Gretal.* One night we snuck around and looked in her windows and discovered she wasn't using her canes. To a bunch of kids this was scandalous. Everything was such a big deal then. There was nothing scarier than walking home in the dark and just at the driveway, getting that hair-raising feeling so that you had to run the last hundred yards to the safety of the house.

There is still one more mystery I have always wanted to solve, and that is the one of Julia West. Miss West was in a murder/suicide that took place at the **Stone Church** around 1945. She and a man were discovered there and her parents put up the arch and cross as a memorial for her *(photo below).* If anyone can find out anything about it for me it would be appreciated.

All in all, Cragsmoor has been a safe and happy place. It can be treacherous in the fog and dead of winter, but there is nothing like it in the summer.

Mountain Lines

Winters in Cragsmoor

by Lucy Muller, *Lu@warwick.net*

(I would like to send my best wishes to Dianne Turner, who was recently badly hurt in a car accident. Dianne will recover, but her dear little dog Kisses was killed in the accident. Our heartfelt sympathy goes out to her.)

A friend of mine at *St. John's Episcopal Church* asked me the other day if I had any memories of the holidays in Cragsmoor over the years.

I have spent 59 summers in Cragsmoor, but it wasn't until 1958 that I spent a winter here. My mother decided to stay all year round so I could go to high school in Ellenville. That was the best decision she ever made. It was truly the best time of my life; the best friends and the best education.

I remember how exciting it was when autumn came in at the end of September. The bus ride down the mountain was so pretty. I met Kate Van Kleeck then and we had many a rollicking time on that bus.

I also met Pete Williams, Mark Levitas, Letty Spadaro, Pat Peters, and so many great kids including Peter Wright. It was in October that Peter died in a car accident. We missed him so, and it was our first experience with death. But being kids, we soon began to enjoy our lives again and my first winter was so much fun. Sometimes we were snowed in for three days, and days when we had to walk through deep snow from the post office, where the school bus dropped us off, to our homes a half-mile away. It took us an hour.

Sometimes it would be raining in Ellenville and, about half way up the mountain, the precip would turn to snow. Every day was more beautiful than the next. When the ice formed on the branches of all the trees, and the sun came out, it was as if you were inside a crystal palace.

My friends in Cragsmoor taught me to cross-country ski and we would literally ski out the back door and visit all the places we had roamed in the summer.

In those days, the *Cragsmoor Inn* was still there, and it had the best wide-open sledding hills anywhere. We had toboggans too, and that was hilarious to climb on, go shooting down the hill, and end up in a pile of laughing kids. I loved ice skating, too, and we once went over to a big tennis court that was ice covered, built a huge bonfire and skated around in the light of the fire. Then we walked home to my house and my mother had hot chocolate for us.

In those days, every Wednesday was religious education day. After lunch four of us, Bruce Bowler, Nelson Loucks, Sara Winterburger, and I, would walk to *St. John's* for our class. That was a trip and the discussions are confidential. The **Stone Church** in Cragsmoor didn't have heat in it then, so the chapel was not used.

Ellenville looked so adorable decorated for Christmas, but I spent the actual day with relatives in another state. I always spent New Year's Eve in Cragsmoor and we had some memorable parties. One was at the home of Henry Munson. It was not really a party, but an event with music and the living room turned into a ballroom. We waltzed around in our fancy clothes like something in "War & Peace." The food was spectacular, as Mrs. Munson was a great cook. Then out into the cold, starry night and the enchantment of the snow-covered mountain. I will never forget the night I saw the Northern Lights. It was January, and colder than anything I felt before, but the sky was pulsating with red, green, and white lights. We felt so humble and tiny.

Since I returned to the mountain in 2002, I've enjoyed the caroling, lights and mounds of snow again. But I am a grown-up now (sort of) and although most of my Christmas memories are from elsewhere, nothing can compare with living here all through the winter when I was young.

Mountain Lines

A Tribute to Good Things

by Lucy Muller, *Lu@warwick.net*

This column is a tribute to the good things about Cragsmoor and Ellenville.

Now to Cragsmoor.

Sally and Chuck Matz saved the **Stone Church** from being turned to rubble and you can enjoy different kinds of services all summer long. Sally also works with Tom Bolger to arrange theater and readings in the *Historical Society*.

Rudy at the post office is always a friendly, fun person who can cheer you up when you need it most.

We have **Bear Hill** and **Sam's Point** to hike to. These natural sites are breathtaking and many people worked hard to be sure they would be preserved.

I wouldn't mind a bed and breakfast and a little Mom and Pop store, but I guess that won't happen.

Bill Shamro keeps our driveways clear in winter and also works to keep the Ellenville schools humming along.

I have friends back in New Jersey who have been here and although they think it's beautiful, they still ask, "How can you live there all winter? It's so far from everything." My answer is, "I wouldn't live anywhere else and maybe everything... *isn't* everything!"

NOTE:

The article appearing above is not printed in its entirety.

Letters to the Editor

To the Editor:

After reading the articles on Cragsmoor by Lucy Muller in the *Wawarsing.Net*, I thought maybe people might be interested to know what it was like in Cragsmoor in the early 1900s.

I lived in Cragsmoor the first 25 years of my life (1910 to 1936) and had ties to Cragsmoor for the next 25 years through my parents who lived here most of their married life (60 years).

This was before electricity, indoor plumbing, radio, TV, snowplows, and school buses. There were about 12 families who called Cragsmoor their home. They didn't leave in September and return in May or June the next year, but lived there and kept Cragsmoor alive. Some of these people were born there and spent their whole life there. They really kept Cragsmoor alive during the winter months.

When the heavy snows came, the men got together with horses and shovels and opened a road to Ellenville by way of the **Gully Road**. This was volunteer work with no pay. When automobiles became more plentiful in the 1920s, the road to Ellenville was opened by way of the **Plank Road**. Snowplows finally came in the late 1930s.

For entertainment, we made our own. There were a few radios in the 1920s but they weren't used much because the batteries had to be taken to Ellenville to be recharged. Electricity finally came to Cragsmoor in the middle 1920s, but not everyone had it. The younger people had sleigh-riding and ice-skating on the ponds and, if the snow was too deep, hiking to **Sam's Point** and skating on **Lake Maratanza**. There were house parties and dinners at the *Federated Church* and just visiting your neighbor for talks and gossip.

The children walked to the one-room school (now a private home) in all kinds of weather. There were no snow days. Several of us walked to high school in Ellenville, also, in all kinds of weather. (No snow days there either.) Snow could be 2 inches to 2 feet in those days. These people didn't complain about the cold, the snow, or the condition of the roads either. People didn't have to go to Ellenville much for groceries because they bought their staples, like flour, sugar, and coffee, before the snows came. They grew and canned their fruit and vegetables and items like eggs, fresh milk, and meat they could buy or trade with their neighbor who had them.

Cragsmoor had artists like Geo. Ennis, Jr., Chas. Curran, EL Henry, Miss Turnasthan. In a way, Cragsmoor had their own local artists of special works: The Keri Bros, Lawrence & Colin, for their masonry works; Bert Goldsmith, with carpentry and moving houses; Lenard Marl, for his stone walls and stone steps. Visit the **Library** and you can see some of their work.

Cragsmoor has grown since those times, but it has also lost some of its charm and a lot of landmarks, like the **Harnhut** (Kite House) with the view of **Mt. Mongola**, Ellenville, and the **Catskills Mountains**, *Barnstormers Theatre*, *Blakely Fields Restaurant, the Frank B. Roadhead Boarding House* (with its bungalows), the *Mance* and *Kinberg Boarding Houses*. In 1930, two local young men, Liels Goldsmith and Bud Marl, had a garage with a gas pump out front on the corner of **Gully Road** and **Sam's Point Road**. They even had a taxi service during the summer months. Across the road from the *Federated Church* was *Garritt's Store and Post Office*, a place you could buy candy, tobacco, and ice cream in the summer. It also had gas pumps out front.

Then there was the *Cragsmoor Inn*, a real hotel with pavilion, theatre and a building called the Casino with a bowling alley, pool tables, and guestrooms. These buildings were connected to the hotel by a covered boardwalk. Then there was a well-kept 9-hole golf course and Mrs. Sturdevant's (the owner) famous Rose Garden.

Another great place was Mr. And Mrs. Ennis's summer home (later known as *Vista Maria*); *Chatolla*, as it was called, had a large picture gallery and Ms. Ennis's studio, terraces, and flower gardens. From there, one had a wonderful view of Orange County. On clear days, you could see Bear Mountain and Northern New Jersey. Their home was opened to the public one day a week during July and August. There were other things to see like the **Stone Pigeon Tower**, **Laly Pond** with a statue and lots of gold fish, the **Lily Pond** full of pond lilies and giant frogs, the gate houses with their huge gates, and a pigeon loft under the garages.

The people of those families who kept Cragsmoor alive during the winter months were interesting people doing interesting things. I'm sure great stories could have been told about their lives in Cragsmoor. I have many fond memories of those people and places of Cragsmoor way back then. Yes, and with the 25 years there, I am still living within 15 miles of Good Old Cragsmoor.

Walt Little
Ellenville, NY

Wawarsing.Net Magazine • 2005 May   **Issue 30** • **Page 21**

88

Mountain Lines

Summers in Cragsmoor

by Lucy Muller, Lu@warwick.net

Cragsmoor may be a little slower than other areas around here when it comes to dressing up for spring, but once she gets going, it is so beautiful.

The pink on the tops of the hardwoods have turned to a light green as I write this on May 14th and here and there are fruit trees in bloom. Our tamaracks, the prettiest of pines, that are not evergreens, have their new soft needles out. The daffodils are finished, but the irises are puffing up and ready to show off.

I have seedlings on the windowsill, but it's still way too cold to put them out. The law around here is to wait until Memorial Day to put out house plants or young plants. You might think that it will never get too cold again, but oh, boy, it can still go down to 35 at night. We walk the dogs down into the woods as much as possible and in the morning, you can hear every kind of bird, announcing his territory. We make sure we never let the dogs go too far into the woods in this season, as fawns may have just been born.

The other day, a Great Horned owl kept flying from tree to tree to make sure we did not get too close to his owlets. A good-sized garter snake startled me on a very warm day, so we know that species is abroad already. I saw a unique woodpecker today. He looked like the ivory-billed one rediscovered in Arkansas. You know, exactly like Woody Woodpecker with the classic head and very big.

Warm weather also brings back memories of games we played as kids. We never had a television until I was eight years old in our winter house and in Cragsmoor, our summer home, we never had one until I was 30. So we had books, radios, records and our imaginations for entertainment. There were always people visiting in the summer, picnics and dinners, so we never missed it.

We also played a lot of games made up by my sister and her friend.

They were older and had willing pawns to boss around.

One game was called Body. It starts with two kids who were the parents and then the rest were the kids. The mother would say, "Now there is a dangerous body hiding in the woods, but we still have to go to the store for our daily bread." Now, one kid was the body and would be hiding somewhere along the driveway. We had to walk to the end, touch a tree and run back to the porch. At some point the body would jump out and grab a kid, take him back to the woods and it would start again. The last kid caught was the next body. It was lots of fun and so scary when we played it after dark.

Another game was called Gascoigne. In this game kids would stand in a circle. The one in the middle had to keep his eyes closed, would be turned around and then have to identify whomever she or he touched, by feeling their face.

We also played Sardines, where one kid would hide, and the others would try to find him; when he did, you would squeeze into the space and the next kid would try to find them and so on.

We played Charades and cards, too.

Once a year, the older kids would make up a funhouse in someone's attic. Grapes were eyeballs and spaghetti was brains.

What is strange and sad to me though is I have no photos of those days. I know we had a camera, but no photos remain.

Our mother also took us to Yankee Stadium once a summer and we got to see the original "West Side Story" and "Destry Rides Again" on Broadway.

We never missed not having TV in the summer and learned to love books. Even today, my sister and I are reading the classics. I feel sorry that most of the children won't bother with Thomas Hardy and A. J. Cronin. But then, why should they? Most people don't live in a place that is so close to the settings of Hardy. Since Cragsmoor is so like Egdon Heath, I would hope all Cragsmoor kids would read, at least, "Return of the Native" and "Far From the Madding Crowd." You have to be prepared to really get into these stories as they are big books, but it is worth it once you're committed.

In the day, we went on hikes or to the swimming pool on **Henry Rd**. I never heard anyone say he or she was bored or had nothing to do. Of course, we were fortunate in having a lot of very close friends and cousins around. The pool was where I met kids from Brooklyn for the first time and what fun they were.

What a childhood! No one in our group was ever very sick or injured. No one was abused, as far as I know, but I think we would have been able to tell. Because of that I never remember anyone being cruel to an animal or another child.

We had no pressure to perform; the dancing class was kind of free-spirited, the art class was fun; there was nothing over-organized. The baseball games were made up by the kids, not the parents – we were just allowed to grow and become who we were.

I guess our parents knew we would observe and be like them, rejecting what we didn't like, and copying what we did.

You know the saying "It takes a village" to raise a child. Cragsmoor was a good example of that. When we left home in the morning, we would meet up with older people at the post office, the library, and the theater or *The Inn*. Almost all of them were nice and the odd balls were harmless. I realize the world has changed, but I still think Cragsmoor has retained some of that same flavor.

One final observation that is going to sound like a grouchy old woman. When I was a child we had to behave. We sat up straight at a restaurant and we had good manners. We giggled in church, but not enough to be annoying. We never threw food or anything at each other; we didn't interrupt or sass the adults. We had lots of loud, wild times together, but with adults we were good. And none of it caused any harm. Actually, it made life a lot easier as adults.

But enough about me.

This morning, May 15th, I was pretty ticked off that both **Center** and **Canal Streets** were closed at 10 AM, when I was trying to get to church. But as fate would have it, I had to take the **Berme Road**. Not too far from **Rte. 52**, I saw a horse in a paddock. He looked OK at first and then I saw his ribs showing. A horse should never have ribs showing. I am going to report this to the SPCA and the owners had best get a vet to check him for worms or they will have some explaining to do.

I plan to report all my sightings of animal neglect. There is also a case of two dogs in Cragsmoor without adequate shelter. Oh, they have doghouses, but according to NY State Law, they do not meet the requirements. I'm about to call Sheriff King as soon as I send this article in. If you can't care for your pets, then give them to a friend or a local shelter.

Forward, into the Past

Summary Homes and the O&W

by Marion M. Dumond
Former Town of Wawarsing Historian
& Ellenville Public Library Director (Retired)

Early commercial transportation in Ulster and Sullivan Counties was limited to foot paths, then dirt roads suitable for animal-drawn wagons – which made commercial transport of products possible – and then turnpikes commissioned by businessmen. Water travel in Sullivan County began with rafts on the Delaware River to transport logs as early as 1764, followed by the moving of bluestone for sidewalks and curbs in New York.

Ulster County had access to the Hudson River, but that was 30 miles away from Ellenville. The construction of the **Delaware & Hudson Canal** opened a new transportation route from Pennsylvania to the Hudson. Coal mined in Pennsylvania was transported by canal to the barges on the Hudson River. So were many other natural and manufactured products in the communities that developed and flourished along the canal. The major drawback to water transportation, be it rivers or canal, is the restriction winter temperatures place on its use when the water freezes.

The development of railroads offered another option to Sullivan County in 1847 when the New York & Erie Railway entered Sullivan County at Tusten Depot. Passenger trains of the *New York & Oswego Midland Railroad* were using the new tunnel opened in 1871 under the Shawangunk Mountains at Wurtsboro, a development that would be of tremendous benefit to Ellenville and the Town of Wawarsing.

The *New York & Oswego Midland Railroad* extended a branch into the Town of Wawarsing in 1871, establishing stations in Ellenville and Homowack (Spring Glen). For almost thirty years, the railroad and the **D&H Canal** ran side by side for miles between Ellenville and Wurtsboro.

In April 1878, the Liberty Register had carried an advertisement directed to proprietors of summer boarding houses and hotels, announcing a proposal to issue a pamphlet entitled *Summer Homes on the Midland*, which would be distributed in New York, Brooklyn, and vicinity. "The object of this publication is to offer the thousands who annually look for Summer homes in the country, detailed information concerning the accommodations and facilities offered along the line of the Middle Division and Branches of the Midland Railroad." After describing the nature of the information needed, the advertisement continued "Station Agents will (until April 25th, but not later) receive the names of all wishing to register themselves as having accommodation to offer... on payment of $2.00. A limited amount of space will be reserved for Hotels, or

Summer Boarding Houses, whose Proprietors wish to pay for inserting displayed advertisements."

The emergence of railroad service hastened the decline of the **D&H Canal**, since the canal could not compete with the year-round service offered by the railroad, or its speed. The last boat to run the full length of the canal completed its run in 1898, although some local runs occurred after that year.

Railroad service had brought a new business to the Town of Wawarsing. The clean air, pure water, and impressive natural beauty of the **Shawangunk Mountains** and the **Rondout Valley** drew residents of New York City, and the summer resort economy blossomed. Farmers opened their large farmhouses to summer boarders, small and large boarding houses were built to accommodate the increasing number of summer visitors, and the economy of the Town of Wawarsing benefited.

However, all was not well with the *New York & Oswego Midland Railroad,* so the *New York, Ontario & Western Railway* took over the operation of the bankrupt Midland. The *O&W* management recognized the growth potential of the summer resorts, thanks in large part to *Summer Homes on the Midland,* and continued its publication as *Summer Homes Among the Mountains of the New York, Ontario & Western Railway.*

Summer Homes is an interesting publication and a fine historical resource. The *Ellenville Public Library & Museum* possesses several different issues that provided the information and graphics for this article. *(The picture above is from the 1905 cover; the picture at left heads the Ellenville Station section).* It is organized by station name, subdivided by post office address, and each community is described with a narrative, usually quite brief.

Until the early years of the twentieth century, railroad service was available only into Ellenville, which was the end of the branch line running from Wurtsboro. In ↗

ELLENVILLE

1902, the *O&W* was extended to Kingston, and a whole new territory opened for the summer visitor. Four trains ran daily each way between New York and Kingston, through the Town of Wawarsing.

The 1891 *Summer Homes* (the earliest in the library collection) describes Ellenville as "a charming village of about 3500 inhabitants, situated in the heart of the Shawangunk region, 340 feet above the sea. It has many delightful drives, and from nearby points are to be gained the most magnificent views of natural scenery to be found in the East." A tiny insert informs the reader that Ellenville is 101 miles from New York, with a fare of $2.37; excursion rate is $4.12.

"Among the bits of natural scenery of the immediate vicinity are Sam's Point, a rocky ledge crowning the highest of the Shawangunk summits; the Ice Caves – natural openings in the mountains – where ice and snow are found the year round, and Minnewaska, Honk, Hanging Rock, and other beautiful cascades and water-falls." The paragraph refers to trout streams and fishing lakes being within easy driving distance, after naming Mohonk, Minnewaska *(painting above, showing lake and* Cliff House*)*, Meenahga, and other "celebrated resorts."

As for Ellenville, "the village of Ellenville has well-paved and shaded streets, and is lighted with gas. Many of the hotels and boarding houses of the region are connected by telephone with one another and with the Hudson River system. There are many fine residences, six churches, excellent schools, and the place is noted for the intelligence, refinement and sobriety of its people and the healthfulness of its climate."

Each boarding house or hotel entry usually includes the name of the proprietor as well as the name of the accommodation, distance from the railway station, capacity and number of rooms, and often the rate. Then there will be a list of the special services or attractions, such as "table supplied with products of my own farm; horses and carriages for use of guests at moderate rates; good stable for guests desiring to bring their own horses." That partial description is taken from *N. Lefever's Maplewood Boarding House and Cottage*, only 1/4 mile from the station, which would accommodate 50 in 26 rooms. Adults would be charged $8 to $12 (presumably per week), transients $2.00 (per night). Names and addresses of individuals, often in New York, are listed for references.

A sample: "William H. Weser - P.O. Box 338. Farm house; accommodate 50; adults $5 and upwards, children $4, transient $1.25; special arrangement for season guests; finely situated on the western range of the world renowned Catskill Mountains, 1800 feet above the sea level; one hour's drive from Ellenville station over a beautiful mountain road; fine scenery; fine view of Lakes Mohonk and Minnewaska, Roundtop, and High Peak; Hanging Rock Falls three miles distant. Refer to R. Cable, 457 West 34th Street, New York; R. I. Bush, 255 West 52nd Street, New York; F. Cassing, 123 East 50th Street, New York; and Dr. Lawrence, Bedford Avenue and North 6th Street, Brooklyn." It sounds like a fine place to stay, doesn't it?

Mount Meenahga is listed with 22 other resorts accessible from the **Ellenville Station** and using the **Ellenville Post Office**, but also has its own very lengthy description and a full-page picture *(etching below)*, which may indicate its prominence in 1891, or U. E. Terwilliger's recognition of the power of advertising. At that time, the hotel could house 100, including the six cottages designed for family occupancy. Each cottage had a sitting room with an open fireplace, plus three to five "sleeping rooms, furnished plain but complete with necessary furniture." The property included 250 acres of wild mountain land. The June 1-October 15 season was fairly standard. (Meenahga was the subject of *Forward, into the Past* in Issue #9, August 2003, of *Wawarsing.Net*).

Other entries under the Ellenville Station heading include two using the **Ulster Heights Post Office** and one each at Mombaccus, Montela, and Mettacahouts post offices.

Greenfield, Ulster County, has its own description, almost as lengthy as Ellenville's. It is identified as having "an elevation of 1100 feet,...situated four miles from Mountain Dale station on the main line, and five miles from Ellenville, the terminus of the branch to that place." The drive from Ellenville to Greenfield is described as being "one of the most attractive drives in the country." along the **Beerkill** stream. In 1891, it had "post-office, stores, church, and telephone communication with Western Union Telegraph Co. at Ellenville." Its listing ↗

MT. MEENAHGA HOTEL.

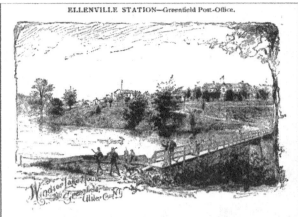

ELLENVILLE STATION—Greenfield Post-Office.

Past. Nichols—Windsor Lake House. 5 miles ; accommodate 75 ; terms $7 to $10, transient $2 ; hotel stage meets guests on arrival of trains—transportation 50 cents, trunks 25

includes the *Windsor Lake House (etching above)* and six others.

Napanoch has only a one-sentence summary: "This little village is about two miles distant from Ellenville, is very beautiful, and the entire region abounds in 'Summer Homes'," but not too many are listed. Is it possible that the length of the community description is tied to the number of advertisers?

The 1901 *Summer Homes* entries for the Town of Wawarsing total more than 60 under 11 post office headings, but still under the Ellenville Station main heading, since the extension to Kingston did not occur until 1902.

By the time of the 1907 edition, a full page of "purple" prose extols the merits of Ellenville's water, "Ellenville is destined to become famous through the location of the bottling works and plant of *The Huntoon Spring Water Company*. The water of this spring is probably the purest ever analized. The history of the spring is almost legendary..." At this point, legends are presented as accepted fact and probably enticed many visitors to Ellenville, where "The largest, most extensive and modern bottling works in the world are in operation..."

An extensive list of hotels, inns, and boarding houses begins with *Mount Meenahga* which now (1907) can accommodate 150 to 175 guests, and includes *Ulster Villa Inn, Mount Mongola House, the Wyndmere, Breeze Lawn* at Leurenkill, the *Marshall House* on Maple Avenue, James A. Myers' *Terrace Hill House*, John D. Wager's *Hanging Rock Falls Farm House*, George McDowell's *Western View*, and a host of others in the 42 entries under the **Ellenville Post Office**.

· ELLENVILLE ·

Cragsmoor has its own post office listing and *The Cragsmoor Inn* on the *Cliff Farm* has an impressively long narrative, concluding with "Reasons Why You Should Go To Cragsmoor Inn: It has the same altitude as Lake Placid in the Adirondacks, and is only 100 miles from New York. It stands on an elevation commanding unsurpassed views of three extensive valleys... and is swept by cool breezes from every point of the compass. It chambers are thoroughly renovated, repainted and recalcimined yearly. It provides certified milk, and serves no canned vegetables. It is especially suited to week-end guests, who can reach their offices in New York by 10:30 A.M. Monday."

Landbohove (John Kindberg & Son), *Lakwelend and Cottages*, and Robert J. Geilhard's two furnished cottages complete the Cragsmoor entries.

Ulster Heights has its own expanded entry, with mention of Cape Pond, "a narrow sheet of water some two miles long, affords most excellent boating, fishing and bathing. John W. Hoff's *Mountain View Farm House*, O. Johnson's *Lake Side Crest House*, E. M. Dill's *Pleasant Hill Farm House*, G. D. Rode's *Terrace Lawn House*, E. H. Hennige's *Mountain Top Orchard Farm House*, *Michael Klass' Farm House*, and the *Rampe Villa* are the "summer homes."

Napanoch Station, Wawarsing Station, and **Kerhonkson Station** all have entries that show how the summer visitor business had expanded in only 16 years. Perhaps the pamphlets also show how Town of Wawarsing proprietors had accepted the value of advertising.

Railroad management also produced other promotional booklets that had a purchase price of 25 cents, composed of little or no text, but black and white photographs of some of the resorts advertised in *Summer Homes (photo above, from Ellenville area, including Meenahga)*. The *Museum* has two different editions in its collection.

The first, purported to be the 1896 edition, has the title *Supplement to Illustrated Homes on the New York, Ontario & Western Railway: A Companion to Summer Homes*. It includes 11 pages of black and white plates.

The second copy has no date at all, but includes more photographs. The title on this one is minimally shorter, beginning *Illustrated Homes on the New York, Ontario & Western...*

In her history of the Town of Wawarsing, *Wawarsing: Where the Streams Wind*, historian Katharine T. Terwilliger published lists of boarding houses from various years with some of her own location information in "Appendix A." Her quote from one of the pamphlets gives the purpose of *Summer Homes* "to bring those residents of our cities, who have not only the desire but the intention of finding a desirable summer home, into ⏴

Wawarsing.Net Magazine · 2005 August   **Issue 33 · Page 12**

92

communication with those having such to offer."

The collections of the *Ellenville Public Library & Museum* include much more about the individual boarding houses and hotels, including pictures. Many additional scenes can be found in the extensive postcard collection, which is indexed.

In *To The Mountains By Rail*, Manville B. Wakefield commented that "In 1898, *Summer Homes* appeared in hard cover and was used extensively in the depots at the various resort points as a ready reference book that generally hung on a nail near the ticket window. They were also available for reference in all the leading New York hotels." His summary of *Summer Homes* was that "During its long tenure of publication, *Summer Homes* could indeed be read as a barometer of passenger travel and the economic stability of the railroad company."

We in this area probably read *Summer Homes* as a measure of the growth of the resort industry in the Town of Wawarsing at the turn of the century and a very valuable local history tool identifying family names and buildings that, one hundred years later, still stand.

93

Library and Post Office

SO MANY BOOKS, SO LITTLE TIME

A library is always a much needed facility, not only for gaining knowledge but for the relaxation granted by the reading of a good book. It is a place for socializing, as well.

The very first Cragsmoor Free Library was housed within the Pines Casino in 1912. The young folks enjoyed it almost as much as the older ones. Then until about 1923 the library was set-up in various establishments. Many thanks to Mr. Dellanbough for designing a new library and also for donating the land on which it was to be built. And, so it was, in 1923, that the trustees did, in fact, arrange for construction to begin on the new library.

The building has a very quaint interior with hand-hewn chestnut beams (similar to the ones that will be seen in the home built by Carroll Butler Brown), a magnificent fireplace and a typical "Dellenbaugh" stairway which is very narrow and leads to a narrow U-shaped balcony.

Many paintings of local artists adorn the walls. The atmosphere within is so pleasant, even upon first entering, when greeted warmly by our new Library Director, Hattie Grifo. Eileen Kolaitis, former Director was a monumental help in guiding us during our research -- and always with a smiling face.

Cragsmoor Free Library remains a focal point within the community and offers many varied activities, for young and old alike. It also publishes the Friendship Calendar on a monthly bases. Please take note of all the scheduled events under the heading of Community Bulletin Board on page

All community events are very well attended.

THE LIBRARY - Late fall 2004

A GLIMPSE OF A TYPICAL DELLENBAUGH STAIRWAY (on the left) LEADING TO THE U-SHAPED BAL-CONY. NOTE THE HAND-HEWN BEAMS AND THE PAINTINGS WHICH ADORN THE WALLS.

THE MAGNIFICENT FIREPLACE - 2004

95

FOOTNOTES

The Newsletter of the Cragsmoor Free Library

Fall 2002

Established 1913

Winter Hours

Monday	9:30 ~ 5:00
Thursday	9:30 ~ 5:00
Saturday	9:30 ~ 2:30

Summer Hours

Tuesday	9:30 ~ 12:30
Wednesday	9:30 ~ 4:30
Thursday	4:30 ~ 7:30
Friday	9:30 ~ 12:30
Saturday	9:30 ~ 1:30

Published by the
Cragsmoor Free Library
PO Box 410
Cragsmoor, NY 12420

Phone (845) 647-4611
Fax (845) 647-4611
E-mail ekolaiti@rcls.org
Web site:
ansernet.rcls.org\crg\

Bear Hill Nature Preserve to be Taxed

It's budget time, and this year presents a new hurdle for Cragsmoor's library.

As most of you know, the library owns the Bear Hill Nature Preserve; a 50 acre parcel purchased by the Cragsmoor community with the aid of David Croyder and a 67 acre parcel given to us by Clarissa Dryden.

These properties are held as the Bear Hill Nature Preserve by the library, because it was the only tax-exempt, 501(c)(3) organization on the mountain at that time. The deeds of both properties stipulate they are to be forever wild and can never be sold for development.

This year, the Town of Wawarsing tax assessor has declared that because the preserve is not contiguous to the library, and because the library's charter does not specifically state that property can be held for the educational purposes related to our mission, the library must pay property tax.

The taxes this year amount to nearly $5,000, a sum almost equal to the library's yearly budget for books, periodicals, and Cassettes; more than we can absorb in a budget with income of $50,000.

On September 28, library board members hosted a tour of the library and Bear Hill for the supervisor and board of the Town of Wawarsing, and appeared at a town workshop on October 3 to explain our dilemma and ask for assistance.

Coming Attractions

THE CRAGSMOOR
HISTORIC HOUSE TOUR

October 19, 2002

All tours begin at 10 am
at the Post Office

This year's tour includes six historic houses and properties, glorious fall foliage and brunch at Orchard Cottage

* Bear Cliff House
* Crow's Nest
* Gardiner Cottage Grounds
* Simonelli Residence
* Sonsy
* Takusan

Tour & Brunch $20
Brunch Only $8

Bear Cliff House

Bear Hill is open to the public, but maintained by Cragsmoor residents who volunteer their time to keep the preserve clean.

Bear Hill, *continued from page 1*

Bear Hill belongs to the community. Resolution of this complex issue will come not only from our board, but from you.

The library accepted the property on the basis that it was tax-free, due to our tax exempt status, and finds the payment of more than $5,000 a year in taxes an unacceptable burden.

There are several alternatives to consider. The deed restrictions allow the property to be conveyed to another Cragsmoor philanthropic organization, or to a government entity such as the Town of Wawarsing or the Palisades Interstate Park Commission.

It is also possible to make a second appeal to change the tax classification, although our first effort with the town board of assessments resulted in a decision upholding taxation.

A committee of community members was formed at the last library meeting to explore the possible alternatives and help to make the best possible choice for the Cragsmoor community. If you'd like to be involved in this working group, you are invited to join the committee as it studies the issues. Call Eileen at 647-4611 to offer your services. We'll keep you posted on future developments.

Worth Noting

Thanks to all who consistently donate books!!

Of special Interest:
Byron Hollinshead was kind enough to have his neighbor, Oscar Hijuelos, autograph his newest novel, A Simple Habana Melody: (From When the World was Good).

Thanks to Mary and Michael Davidson for the wonderful books on Egypt, many of which were made part of the library's permanent collection.

Author Amine Wefali came to Cragsmoor this summer to read passages from her novel, Westchester Burning.

Help Wanted
We need a cleaning person! Call Berle at 647-7182 to make a proposal on cleaning the library.

Coming Up

Cat Talk! An informative presentation by Susan Clarke and Carolyn Peters-Baker, Cragsmoor residents who operate their own animal welfare program. Since beginning in April, they've had 85 cats neutered and rabies vaccinated. Saturday, November 2 at 7 pm.

Board Vacancy

The library has a vacant seat on its 7 member board. If you would be interested in a two year term, call Paula Medley at 754-0743.

Eileen Kolaitis
Library Director

From the Director

I was so happy to see all the community members who attended the recent meetings at the library. As you know, all Library Board meeting are open to the public. It usually falls on the first Sunday of every month.

I would like to take this opportunity to encourage all Cragsmoor residents to come to the library and register for a library card. As you may have heard, our population declined on the 2000 census. This has caused a decrease in funding from Ulster County. Being a registered member of the library is a way you can help simply by being counted.

The library board has begun a long range planning process. If you're interested in contributing your thoughts and suggestions, call Eileen to sign on.

The library's fundraising events include the Bird Cage Party, where new Cragsmoor residents get acquainted, and long-time residents visit with old friends.

This summer, the library's annual festival raised $1800. The rummage and book sale, managed by Alex Jakubowski, a former Cragsmoor resident, accounted for $ 900 of that total.

Other fundraising events include the Mother's Day plant sale, the Valentine and Holiday parties, the Historic House Walking Tour, our annual appeal and sale of library-related merchandise and publications.

The Turner Tapestry of Takusan

The Turner Tapestries

Last year the library received a Conservation Treatment Grant from the NYS Council on the Arts to restore one of the two tapestries created by Helen and Lettie Turner. That tapestry (shown at left) is of Takusan, Turner's house. Peter Harrison crafted an appropriate frame for it.

This year, we have been awarded a grant of $6688 to conserve and restore the second Turner Tapestry, which depicts the old Cragsmoor Post Office and The Chapel of the Sacred Heart. If you haven't had a chance to see the results of last year's grant be sure to see this beautifully restored treasure when you next visit the library.

Library Board Welcomes New Member

Berle Driscoll, a resident of Cragsmoor for 13 years, joined the board in September and holds the office of treasurer.

She brings experience from a successful career in nonprofit organization and development. As the library's treasurer, she is responsible for preparing the budget and participating in long range planning and development of strategies for a funding program to secure the fiscal well-being of the library.

Our Library serves as a gathering place for the community. While kids work on their projects, other patrons are browsing for books and videos, using the archives for research and making use of the library's computers.

Over 66% of the community uses the library on a regular and frequent basis. The support of the community is essential. If you're not a regular, visit us and see what we have to offer.

When the supervisor and board of the Town of Wawarsing toured our library, they were impressed with our ability to provide such a wide variety of services and our efforts to obtain broad-based support through community fundraising and obtaining grants. They also observed that we are in need of more space, and offered the town's assistance in helping us expand our physical capacity as our programs and patronage increase.

A few statistics:

- Circulation has increased every year since we automated services at the
- end of 1999, and continues to rise – more than 6100 items circulated in 2001! In the last two months, over 1500 items were checked out. We add approximately 500 books to the collection each year. Many are outright gifts, but purchases cost an average of $38 per volume.
- While we have over 350 registered patrons, and another 250 users, financial support from Ulster County is calculated on the basis of the US Census. Based on the 2002 report, the library's funding from the county will be reduced from $8192 in 2002 to $6649 in 2003.
- Each year the library pays the Ramapo Catskill Library System (RCLS) $2650 for the Network ANSER program, allowing us to be part of the inter-library loan system, which accounts for 1 in 5 of the materials checked out of our library.
- Volunteers spent over a year bar-coding the library's books and tapes so that we would be fully computerized and have access to inter-library loans.

Cragsmoor Free Library
PO Box 410
Cragsmoor, NY 12240

NOTICE

Our regular December 1 library board meeting is scheduled for 1:00 pm.

We hope the time change for this meeting will make it possible for you to attend

Opening the meeting will be a review of the library's internet policy.

Please join us.

Cragsmoor Historic House Walking Tour

to benefit the Cragsmoor Free Library

Walk 1 - 2 miles (moderately difficult) through Cragsmoor's Historic District enjoying the fall foliage while touring six historic houses, "Hillcrest" (Gale), Hollinshead residence, "Orchard Cottage" (Maurer/McKenney), "Winahdin"/ "Blithwood" (Shulman) and the Wiebe residence, ending with a sumptuous brunch.

"Orchard Cottage"

"Winahdin"

Date: Saturday, October 11, 2003 (No Rain Date)

Starting Place: Cragsmoor Post Office

Times: 2 groups leave at 10:00 am, 1 group leaves at 10:30 am

All tours begin promptly. There are no ongoing tours throughout the day. Pre-registration is greatly appreciated.

Entry Fee: $20.00
Brunch only: $8.00

Parking: Cragsmoor Free Library and vicinity of Post Office.

PRIZES AWARDED!

Participating Organization:
Cragsmoor Volunteer
Fire Company

For more information call
The library at 647-4611
or Event Director:
Paula Medley at 754-0743

Cragsmoor Historic House Walking Tour & High Tea

Attention House Peepers & Leaf Peepers! On **Saturday, October 9th**, the *Cragsmoor Free Library* presents the annual *Cragsmoor Historic House Tour*. The tour begins at **1:00 PM** at the **Cragsmoor Post Office**, followed by *High Tea* at **Orchard Cottage**.

The summer home of artists since the turn of the century, Cragsmoor is still the home of artists, writers, actors, and other creative folks. A one-mile walk through the community takes visitors to four historic Cragsmoor homes. Visitors can also tour the **Cragsmoor Free Library** building, a rustic, early 20th century building designed by Frederick Dellenbaugh, one of the artist colony's founders, and still the cultural center of the Cragsmoor community. The *Library* also serves as a gallery for the work of Cragsmoor artists, past and present.

One of the highlights of the day this year will be the drawing for the *Library*'s big money raffle, the *"Rake It In" Raffle*. Winners receive a 1st prize of $10,000, with a 2nd prize of $750, 3rd prize of $500, 4th prize of $250 and 5 prizes of $100 each. Only 200 tickets will be sold, so the odds are in your favor. Send your $100 check to **Cragsmoor Free Library, PO Box 410, Cragsmoor, NY 12420**, or buy your ticket any Saturday at the *Library* from 9:30 AM to 2:30 PM.

The cost of the tour and the *High Tea* is $25 per person in advance and $30 on the day of the tour. Cragsmoor is located on **Rte. 52**, between Ellenville and Pine Bush, one mile north on **Cragsmoor Road**.

Call Paula Medley at 754-0743 or Eileen Kolaitis at the *Cragsmoor Library*, 647-4611 for reservations.

Wawarsing.Net Magazine   October 2004
Issue 23   Page 22

"The Barnacle"   House tour 2004

"The Boulders" House tour 2004

The Library On The Mountain
Established 1913

Cragsmoor Free Library	Cragsmoor Free Library
P. O. Box 410	P. O. Box 410
355 Cragsmoor Road	355 Cragsmoor Road
Cragsmoor, NY 12420	Cragsmoor, NY 12420
845-647-4611	845-647-4611
Hattie Grifo, Director	Hattie Grifo, Director
www.rcls.org/crg/	www.rcls.org/crg/
hgrifo@rcls.org	hgrifo@rcls.org

SUMMER HOURS   WINTER HOURS

SUMMER HOURS	WINTER HOURS
Tuesday: 9:30 – 12:30	Monday: 9:30 – 5:00
Wed & Sat: 9:30 – 4:30	Thursday: 9:30 - 5:00
Thursday: 4:30 - 7:30	Friday: 3:30 – 5:30
Friday: 9:30 – 12:30	Saturday: 9:30 – 4:30

Two-sided Library
bookmark

101

Cragsmoor Free Library

355 Cragsmoor Road, PO Box 410
Cragsmoor, NY 12420

The Library On The Mountain
Established 1913

Telephone/Fax (845) 647-4611

December 11, 2004

After 10 years as our Library Director, Eileen Kolaitis is leaving us to pursue a full time teaching career. She is caring and professionai and has been a wonderful asset to our Library and the community. We will miss her.

*The **farewell party** for Eileen*
is Saturday, December 18th
from 12:30 - 4:30pm
Join us for lunch
and say "good bye" to Eileen
or just send a card or note.
Shhh! It's a surprise!

also   The Library Board is pleased to announce that Hattie Grifo will succeed Eileen as the new Library Director.

Hattie has been volunteering her time at the Library for over 20 years and is familiar with our library's daily procedures, practices and computer systems. She is a respected member of the Cragsmoor community and her knowledge of our community and its' history, along with her working knowledge of the library makes her an ideal choice as our new Library Director.
Welcome Hattie.

A Note from Hattie

The transition has been made and my thanks go out to Eileen, the Board, and our patrons for making it so easy. Thank you for your confidence in me as the Library Director. I am thrilled, and feel like I 'm right where I belong.

Eileen and I tried to take the broader community's reading tastes into account when buying books and magazines. Barbara Harris, the new chairperson of the Book Committee, and I, would like to invite any one who feels their favorite authors or magazines have been ignored, to let us know and we'll work to include them. I am also interested in knowing about any craft magazines that you may want.

FROM: The Friendship Calendar
←   February 2005
       Vol. 13 No.7

Hattie Grifo
March 2006

102

The Ellenville Public Library and Terwilliger House Museum were most attentive to our desire to learn all that we could about Cragsmoor and our artist "friends" of old.

Many, many hours were spent in both the library and museum, which has quite a large collection of local history. The library has on display a wonderful collection of E. L. Henry's paintings, most of which are copies. It is very worthwhile and fascinating to view so many of his works in one place.

Carroll Butler Brown is also a featured artist at the library and his well-known painting, View of Ellenville From Cragsmoor, holds a place of honor near the entry way to the library.

Wawarsing.Net Magazine • 2004 April   Ellenville Public Library   Issue 17 • Page 13

Terwilliger House Museum

Wawarsing.Net Magazine • 2004 April   Issue 17 • Page 14

103

An October Day aka Cragsmoor Post Office –
(Edward Lamson Henry – 1903)

UNITED STATES POSTAL SERVICE®

Home

Introduction
National Archives
Personnel Records
Center

Geographic Names

Postmaster Finder
Postmasters by City

**CRAGSMOOR POST OFFICE
ULSTER COUNTY, NEW YORK**

Keyword/Search

keyword | search

Name	Title	Date Appointed
George Bleakley	Postmaster	08/20/1892
John C. Ecker	Postmaster	10/10/1896
John H. Beckmann	Postmaster	01/21/1899
Warner R. Garritt	Postmaster	01/21/1909
W. Harold Garritt	Acting Postmaster	10/23/1938
Mrs. Naomi C. S. Garritt	Postmaster	05/22/1939
Robert F. Van Kleeck	Acting Postmaster	07/18/1958
Mrs. Jean N. Van Kleeck	Acting Postmaster	09/16/1959
Mrs. Jean N. Van Kleeck	Postmaster	08/30/1965
Gladys A. Hendrickson	Postmaster	01/10/1981
John A. Caparaso	Officer-In-Charge	12/30/1982
Grace C. Stewart	Officer-In-Charge	02/04/1983
Mary L. Saunders	Officer-In-Charge	03/23/1983
Salvatore A. Filippone	Officer-In-Charge	08/05/1983
Irene I. Savage	Postmaster	01/21/1984
Darryl Castellana	Officer-In-Charge	05/08/1992
Jeanne Horowitz	Officer-In-Charge	11/02/1992
Rudolph A. Travali	Postmaster	04/03/1993
John Hendrix	Officer-In-Charge	08/03/2005
Karen Zappala	Officer-In-Charge	11/05/2005

CRAGSMOOR POST OFFICE - 2005

CRAGSMOOR POSTMASTER-Rudy Travali
2005

Art and Artists

BRUSH AND PALETTE

In the early 1880's, Cragsmoor was already becoming quite an elite artist community.

Edward Lamson Henry was the first artist to build a summer home in Cragsmoor after having boarded at The Bleakley Farm in 1879. During 1880 and 1881, he boarded in Ellenville and moved into his Cragsmoor home in 1882 with his wife Frances Wells Henry. Their home was named by Mrs. Henry and called "NA-PEE-NIA". The Henry's also built two other cottages in Cragsmoor, one being named "Shinglenook" and the other "I-E-NIA". One of Henry's homes still remains and is located on Henry Road and is owned by The Blumbergs.

E. L. Henry was born in Charleston, South Carolina on January 12, 1841 and died on May 11, 1919 in Ellenville, New York. Mr. Henry was a very short and extremely frail person, standing at only five feet, two inches and weighing a maximum of one hundred fifteen pounds. He was also known to be quick tempered, swore frequently and was a big tease to the Mrs. However, they seemed to adore each other. He enjoyed music, loved animals, in particular, horses, which appear in many of his paintings.

Much information regarding E.L. Henry, who was by far, the most well-known and financially successful artist of Cragsmoor, has had much written about him. He was a world traveller but enjoyed the charm and serenity of Cragsmoor.

A sizable collection of Henry's paintings are currently on exhibit in the Ellenville Public Library, a couple in the Cragsmoor Free Library and a more complete gathering is contained at the New York State Museum in Albany, including materials such as sketchbooks, letters, photographs, books and other memorabilia.

He was a member of the National Academy in New York City, which is a most honorary bestowment. (A portion of the aforementioned facts were taken from The Life and Works of Edward Lamson Henry, published by The University of New York in Albany - 1945.)

It is without a doubt that his paintings are so precise, detailed and sophisticated that they appear to be photographs. Most of his works seem so alive that one can almost feel a sense of being part of the scene or activity. He is absolutely our favorite Cragmsoorian artist!

Many artists followed E. L. Henry to Cragsmoor, a partial listing follows, chronologically.

1. Eliza Pratt Greatorex 1820-1897 A.N.A.

2. William H. Beard 1824-1900 N.A.

3. J. G. Brown 1831-1913 N.A.

4. Edward Gay 1837-1928 N.A.

5. Edward Lamson Henry 1841-1919 N.A.

6. Frances Wells Henry 1845-1928

7. Frederick S. Dellenbaugh 1853-1935

8. George Inness, Jr. 1854-1926 N.A.

9. Austa Densmore Sturdevant 1855-1936

10. Colin Campbell Cooper 1856-1957 N.A.

11. Helen M. Turner 1858-1958 N.A.

12. Emma Lampert Cooper 1860-1920

13. LeGrand Botsford 1860-1937

14. Charles C. Curran 1861-1942 N.A.

15. Arthur I. Keller 1866-1924

16. Carroll Butler Brown 1868-1923

17. Eugene Higgins 1874–1958 N.A.

18. Alfred Rowley 1878–1962

19. Patricia Gay 1882–1964

20. Ruth Jeffries 1884–1982

21. Paul Bronson 1885–1955

22. Alice Browning 1887–1916

23. Helen Tichenor Mills 1889–1974

24. Charles Peters 1891–1974

25. Edith Winston 1896–1971

26. Arthur Keller 1897–1974

27. Edwin L. Oman 1905–

And others: Frederick Baker

                William Otis

                Ella B. Sherman

                Rachel Taylor

Today there are many artists of all types living in Cragsmoor, from painters, potters, writers, poets, musicians, actors and many more.

Fine Art and Antiques

Welcome to The Barnacle! Located in historic Cragsmoor, NY, we offer Fine Art, Scottish, Vintage and Antique Jewelry, Rare Art Books, Sculpture and Antiques! Proprietor Kaycee Benton is a knowledgeable art historian as well as a dealer in antiques. Cragsmoor was the site of an early American art colony. The Barnacle itself has been declared a historic landmark! We are currently compiling catalogue raisonnes for two of the early artists of Cragsmoor, Charles Courtney Curran and Helen M. Turner.

Click here to help us with the Curran and Turner catalogue raisonnes

View the Helen Turner Masterpiece "The Dreamer"

Cragsmoor was founded in the early 1870's by artists who wanted to escape from the big city in the summer. This lovely village has been called home by artists such as William H. Beard, LeGrand Botsford, Carroll Butler Brown, Winfield Scott Clime, Emma Lampert Cooper, Colin Campbell Cooper, Frederick S. Dellenbaugh, Edward Gay, Eliza Greatorex, Edward Lamson Henry, Frances Wells Henry, Eugene Higgins, George Inness, Jr. Arthur I. Keller and Helen M. Turner. To learn more about the history of Cragsmoor and its famous denizens, click here.

We are interested in purchasing quality pieces of jewelry and art. In addition, we offer appraisal, consignment and estate services. For more information, or if you would like to visit The Barnacle in person, please click here for contact information.

We have fine antiques, jewelry, art and more for sale so please browse our pages.

Featured at The Barnacle! Sculpture by the renowned artist Robert Jeronimo

CRAGSMOOR ARTISTS' VISION OF NATURE   Sept. 1977

Price List

Cat. #	Painting	Price
2.	BEAR IN A FOREST 1863, Wm. H. Beard Oil/canvas, 11½ x 18"	$ 2,250.
11.	FLORAL GROUP, Colin Campbell Cooper Oil/board, 16 x 12"	$ 500.
12.	THE GEORGIAN HOUSE, C.C. COOPER Pastel, 22 x 19"	$ 450.
13.	LOTUS POOL, Colin Campbell Cooper Oil/canvas, 29 x 36"	$ 1,500.
18.	EARLY MORNING IN JUNE, C.C. Curran Oil/canvas, 18 x 22"	$ 950.
19.	THE SCENT OF THE ROSE, C.C. Curran Oil/panel, 4½ x 12 1/8"	$ 1,500.
20.	BOULDERS AND CLOUDS, C.C. Curran Oil/masonite, 20 x 30"	$ 750.
28.	VIEW OF NEWPORT, F.S. Dellenbaugh Oil/canvas, 5 x 9"	$ 1,000.
33.	LANDSCAPE, Edward Gay, 1897 Oil/canvas, 20 x 27"	$ 1,500.
34.	LANDSCAPE, Edward Gay Oil/canvas, 28 x 33"	$ 2,500.
35.	LANDSCAPE, Edward Gay, 1908 Oil/canvas, 33 x 44"	$ 3,000.

The Library On The Mountain

CRAGSMOOR ARTISTS' VISION OF NATURE   Sept. 1977

Price List

Cat.#	Painting	Price
36.	GOLDEN AUTUMN, Edward Gay 1912 Oil/canvas, 25 x 30"	$ 1,500.
37.	IN THE SPRINGTIME, Edward Gay Oil/board, 21 x 30"	$ 1,500.
63.	SHEEP HERDER AND FLOCK, G. Inness Jr. Oil/canvas, 20 x 30"	$ 3,500.
64.	SPRING ON THE MOUNTAIN, G. Inness Jr. Oil/panel, 8 3/4 x 7 3/4"	$ 1,500.
73.	MORNING, 1917, Helen M. Turner Oil/canvas, 34 x 44"	$15,000.
76.	GOLDEN AFTERNOON, Helen M. Turner Oil/canvas, 18 x 24"	$ 1,300.

10% of the sale of each painting will go to the benefit of
the Cragsmoor Free Library.

The Library On The Mountain

Edward Lamson Henry (1841-~~1913~~)

(Correct year of death was 1919)

"Unexpected Visitors"

Signed and dated *E. L. Henry, 1909*, l.l.

Oil on canvas

17 1/4" X 25" (23 1/2" X 31 1/4" overall).

Provenance: Mrs. George Arden, New York

Exhibited: New York, National Academy of Design, 84th Annual Exhibition, March-April 1909, no. 5; Yonkers, New York, The Hudson River Museum; Rochester, New York, The Margaret Woodbury Strong Museum, *Domestic Bliss: Family Life in American Paintings, 1840-1910*, May-November 1986, no. 27, p. 77, illustrated in color.

Literature: Elizabeth McCausland, M.A., *The Life and Work of Edward Lamson*

Figure 189 *The Pedler*, 1879: CAT. 139. Collection,
William B. Kirkham   Page 295

Reference: THE LIFE AND WORK
                        OF
                EDWARD LAMSON HENRY N. A.
                    1841-1919

                        by

            Eliaabeth McCausland M.A.

            NEW YORK STATE MUSEUM

            Bulletin Number 339

    Published by The University of the State of New York
    Albany, N.Y.   September 1945

114

Edward Lamson Henry, 1841-1919

The Peddler, 1879

(Oil on canvas, 13 5/8 X 19 1/2 inches, Inscribed at lower right: E L Henry / 79, George Walter Vincent Smith Art Museum, Gift of Louis Cutler Hyde in memory of his wife, Marguerite Kirkham Hyde, 1.76.1)

Perhaps no artist played so consistently and so durably to the American cult of nostalgia in the last quarter of the 19th century as Edward Lamson Henry. Henry devised laboriously researched and detailed images intent upon preserving appearances and experiences that disappeared in reality even as they appeared in fiction in his art. He worked to shape a collective memory for a society anxiously conscious of obsolescence. The Civil War was past, but the present was in crisis, especially as science and technology -- the dominant forces at the Centennial Exhibition held in Philadelphia in 1876 - -remade society. Enough collectors responded to Henry's vision of an American ethos sited in rural experience, an American identity that originated in colonial achievement, and an American present on the cusp of fundamental change to make him a successful artist, perhaps the most successful in the specialized vein of historical genre. When Henry died in 1919, artist Will Low reported in the *New York Evening Post* that "few American artists ... have better served their country in preserving for the future the quaint and provincial aspects of a life which has all but disappeared."[1] In the early modernist age, Henry seemed the last anachronism, but he painted with conviction and sustained a strong following until his death.

Henry was born in Charleston, South Carolina, but, an orphan by seven, he grew up with cousins in New York. He studied painting there and in Philadelphia. While in Europe from 1860 to 1862 he worked with Charles Gleyre and Gustave Courbet in Paris. He served briefly in the Civil War as clerk on a Union transport ship, sketching African Americans and Union camps along the Virginia rivers. When he translated these experiences to paintings, he tapped a vein of interest that led to recognition as full academician at the National Academy of Design in 1869.

In New York, Henry was a fixture of the artistic community. He rented space at the Studio Building at 51 West Tenth Street, the hub of the American art scene, and later kept a studio at 3 North Washington Square. He joined the essential roster of clubs (Century, Salmagundi, Lotus, Union League) and artists' organizations (American Watercolor Society, Artists' Fund Society), and he was a central figure in the artists' colony at Cragsmoor in the Catskill Mountains, where, beginning in 1884, he established his principal residence. Henry was an avid collector of Americana, stuffing his house and studio with antique furniture, textiles, ceramics, metalware, architectural fragments, a research library and photographic archives, and, out back, an array of old carriages. Art critic Clarence Cook described the Cragsmoor house as "a museum of antiquarian curiosities in the field of relies of colonial life."[2] Henry used his collections as primary source material in devising his paintings, aiming for an unassailable historical authenticity. "Nothing annoyed him more," his wife Frances recalled, "than to see a wheel, a bit of architecture etc. carelessly drawn or out of keeping with the time it was supposed to portray."[3] An active member of the New-York Historical Society, Henry was regarded as an authority on American material culture, social history, and historic preservation, and his paintings were accepted as authoritative reconstructions: "in depicting scenes from the quiet, domestic life of a hundred years ago ... he is entirely in his element, and no one can be more familiar than he with all the details of the furniture, dress, and architecture of that time."[4] Henry's art and professional activities both derived from and contributed to the Colonial Revival of the postwar period. [5]

From: http://www.tfaoi.com/aa/3aa/3aa167.htm

The Peddler is unmistakably typical of Henry's art. The painting is small, closely crafted, and characterized by clear lines, bright colors, and a straightforward narrative that is annotated with myriad authentic-seeming details and enlivened by touches of humor and local color. In 1880, critic S. G. W. Benjamin did not find such elements especially praiseworthy, slighting "the elaboration of his work," "the crudeness in color and hardness in outline," yet Benjamin placed Henry in context with admired genre artists John George Brown (Henry's particular friend) and Thomas Waterman Wood in a field dominated by Eastman Johnson and Winslow Homer.[6]

The peddler has arrived at a substantial old farmhouse on a warm and sunny summer's day (a door and several windows are open, and the flowers -- many of them staked or potted -- are in full bloom). His horse grazes, still harnessed to the wagon; lying on the seat, his dog nonchalantly regards the farm watchdog chained to the doghouse. An African-American woman carrying a basket of produce approaches from the left with a droopy-drawered child. The composition centers on the peddler himself and two white women, one young, the other older and presumably her mother. The peddler leans slightly backward to read the numbers on the scale from which is suspended a white sack containing angular objects. The older woman, who wears a pocketbook outside her apron, frowns slightly and makes a point by raising her left hand. On the ground behind the peddler is an assortment of shiny new tin hollowware; more tinware hangs from the wagon, which also contains dusters, brooms, and other household items. The story seems clearly told. The Yankee peddler and his characteristic wagon with racks, drawers, and cabinets are midway out on the circuit (he has sold a number of his Hadley brooms) from Connecticut (where most tinware was made) to points south and back. His main commodity, the gleaming tinware, may be of special interest to the young woman, whose age and pink dress suggest her eligibility for marriage; tinware was essential to setting up housekeeping in the mid-19th century.[7] The older woman, however, is directing the bargaining, arguing for a better price for the contents of the sack being weighed.

If the negotiation is the focus of the composition, the main figure is the house. The house brings to mind Quaker domestic architecture of southeastern Pennsylvania, in Chester, Montgomery, and Bucks counties: the random masonry, overall asymmetry of conjoined units, discontinuous stringcourse, layered cornice molding on the facade, several chimney stacks, forked lightning rod, dormer windows, the sequence of doorways, flag terraces, porches, and numerous other details are typical of the stone farmhouses of that area. At the peak of the gable the characteristic stone tablet bears the date 1741, clearly signifying the structure's colonial origins.[8] Henry was familiar with the region's architecture, having served on the committee charged with the restoration of Independence Hall for the Centennial. In 1880, furthermore, he exhibited what must have been a similar painting, *The Old Trimble House, Chester Co., Penn: Built in 1741* (unlocated), at Gill's Gallery in Springfield, where *The Peddler*, too, may have been shown (indeed, Henry was "a particular favorite" at the Gill annual, showing a total of 20 paintings at 16 exhibitions there from 1878 to 1919).[9] Though the architecture is colonial, the scene is antebellum, for the peddler's wares and dress, especially the derby, likely date the narrative to around 1840.

According to Henry's wife, Frances, Henry "always tried to give some deeper meaning to a painting than to show just a pleasing picture."[10] Often he generated contrasts between male and female, rich and poor, black and white, old and new. Such contrasts are at play in *The Peddler*. The long-established homestead, the fixedness of the assiduously cultivated flowers, and the immovability of the white women stand against the transience of the traveling salesman and his vehicle, only momentarily stopped. The women's presumed virtue and natural conduct contrast with the stereotype of the Yankee as cunning, manipulative, and unlikely to conclude a fair trade. The white women, associated visually with the house and garden which they tend, contrast with the black woman and child, who wait at the margin to trade with the peddler (since, Henry suggests, the peddler will not stop at their house) and are associated with the stone carriage steps, now unused but alive with connotations of servitude. Perhaps the most stark confrontation is between a self-sufficient agrarian life and the increasingly intrusive, but not necessarily unwelcome, world of commerce and factory-made goods.

116

Endnotes

1. Quoted in Elizabeth McCausland, *The Life and Work of Edward Lamson Henry, N.A., 1841-1919*, New York State Museum Bulletin, no. 339) (Albany: 1345), p. 65.

2. Clarence Cook, *Art and Artists of Our Time* (1888; reprint, New York: Garland, 1978), Vol. 3, p. 267.

3. McCausland, p. 340.

4. Cook, p. 267.

5. See Alan Axelrod, ed., *The Colonial Revival in America* (New York: W. W. Norton & Company for The Henry Francis du Pont Winterthur Museum, 1985).

6. S. G. W. Benjamin, *Art in America: A Critical and Historical Sketch*, H. Barbara Weinberg, ed. (1880; reprint, New York: Garland, 1976), p. 115. For *The Peddler*, see McCausland, p. 174, no. 139, fig. 189; Christian Klackner, *Reproductions of the Works of E. L. Henry* (New York: 1906), no. 47; Dean Flower and Francis Murphy, *A Catalogue of American Paintings, Water Colors and Drawings (to 1923) in the George Walter Vincent Smith Art Museum, Springfield, Massachusetts* (Springfield, Mass.: George Waiter Vincent Smith Art Museum, 1976), p. 49.

7. See J. R. Dolan, *The Yankee Peddlers of Early America* (New York: Ciarkson N. Potter, 1964), pp. 141-148, 181-182.

8. See Aaron Siskind and William Morgan, *Bucks County: Photographs of Early Architecture* (New York: Horizon Press for The Bucks County Historical Society, 1974), c.g. pp. 28, 65, 71.

9. McCausland, p. 56.

10. Ibid., p. 339.   Edward Lamson Henry, 1841-1919 The Peddler, 1879; essay by William T. Oedel

About the author

At the time of publication of the essay, these biographical notes for the author were included in the catalogue.

William T. Oedel (Ph.D., University of Delaware) is associate professor in the Art History Department at the University of Massachusetts at Amherst. A former museum curator, he has contributed to several exhibitions and their catalogues, including *The Peale Family: Creation of a Legacy, 1770-1870* (1996). Professor Oedcl is preparing a monograph on the artist John Vanderlyn and to that end was Smithsonian Senior Postdoctoral Fellow at the National Portrait Gallery, Washington, D.C. He has held a Rockefeller Foundation Fellowship in American art and a National Endowment for the Humanities Research Fellowship at the H.F. du Pont Winterthur Museum.

The Civil War Drawings of Edward Lamson Henry

"War Sketches Oct & Nov - 1864"

The New York State Museum administers an outstanding collection of the works of Edward Lamson Henry (1841-1919), one of the country's most popular and prolific genre artists at the end of the nineteenth century. His meticulously crafted paintings of domestic life appealed to an audience nostalgic for idyllic images of a vanishing America, an America unsullied by rampant technology and the effects of a devastating Civil War. The Henry collection at the New York State Museum contains a significant group of Civil War images sketched on-site from "nature."

As a youthful artist, Henry experienced the Civil War in the autumn of 1864 when he served briefly as a captain's clerk aboard a Union Quartermaster's supply transport on the James River in Virginia. In a series of penciled "War Sketches" and pastel crayon studies he documented behind-the-lines scenes of a Federal occupation force during the siege of Petersburg. His images of the confiscated, fortified plantation houses of "Westover" and "Berkeley" combine with studies of the sprawling Union supply depot at City Point to chronicle a non-combat side of soldiering important to a fuller understanding of events of the period.

In a posthumous "Memorial Sketch" published by the New York State Museum in 1945, Henry's adoring wife Frances admitted that after a potentially dangerous encounter with a combative guard while sketching on shore, Henry discreetly "made his drawings on deck afterwards and at a safe distance." This distanced viewpoint, however, does not fail to complement the work of other Civil War "Special Artists" like the Waud brothers and Vizetelly, or photographers like Gardner, Brady, and O'Sullivan. In addition, Henry's details of soldiers, horses, wagons, and accoutrements are often sprightly and appealing.

Henry's reasons for rendering war service are as yet speculative. A turn-of-the-century biography states that he "desired to see the pictorial side of the Civil War, and in 1864 obtained a nominal place as a Captain's clerk on a transport, with full liberty to sketch." Frances Henry's contention that at "the breaking out of the War of the Rebellion Mr. Henry was very anxious to go but was too young to enlist" seems naive since he was twenty-three years old by the time "there was a position found for him as captain's clerk". He was, however, a young artist quartered in the Tenth Street Studio Building in New York City at a time when the city witnessed not only the infamous draft riots of 1863 but also the gala sendoff parade for the 20th Infantry United States Colored Troops in the spring of 1864. (In 1869 Henry was commissioned to paint the scene by the Union League Club of New York). In the spring of 1864 the city also was caught up in the fervor surrounding the famous "Metropolitan Fair" Army Relief Bazaar held to raise money for the U. S. Sanitary Commission. In this milieu, perhaps Henry, who had been born in Charleston, SC, and still had family connections in the South, felt compelled to "show his colors." Perhaps he toyed with the idea of becoming a "Special Artist."

No record of enlistment for E. L. Henry has yet surfaced. It is probable that he served, as other artists did, in civilian garb. Had he been in uniform when accosted by that shore guard - had he looked more like a soldier and less like a civilian spy, perhaps - Henry might have felt less compelled to remain "at a safe distance" from potential injury. That his biography refers to his clerk's position as "nominal" is further implication that he possibly was not a uniformed enlistee.

Henry's "War Sketches" and pastel crayon studies document details of site deployment and features which post-Civil War decades erased or obscured. For example, two tiny pencil sketches document river views of "Fort Powhatan" and "Camp Wilson's Landing" (Fort Pocahontas), which provide rare if not unique surviving visual documentation, albeit "at a safe distance," of positions manned by African American troops. The locations are now archeological sites.

Bibliographical note: Elizabeth McCausland's *The Life and Work of Edward Lamson Henry N. A., 1841-1919.* (Albany: The University of the State of New York, 1945. NYS Museum Bulletin No. 339) remains the primary reference and catalogue raisonne for this artist. It includes "A Memorial Sketch: E. L. Henry, N. A., His Life and His Work" by Frances L. Henry, his wife of forty-four years. Kaycee Benton Parra contributed additional insight into the artist's life in her text for the exhibition catalogue *The Works of E. L. The Henry: Recollections of a Time Gone By* (Shreveport, LA: The R. W. Norton Art Gallery, 1987). Henry apparently contributed biographical information on himself for the 1894 edition of *The National Cyclopedia of American Biography* (New York: J. T. White Company). See also: William A. Frassanito, *Grant and Lee, the Virginia Campaigns, 1864-1865* (NY: Charles Scribner's Sons, 1983); Harold Holzer and Mark E. Neely, Jr., *Mine Eyes Have Seen the Glory: The Civil War in Art* (NY: Orion Books, 1993); and Allen Johnson, ed., *Dictionary of American Biography* (NY: Charles Scribner's Sons, 1928-1937).

RESTING BY THE ROADSIDE, ca. 1880 (Henry Road, Cragsmoor)
Edward Lamson Henry, N.A. (1841-1919)
Oil on canvas, 10 x 14 inches
D. Wigmore Fine Art, Inc., New York, N.Y.

Copied from WINDY SUMMITS FERTILE VALLEYS
An Artistic Journey Through the Shawangunk Mountains

Presented by the Cragsmoor Free Library

19

A Hard Road to Travel

By Emily August

January 27, 2004

I've got a road to travel,
A hard one it shall be.
It's only made of pebbles,
And narrow, as you see.

It's quiet in these woodlands,
The only noise I hear,
Are sounds of horse hooves
trotting,
And crackling leaves from deer.

There's open fields around me,
And scattered here and there,
Are shallow streams for
drinking,
For animals to share.

There's mountains in the
distance,
And leaves upon the ground,
The wind is whipping quickly,
And makes them fly around.

The sun is slowly leaving
And setting in the West,
I might not beat the darkness,
But I shall try my best.

I've got a road to travel,
A long one it shall be.
I'm going on a journey,
To where I will be free.

E. L. Henry's "A Hard Road to Travel"

NOTE: EMILY IS THE GRANDDAUGHTER OF HAROLD AND CHRISTINA CLARK OF 421
        HILLSIDE ROAD, CRAGSMOOR.   EMILY RESIDES WITH HER PARENTS, SCOTT
        AND CORAL AUGUST OF CENTREVILLE, VIRGINIA;   ALSO HER BROTHER MITCHELL.
        EMILY WAS THIRTEEN YEARS OLD AT THE TIME OF THIS WRITING.   E. L. HENRY
        PAINTED "A HARD ROAD TO TRAVEL" IN 1882.

To the Editor:

My friend Marie Bilney and I have been doing research on one of the original *Cragsmoor Art Colony* artists, Carroll Butler Brown (1868-1923). My husband and I own the house built on the mountain that is registered in the Historical Houses of Cragsmoor. His aunt and uncle, Kenneth and Helen Clark, were the 3rd owners of the house named by Brown as the "Falcon" until their deaths in the early 1980s.

As is commonly known, Carroll Brown was a contemporary of the most famous artist from that colony, Edward Lamson Henry.

During our research, my grand-daughter Emily August (age 13, of Centreville, Virginia) became interested and helped me access Internet information. She enjoyed looking at the E.L. Henry paintings, some of which she also saw at the *Ellenville Museum*.

As an art class project, she wrote a poem to go along with one of his paintings.

I thought your magazine might be interested in printing this, as I noticed it does print some poems from local children. She's not local, but has visited Cragsmoor and Ellenville several times and always enjoys her time spent there.

Christina Clark
Hamburg, New Jersey

A Hard Road to Travel

by Emily August

(Based on E. L. Henry's painting,
A Hard Road to Travel, photo below)

I've got a road to travel,
A hard one it shall be.
It's only made of pebbles,
And narrow, as you see.

It's quiet in these woodlands,
The only noise I hear,
Are sounds of horse hooves trotting,
And crackling leaves from deer.

There's open fields around me,
And scattered here and there,
Are shallow streams for drinking,
For animals to share.

There's
mountains in
the distance,
And leaves
upon the
ground,
The wind is
whipping
quickly,
And makes
them fly
around.

The sun is
slowly leaving,
And setting in
the West,
I might not beat
the darkness,
But I shall try
my best.

I've got a road
to travel,
A long one it shall be,
I'm going on a journey,
To where I will be free.

The Mountain Echo

Volume I. No. 3.　　　　CRAGSMOOR, N. Y.　　　　August 6, 1928

Cragsmoor Mourns the Death of Mrs. E. L. Henry

With deep regret Cragsmoor heard that Mrs. E. L. Henry had passed on into the Great Unknown on July 23d. Mrs. Henry had for some time been suffering of angina pectoris, and had been taken to the hospital three weeks before her death. We are indebted to Mr. F. S. Dellenbaugh for the following sketch of her life:

"One of the oldest families in the state of New York is the Wells family of Johnstown. N. Y. There Frances Wells was born in the year 1845, and when she grew up and developed a marked talent for drawing and painting she was sent to New York to study art.

She became a pupil of the late Edward Lamson Henry, even then a noted painter, and a love affair developed which led to marriage.

Mr. and Mrs. Henry went to Paris for a while and there Mrs. Henry made an impression on all who met her by her brilliant conversation, her charming manner and her great beauty. A prominent New York artist and Academician who was there at the time declared she was one of the most beautiful women he ever saw.

The Henrys finally came to this region through the Otis family then living in Ellenville, and in 1881 they came to "the Mountain," as Cragsmoor was then called, and boarded with the Blakeleys in the house now belonging to Mrs. Rust.

Mr. Henry painted some of his old time pictures at that time and Mrs. Henry sketched and painted also.

In 1884 they decided to build a cottage and the present house where Mrs. Henry died on July 23d, 1928, was the outcome of this decision. It was the first "real" summer residence on the mountain.

Mrs. Henry's personality and the attractiveness of her husband soon brought others to the mountain and through all the years until Mr. Henry's failing health interfered their home was one of the centres of attraction.

Numerous concerts and entertainments of various kinds were held there, before the Barnstormers Theatre was opened, and Mrs. Henry was always a charming hostess. But not only on these occasions did she receive visitors but at many other times for E. L. Henry's pictures were known throughout the country and when possible visitors came up especially to call on him and Mrs. Henry who generously made them welcome. Some of these visitors were entire strangers and on one occasion when Mrs. Henry could not come down to meet a party of "unknowns" they ranged the house and satisfied their curiosity to the full, which Mrs. Henry was pleased to have them do.

Mrs. Henry did some decorating in oil colors in their house, notably the rhododendron blossoms painted on the glass doors leading from the living room to the little library. Mrs. Henry was a musician, too, as was Mr. Henry, and he played the flute while she accompanied him on the piano.

It is safe to say that Mrs. Henry's attractive conversation and personality combined with Mr. Henry's equally attractive personality, was a leading factor in bringing to Cragsmoor people of artistic and literary tastes—laying the foundation, as it were, of the delightful society for which the place has been noted.

Mrs. Henry is buried alongside her husband in the cemetery at Johnstown, N. Y., where she first saw the light of day."

The Barnstormers to Present Two Plays

On the evenings of Thursday and Friday, August 9th and 10th, at 5:30 o'clock, the Barnstormers will present their first group of plays: the first is "The Land of Heart's Desire," a fanciful creation of W. B. Yates, the other is "The Trysting Place," a rollicking comedy such as only Booth Tarkington can write. The net proceeds of both evenings will be given to the roads fund. Concentrated effort has been applied to both plays, which promise to be finished productions for they are under the professional direction of Emilia Joan Schneider, the dramatic director of the organization. A great deal of time is being spent not only in the daily rehearsals, but also in building scenery, and collecting properties.

As Mr. Chas. Curran found it impossible to accept the presidency of the organization, Mrs. Langstaff graciously undertook the responsibility, and under her enthusiastic leadership things are running quite smoothly.

Those acting in the "Land of Heart's Desire" are Helen Turner, George R. Montgomery, Meredith Langstaff, J. Corona Sutton, Siegwalt O. Palleske, and Esther Gordon. The cast of "The Trysting Place" is Esther Langstaff, Billy Sutton, Julea C. Sutton, Chas. C. Curran, Julia Polk and Hugh McCandless. Tickets for these plays may be obtained from Mrs. Langstaff or Mr. S. Palleske.

Last Thursday evening tryouts were held at the home of Mrs. Langstaff for the casting of the next production which will be "Enter Madame" by Gilda Varesi.

_ 252 -

NOTE: As with many dates in history, there are discrepancies here also. In Cragsmoor Library (Book 16, page 92), there is a Testimonial Letter by Dellenbaugh regarding E. L. Henry's death, stating that he died of pneumonia on May 7, 1919 while Kingston, New York records claim his death to have been on May 11, 1919. He left no apparent will, most likely because his only heir was his beloved wife, Frances.

It was not our intention to delve into the depths of the Henry's personal affairs, but we found it so interesting and fascinating that we decided to share our findings.

LAST WILL AND TESTAMENT,

I, FRANCES L. HENRY of Cragsmoor, in the County of Ulster and State of New York, being of sound mind and memory, do make, publish and declare this my last WILL AND TESTAMENT, in manner following that is to say:

FIRST. I direct that all my just debts and funeral expenses be paid.

SECOND. It is my desire that the enclosure in the Johnstown, Fulton County, New York Cemetery, in which the body of my husband, Edward L. Henry, is now laying, be opened and by body laid close beside him in a new enclosure large enough for two.

THIRD. I give and bequeath to the Trustees of the Johnstown, Fulton County, New York Cemetery, the sum of FIVE HUNDRED DOLLARS, ($500.), to be held by them and their successors in office in perpetuity in trust. I direct that the said Trustees and their successors in office do invest the said moneys in accordance with the laws of the State of New York for the investment of trust funds, and to use the income arising therefrom for the purpose of keeping the lot where I or the members of my family may be buried in good order; the ground well turfed, the turf properly cut and fertilized, and to apply the surplus of such income, if any, to the approaches thereto.

FOURTH. I give and bequeath unto the Presbyterian Hospital in the City of New York, incorporated by the legislature of the State of New York in the year 1868, the sum of TWENTY THOUSAND DOLLARS, ($20,000.), for the purpose of endowing a private room in said Hospital for the use of Artists under such rules and regulations as to endowed beds as the Hospital authorities may from time to time adopt. It is my understanding that the present Hospital buildings at Madison Avenue and 70th Street do not permit of the setting aside of any private room for such purpose. I am therefore quite willing that until such time as a new Hospital building shall have been erected and completed, that there shall be assigned to the use of Artists two (8) free beds in the common wards of the existing Hospital buildings. I designate and appoint the President of the Academy of Design and the President of The Artist Fund Society of New York City to nominate from time to time patients to use and occupy such room or beds, and in default of such appointment, the right to nominate patients to use and occupy such room or beds shall best in the said Presbyterian Hospital. It is my most earnest desire and wish that these two beds or room shall always be known as the free gift of E. L. Henry, N. A., who was for many years a member of The Academy of Design and Artist Fund. I wish, if possible, that a silver plate with his name engraved thereon be fastened upon the bed as it is my great desire that it shall be a memorial to my husband, E. L. Henry.

FIFTH. I give and bequeath unto the Foreign Mission of the Presbyterian Church of America the sum of FIVE HUNDRED DOLLARS, ($500.).

157

124

SIXTH. I give and bequeath the sum of FIVE HUNDRED DOLLARS, ($500.), to the Home Mission of the Presbyterian Church of America.

SEVENTH. I give and bequeath unto the General Synod of the Reformed Church in America the sum of FIVE HUNDRED DOLLARS, ($500.), for the Disabled Ministers' Fund.

EIGHTH. I give and bequeath unto the Reformed Church of Ellenville, N. Y., the sum of FIVE HUNDRED DOLLARS, ($500.).

NINTH. I give and bequeath unto my niece, Mrs. Alida Stetson, my cluster diamond ring and a black cabinet with three carved drawers and one glass door with the contents thereof. And I also give and bequeath unto my said niece, Mrs. Alida Stetson, a mahogany piece of furniture with carved legs and drawers.

TENTH. I give and bequeath unto my grand-nephew, Edward Wells, Jr., the sum of ONE HUNDRED DOLLARS, ($100.), also any painting that he may choose of my late husband, E. L. Henry, and also any choice of sketches made by the late E. L. Henry.

ELEVENTH. I give and bequeath to my grand-nephew, William Wells, the sum of ONE HUNDRED DOLLARS, ($100.), and any choice of paintings and sketches from my collection that he may choose.

TWELFTH. I give and devise to my nephew, NATHAN FRANK WELLS, of Johnstown, Fulton County, New York, all that piece and parcel of land, situate at Cragsmoor, in the County of Ulster and State of New York, known as "Singlecook". The said premises being bounded in front by the main highway known as the Plank Road, in the rear by what is known as the first Privet Hedge, on the one side by lands and premises of Katie Broadhead and on the other side by a road leading from the said main Plank Road through the E. L. Henry property. To have and to hold the same unto the said Nathan Frank Wells, his heirs and assigns, forever.

THIRTEENTH. If in my lifetime I should sell and dispose of the said property known as "Shinglecook" devised in paragraph "Twelfth" of this, my last Will and Testament, then and in that event and not otherwise, I give and bequeath unto my nephew, NATHAN FRANK WELLS, the sum of ONE THOUSAND DOLLARS, ($1000.).

FOURTEENTH. I give and bequeath unto my niece, Margaret Wells, my diamond ring set with one diamond.

FIFTEENTH. I give and devise unto my nephew, EDWARD WELLS, Sr., of Johnstown, Fulton County, New York, all the rest, residue and remainder of my real property and estate situated at Cragsmoor, Ulster County, New York, being all of my real estate at Cragsmoor, New York excepting only that part thereof devised unto my nephew, Nathan Frank Wells, of Johnstown, New York, under the "Twelfth" paragraph of this, my last Will and Testament.

SIXTEENTH. All the rest, residue and remainder of my estate and property, both real and personal, of whatsoever kind or nature, and wheresoever situated, I give, devise and

156

125

bequeath unto my nephews, EDWARD WELLS, Sr. and NATHAN FRANK WELLS, and my niece, ALIDA STETSON, to be divided among them equally, share and share alike.

LASTLY I hereby appoint my nephews, EDWARD WELLS, Sr. and NATHAN FRANK WELLS, executors of this, my last will and Testament; hereby revoking all former wills by me made.

IN WITNESS WHEREOF, I have hereunto subscribed my name the 9th day of September, in the year Nineteen Hundred and Twenty-five.

FRANCES L. HENRY   L.S.

We, whose names are hereto subscribed, DO CERTIFY that on the 9th day of September, 1925 FRANCES L. HENRY the testatrix above named, subscribed her name to this instrument in our presence and in the presence of each of us, and at the same time, in our presence and hearing, declared the same to be her last WILL AND TESTAMENT, and requested us and each of us, to sign our names thereto as witnesses to the execution thereof, which were hereby do in the presence of the testatrix and of each other, on the day of the date of the said will, and write opposite our names our respective places of residence.

RAYMOND G. COX   residing at   ELLENVILLE, N. Y.

FRANK H. SPRAGUE   residing at   ELLENVILLE, N. Y.

159

SCHEDULE A-1.

Pieces or Parcels of land on top of Shawangunk Mountain
in the Town of Wawarsing, Ulster County, New York, at or
near a place called Cragsmoor as described in three certain
deeds of conveyance as follows, viz:-

Deed, Full Covenant, Hattie L.
Keir, formerly Hattie L. Stymers to
Edward L. Henry. Dated August 3rd,
1883, ack. August 9th, 1883; recorded
in Ulster County Clerk's office, in
Book 245 of Deeds at page 631, Sep-
tember 4th, 1883. Cons. $200.00
Conveys Lot at Cragsmoor, N. Y.

Deed, Warranty, Harriet L. Keir and
John Keir her husband to Edward L.
Henry. Dated December 1st, 1888, ack.
29th day of December, 1888; recorded
in Ulster County Clerk's office, in
Liber 282 of Deeds at page 378, January
22, 1889. Cons. $150.00. Conveys
Lot at Cragsmoor, N. Y.

Deed, Warranty, Harriet Keir to Edward
L. Henry. Dated March 26, 1894, ack.
April 9th, 1894; recorded in Ulster
County Clerk's office in Liber 317 of
Deeds at page 333, May 9th, 1894.
Cons. $500.00. Conveys Lot at Crags-
moor, N. Y.

All combined as one property. On this land is erected
two houses, one called "Shinglenook."

Whole property is valued at $5000.00, and
the part thereof devised to Edward Wells,
Sr., is valued at $2500.00, and the part
thereof devised to Nathan Frank Wells, is
valued at $2500.00, in all, $5000.00

127

Amount brought forward	$46701.95 (VALUE OF STOCKS)
1 Cluster diamond Ring (9 small Diamonds),	60.00
2 Rings white Gold Value of gold only,	2.00
2 Rings Gold " " " "	2.00
1 Small Diamond Ring,	10.00
1 Three Stone Diamond Ring Old-Fashioned,	250.00
1 Four " " " " "	300.00
34 pieces old table silverware,	25.00
6 chairs,	6.00
1 Dresser,	5.00
1 Bookends,	5.00
1 Table,	2.50
1 other Bookends	2.50
1 Oil Stove,	3.00
4 Rugs,	1.50
39 Sketches, Pictures & Photographs,	20.00
1 Old wall Clock,	23.00
1 old stove,	3.00
Cabinet drawers,	1.50
1 trunk,	5.00
6 Chairs,	3.00
1 Couch,	.50
3 Tables,	1.00
1 Cabinet,	1.00
1 Clock,	3.00
1 Piano,	20.00
1 Easel,	3.00
Sketches, Photos, & unfinished picture,	40.00
1 Large Oil Painting, George Barrett,	25.00
1 Chest of Drawers,	2.50
1 Dinning Room Table,	3.00
1 China Closet,	5.00
1 Dresser,	2.00
Old lot of dishes and tray,	3.00
1 Ice Chest & Refrigerator,	5.00
1 Oil Stove,	3.00
1 Kitchen Table and 2 Chairs,	1.00
Kitchen Utensils,	.50
Ax, Scythe, Lawn Mower & Rake,	2.00
Step, Ladder,	.50
1 Iron Bed & Mattress & Bedding,	3.00
3 Chairs,	1.00
1 Dresser,	2.00
1 Chiffonier,	5.00
Bed & bedding, two stands, & Dresser,	10.00
Writing Desk, Bureau, Stand, Cot, 2 Chairs,	10.00
8 Chairs & Table,	10.00
2 Setees & 2 Rocking Chairs for Porch,	2.00
1 Stand,	1.00
1 Table & 6 Chairs,	5.00
1 Sideboard,	5.00
1 Range,	5.00
2 Kitchen Tables,	1.00
6 Lamps,	1.50
Lot of Bedroom Furniture in summer cottage,	25.00
Picture by Mr. Henry, Automobile,	300.00
" " " " Story of Blue Beard (water color),	100.00
" " " " Waiting for the Stage,	100.00
" " " " Four Seasons,	400.00
Old silver,	2.00
TOTAL	$47543.45

58

128

At a Surrogate's Court, held in and for the County of Ulster, at the Surrogate's Office in the City of Kingston, on the 8th day of October in the year one thousand nine hundred and twenty-eight.

Present, Hon. George F. Kaufman, Surrogate.

In the Matter of the Appraisal, under the Taxable Transfer Act, of the Estate of

Frances L. Henry,

Deceased.

Decree, Assessing and Fixing Tax.

The Surrogate of the County of Ulster, having heretofore appointed the County Treasurer of the County of Ulster, Appraiser, under and in pursuance of the Taxable Transfer Act, to appraise the property of Frances L. Henry, deceased, who died on the 23rd day of July, 19 28, and the said Appraiser having made and filed his report in the office of said Surrogate on the 5th day of October 1928;

IT IS ORDERED, that the said report be and the same is hereby approved and confirmed and the cash value of the property of said deceased which is subject to the tax imposed by said Act; and the tax to which the same is liable, are hereby assessed and fixed as follows:

PERSONS ENTITLED TO SUCH PROPERTY	CASH VALUE	TAX
Trustees of the Johnstown Cemetery, Fulton Co., N.Y.	500.00	Exempt
Presbyterian Hospital, Madison Ave., & 70th St., New York City	20000.00	"
Board of Foreign Missions Presbyterian Church, N.Y.City	500.00	"
Board of Home Missions, Presbyterian Church, N.Y.City	500.00	"
General Synod of Reformed Church in America, N.Y.City	500.00	"
Reformed Church, Ellenville, N.Y.	500.00	"
Alida Stetson	7415.98	370.80
Edward Wells, Jr.	100.00	Exempt
William Wells	100.00	"
Nathan Frank Wells	9853.49	492.67
Margaret Wells	10.00	Exempt
Edward Wells, Sr.	9853.49	492.67
	49852.96	1356.14

COURT.

106

Estate of Mrs Frances Henry

1 Finished, Cypress, Outside Burial Case _____ 100⁰⁰
Extra Size. 9ft 3 long 5ft 3 wide 1½ in Thick. Same used to
place Caskets of Mr & Mrs Henry inside

1 Chestnut, finished Casket, for remains of Mr Henry — 50⁰⁰
Made necessary by breaking leg of original casket, after
grave was opened and change made

use of Auto Hearse at funeral of Mrs Henry — 10⁰⁰

use of 60 Folding chairs at residence, also use
of Matting — Grade, Grave Lowering, and Storm Tent
and Labor of 3 men at Cemetery _____ 25⁰⁰

Flowers on door of residence _____ 3⁵⁰

Paid Rev Andrew Dillenbeck _____ 10⁰⁰
Charge of Cemetery Association Grave & Extra Labor 35⁰⁰
Service of Undertaker. Attending to all Cemetery arrangments
and to burial, & funeral service of Mrs Henry — 25⁰⁰
Service of 2 assistents _____ 10⁰⁰
1 Auto for minister _____ 147⁰⁰ 5⁰⁰

Sept 10 paid A. B. Wassung 268⁰⁰

130

Irving Ostrander
Mortician

Ellenville, N.Y., 8/15/20

ESTATE of FRANCES WELLS, HENRY,

Cragsmoor. N.Y.

BURIAL of FRANCES WELLS. HENRY, Dec'd

Removing Body, Cragsmoor to Ellenville.   15.00

Embalming Body   25 00

1/2 Couch Mahogany Casket, trimmed complete   410 00

Casket Coach to Johnstown. N.Y. (Special)   50 00

Personal Service   25 00
                                                 $525 00

Rec'd Payt in Full

Irving Ostrander

131

Cragsmoor, an early American art colony

BY BARBARA BUFF

ABOUT SEVEN MILES from Ellenville in Ulster County, New York, on a plateau in the Shawangunk Mountains, a summer art colony was established in the early 1870's. Cragsmoor was the first of a number of such colonies that sprang up in the late nineteenth century in reaction to industrialization in the United States and a concommitant yearning by American artists to return to nature. The grimy cities provided a market for the work of the very painters who wanted to escape from them during the hot summer months.

Throughout the nineteenth century, when Cragsmoor was called Evansville, farmers had been clearing the land so that by 1872 there were superb views of surrounding valleys and mountains in every direc-

tion. The light and the sky were wonderfully clear and changed often; the air was pure; and breezes blew almost constantly. These were the qualities that attracted artists to the plateau which in the 1890's came to be called Cragsmoor. Throughout its history and even today the place is also referred to simply as "the Mountain."

Edward Lamson Henry was the first artist to choose Cragsmoor as his summer home. He and his wife stayed in Ellenville and Cragsmoor boardinghouses from 1872 until in 1883 they began to build a house of his design (see Fig. 1). Even before they embarked on this project, the Henrys' enthusiastic descriptions had enticed to Cragsmoor such leading artists of the day as Eliza Pratt Greatorex (1820–1897); Frederick S. Dellenbaugh, who served as topographer on John Wesley Powell's second expedition down the Colorado River from 1871 to 1873; and William H. Beard (1824–1900) and John G. Brown (1831–1913), both members of the National Academy.

Word spread among artists about "... Cragsmoor, with its stimulating air, its distant horizon, its wide expanse of landscape, valley and mountain, the brilliancy of its sunset skies, and the grandeur and awfulness of its summer storms!"[1] The colony did not attract the struggling artists of tradition. It drew people who were already successful and who for the most part lived staid, prosperous family lives. Cragsmoor was an extension of this way of life, the long summer days and the atmosphere of sociability providing inspiration for the canvases that sold so well in winter. E. L. Henry had first exhibited at the National Academy at the age of eighteen. Charles Courtney Curran, a member of the Academy at the age of twenty-nine, induced Helen M. Turner, a fellow New Yorker and academician, to come to the Mountain. Arthur I. Keller (1866–1924), whose descendants still summer on his property in Cragsmoor, was one of the founders and an early president of the Society of American Illustrators. When the academician Edward B. Gay built his house Gaylands at Cragsmoor in 1905 many members of the art colony were among

Fig. 1. Stair hall of Edward Lamson Henry's (1841–1919) house, begun 1883. Henry designed the house, the first summer place in Cragsmoor, incorporating elements from houses being demolished in New York City. Joseph Mance, the local carpenter who built the house and who frequently posed for Henry (see Fig. 3), wrote, "your Door and Frame and Box etc arived by Canal all in good shape." Quite possibly "etc" includes these handsomely carved newel posts, handrails, and turned banisters. Salvaged items were brought from New York City to Ellenville by boat up the Hudson River and the Kingston-Scranton Canal. From there they were hauled up the mountain to Cragsmoor by oxcart. *Photograph by Helga Photo Studio.*

From ANTIQUES MAGAZINE
November 1978

Fig. 2. *Peter Brown*, by Henry, 1886. Signed and dated at lower right, *E L Henry/1886*. Oil on canvas, 17½ by 14¾ inches. Brown was a member of one of the oldest farming families in the district. He frequently modeled for Henry's genre and history paintings. *Ellenville Town Hall; Helga photograph.*

the party that wended its way through the evening by lantern light to a surprise housewarming.[2] Another academician, George Inness Jr., and his wife bought Eliza Greatorex's property from her daughters in 1900 and turned it into the largest and most elegant summer estate in Cragsmoor, where tea was served in porcelain that was said to have belonged to Napoleon.

In its July 1905 issue the *Cragsmoor Journal*, a summer publication of the period, noted that there were no less than five members of the Salmagundi Club resident in the town. The records of that New York City artists' club have burned, but four of the five would have been Keller, Henry, Curran, and Frederick V. Baker (1876–1964).[3]

As was true in the later summer art colonies, Cragsmoor attracted artistic people other than painters. The *Journal* on August 15, 1910, for example,

reported that "the magazine of Arts and Crafts, 'Pallette and Bench,' has its summer editorial office on the mountain, and a recent exhibition of Crafts work ... has set a high standard of merits." Charles Curran was on the editorial board and his wife, Grace, was the editor of the magazine, which had been established in 1908 by Adelaide Alsop Robineau of Syracuse. The *Journal* also carried notices of craft exhibitions as well as descriptions of some of the pottery, wood and horn carving, needlework, and weaving created by the exhibitors.

The paintings done at Cragsmoor reflected the current taste in academic art and, not surprisingly, often were awarded prizes and sold well. Helen Turner's *Summer* of 1919 was "invited" to exhibitions around the country and won several prizes, while her *Girl with the Lantern* of about 1921 was bought by the Corcoran Gallery of Art in Washington, D.C. Charles Curran's *At the Piano* of 1903 was shown for the first time in Cragsmoor and was subsequently exhibited at the Pennsylvania Academy of the Fine Arts. It too won a number of prizes.

The awesome natural scenes painted by the Hudson River school were less in demand at the time than a tamer version of nature in which human figures are prominent. Cragsmoor's artists specialized in these gentler, more sentimental paintings of country life and scenery. The Mountain was important to

Fig. 3. *Joseph E. Mance*, by Henry, c. 1887. Signed at lower left, *E L Henry*. Oil on canvas, 18 by 14 inches. Mance, a member of a long-established Cragsmoor family, was a carpenter who built Henry's house as well as Frederick Dellenbaugh's. *Ellenville Town Hall; Helga photograph.*

Pl. I. *Landscape*, by Edward B. Gay (1837–1928), 1908. Signed and dated at lower right, *Edward Gay, 1908*. Oil on canvas, 33 by 44 inches. This view of Cragsmoor in autumn was probably taken near Gay's studio. *Private collection; photograph by courtesy of Marbella Gallery, Inc.*

Pl. II. *Through the Gate*, by George Inness Jr. (1854–1926), c. 1905. Signed at lower left, *Inness Jr.* Oil on canvas, 29 by 36 inches. Inness and his wife bought the house and property belonging to the daughters of Eliza Greatorex and added adjoining land until they owned about five hundred acres. Their house, Chetolah, was an elaborate show place. In this painting Mr. Marl, a local man who worked for the family, is shown in the saddle. He also appears in other Inness paintings. *Collection of Mr. and Mrs. Cornelius Watts. Except as noted, color photographs are by Helga Photo Studio.*

The painters of Cragsmoor rendered the surrounding scenery in many aspects and at many seasons and times of day. Some of the titles of Charles Curran's paintings describe the qualities of light and atmosphere he was attempting to capture on canvas: *Wind on a Cliff* (1917), *After the Storm* (1930), and *On the Heights* (Pl. V and Fig. 5). Carroll Butler Brown, who was confined to a wheelchair, had himself taken to sites around Cragsmoor where he could paint the colors and light of autumn in such canvases as *Cragsmoor Landscape* (c. 1915) and *View of Ellenville from Cragsmoor* (Pl. VI). LeGrand W. Botsford, a member of a local family and a year-round resident, left a more primitive record of Cragsmoor scenes and landmarks (see Pl. VII).

The intimate style and leisurely pace of life in Cragsmoor can be sensed in the paintings of the art colony. Turner's *Morning* (Pl. VIII), for example, breathes tranquility; Curran's *Lanterns* (Pl. IX) draws the viewer into the velvety warmth of a summer evening party; and Henry's *Mrs. Henry on the Porch* (Fig. 6) is the essence of a familiar figure in a homely setting.

A primary mover in the development of Cragsmoor was Eliza Hartshorn, a wealthy lady from Newport who was related both to Frances Wells (Mrs. E. L.) Henry and Harriet Otis (Mrs. Frederick) Dellenbaugh. She first came to Cragsmoor in 1886 to visit the Henrys and she immediately bought land. She built a succession of houses, barns, public buildings, and roads, using Frederick Dellenbaugh as her architect.

Pl. III. *Grandpa Coddington*, by Frederick S. Dellenbaugh (1853–1935), 1890–1900. Signed and dated at lower right, *F. S. Dellenbaugh, 189*[?]. Oil on artist's board, 14 by 10 inches. Coddington was an Evansville farmer who worked as a handyman and gardener for the summer people. *Collection of George Thompson.*

them not only for its great scenic beauty (Pls. I, II) but also as a source of local characters to use as models. The *Journal* for September 1, 1912, for example, noted that "Peter Brown died . . . a great loss to Mr. [E. L.] Henry, for he had utilized him as a model in some of his most striking pictures" (see Fig. 2). Frederick Dellenbaugh recorded "Grandpa" Coddington, a local farmer who worked as a handyman and gardener for the summer people (Pl. III). E. L. Henry painted Joseph E. Mance, a Cragsmoor carpenter (Fig. 3). And, of course, the painters painted each other (see Pl. IV and Fig. 4) and themselves.

Pl. IV. *Edward Gay*, by Augusta Densmore Sturdevant (1855–1936), c. 1920. Signed and dated at lower right, *A. D. Sturdevant, 19*[??]. Oil on canvas, 30 by 23 inches. Sturdevant was trained in Italy and specialized in portraits. In 1904 she bought a boardinghouse which she developed and ran for a number of years as the Cragsmoor Inn. *Collection of Ingovar*

Although Dellenbaugh was a man of many interests and accomplishments, he was never trained as an architect, so that while his houses have charm and some innovations (such as closets in otherwise wasted space) they also have some idiosyncracies. Stairs in particular seem not to have interested him greatly. Hardly any flight permits the passage of large pieces of furniture, and some have had to be rebuilt to make them usable at all. In one extreme case an enclosed stair had to be built onto the outside of a completed house. Often a Dellenbaugh house has no two windows alike, for he was fond of salvaging windows from houses being demolished in New York City and working them into the design of his Cragsmoor houses. Today, despite alterations inside and out, Dellenbaugh's houses of stone and dark cedar shingles give Cragsmoor a look all its own (see Pl. XI). It was Dellenbaugh, too, who gave Cragsmoor its name, winning the battle against Frances Henry's suggestion of Baim-Wa-Wa when the residents petitioned for a post office in 1893. Mrs. Henry maintained that Baim-Wa-Wa was Indian for "passing thunder," but Dellenbaugh vowed he would never live in a place with such a name.

"It is seldom one finds so many congenial people in a small community as in Cragsmoor," stated the *Cragsmoor Journal* on August 15, 1904. "The features of the place, its situation, climate and healthfulness are very attractive. At the same time, one cannot live on views, air, and health-giving attributes without companionship." And companionship they had. The pages of the *Journal* record a steady round of teas, card parties, recitals, theatricals, picnics, and fancy-

Fig. 4. *E. L. Henry, N. A.,* by Charles Courtney Curran (1861–1942), 1909. Signed and dated at lower right, *Chas. C. Curran/1909.* Oil on canvas, 20 by 12 inches. Curran captured his subject in what he described as a characteristic pose while Henry worked in his Cragsmoor studio. *New York State Museum, Albany; photograph by courtesy of the museum.*

Fig. 5. Curran works on *On the Heights* (Pl. V) near the tennis court of the Boulders (see Pl. XI) in a photograph of c. 1909. His daughter Emily lies in his shadow. *Collection of Kaycee Benton.*

Fig. 6. *Mrs. Henry on the Porch at Cragsmoor*, by Henry, 1914. Signed and dated at lower left, *E L Henry./1914*. Oil on canvas, 7½ by 9½ inches. The small size of the painting and the casual pose give this canvas an air of intimacy and serenity. A photograph of the scene that is almost identical to the painting is in the Henry collection in the New York State Museum. *Collection of George Thompson; Helga photograph.*

dress parties (see Fig. 9). When the Henrys entertained, "The program . . . was a series of old-time songs rendered by a group who looked as if they might have stepped out of Mr. Henry's famous *Wedding Party*." [4] Most of the costumes came from Henry's enormous collection of Americana, including clothing, which is now in the Brooklyn Museum. Henry used the collection frequently to ensure the accuracy of detail in his paintings.

There must have been a lot of music during these summers at Cragsmoor, for the *Journal* reports the presence of a number of musicians and music teachers. The best known was Maud Powell (1868–1920), the greatest woman violinist of her day and a good friend of the Henrys. Theater people too were attracted by the Barnstormers Theater, an outgrowth of the readings, amateur theatricals, and tableaux that were popular at Cragsmoor from its earliest days as a summer colony. Indeed, Thornton Wilder is said to have written *The Skin of Our Teeth* while a guest of Jessica Bruce at Cragsmoor.

Fig. 7. *Sam's Point, Cragsmoor*, by Curran, c. 1910. Inscribed *C* at lower left. This lithograph illustrates a dramatic moment in an epic poem written by Blanche Densmore Curtis, Augusta Sturdevant's daughter. The poem concerned an eighteenth-century legend about Cragsmoor and was privately published in 1910. *Benton collection; Helga photograph.*

Fig. 8. Orchard Cottage, the oldest house in Cragsmoor. It was built in 1834 as a tavern on the road from Newburgh to Ellenville. Then for many years it was lived in by the Bleakley family, who farmed the land and, when people began summering in Cragsmoor, took in boarders. About 1893 George Bleakley built an addition to the house to serve as the local post office (see Pl. VII). The Bleakleys' fruit trees inspired Belle Dellenbaugh's name for the house when she bought it and had her brother Frederick convert it into her summer house. Behind the lattice at the left are some of the stone walls of the old tavern. The dormers date from Dellenbaugh's conversion. The house now belongs to Kenneth Hasbrouck. *Helga photograph.*

Pl. V. *On the Heights*, by Curran, 1909. Signed and dated at lower left, *Chas C. Curran,/1909*. Oil on canvas, 30⅛ inches square. In this romantic scene at one end of the Cragsmoor plateau, Curran repeats one of his favorite themes: graceful young women, wind blown and sun drenched against the blue sky and fluffy clouds typical of summertime in Cragsmoor. *Brooklyn Museum, gift of George D. Pratt; photograph by courtesy of the museum.*

Pl. VI. *View of Ellenville from Cragsmoor*, by Carroll Butler Brown (1860-1923). Signed at lower right, *Carroll Brown*. Oil on canvas, 30 by 38 inches. Although Brown was never a member of the National Academy of Design, his work was occasionally exhibited there. This view can be seen today from Route 52 between Ellenville and Cragsmoor. *Ellenville Public Library and Museum.*

(1868)→

VII. *First Post Office in Cragsmoor at Bleakley Farm,* LeGrand W. Botsford (1860–1937), 1893–1895. Oil on canvas, 11¾ by 20¾ inches. Botsford was a lifelong resident of Cragsmoor and a member of an old local family. He built roads, took photographs for E. L. Henry to use while painting, and left his own artistic record of his home town. George Bleakley built an addition to his house c. 1893 to serve as the town's post office, and was the first postmaster, from 1893 to 1895. When the house was bought by Belle Dellenbaugh her brother Frederick designed the alterations that turned it into her much beloved summer house, Orchard Cottage (see Figs. 8, 9). *Cragsmoor Free Library.*

Often the entertainments were of a simple country kind. On August 15, 1904, the *Journal* reported "a very jolly *bon fire* at Ruhberg, on Thursday evening. . . . Marshmallows were toasted, corn popped, stories told, songs sung and conundrums propounded." On another occasion "the evening ended with Dr. Lewis playing on the guitar and everybody singing old songs."[5]

VIII. *Morning,* by Helen M. Turner (1858–1958), 1919. Signed and dated at lower right, *Helen M. Turner, 1919 N. Y.* Oil on canvas, 34 by 44 inches. The sunlight filtered through rhododendrons and the relaxed, almost langorous pose of the model on the porch of Turner's studio in Cragsmoor convey the sense of summer at the art colony. *Helga photograph, by courtesy of Ira Spanierman.*

Cultural events, too, dotted the social calendar. In 1906 Edward Gay's wife, Martha, gave an evening talk "to the young people of Cragsmoor. Last winter she was in Athens and saw the Olympic Games; so she told her friends about it."[6] And every summer Saturday morning Harriet Dellenbaugh, an actress in New York City during the winter, gave readings from classical and modern plays.

The pride and the pleasure the summer people took in Cragsmoor made them very civic minded. The Cragsmoor Free Library was originally housed in the Pines Casino, which Eliza Hartshorn had built in 1899 for the use of the young people. About 1912 Frederick Dellenbaugh and one of the year-round residents inaugurated a library for both summer and permanent residents that was housed at various locations until 1923, when the trustees built the library shown in Figure 10 which was designed by Dellenbaugh and erected on land donated by him. The Cragsmoor Improvement Association was formed in 1908 to improve lighting and roads. Curran and Dellenbaugh were president and treasurer, respectively, and Martha Gay and Augusta Sturdevant served on the executive committee.

The summer people also looked to their churches. Dellenbaugh in 1895 and 1896 designed and built the Episcopalian Chapel of the Holy Name with funds supplied by Eliza Hartshorn (Figs. 11-13), and the construction of the Federated Church in 1903 was heavily supported by the Innesses. Charles Curran served as a deacon.

Fig. 9. Belle Dellenbaugh presides on the porch of Orchard Cottage in a photograph of c. 1909. Her guests are, from left to right, Frederick Dellenbaugh, E. L. Henry, Charles C. Curran, George Inness Jr., Arthur I. Keller, a Dr. Northrup, Edward Gay, a Mr. Cownig, and Carroll Butler Brown. *Collection of Kenneth Hasbrouck.*

Fig. 10. Cragsmoor Free Library, designed by Frederick Dellenbaugh, built 1923–1925. The roof is supported by trunks of native chestnut trees, and the fireplace, like other masonry in Dellenbaugh's buildings, is of local stone. The large landscape at the right, *The Rainbow*, is by George Inness Jr. *Helga photograph.*

ANTIQUES

140

had the chapel built to serve the nearby Episcopal monastery, Ruhberg, as well as the residents of Cragsmoor. The stained-glass window in the gable end was donated in 1932 by Dellenbaugh in memory of his wife, Harriet Otis, who died on November 15, 1930. From the date and appearance of the chapel it is safe to assume that the Italian Tony was the mason (see Pl. XI). *Helga photograph.*

The *Journal* too benefited from the involvement of the summer people. The energetic Dellenbaugh covered the games played by the Cragsmoor baseball team, and during a six-week trip to Iceland in 1906 he "consented to be the Icelandic correspondent to THE CRAGSMOOR JOURNAL."[7] When his son Frederick wrote long letters describing his Army experiences during World War I, the *Journal* published them. Articles by Martha Gay included critiques of Harriet Dellenbaugh's Saturday morning dramatic readings.

Describing the Cragsmoor summer colony in 1906, the editorial writer in the *Journal* found "a harmonious community . . . active-minded and deeply interested in the best art, literature, drama and music; so that mingled with the atmosphere of relaxation is also one of pleasant mental activity. These people have seen the world far and wide, yet they find the charms of Cragsmoor undimmed by comparison."[8] Despite the fact that six years later the *Journal* complained that life in Cragsmoor was becoming "too formal,"[9] very little changed there throughout the war years and beyond.

Fig. 12.   Interior of the chapel shown in Fig. 11. *Helga photograph.*

The impending demise of Cragsmoor as an art colony may be sensed in this passage from the August 6, 1928, *Mountain Echo*, the successor to the *Journal*: "Both summer and all-year residents of Cragsmoor congregated in the Barnstormers Theater . . . at the reception tendered to Mrs. George Inness, Jr. While everyone was glad to meet everyone else . . . a note of sadness hovered in the air, for we all realized that we were saying farewell to an honored friend and an invaluable member of our community. . . . There are rumors . . . that a club of engineers have bid for the Inness estate."

It was not, in fact, a club of engineers that bought Chetolah from Inness' widow, but a religious order which converted the large and elaborate mansion into a rest home. Today it is abandoned and decayed, brooding over the valley view that caused it to be built.

In 1928 Edward Gay, Eliza Greatorex, E. L. Henry, and Arthur Keller were dead. Carroll Brown and Dellenbaugh outlived them by only a few years. Until World War II some of the old guard continued to come to Cragsmoor, but by the time Charles Curran died in 1942, the day of the community of kindred souls that sustained the place as an art colony had long been over.

I would like to express my thanks to Kaycee Benton of Cragsmoor for sharing her extensive research materials with me in the preparation of this article. A list of other artists known to have spent summers at Cragsmoor will be found on page 1106.

* Carroll Brown died June 4, 1923.

1065

141

Pl. XI.   The Boulders, designed by Dellenbaugh and built for Judge Addison Brown (1830–1913) in 1898. In his *Autobiographical Notes for His Children* (Boyce, Virginia, 1972, pp. 10-11) Judge Brown relates that "the stone work was done by 'Tony' an eccentric Italian, whose treatment of the joints of the rough mason work were new in this region." The judge also noted that the front door and its surround were "taken from an old building, No. 69 Christie St., New York City, then recently torn down, but originally built about 1825. The carved wooden mouldings of the dining room were also taken from old torn down buildings in New York City." Considering the many sizes and shapes of the windows it is reasonable to assume that they were salvaged from the same sources as, possibly, were the ironwork on the lower roof and the colonnettes supporting the porch roof. In any event, the variety of building materials makes this one of Cragsmoor's more fantastic houses.

Fig. 13.   View toward the Chapel of the Holy Name and the monastery Ruhberg to the left of it. The photograph was taken c. 1887. Even at this time farming had largely ceased at Cragsmoor, and today these fields have been reclaimed by large trees and dense underbrush. *Collection of Mr. and Mrs. R. C. Ernst.*

Pl. IX. *Lanterns*, by Curran, 1913. Signed and dated at lower right, *Charles C. Curran, N. A., 1913.* Oil on canvas, 30 inches square. The summer residents of Cragsmoor habitually lit their way at night with lanterns such as the one shown here. The soft, romantic glow illuminates the painter's two children and Elizabeth Allen, a neighbor, and captures the magic of summer evenings remembered. *Benton collection.*

---

[1] Addison Brown, *Autobiographical Notes for His Children* (Boyce, Virginia, 1972), p. 4.

[2] *Cragsmoor Journal*, August 1905.

[3] In various summers the following members of the Salmagundi Club also visited Cragsmoor: Edward Dufner (1872–1957), Colin Campbell Cooper (1856–1937), and Edmund Graecan (1876–1949).

[4] Elizabeth McCausland, *The Life and Work of Edward Lamson Henry, N. A. 1841–1919* (Albany, New York, 1945), lists three pictures of weddings but none called *Wedding Party*. They are *A Wedding in the Early Forties, Colonial Wedding,* and *Country Wedding.*

[5] *Cragsmoor Journal*, August 1906.

[6] *Ibid.*

[7] *Ibid.*, July 1906.

[8] *Ibid.*, June 1906.

[9] *Ibid.*, August 1, 1912.

Pl. X. *Spring*, by Henry, 1904. Signed and dated at lower left, *E. L. Henry, May, 1904.* Oil on canvas, 11 by 20 inches. As a history and genre painter Henry left not only a record of what Cragsmoor looked like while he lived there, but a suggestion of what it was before it became an artists' colony. The Coddington cottage shown here was on the road from Ellenville to Cragsmoor. Mrs. Coddington is churning while Harry Cook, a local farmer, looks on. *Collection of Ruth Giriat.*

Cragsmoor, The Art Colony (?)

by Walter Little

Was Cragsmoor really an Art Colony or was it a nice place where people came to spend the summer? In 1920-21, there were fifty or more summer homes, six boarding houses, and one real hotel (*Cragsmoor Inn*). The people who came to these places began to arrive in late May or June, just for the summer, and leave for their real homes before cold weather arrived. Yes, we did have several artists in Cragsmoor but they, too, only came for the summer. These were the years that my older sister and I began to deliver milk to most of these homes and a couple of boarding houses.

Most of these buildings, including the hotel, were not built and equipped for cold weather living. By October, they were closed for the winter months to be reopened the following spring. When the snows arrived, most of these homes and boarding houses, even the *Cragsmoor Inn*, were pretty much isolated because most of the roads leading to these places were either privately owned or were owned more or less and maintained by the *Cragsmoor Improvement Association*, an organization formed and ruled by the summer residents only. The only maintenance was done in the spring and summer, nothing in the winter. Some time around 1940, the *Town of Wawarsing Highway Department* took over and maintained these roads.

According to my old Webster Dictionary, I don't believe that Cragsmoor really fit the description of an Artist Colony. This is just my opinion of Cragsmoor as an Art Colony and maybe, too, of some of the other people who made Cragsmoor their real home back then. After living there for the first 25 years of my life, I still live within less than 15 miles of Cragsmoor. I have a lot of fond memories of the wonderful people who made their home there and kept Cragsmoor alive during the cold, snowy winter months back then. (Having never used a typewriter and not owning a computer, I write the way people did in Cragsmoor back then.)

From Antiques Magazine
November 1978

Queries

EDITED BY ALLISON M. ECKARDT

AMERICAN ARTISTS who painted at Cragsmoor, New York, during the summer months in the late nineteenth and early twentieth centuries are the subject of an article in this issue (see pp. 1056-1067). Other artists known to have worked there are: George Rufus Boynton (1856–1945), Charles Francis Browne (1859–1920), Margaret Fitzhugh Browne (1884–1972), Alice Browning (1887–1916), Clarence K. Chatterton (b. 1880), Katherine C. Chipman (d. 1915), Sarah Eakin Cowan (1875–1958), Frank DeHaven (1856–1934), Esperanza Gabay, Charles Alden Gray (1857–1933), Eleanor Greatorex (b. 1854), Kathleen Honora Greatorex (b. 1851), Eugene Higgins (1874–1958), Martin Justice, Ernest Wise Keyser (1876–1959), Isabel Moore Kimball, James J. McAuliffe (1848–1921), Ross E. Moffett (1888–1971), Mrs. A. O. Moore, Dora Louise Murdoch (1857–1933), Arthur Parton (1842–1914), William S. Robinson (1861–1945), Franklin Lewis Schenck (1855–1926), Ella Bennett Sherman, Zulma Steele (b. 1881), Maria Judson Strean (d. 1949), and Ella Snowden Valk. Any information about them, including the whereabouts of any of their works, would be of interest.

BARBARA BUFF
27 Walbrooke Road
Scarsdale, New York 10583
KAYCEE BENTON
The Barnacle
Cragsmoor, New York 12420

In May of 1902, Mr. and Mrs. Anderson Polk came to Cragsmoor, New York, from New York City to stay at the boarding house called "Hermhut" which was owned and managed by Miss Abigail Kite. Miss Kite was a Quaker from Philadelphia, Pennsylvania. She was devoutly religious and thought the name Hermhut meant "Blessed by God." Others insisted it meant "Gentleman's Hat." I think they were teasing Miss Kite. Mr. and Mrs. Polk brought with them their six-month old son, David Stewart, and bought a half-acre of the Kite property with a four-room cottage at one end. The cottage was put on rollers and moved, intact, to the northern few yards of the property and there it is today in 1983.

My mother improved the house, but it is a seasonal dwelling with no cellar. A Pennsylvania carpenter named Mr. Penney built the cottage with all the inner walls made of wainscoting.

In 1906, I was born in May and before I was two-months old taken to Cragsmoor. Except for the summer of 1924 and the years just before our entering World War II, I have never missed a July and August. In my youth Cragsmoor was a really dedicated artists colony. The first artist I remember vividly was Carroll Brown. He gave me lessons in oil painting, once a week, when I was eight years old. Now I think I was too young, because we didn't have a very happy time. His landscapes were sensitive, subtle and cheerful and his technique was admirable. All those artists who peaked from 1900 to 1935 knew how to "draw." Not one fumbled, as I remember. So Carroll Brown's paintings were and are a delight. Mr. and Mrs. Miller, she nee Helen Tichenor, possessed many Carroll Browns in their home here in Cragsmoor and no doubt, young and older Tichenors have inherited them.

Three years before my lessons with Carroll Brown, I was very much aware of the artist Edward Gay. He was Irish, tall, thin, handsome, wore a Van Dyke beard and he and his small wife had nine children! Their house was west and downhill from Carroll Brown's. Mr. Gay was an artist of renown; he used his brushes and colors in the manner of the great Carot. Somber landscapes with wistful message to the viewer, of autumn to come all too soon. He liked cloudy skies, lonely little lanes and ponds amid uncultivated meadows. Cragsmoor was mostly meadows in those days. His paintings spoke; he was truly great; an artist's artist.

I suppose the most revered artist of the nation and the Cragsmoor colony was E.L. Henry. I knew him as a small, old man; sideburns on his cheeks and a very pleasant person. His studio was and is lovely. Very high ceiling and a magnificent skylight was the entire north wall. If he had children, I was unaware of it, but Mrs. Henry was the most appealing little old lady I ever saw. Distinctly, I remember an evening walk with her when I was five-years old. She was part seventy and I kept thinking, "How can anyone so old be so lovely?" I remember a sweet face and bright blue eyes.

E.L. Henry painted in great detail; right down to the shiny feathers of chickens pecking around. He used oils, but liked black and white sketches too. Hardly spare time scriblings, but exquisite works of art. Not being an expert

Memories
of the
Cragsmoor
Artist Colony

by

Julia Polk Hunsicker

Edited by Susan Houghtaling

Published by the Cragsmoor Free Library

Indian in New York City are two of Mr. Dellenbaugh's desert paintings, one on each side of the entrance. An almost naked Indian is facing you, bow and arrow at alert, and the background is the yellow desert sand and the great clear blue bowl of sky that one sees in the West.

There was a self-portrait of Dellenbaugh, very dashing, which hung in the Cragsmoor home for years. Eventually Mr. and Mrs. Dellenbaugh died, their one son does not return to my knowledge and new owners occupy the house. But I still love that house and my memories of lovely people.

Down the hill going Northwest lived an artist and family, the Arthur I. Kellers. Mr. Keller illustrated novels. If I remember correctly, when novels were published before World War I they were almost always illustrated. Arthur I. Keller's figures were full of action; his technique and anatomical knowledge were flawless. He had on hand period clothing if needed. He was a lovely, kind man with a second wife and lots of children.

His first wife had died and he was a widower with half-grown children. He married again, Miss Edith Mason from Newport, Rhode Island. Their first baby, Liona, was born in 1909. I was older but I played with Liona constantly from the time she could understand play. Three more babies appeared: David, Edith and Cecilia. So I was in and out of that home constantly summer after summer, and around 1920 I began to pose for him. He was very thoughtful in that he understood how posing in an action position becomes painful very quickly. So he gave me breaks constantly.

Once he was going to put some period clothing on me for an 18th century illustration and told me to take off my 20th century dress. I didn't want to since I was going through a prudish stage. Also I knew I had on a boy's undershirt. Why would my mother dress me like that? A hand-me-down from big brother? Also, though thin, I was old enough to have a girl's figure. I argued and suffered, but he won. He called me "silly" and finally, there I stood in panties and undershirt, and Mr. Keller painted away happily. He drew me frequently in a soft black pencil. His male model was his gardener, chauffeur and handyman, all in one person.

Mr. Keller was a handsome, dark-eyed man with a luxuriant moustache, lots of dark hair and full of vigor. But when he was in his forties, to our immense dismay and sorrow, he died of pneumonia in a few days. No antibiotics. The middle child of his first family, Edward Keller, was very talented in drawing. He liked to draw figures and faces. When I knew him he limited himself to portraits in sepia pencil. Eddy had to have a photograph of his subject to work from. He wouldn't work from real life.

Another artist who never achieved fame but may have, was Charles Peters. Charlie worked hard enough and he loved painting. But his career was professional house painting. He had a wife and four sons and couldn't give much time to his artistic work. Charlie was a real Cragsmoorian since his house served him every day of the year. So he had the opportunity to paint snow pictures, and they are charming. I doubt if Charlie went to art school. But he had a gift of knowing how to compose his landscapes. If a tree was in the wrong

-3-

and without research, I still am of the opinion that E.L. Henry is known and his work revered around the world.

George Inness, equally renowned, was before my time, but his son, George Inness Jr., lived in a gorgeous estate on the southern slopes of Cragsmoor overlooking Orange County. The back roads on the way to Walker Valley are very steep, but George Inness Jr.'s acres were fields and meadows open to the sun all year round. The mansion itself was a low profile building, all spread out; the formal French gardens, walls and steps and statues went gently downhill. Some fountains too. Cragsmoorians were invited on Tuesdays to a tea given by Mrs. Inness. The refreshments were served on a long table in Mr. Inness gallery with his own framed paintings around. The room was down a few steps from the hallway. It was large, beautiful and immaculate. It could not have been his studio, because artists' studios have one thing in common—they are messy. Sandwiches were served on a table with a lace cloth and gleaming silver dishes. Mrs. Inness was such a hospitable, lovely person that all the people of Cragsmoor always went to her "Tuesday." She was as big as her personality. I think 6 feet 1 inch and heavy too. I remember her in purple taffeta with a purple hat, looming over all the women and many men too. Mr. Inness was not her height.

Mr. Inness was genial and much loved. If he didn't equal his father in talent, he was still an awfully good painter. I can't forget how he captured sunlight in the woods. Any reader who likes to paint and who has tried to picture summer sunlight coming from heaven, through innumerable shining leaves, knows all too well what a job it is. George Inness Jr. could do it and so beautifully.

I had no personal relationship with Mr. and Mrs. Inness because I was very young when I went to the "Tuesdays." Just one of the Cragsmoor teenagers who loved to see the beautiful home and, of course, eat up everything in sight.

A real friend of mine was Frederick Dellenbaugh who lived nearby. Cragsmoor was bigger than it seemed. "Our end" of the mountain which seems to have begun with Judge Addison Brown's estate and extended to Hermhut was comprised of roughly a dozen families. The ladies "called" on each other from 4 p.m. on. There were no phones. A lady dressed very carefully at 4 p.m. and waited hopefully, I suppose. Everyone walked, so she called came silently and suddenly. Mrs. Frederick Dellenbaugh didn't call much but she gave great pleasure to her friends by conducting a reading every Saturday morning in her home. I think she read from Charles Dickens' novels.

Mr. Dellenbaugh was an artist, explorer, geologist and architect. Maybe he had other skills I never knew of. His own home in Cragsmoor (he being the architect) is about the loveliest house to live in imaginable. I lived in it for four winters and how I did enjoy it. The attic is floored and even in the worst weather is cozy. But the Dellenbaughs used it for a summer home.

As a boy of 16 he went through the Colorado River, a member of the first group of explorers to complete the journey in the Grand Canyon. The leader was a mature man named Major Powell. In the Museum of the American

-4-

place, move it, replace it with a little brook or a small house. Make your scene more appealing than it really is.

Charles Curran. I remember a plump, medium height man with so kind a disposition that everyone was his friend. Cragsmoor loved him and vice-versa. He had a child's red wagon in which he packed his painting needs and about every day he was off to Bear Hill. His ability to paint clouds was so unusually excellent that one stands before his pictures stunned and delighted

The first twenty years or so of the 20th century he had a pretty young lady, Dorothea Story, for a model. She was a fixture in the community, or so it seemed to me, a child Miss Helen Turner painted her also in "Girl With A Lantern." Mr. Curran had her pose on the rocks of Bear Hill in different kinds of weather. There is a picture we all know of a girl in a blue dress leaning against one of the boulders, and there are several children here and there. The day was an exquisitely cloudless hot dream. Indeed the whole week was, I remember well because I posed for that painting along with my friends Mary and George Lewis and Helen Butterick. Mr. Curran gave us breaks. But I was not a happy model. To lean on a hot rock under a boiling sun and to feel perspiration trickling down my neck and back, beginning to ache all over, wasn't my idea of the good life. I didn't pose for him much.

By the way, do Cragsmoorians know that he painted fine portraits? He painted a beautiful portrait of Mrs. Sturdevant, the owner of the Cragsmoor Inn, who when she sat for that painting was old but lovely. He painted a handsome portrait of a Mr. Welling, a great gaunt and handsome old man, an important person in New York City. I was 21 or 22 years old at that time. He and his sister came to the Inn, summer after summer, and I began to doubt their mortality. But alas, I am now their age and where they are, who knows?

The artist I knew best in Cragsmoor beginning in 1923 was Miss Helen Turner. Every weekday from 10 a.m. to noon I posed for her, all summer long. I kept at it, sporadically, until I was 24 years old and began to sell my own small oil landscapes and pastel drawings of little children's heads.

In the summer of 1923, I was 17. No beauty, but I did have a good complexion and light gold hair. I had a sturdy but slim figure and pretty legs. Miss Turner didn't care about legs at that time. She kept putting clothes on me that were size 40 and hats that must have been her grandmother's. So in her pictures of me and her other young models one sees that face, lots of hair, flowers in profusion and a dress. But, oh the life, color, brilliance, light and sparkle. She painted in mosaics and patches of color with the brushwork remaining rough. But all of a sudden, there was a gorgeous three-dimensional painting. The world honored her, a member of the National Academy, and I suppose, she asked any price she cared to.

She had one of the prettiest houses in Cragsmoor, the whole second floor to the North was her studio. I think she was one of the happiest people I've known. As she painted she danced and sang back and forth, near me, then back to the canvas. I thought of her as being odd but I loved her. Teenagers are often critical. She came from New Orleans, our only artist from Dixie, I think

I used to bicycle from home to Miss T's and with me went my fuzzy haired dog. She put up with him and once she painted us together. This is a fact. We sat on a porch bench side-by-side. The dog was painted roughly, a sort of hairy blob, but if he had known the honor of being in a Helen Turner painting, his little head would have swelled up. His little pink tongue panted from his tannish face. I wonder about that painting, who has it? (Ed. note: Chrysler Museum, Norfolk, Va.)

I want to mention Miss Patricia Gay's work. I remember best her brilliant still life's of flowers. They were dazzling. My daughter, Nina Hunsicker Lockwood of Rochester, N.Y., has a lovely Patricia Gay landscape of the Stone Church and grounds. Miss Gay worked for Tiffany & Co., New York City. She made gold leaf frames for paintings, large and small. She handled in her expert way the small, fragile, paper-thin leaves of gold, and when completed, the frame was a work of art, fit to surround the world's best in oils. Her frames, were unsuitable for water colors, etchings, drawings, etc.

In this long introduction (Ed. note: Julia wrote these memoirs to be an introduction to a history booklet. Fortunately, she wrote more than was required.) did I mention the paintings of Mrs. Sturdevant, the owner and manager of the popular Cragsmoor Inn? I never knew about her youth, her circumstances, her home, her schooling in art. She was my grandmother's age. But I found out in my teen years that not only did she manage to give her guests a delightful "home away from home" complete with lots of entertainment, but also superb food three times a day, suites for families, a tennis court, bowling alley, ballroom with stage, and in 1925 a beautiful 9-hole golf course plus putting green on the front lawn. She also had innumerable bridge tournaments complete with refreshments and prizes. At this time, she was not painting. Active as she was, she couldn't add hours to each passing day. Her paintings were sentimental, skillfully executed and perfectly delightful.

At present, my memory is drained. There were amateur artists doing their best to catch some aspect of the beauty around them. Miss Edith Browning painted tiny endearing landscapes and a nameless miniature portrait painter visited Miss Turner in 1921.

So Cragsmoor was once a truly important artists' colony. Snow closed it down in winter, before the blacktop roads and gasoline snow plows. But the summer returned and the summer homes opened their doors and windows to light and sunshine and leaves and flower gardens and one more happy season began. I loved the place and still do, even more

147

NOW, THAT'S TALENT!

Impressed we were in 2002 as we were travelling route 52 and saw several vehicles stopped at one of the turn-offs, only to find "Elvis in the field". It is such an amazing feat to create art by mowing/cutting a field of hay that we felt a great need to speak with or meet the artist and bestow on him the notariety he so well deserved. We had hoped to contact the "powers that be" to write an article or give "air time" to Roger Baker, whom we by now learned lives in Cragsmoor. But.....we didn't even know him!!

Later that day we called Eileen at the Cragsmoor Library to ask how we could go about contacting Mr. Baker and as luck would have it, he just happened to be in the library at that very moment. And, yes, we spoke to Roger, who politely declined our offer of making him a household name across the U.S.A., but it was so exciting just to speak with him.

A couple of weeks or more later, we were admiring the art on exhibit in the walkway between the Ellenville Library and the Terwilliger House Museum, when we heard a gentleman asking if Marie Bilney was present at the time. I was very surprised to hear my name called since I really wasn't acquainted with many folks in the Ellenville area at that time. I identified myself and was delighted to meet Roger Baker, in person, realizing a moment later that I had signed the guest registry in the art area.

In 2001 Roger cut the Statue of Liberty; in 2002 Elvis appeared; in 2003 Albert Einstein grew in the field and in 2004 Jimmy Hendrix played his guitar. Roger performs his artistry in late June or early July, annually, we hope, as we all look forward to seeing his latest creation.

Roger's talent can be seen in many places in Cragsmoor and Ellenville such as the sign at the Stone Church, the Top Shelf, the Lighthouse restaurant, the five panel mural on the old Ellenville National Bank, which is beautiful! and many others.

This Roger, is our small tribute to you because we feel that you are an amazing artist and individual and we will look forward to seeing what or who is next to liven up the field!!

The next few pages are pictures of a couple of R. Baker's "field cuts". Unfortunately, we were unable get copies of his other field works of art.

The following are to his credit:

2001 - Statue of Liberty

2002 - Elvis

2003 - Einstein

2004 - Jimi Hendrix

2005 - Indian Larry

Sign by Roger Baker in Cragsmoor, New York

Five panel mural by Roger Baker on the old Ellenville National Bank

AOL News

Explore AOL News [Go]

The Children of Angola
PHOTOGRAPHS BY SEBASTIAO SALGADO
Click Here
TIME

LIFE
BOOKSTORE
click here

RENT DVDS ONLINE!

TIME.com

HOME
NATION
WORLD
BUSINESS
ARTS
SCI-HEALTH
PHOTOS
MAGAZINE
ARCHIVE
COLUMNISTS
SPECIALS
DAILY E-MAIL
SUBSCRIBE
HELP
LIFE Magazine

Action
Comedy
Drama

SEARCH THE TIME ARCHIVE:

● Magazine ○ All of TIME.com

Topical Searches Sept. 11 Iraq Covers

> Try 4 issues of TIME free!
> Gift Subscriptions
> Magazine Customer Service

PROMOTION

TIME
GREEN CENTURY
A TIME special report on the state of the planet and how to save it
click here

TIME
GREEN CENTURY
click here

RELATED STORIES
The Official Elvis Website
Elvis on the Web

CNN: Tribute to a King
CNN

Friday, September 20, 2002

Person of the Week: Elvis Presley

Twenty-five years after his death, the King lives on in America's hearts

BY JESSICA REAVES

PRINT E-MAIL SUBSCRIBE

AT A GLANCE

Name: Elvis Aaron Presley
Profession: The King of Rock and Roll
Why We Chose Him: Two and a half decades after his death, Elvis remains an all-American phenomenon

Thursday, Aug. 15, 2002

SPENCER AINSLEY/POUGHKEEPSIE JOURNAL/AP

ELVIS LIVES... in Roger Baker's field in Ellenville, N.Y.

Wise men say only fools rush in
but I can't help falling in love with you.
Shall I stay
would it be a sin
If I can't help falling in love with you?
—Elvis Presley, "Can't Help Falling in Love"

Twenty-five years to the day after his death at the age of 42, Elvis Aaron Presley's name fairly droops under the weight of its acquired cultural significance. Briefly tagged a teen idol, the King of Rock and Roll swiftly transitioned into category-defying superstar. Today, college professors devote whole careers to examining Elvis's influence on America's cultural mores, his impact on American sexuality and most of all, our apparently unflagging passion for his music.

Even in death, Elvis's commercial success is unparalleled; he's sold more records (1 billion worldwide) than any other artist in history, and his estate is priceless. Given his spectacular popularity, it's easy to forget that when he first came on the national scene in the 1950s, Elvis was considered highly subversive.

Middle America was flummoxed by his singing, which didn't fit with the era's squeaky-clean bill of fare. It wasn't just his lyrics; it was what he introduced vocally — appropriating the blues and gospel styles of the African-American South, he brought "black" music to white Americans. Then there was the matter of his stage presence. Elvis Presley, the performer, was all about sex — it may have only been the suggestion of sex, but it was there all the same, in the sneer, the gyration, the raised eyebrow. And that unfettered sex appeal represented everything American parents wanted to suppress in the mid-1950s. Wanted to — but couldn't.

Born in 1935 in Tupelo, Mississippi, Presley showed an early aptitude for music. By the time he was 19, he was recording his own music, and at 21 he was an international star.

You ain't nothin' but a hound dog cryin' all the time
You ain't nothin' but a hound dog cryin' all the time
Well, you ain't never caught a rabbit and you ain't no friend of mine.
-"Hound Dog"

In 1956 and '57, Elvis appeared several times on television variety programs hosted by Ed Sullivan and Milton Berle. During his second appearance on the Berle show, he sang "Hound Dog" and engaged in a bit of his trademark hip swiveling. The broadcast generated shock nationwide, and sparked a flurry of hysterical press.

In 1957, the famously stiff Ed Sullivan, who'd once vowed never to have Elvis on his show, was so thrilled by his guest's effect on the show's ratings that he announced on camera, "I wanted to say to Elvis and the country that this is a real decent, fine boy." Such sentiments did not keep the network brass from issuing an historic decree to the cameramen: Elvis was to be shot strictly from the waist up.

The Elvis revolution was on — and as parents around the world quickly realized, the sultry crooner wasn't just a temporary distraction. As the singer's popularity exploded, his risque dance moves sent girls into paroxysms of excitement and his slightly suggestive half-snarl made mothers everywhere a little bit nervous.

Much as he loved music, Elvis also wanted to be an actor — a serious actor, like his idols, James Dean and Marlon Brando — but producers and directors kept sending him puff scripts. He appeared in 33 films, and while all of them were profitable, only a few (the mega-hits "Jailhouse Rock" and "King Creole" included) truly satisfied their star.

Well, since my baby left me,
I found a new place to dwell.
It's down at the end of lonely street
at Heartbreak Hotel.
—*"Heartbreak Hotel"*

The end came for Elvis during the 1970s, a time when no worthwhile American Dream stumbled to a halt without first exposing its dark side. Elvis, despite his tremendous success, is generally believed to have been a depressive, even, it has been suggested, manic-depressive, or bipolar. When he died in 1977 from a cardiac arrhythmia, his finances were in wild disarray, he was overweight and (it is believed) he had been abusing alcohol and prescription drugs for years. His private life was also a mess; his marriage to Priscilla Presley had hit the rocks four years earlier.

It is testament to Elvis's appeal that none of the less-than-glamorous trivia of his final years and death has marred his sheen. If anything, in fact, it's the excruciatingly human details of Elvis's sad last days that has endeared him to so many fans. It makes him more like one of us: life-size, even vulnerable. It even enhances the pleasure of listening to his music, reminding us that the voice that brought us all those heartbreakingly beautiful tunes belonged to a person who ached and longed and lost.

Get the Magazine
Try 4 Issues Free!
▸ Click here to try.

SEARCH THE ARCHIVE

[Search]

◉ Magazine ○ All of TIME.com

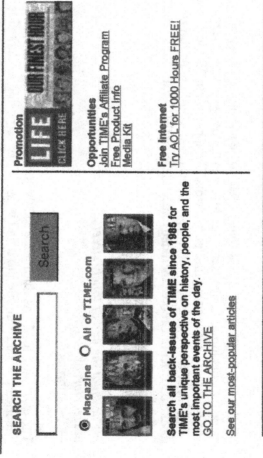

Search all back-issues of TIME since 1985 for TIME's unique perspective on history, people, and the most important events of the day.
GO TO THE ARCHIVE

See our most-popular articles

Promotion

LIFE
CLICK HERE

Opportunities
Join TIME's Affiliate Program
Free Product Info
Media Kit

Free Internet
Try AOL for 1000 Hours FREE!

http://www.time.com/time/pow/article/0,8599,337778,00.html

9/20/02

Village Views

Resnick Park & Baker Mural Dedicated

The Mayor and Board of the Village of Ellenville invited the public to join them on Sunday, November 21st, 2004, at the Village Park at the corner of **Main and Canal Streets** for a brief ceremony to dedicate the Park as the **Mildred & Louis Resnick Park** in their honor, and officially unveil Roger Baker's new mural on the wall of the old *Ellenville National Bank* building *(bottom right)*.

Upwards of 60 persons enjoyed the mild weather, and admired the mural while waiting for the ceremonies to begin *(photo above)*.

Mayor Jeffrey Kaplan *(below)* welcomed and greeted the assembled guests, which included numerous public officials and private citizens, many making it their special

business to attend as their way of thanking the Resnicks for their many contributions to the community over the years. Among those speaking were US Congressman Maurice Hinchey *(below)*, who recalled his early and continued association with the Resnick family starting

with work on Joseph Resnick's congressional campaign in 1964; NY Assemblyman Kevin Cahill *(below)*, who noted that this was one of the busiest corners in Ulster County,

and revealed his particular fondness for old, analog clocks, such as the one provided to the Park by *Provident Bank*, as they remind you not just of the present moment, but also where you've been and where you will be; Village Manager Elliott Auerbach *(top right)*, who called the

new mural an "autograph" for the community; artist-in-residence Roger Baker *(below)*, whose five-panel mural combines iconic views of the area with an iconoclastic and fanciful blending of past and

present elements; and Myrna Jargowsky *(below)*, who spoke on behalf of her parents and the Resnick family.

Mildred Resnick *(below)*, making her first public appearance since a recent hospitalization, was clearly overwhelmed with emotion as the plaque bearing the Park's new name was uncovered. The large "Shawangunk grit" conglomerate stone on which the plaque is affixed was personally selected by Baker and brought down the mountain by members of the *Ellenville Street Dept.*, who also provided cider and donuts for the crowd.

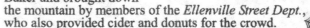

Local Artist, Roger Baker Exhibits at Aroma Thyme

By Norma Jean Wood

THERE ARE SIGNS EVERYWHERE. Big signs. Little signs. Glowing signs. Moving signs. Signs are a part of American culture. We see signs everyday. They guide us—act as landmarks. They spark our memories and take us back in time.

In today's technological-reliant world, signs have lost their character. Nothing stands out. There is no craftsmanship. No individuality. All vinyl. Screen printed. Computer graphics. What ever happened to the sign painter?

"Back in the 1930s, 1940s and 1950s every town had a sign painter," said local artist Roger Baker. "A handful of sign painters in each town and you could tell who made the sign by just looking at it."

Roger Baker is a Cragsmoor resident, and artisan specializing in hand painted sign design all his life. Originally from New Jersey, central shore area, he was drawn to the Ellenville area through hang gliding.

He is a hang gliding pilot and a member of the State of New York Hang Gliding and Paragliding Association. A celebrity due to his famous field cuttings seen from the mountain on Route 52 since 2000—he's

One of Roger Baker's hand-painted signs found at the Aroma Thyme Bistro on Canal Street in Ellenville.

Jamie and Marcus Guiliano, owners of Aroma Thyme Bistro in Ellenville, are featured in 'Celebrity Chefs' Tastings' at the Museum of the Hudson Highlands February 4.

painted motorcycles, he is also a master of gold leaf design—and his hand painted signs are exquisite.

What began as an idea to spruce up Hudson Valley's Best New Restaurant 2004, the Aroma Thyme Bistro of Ellenville (a favorite spot of Baker's) several of Baker's hand-painted signs were on loan to the restaurant from his wife's collection. (Whether a commissioned sign or one he does for pleasure, Baker's wife has first pick for her personal collection of his signs in their home.)

Familiar signs like "CLOCKS REPAIRED", "FRESH JAMS & JELLIES" and "THE WAWARSING CHOCOLATE CO." line the walls not only as decorations—but conversation pieces. The signage has gotten such positive responses an exhibit couldn't be far behind.

For the month of March, Roger Baker will hang dozens of his hand painted signs on the walls of the Aroma Thyme Bistro. The collection of works to be displayed includes some of his favorites made for

clients, pieces from his wife's personal collection, as well as a group of new ideas still in the works.

It's amazing how signs painted three weeks ago could look like antiques from the 1920's. He does his research in libraries, museums and anywhere else he can get his hands on pictures from old-time Ellenville. He described the town to me as a blank canvas. Baker's signs are taking 'Ellenvillians' on a trip back in time to places—real and imaginary, no one knew existed.

Seeing Baker's hand-painted signs jogged my memories of other old signs I've seen in my travels. Hand made signs really are a lost entity. Each sign I saw reminded me of something—created a fantasy. Had I seen it before? It's strange how a sign can stimulate our senses but it does everyday without our ever paying much attention.

Baker's sign exhibit will run throughout the month of March. Aroma Thyme Bistro is located at 165 Canal Street, Ellenville. For information call the Aroma Thyme Bistro 845-647-3000.

Delaware & Hudson

CANVAS

Community Arts: News, Views And Schedules

SERVING ORANGE, PIKE and SULLIVAN COUNTIES

Vol. 1 No. 7

February 2005 Edition

Complimentary

SPRING 2005 SIGN SHOW

by Roger B. Baker

1. Village Book & Periodical   oil wood   31.5 h x 25.5w   400
2. Equational Tourist w/equation   oil wood glass gold   20 h x 47 w   NFS
3. Physics Dept.   oil wood   10h x 32w   collection of c.flueck   NFS
4. Old Rare Books   oil wood   6h x 96w   345
5. Fishing Pier   oil wood   10h x 35w   180
6. Halibut Haddock Sole etc.   oil wood   20w x 75h   16 pcs.   900
7. Fountain Service   oil metal gold   18h x 36w   375
8. Trout Brook   oil wood smalts   9.25h x 120.25w   850
9. French Lake   oil metal   42 dia.   880
10. Cragsmoor Lettering Service   oil wood   22h x 27w   285
11. Reds Motorcycle Shop   oil metal   34 dia.   410
12. Cragsmoor Curio Shop   oil wood   11.5h x 34.75w   250
13. Pot Luck Supper   oil wood   16.5h x 50.5w   570
14. Shawangunk Huckleberries   oil wood   7.5h x 47w   175
15. Mandolins Bought & Sold   oil wood   8.25h x 39.75w   260
16. Fish Frog Chicken & Steak   oil wood   7.5h x 134.5w   420
17. Saxophones   oil wood   12h x 50w   290
18. Clocks Repaired   oil wood   11.25h x 48w   310
19. Paint & Art Supply Company   oil wood   10.5h x 38w   435
20. Indian Motorcycle Parts   oil wood   12h x 31w   collection of g. murello   NFS
21. Wheezers Crab Stand   oil wood   18.5h x 30.25w   290
22. Wawarsing Chocolate Co.   oil metal   42 dia.   1250
23. Town Hall   oil wood 8h x 40w   180
24. Cherries   oil wood   6.75h x 28.5w   125
25. No Vehicles Or Camping   oil wood   7h x 80w   collection of snyhgpa   NFS
26. Barn Sale   oil wood   18h x 36.25w   345
27. Cragsmoor Botanical   oil wood   29.75h x 47.5w   collection of c. peters   NFS
28. Pies & Jams   oil wood   5.5h x 43w   125
29. Fresh Cut Asparagus   oil wood   5.5h x 43w   125
30. Cranberries   oil wood   7.5h x 52.5w   155
31. Blueberries   oil wood   6.5h x 51w   145
32. Fishing & Hunting   oil wood   22h x 22w   285
33. Library w/arrow   oil wood smalts gold   12h x 45.5w   465
34. Fishing Rod & Reel Repairs   oil wood   5.25h x 79.5w   210
35. Bring It On Home   oil wood   10h x 83.75w   265
36. Billiards & Tap Room   oil wood gold   11.25h x 47.25w   485
37. Christmas Tree Farm   oil wood   26h x 32w   collection c. peters   NFS
38. Snedens Landing   oil metal   25h x 40w   485

39. Fresh Eggs   oil wood   18h x 45h   230
40. Nurses Office   oil wood   15h x 28.25w   165
41. Railroad Crossing   oil wood glass   40h x 68w collection c. peters   NFS
42. Circle Inn Dancing   oil metal   36 dia.   510
43. Principals Office   oil wood   19h x 28.25w   190
44. Micropterus Giganticus   oil wood   7h x 65w   collection of r. baker   NFS
45. Postcards/Kitchen/Sporting   oil wood   32h x 16w 3 pcs.   320
46. Pomegranate   oil wood   6.5h x 42w collection c. peters   NFS
47. Sandburg Sweet Shoppe   oil wood smalts gold 26.5h x 49w   895
48. Piano Tuning   oil wood   10.25h x 45.75w   365
49. Silent Auction Cragsmoor Artists   oil wood 10h x 72w   350
50. Bressler Dairy oil wood   8.5h x 56w   210
51. Basil/Garlic/Kale   oil wood   5.75h x 78w   collection c. peters   NFS
52. Persimmons   oil wood   10h x 50w collection c. peters   NFS
53. Land For Sale   oil wood gold   11.25h x 47w   450
54. Groceries & General M'dse   oil wood   12h x 31.5w collection c. peters NFS
55. Bements Market   oil wood   16.75h x 20w   collection h. peters   NFS
56. Picnic Grove   oil metal   33 dia   380
57. Please Keep To The Right   oil wood   5.75h x 24w   65
58. Peaches Pears Pies & Jams   oil wood   13h x 14.75w   135
59. MVC   oil glass gold   40h x 10w   collection m.vancleeve   NFS
60. Jullune   oil glass gold   40h x 10w   collection m. vancleeve   NFS
61. Napanoch Fly Shop   oil metal gold   42 dia.   1500
62. Shallots Garlic Parsley Basil   oil wood   collection j.weber   NFS
63. Peach Cobbler Pecan Pie   oil wood   8h x76w   collection j.weber   NFS
64. Parking For Our Customers   oil wood   10h x 40w   collection c.delfalco NFS

Ellenville Film Reaches The 2005 New York International Independent Film Festival

By Norma Wood

Indie Filmmaker, Gary Planken teamed up with local phenomenon, Roger Baker to create "The World's Largest Portraits" a reality documentary about the giant field portraits Baker has been creating on the hang-gliding landing zone in Ellenville since 2000. The film's focus is Baker's enormous Jimmy Hendrix he cut with only a few hand mowers, a tractor and some imagination.

In the film, to complement Baker's World's Largest Portraits is the "World's Smallest Sculptures" done by Dalton Ghetti. No-magnifying glasses needed as he uses needles for hand-made chisels and sculpts pencil graphite.

The film received an honorable mention

"The World's Largest Portraits"
Pre-screening show on April 10
Shadowland Theatre
845-647-5511

~~~

Roger Baker's 'Sign' exhibit
Opening Reception April 10
Aroma Thyme Bistro
845-647-3000

---

when it was on view with the festival in Miami this past February. It made it to Los Angeles in March and now is back in New York City for the festival April 28 through May 8. "The World's Largest Portraits" got a key slot; 8 p.m. Saturday night, April 30 at the East Village Theatre (The Old Fillmore East) in Manhattan. Tickets are only $10. Call 866-468-7919. After NYC

the film is on to Las Vegas.

The Shadowland Theatre in Ellenville will host a pre-screening Sunday, April 10 to run along side Baker's opening reception for his 'Sign' exhibit next door at the Aroma Thyme Bistro. For times call The Shadowland Theatre 845-647-5511 or Aroma Thyme Bistro 845-647-3000.

Indie Filmmaker, Gary Planken teamed up with local phenomenon, Roger Baker to create "The World's Largest Portraits".

Cragsmoor Journal Excerpts

PLAIN AS BLACK AND WHITE

It has been noted throughout this writing that Cragsmoor's citizenry was extremely active in all phases of community and social awareness, and so developed a library, schools, a post office, theater and held numerous social activities. So, wouldn't it be only a "natural" for a local newspaper to be born?

On August 14, 1903 the very first issue of The Cragsmoor Journal was printed and contained all the news that was fit to print -- Editorials, Society Notes, Church Notes, Local Happenings and, even humor. And, of course, advertisements! It was a wonderful little paper, so delightful and joyful to read that even today it brings much pleasure. Sadly, the final issue of The Cragsmoor Journal was dated September 18, 1916. The Mountain Echo followed beginning on July 9, 1928 but was published only briefly.

The following excerpts from The Cragsmoor Journal, highlight mostly visits to Cragsmoor by Carroll Butler Brown and his mother, since he is a very important person to us.

Pertaining to Carroll Butler Brown

1. Volume VI, No. 1 July 1908 - Social Notes Page 74A
   "Mr. Carroll Brown & Mr. Frederick Baker are a pleasant addition to
   the artist colony."
   This is also found in Volume VI, No. 2 August 1908 - Social Notes
   Page 74A

2. Volume VI, No. 3 August 1908 - Social Notes Page 77
   "Mr. Carroll Brown & Mr. Edward Gay are to be thanked for the pleasure
   they have given everybody by their weekly "At homes" where at the same
   time one could feast one's eyes on masterpieces in art. Occasional
   artistic discussions" were partaken of, which were enjoyed as well
   as benefited of by all. Mr. Brown has distinguished himself by his
   powerful sunset scenes."

3. Volume VII, No. 1 June 1909 - Society Notes Page 80 & Editorial
   "Mr. Carroll Brown and his mother were in the Pines Casino last year,
   and we are glad to see them again this summer." (Editorial)
   "Mrs. Brown and Mr. Carroll Brown were among the first comers."
   (Society Notes)

4. Volume VIII, No. 1 July 1910 - Society Notes Page 93
   Mr. Carol (Carroll) Brown and his mother arrived at Mrs. Hartshorn's
   Casino on May 3."

5. Volume IX, No. 1 July 1, 1911 - Society Notes Page 117
   "Mrs. Theodore F. Brown and her son Carol (Carroll) Brown, have been
   at the Casino since the 1st of May."

6. Volume X, No. 1 July 1, 1912 - Society Notes Page 143
   "Mr. Carol (Carroll) Brown and his mother also arrived in early May,
   and are again at the Casino."

7. Volume XII, No. 1 July 1 1914 - Society Notes Page 200
   "Mrs. Brown and her son, Mr. Carol (Carroll) Brown, were the first of
   the summer colony to arrive this year -- having braved the cold of
   May 1st."

8. Volume XIII, No. 1 July 1, 1916 - Society Notes Page 224
   "Mrs. Theodore Brown and Mr. Carol (Carroll) Brown were also among
   the early arrivals of the season. They have been in their cottage since
   May 10th." (According to records, the Browns summered in The Hartshorn
   Casino at this time, as they had not yet acquired property in Cragsmoor.)

14a

A college heart party was given at the Inn by Miss Winifred Sturdevant. to meet her friend Miss Pressinger. The pavilion was prettily decorated with lighted lanterns. flowers. and flags. Four colleges were represented. each person playing for one college. At every place were dainty tally cards and a little bunch of flowers representing in color one of ten colleges. After much fun and excitement. Princeton won the day. at which those Princeton men who had been represented slipped outside and gave a locomotor cheer. Light refreshments were then served. and thus the delightful evening came to an end.

Mr. Carroll Brown and Mr. Frederick Baker are a pleasant addition to the artist colony.

Miss Turner is having a sale of delightfully unique water colors. representing Cragsmoor scenes. at the Inn.

The following guests are staying at Mr. Charles Mance's: Miss H. E. Brown. Mrs. Hall and daughters. Miss Losee. Miss Rohrs. Mrs. Olsen and daughters. Captain Robert. Mr. and Mrs. Elliot. Miss Lulu Freileweh of New York; Mrs. J. S. King. Mrs. T. F. McCarthy. of Ridgewood. N. J.; Mrs. H. J. Fonda and Miss Fonda. Miss Miller of Newburgh.

Miss Margaret Harmon is visiting Miss Albert.

Miss Gertrude Wood. of Trenton. N. J., is visiting her grandmother. Mrs. Rushmore.

Miss Mary Woodruff is to be Miss Ham's guest at the end of August.

Mr. and Mrs. Frank M. Tichenore. of Mt. Vernon. are in Mrs. Keir's cottage. All are looking forward to the time when Mr. and Mrs. Tichenore and son and daughter will be "Cragsmoorians" in the true sense. namely, possessors of their own home.

☞HEATHCOTE HALL. Scarsdale. New York—the Misses Lockwood's collegiate school for girls. Beautifully located among the hills of Westchester County. 40 minutes from Grand Central Station. General course of study. offering fullest opportunities in Literature. Languages. Art and Music. Certificate admits to leading colleges. Outdoor life a specialty. Send for catalogue.

We regret the departure of Father Dana. whose return to Cragsmoor was a pleasant feature of this season. We also extend a hearty welcome to the Rev. Father Sweatland and his wife. for whose recent bereavement we feel the keenest sympathy.

In the evening of August 7th, Mrs. Fox gave a vaudeville in her casino. for the benefit of one of the Philadelphia charities. The program was as follows:

Kipling. Reading	Miss Cowing
Violin	Miss Ham
Kipling. Song	Mr. McClelland
Ophelia	Miss Leavitt
Monologues	Miss Schenck
Song	Miss Prahl
Guitar	Miss Hagedorn
Recitation	Miss Maynard

HUMOROUS ?

Kind Mrs. Brown. wishing to console Willie upon the death of his father. said: "Dear little boy. what were your father's last words?"

The much disgusted Willie: "He didn't have none: ma was there to the finish."

JOHNNY'S CONFESSION

"Why, Johnny, dear. how very queer.
    That you should be in bed!
The sun is high up in the sky."
    Dear Johnny's mother said.

"You must be very ill. indeed.
    To go to bed at noon;
We'll have the doctor in to see
    You very. very soon.

"Put out your tongue. I'll feel your pulse."
    The anxious mother cried—
"It must be measles. or the croup."
    Poor Johnny's mother sighed.

*   *   *   *   *

"No. muvver dear. jus' look a' here.
    I really am not ill;
I don't need squills er ipecac.
    Er any kind o' pill.

"I fought I'd have a little fun.
    W'en you wuz gone away.
So I took ve hose out in ve yard.
    An' turned it on t' play.

"An' nen I couldn't turn it off.
    An' ve yard got awful wet—
It mus' 've made a lake by now.
    Fer I guess it's runnin' yet.

"An' nen I just got nearly starved
    Fer sumpin' good t' eat;
Do you fink ver is a hole in me
    F'm my mouf down to my feet ?

"So I went into ve suller.
    'Cause 't was vewwy handy by.
An' vare I found a pot uv jam
    An' a piece er two uv pie.

"An' nen I 'membered where I wuz.
    An' what I'd been about;
An' my feet wuz awful. awful wet.
    An'—you wuz all gone out.

"So I stealed upstairs and found a switch.
    An' spanked myself. I did;
An' nen I took my wet clo's off.
    An' inter bed I slid.

"Now. muzzy. wuz n't 'at just right
    An' what y'd have me do?
I fink I've caught a nawful cold—
    A-chew! A-chew!! A-chew"

We wish to recall to the minds of old Cragsmoorians that on August 14. 1905. was the sixth anniversary of the CRAGSMOOR JOURNAL.

74A

During August a Bridge Tournament was given at the Inn. The first prize was won by Mrs. George Glaenzer.

On the 31st of August. Mrs. Sturdevant gave a delightful tea in her studio, to exhibit some pictures of Miss Browne. Miss Browne's specialty is work on cattle. The exhibit was an extremely interesting one, and the afternoon was much enjoyed by all.

Miss Helen M. Turner has done some noteworthy work in painting this summer. Attention is particularly called to two of her pictures—one a moonlight scene, the other a view of Miss Dellenbaugh's porch. Miss Turner has attained some marvelous effects in both these pictures.

The collection of miniatures done by Miss Katherine C. Chipman has greatly increased over the summer. Miss Chipman's fine style may be seen in each one.

Mr. F. Baker has been at work on some interesting landscapes, all of which are typical Cragsmoor scenes.

Mr. Carroll Browne and Mr. Edward Gay are to be thanked for the pleasure they have given everybody by their weekly "At homes," where at the same time one could feast one's eyes on masterpieces in art. Occasional "artistic discussions" were partaken of, which were enjoyed as well as benefited of by all. Mr. Browne has distinguished himself by his powerful sunset scenes. Mr. Gay's ever-wonderful landscapes—in particular, his work on rocks—causes one to acknowledge him the great master that he is.

Mr. E. L. Henry has been at work as usual on some interesting pictures, all of which reveal the charming atmosphere peculiar to his paintings.

Mr. Charles Curran has perhaps done more this summer, in number and variety, than any other artist. His exquisite portraits and his delightful scenes of outdoor life, as well as his numerous landscapes, have given the community never-to-be-forgotten memories.

We regret very much that the illness of Mr. George Inness has prevented him from enlarging to any extent his collections of wonderful landscapes.

Mrs. S. Von Eltze closed the social season on Friday afternoon, September eleventh, by giving one of the most delightful teas of the summer in her charming home, Eltz Khue.

Mrs. Slieght and three of her pupils. Miss Marie LaDue, who starred in the "Isle of Spice" last season. Mr. Piersol and Mr. Yagger, have been at The Pines for three weeks. The pleasure which they have been giving the Cragsmoorians by singing for them, we sincerely hope will be repeated another summer.

We wish to express the regret the Cragsmoorians felt that the vacation of Mrs. Harriet Otis Dellenbaugh was unavoidably cut short. May better luck attend both Mrs. Dellenbaugh and Cragsmoor another year.

Mrs. Sturdevant has delighted all by her charming traits, principally of children painted in the open.

HEATHCOTE HALL. Scarsdale, New York—The Miss Lockwood's Collegiate School for Girls. Beautifully located among the hills of Westchester County — min from Grand Central Station. General course at offering fullest opportunities in literature languages and music. Certificate admits to leading colleges door life a specialty. Send for catalogue.

The Cragsmoor Improvement Association

There are a great many in a growing place like Cragsmoor that require the cooperation of all the residents. There being no village organization and the place not requiring it, a plan was proposed for formation of an improvement society, such as is in successful operation in other communities. A meeting of the real estate owners of Cragsmoor was therefore called for September at the "House-of-the-Four-Winds," the home of Miss Cowing, which was placed at the disposal of the committee formation.

A large number of the real estate owners attended this initial meeting, and articles of association adopted. These articles provide that only real estate owners, not minors, are eligible for membership in the association. The officers elected were: President, Charles Curran; Vice-President, Dr. Emmet Densmore; Secretary, Mrs. B. Curtis; Treasurer, F. S. Dellenbaugh; and an Executive committee of five, two being ex officio, the President and Treasurer the other three being Mrs. Edward Gay, Mrs. S. Sturdevant and Mrs. Harriet L. Keir. The meeting adjourned the following Thursday, Sept. 10th, to meet at the same place. At this adjourned meeting by-laws were adopted fixing annual dues at one dollar, and otherwise regulating the workings of the association. Suggestions were made for the executive committee concerning the expenditure of the money on hand. This money was received from those who had previously arranged entertainments, so that the committee has in the treasury a considerable sum. A communication was received from the management of Cragsmoor Inn concerning the improvement of the old long or Horsedale road at lenville so that it will be available for the use of autoists etc. To effect this a large number of watercourses will have to be removed and culverts substituted. The Inn offered to contribute a goodly sum towards this end. Dr. Densmore offered a hundred dollars, and the Association agreed to appropriate about $200 more for the purpose. Other suggestions were lamps in the dark spot on the road near the post-office, the repair of the road from the Morgan cottage to the Episcopal chapel, the placing of receptacles here and there for waste paper and rubbish, and some minor matters, all of which the Executive Committee will carry out.

The Cragsmoor Journal

PENDLETON SCHENCK, Editor   Published Monthly   Telephone Call: Cragsmoor

Vol. VII., No. 1   CRAGSMOOR, N. Y., JUNE, 1909

Editorial

In the CRAGSMOOR JOURNAL of August 14, 1904, there was a long article about Cragsmoorites. Since then many new people have added their names to Cragsmoor's list, and many changes have taken place. At that time Mr. and Mrs. Edward Gay were about to finish their new house "Gayland," to-day it is one of the most picturesque homes of the Mountain. Mrs. Hartshorn put up a garage in 1905, which was opened by a vaudeville for the benefit of the roads. Road Committees have been formed, new roads have been opened, which are all for the good of the place. Entertainments have been held each year at the Cragsmoor Inn, the proceeds from which have always gone for the improvement of Cragsmoor. On the ridge beyond the Barnacle fine new houses have been put up. Last year Mrs. Halsey Wood of Philadelphia, built a cottage there. In front of it, down the hill, Miss Faries and Miss Davis erected a cottage. This year Mr. C. C. Curran's new house is under way. From these cottages a grand expanse of the Mountains is seen. Miss Cowing's "House of the Four Winds," which was built last Summer, is one of the show places of Cragsmoor. Beyond her cottage in the midst of the old Bleakley fields, Miss Ham's attractive cottage "Midfields" is beautifully located. Her new strawberry beds are the envy of the mountain. On the knoll back of Miss Dellenbaugh's "Orchard Cottage," Mrs. Von Eltz and Dr. Hawley have their new cottages. Since last Summer Mr. John Beckmann has sold his store to Mr. W. R. Garritt. Mr. Alexander Terwilliger is putting up a bowling alley near his house. Mr. John Terwilliger has put up a house on the site of his old cottage. Mr. and Mrs. Long of Brooklyn, have erected a cottage by the Crow's-nest Tree, which is back of the Inn. This Tree marks the highest point of Cragsmoor land. The Misses Turner have been on the Mountain for several years occupying Miss Brodhead's corner cottage. Captain Robert comes back every year. He is a great walker, and is an authority on the Mountain paths. Mr. Ernest Wood has moved his cottage to the edge of his lot, giving a more extended view. Substantial houses which have gone up in the past few years are: Mr. Mumm's, Mr. Clark's, and many others on that side of the Mountain. Mr. Carroll Brown and his mother were in the Pines Casino last year, and we are glad to see them again this Summer. Mr. McKinney of Pine Bush, bought the Wray cottage last season, and is making many improvements. The Cragsmoor Inn has been greatly improved in the last five

years by the building of a large pavilion which joins the main house by a covered porch. Below is the casino with a bowling alley. Every Saturday evening the Inn guests and cottage people assemble for dances. Mr. and Mrs. Compton occupy the Inn cottage. People who have been at the Inn year after year are: Mr. & Mrs. Brachvogel with their son and daughter, Mr. Whiteside, Mr. Harlan Pratt, Mr. and Mrs. Duncan and family, and many others. Mr. and Mrs. Inness's place is a beautiful spot on the Mountain. "Chetolah" can be seen from the train before entering the tunnel at Bloomingburg. There is no end to the improvements which Mr. and Mrs. Inness make to their place. The joy of the Cragsmoor of to-day, as of the Cragsmoor of earlier days, is the fact that everybody knows one another so well. Let the motto to Cragsmoor be "Friendship."

Society Notes

The Cragsmoor season of 1909 began early in May.

Mrs. Gay opened "Gayland" on May 9th for the summer.

Miss Sarah Morgan and Mr. Pendleton Schenck arrived at "The Knoll" on May 14th.

Mr. and Mrs. Henry came on May 15th.

Mrs. Brown and Mr. Carroll Brown were among the first comers.

Miss Chipman has been on the Mountain since April.

Mrs. Dellenbaugh and Miss Ham were up for a week in May. Mrs. Dellenbaugh formally opened "Endridge" the first week in June. Miss Ham will return after she has made some visits in Rhode Island.

The early Spring found Mrs. Bleakley happily settled in her Mountain home.

"Chetolah" has been opened since early in May, and is in running order. Mrs. Inness's daughter, Mrs. B. Ellsworth will occupy one of the cottages on the place.

On May 21st the doors of the "House of the Four Winds" were unlocked and Miss Cowing walked in to open her season with two guests, Miss Agnes Cowing and Miss Eddy of Brooklyn. Mrs. James Cowing followed a few days later.

Mrs. Charles B. Foote, Miss Isabel Foote, and Mr. Hastings Foot of New York, have taken Mrs. Clay's cottage for the summer. In June, Mrs. Foote's father, the Rev. Thomas Hastings, LL. D., and Miss Hastings will be their guests.

- 80 -

The Cragsmoor Journal

FOUNDED BY PENDLETON SCHENCK

JULIUS T. VON ELTZ, Editor   Published Semi-Monthly   Telephone Call : Cragsmoor

Vol. VIII., No. 1   CRAGSMOOR, N. Y., JULY, 1910

Editorial

Once more. as in 1908. Mr. Pendleton Schenck has deserted Cragsmoor and the JOURNAL. leaving the latter in the hands of Mr. Julius T. von Eltz.

Although this is the present editor's first attempt in the Elysian fields of journalism. he has decided to enlarge the publication of the paper to six issues.

Readers of the JOURNAL will readily see the advantage of this as affording plenty of space for the many social events of Cragsmoor. several of which. in former years. have had to be omitted through lack of room. This enlargement of the publication means of course much additional work. and the JOURNAL will gladly welcome contributions of any kind whatsoever. The editor will appreciate any notices of guests and social events.

DEAR EDITOR

I wonder if you know the meaning of "gerem pani goozle." It is Hindustani for "hot water bath." and was the first thing I learned out there. The word "goozle" does not sound euphonious to unaccustomed ears. but it is the magic word that makes life endurable in India—that topsy turvy land where you get up in what seems to be the middle of the night to take your horseback ride. and go to bed in the middle of the day. Where you jump. if one exclaims. "The sun is shining on you." as if you were bitten by a tarantula—for in India the rays of the sun are fatal.

Mohammedans and Hindus have many. curious customs. A Hindu is never permitted to see the face of his daughter-in-law. We visited a Hindu family where the greatest ingenuity was exercised in veiling and unveiling the daughter-in-law —a bride. The bride was fair. fat. and probably fourteen. and was perhaps a real Hindu Gibson girl. but our private opinion was that the father-in-law did not lose much in not being permitted to gaze upon her features. Before we made this visit our host was requested not to offer us refreshments as our caste did not allow us to partake of their food. All went well until we came to leave. when two servants approached carrying large perfectly flat straw baskets. filled with fresh and dried fruits. flowers. and on the top of one a bottle of champagne. As we drove along. we were painfully conscious of the bottle perched on the apex of the basket and held aloft by the proud and admiring footman. It is needless to say that our return home was through a labyrinthian maze of narrow and obscure streets.

You wanted one or two side lights on life in India. that fascinating country. but if I keep on you will call me a monopolist and never ask me to write for you again. so goodbye. Yours faithfully.

BELLE DELLENBAUGH.

Society Notes

All are eagerly looking forward to Mrs. Hartshorn's arrival on the mountain. which is still undecided.

Miss Chipman has been on the mountain since April 31.

Mr. Carol Brown and his mother arrived at Mrs. Hartshorn's Casino on May 3.

We are glad to be able once more to number Miss Dellenbaugh among our cottagers. She has been much missed during her two years absence.

Miss Dellenbaugh expects as a guest on July 1. Mrs. John Druar.

Gayland was opened on May 28. Mrs. Gay had as guests for a few days Miss Helen Gay and Mr. Walter Learned.

Winahdin was opened on June 3. Mrs. Curran has had as guests since June. her mother and father. Mr. and Mrs. Wickham of Ohio. and Miss Bessie Smith of East Orange. N. J. Miss Smith intends to sail for Europe on July 0.

Mr. Louis Curran has been spending a few days in Cragsmoor. He expects to leave soon for the South.

Mrs. Frederick Adams has again rented Mrs. Keir's cottage for the summer. and has as a guest her sister. Miss Margaret King of Norfolk. Va.

Captain Robert. who has so long boarded with Mrs. Mance. is this summer to be at Lake Minnewaska

We are glad to know that Mrs. Burt. who occupied Miss Dellenbaugh's cottage last summer. is to be with us again. She has rented the Knoll for the summer

Mrs. Allen and her two daughters have taken El Morichal for the summer.

On June 18 the chimney of the Cragsmoor Inn was struck by lightning. With the exception of two pieces of brick being knocked off. no damage was done.

Miss Julie Husson has rented Mrs. Henry's smaller cottage. I-e-nia. for the summer.

Judge Brown and his family have been on the mountain since June 14.

Franklin Nordoff of California is visiting Addison Brown.

The Cragsmoor Journal

FOUNDED BY PENDLETON SCHENCK

JULIUS T. VON ELTZ, EDITOR
ELEONORE VON ELTZ ASSOCIATE EDITOR

Published Semi-monthly

TELEPHONE CALL
CRAGSMOOR

Vol. IX., No. 1   CRAGSMOOR, N. Y., JULY 1, 1911

Editorial

In this first editorial of the year, we think it only fair to speak a good word for the Cragsmoor Improvement Association. This hard-working organization has accomplished much during the past year, as all will realize if they compare the bumpy, dusty roads of last summer with the smooth shale ones of this, and the former rough trail to Bear Hill with the fine new road along which "picnickers" can go without fear of stumbling and casting their provisions to the winds. All this has of course made a large hole in the Association's treasury, and though Mr. Curran, Mrs. Keir, Mrs. Curtis and the other officers are fairly aching to improve Cragsmoor for you, the necessary funds are lacking. Plainly, it behooves the local talent to do something. If you know of any good skit or play which Cragsmoorians could give for the benefit of the Association, or if you can "make up" and give monologues, dance fancy dances, or do "stunts" of any kind, please report to the Association, and help to start things going.

Just one word more, before you pass on with a sigh of relief (?) to "Society Notes": Please begin the summer right by not buying paint with which to deface the rocks with names and dates—— such inscriptions are for tombstones, and no one wishes to make a cemetery of Sam's Point or Bear Hill. Above all, if you must paint, don't cause any of your friends distress by posting up their names without their permission. On the whole, the safest way will be to leave all decorating to Cragsmoor artists.

Society Notes

Mrs. Curran arrived at Winahdin on June 5th. Mr. Curran's father, Judge W. T. Curran of Ohio, is to be their guest for the summer.

We are happy to learn that Mrs. Burt is to be with us again, occupying the "little Brown cottage" for the summer.

Eltzruhe was opened on June 3th. Mr. William Dea. is the guest of Mrs. von Eltz.

Mr. Demetre and his family are again occupying the Clay cottage.

Mr. Baker and his family have returned to Cragsmoor, and are occupying one of Miss Brodhead's cottages.

Mrs. Hitchings and her daughter, Miss Marjorie Hitchings, Dr. and Mrs. Lewis and their family, and Mr. and Mrs. Munson and family, and Mr. and Mrs. Maltby and family are all occupying cottages in the Brodhead Grove.

Mrs Browning and her daughters have been on the mountain since the first week in June.

We are sorry to say that Miss Helen Turner will not be with us this summer, as she will be traveling through Italy. Miss Laurette Turner, with her sister-in-law, Mrs. Turner, will occupy the cottage.

Miss Cowing arrived at Cragsmoor on May 17th, bringing with her as guests Misses Helen and Katherine Dudley. At present the visitors at "House of the Four Winds" are: Miss Murdoch, Mrs. and Miss Thurston and Miss Agnes Cowing. Dr. Northrop also has visited there twice, in order to watch the building of his house.

Mrs. Theodore F. Brown and her son, Mr. Carrol Brown, have been at the Casino since the first of May.

We are all glad to hear that Miss Ham is expected in Cragsmoor about the 10th of July. Miss Ruth Dudley is to be her guest for the remainder of the summer.

Mrs. Gay arrived at "Gaylands" on May 18th. Her daughters, Misses Ingovar and Helen Gay, are visiting her for two weeks.

The Misses Peters returned to Mrs. Henry's cottage, "Shinglenook," on June 9th, and at present are being visited by Miss Eastman.

Mr. and Mrs. Henry were at Na-pee-nia during the first week in May, and permanently opened the cottage on June 7th.

Miss Husson arrived at I-e-nia on June 22d.

Mrs. Bleakley has been on the mountain since the last of April. She returned to the Mance on June 28th, when Mrs. Suydam and her family arrived.

Miss Dellenbaugh has been in Cragsmoor since May 5th.

Mr. Guy Mount has just graduated from the medical college of Columbia University, and will be engaged in hospital work during the summer.

Mr. _____ the family arrived to their cottage on May 27th.

During the last week in May, Miss Feary and Mrs. Harold

We are glad to extend a hearty welcome to Mrs. Fox, who has been absent from Cragsmoor for several summers. Mrs. Fox and Master Jack Hilliard arrived at Miss Kite's on the 7th of June and moved into the Bungalow on July 1st.

Mrs. Keller made one or two flying visits to Cragsmoor in May for the purpose of overseeing the alterations which were being made on her cottage. The Kellers arrived en masse on June 10th, and are greatly pleased with the new extension and the addition of a tennis court.

Dr. Northrop visited Cragsmoor the first week in June, but The Porches was not opened for the summer until Mrs. Northrop's arrival on June 16th.

It is with regret that we announce that Miss Dellenbaugh has again deserted Cragsmoor for Europe. We are glad to say, however, that Orchard Cottage is occupied by Mr. and Mrs. Benedict, who last year were at The Knoll.

The Misses Turner arrived at Takusan on June 4th, and have as guest over the 4th of July Miss Louise Cushman of New York.

The Brownings followed closely on their heels, and established themselves in their cottage on June 5th.

This year Mrs. Hobbie and her family are at the Clay Cottage, instead of Ruhberg.

Mr. Long and his daughter came to Cragsmoor on June 15th, and Mrs. Long followed on the 21st, bringing with her Miss Edna Aller, who will be her guest for the summer.

Miss Kite was one of the early comers this spring. She arrived May 6th and opened her house on June 6th. At present some of her guests are Mrs. and Miss Clay, Mrs. and Miss VanKirk and Misses Perry and Copeland.

Mrs Wood opened the Rushmore cottage on June 19th, and was joined by Miss Gertrude Wood and Mr. Rushmore on the 22d.

It gives us great pleasure to welcome the Alberts back to Cragsmoor after their absence of a summer. Miss Armstrong is now the guest of Miss Hilda Albert.

For the first time in several years Dr. Harley will be at Windy-Hearth for the entire summer. She arrived on June 18th, bringing with her Mrs. James Sandwin, who remained her guest till June 27th.

Mr. and Mrs. Dellenbaugh returned to Endridge on May 17th, and expect to be able to spend more time here than usual. Mrs. Dellenbaugh was absent from Cragsmoor last week, giving a reading of a Spanish play at the summer home of Mrs Scribner.

Mr. Carol Brown and his mother also arrived in early May, and are again at the Casino.

Miss Emily Wood and Mr. Halsey Wood opened Blythewood on June 18th. Mr. Alexander Wood joined them on the 30th, and Mrs. Wood is expected soon. Mrs. C. B. Berkeley is a guest at Blythewood for the summer.

Judge Brown arrived at The Bowlders the 3d of June, but on account of illness in the family, Mrs. Brown did not reach Cragsmoor until the last week in June.

Mrs. Tichenor made a short stay at her cottage in May and came up with her family on June 20th for the summer.

Miss Buxton and Miss Husson opened I-e-nia early in May. They visited last week at Lake Mohonk.

Mr. and Mrs. Henry were also early comers, arriving at Na-pee-nia on May 5th.

This summer the Prahls' house, El Morichal, will be occupied by Mr. and Mrs. Almirall and their family. The Almiralls were at the Inn during the summer of 1909, and we are glad to have the opportunity of welcoming them to our cottage colony.

To Mrs. McAfee, a newcomer, and her guest Miss Smith we also extend a hearty welcome. Mrs. McAfee is spending the summer at Langundo.

Mr. and Mrs. Inness, except for occasional absences, have been at Chetolah all winter. The first of Mrs. Inness's teas, given in honor of the Rev. Dr. Mix and his daughter, took place on July 2d, and was enjoyed by all on the mountain.

It is with genuine pleasure that we greet Mrs. Burt and Capt. Ralph. They arrived at the Parsonage on June 20th, and expect to be at Cragsmoor all summer.

The Misses Peters are again at Shinglenook, and have as guest Miss Eastman.

Mr. and Mrs. T. Browne and family returned to Cragsmoor the first week in June.

Mr. and Mrs. Gilbert and their daughter are occupying Fairview, one of Mrs. Keir's cottages. The other one, Edgewood, is occupied by Miss Ring and some friends.

Some of Mr. and Mrs. Mance's guests are: Miss Beebe, the Rev Dr. Eldridge Mix and his daughter, Miss Grace Mix, Miss Weinacht and Miss Mats.

Mrs. Lewis is again in Miss Brodhead's corner cottage. The other members of the colony in the grove are the Hoffmans and the Maltbies.

We are glad to say that, although Mrs. Glaenzer went abroad the last of May, expecting to stay in Paris until August, the charms of Cragsmoor have lured her back before that time. She is now at the Inn with Mr. Glaenzer, who has been here since May 27th.

Others of the Inn's guests are: Dr. and Mrs. Savage, Mr. W. E. Blackburn and family, Judge S. W. Clark and family, Mr. and Mrs. F. C. Newhouse, Miss Louise Field, Miss I. V. Martin, Mrs. S. D. Allen, Mr. and Mrs. Tappan and Miss Erkenbrecher.

We must not forget to mention Miss Ham's tea, given on June 22d in honor of Mr. Post. Aside from the fact that the guest of honor was so busily engaged chasing butterflies that he neglected to appear until his guests were leaving, the tea was counted a great success.

Lessons ... this summer. For particulars please address Miss Emily H. Wood, Box 36, Cragsmoor

The Cragsmoor Journal

FOUNDED BY PENDLETON SCHENCK

Published Semi-Monthly

ELEONORE VON ELTZ, EDITOR
LUENNA VON ELTZ, ASSISTANT EDITOR

Vol. XII., No. 1   CRAGSMOOR, N. Y., JULY 1, 1914

Editorial

"This our first editorial of the year" is a distressingly difficult one to write for the reason that we are some hundreds of miles from Cragsmoor and too much cut off from the community life to make sage comments on the current happenings. The gentle reader is thereby spared something, but even so must undergo a milder form of torture, for we promised the other members of the editorial staff (kindly notice - new Journal heading) to lead off in the first issue. The Assistant We (or perhaps "wee" is nearer the mark) has in turn guaranteed to supply all the rest of the copy for the issues of July 1st and 15th and August 1st. Being of a generous nature, she will probably allow any or all of you to join her in this pleasant pastime. Unlike Tom Sawyer she will not even exact a price for the privilege.

With this brief word of introduction we joyfully withdraw for a vacation of six weeks and allow her a clear field for action.

"With glee we warn her from afar;
    The paper's hers to make or mar."

Society Notes

Mrs. Browne and her son, Mr. Carol Browne, were the first of the summer colony to arrive this year—having braved the cold of May 1st.

Mr. and Mrs. Henry, are staying in Ellenville about two weeks opened Nepee-nia on May 14th.

On May, 27, the Misses Frances, Marion and Elizabeth Peters took possession of Shinglenook, Miss Margaret Lawrence was their guest for the first two weeks and Miss Sally Peters is expected the first week in July.

Mr. Mance has been enlarging his house this year to great advantage. His guests for the present are: Mrs. de Percin, Miss Sylvia Sherman, Miss Tiator and Mr. and Mrs. Edmund Greacen with their two children. Mr. Greacen is a well known New York artist.

Miss Anna Boll and Miss Helene Boll with her friend, Miss Mills will spend the month of July at Langundo.

Mrs. Mumm opened her cottage on June 18th.

Miss Feary has been on the mountain since May 21st. Miss Ruth Feary, her niece, arrived on June 4th for a short visit. Mrs. Ahnon Millard of Troy has been her guest for a few days. Miss Davis is expected on July 3d and Miss Feary will sail for Norway the fourteenth of July.

Miss Buxton and Miss Husson arrived the latter part of May. Miss von Eltz was their guest for a week while opening Eltzruhe and returned on June 9th with the rest of the family. Until August 1st Miss von Eltz will be in Wisconsin attending the summer school at the University.

Mr. and Mrs. Gay are now at Gaylands with their daughters, Miss Helen, Miss Ingovar and Mrs. J. C. Coker.

The Misses Turner opened Takusan on June 3d.

. . . . . Mrs. Browning with the Misses Browning arrived.

The same day Mr. and Mrs. Gabriel opened Mrs. Lewis' new cottage. Dr. and Mrs. Lewis with Miss Jean Lewis are expected on the mountain about August 1st.

Dr. Rushmore is now at his cottage. Mrs. Patterson and Miss Margaret Patterson will spend the summer abroad. Mrs. Wood, Miss Gertrude Wood and Master Willis Wood arrived July 24th.

Miss Sellars and Miss Howe are occupying Blythewood this summer. Miss Robertson and Miss McElroy are their guests for the present.

Mrs. Dellenbaugh was here the first week in June putting her house in order which is to be occupied by Miss Otis. She and Mr. Dellenbaugh will spend the Fourth of July here.

The House of the Four Winds was opened on June 1st. Mr. and Mrs. Heaton were guests there from June 11th to the 15th, and Miss Murdock for the last three weeks in June. Dr. Northrup arrived June 20th and Mr. and Mrs. Herbert Cowing with their baby and Miss Gertrude Cowing on June 29th. Miss Agnes Cowing will spend the summer traveling thru the French Provinces and the Pyrenees. She will return home by way of the Channel Islands.

Mrs. Clay and Miss Gladys Clay will occupy their cottage this summer.

It is with pleasure we announce the engagement of Miss Emily Wood to Mr. Robert Harris who, with Miss Wood, will spend three weeks with Mrs. Clay. Other guests at Breezy-Brae will be Miss Lilienthal and Mr. Anthony.

Mrs. Gilbert and her daughter are here again this summer in one of Mrs. Keir's cottages. Miss Gertrude Hawkshurst is visiting them.

The Cragsmoor Journal

FOUNDED BY PENDLETON SCHENCK

ELEONORE VON ELTZ, EDITOR

Published Semi-Monthly

Vol. XIII., No. 1   CRAGSMOOR, N. Y., JULY 1, 1916

Editorials

"Sumer is icumen in."—In this year of widespread jubilance over the Bard of Avon's demise, one must perforce employ "ye olde Englishe" tongue to gain a hearing. Possibly "lend me your ears" would be quite as arresting and more Shakespearian. But after careful deliberation we gave preference to the former phrase in order to reassure and cheer those damp and drooping summer settlers who, since early May have divided their time between cracking the ice in their water pitchers, scraping mud off their rubber boots and placing tubs and buckets at strategic points in their attics. Never before has there been so early an influx of city-dwellers to the mountain, and never have they been more ungraciously received. A few spring showers they might have excused as tears of joy at their arrival, but no such generous interpretation can be put upon the five long weeks of copious weeping. Unless Cragsmoor sees fit to mend her ways, even to those staunch defenders who poetically describe the vague grey forms which settle over her, as "clouds," will turn upon her, and mutter from beneath their rubber hoods, "Beastly fog!" With these words one of Cragsmoor's fondest traditions would be shattered. So we implore the staunch defenders to forbear yet a little while, for are we not promised a warm, sunny (and doubtless dry) August?

And meanwhile, let us smile though nature sulks. We can well afford to laugh her moods to scorn, with almost every cottage full of householders and a goodly gathering of inmates, all of whom can enter into the community life and make it what they will, heedless of winds or weather.

"En avant!" all together, on the road to a good and fruitful season.

The American Red Cross

The American Red Cross was founded "to aid in the p... of human suffering in times of war and peace." It is not a militaristic institution, but one wholly dependent for service in disasters of every kind. The United States, with a population of 100,000,000 has but 27,000 Red Cross members, whereas Japan has a membership of 2,000,000. A campaign is now afoot to enroll 1,000,000 members in America. Annual membership is $1; sustaining, $10; Life, $25; Patron, $100. The primary object of the present campaign is not to increase funds but to build up a membership which will give proof of widespread interest and be somewhat commensurate with the size of the general population.

The above is the gist of an appeal received by Dr. Northrup from a special committee of physicians which is assisting the Executive Committee of the American Red Cross Campaign. He was requested to become a member himself and to enroll four other members. With characteristic energy he scoured the mountain top with an enthusiasm which gained for the cause 26 adherents and $60. Moreover, such warm interest was evinced that it was felt that those with a little leisure would be glad to do some practical work. Accordingly Mrs. Northrup has sent for materials and instructions and upon their arrival, will call for volunteers. The work may be taken home or be done at an established headquarters.

Let us emphasize once more that anti-militarists need have no scruples against aiding in the movement, for the American Red Cross, as its seal proclaims, stands for Neutrality and Humanity.

Most Cragsmoorians have by now read the notice of the Federal Government which calls attention to the paper shortage, and urges everyone to save papers of every sort. In this connection we wish to announce that a second-hand dealer from Ellenville will probably make regular rounds of the mountain to purchase waste paper. Definite information will be published in our next issue. Meanwhile save all kinds of paper, pasteboard and rags. Separate newspapers, magazines and other printed matter from the other kinds of paper.

Society Notes

Mrs. Sturdevant and Miss Fouhy hold first place in the annual spring dash for the mountain. They opened Bear Cliff Cottage on April 4th.

Mrs. Theodore Brown and Mr. Carrol Brown were also among the early arrivals of the season. They have been in their cottage since May 10.

Miss Odell has changed her residence from Hillcrest to Ruhberg. She arrived there on May 15th, with the Rev. Odell, who spent ten days with her. The Rev. B. Stewart Bert of the Chapel of the Holy Name will be her guest for the summer.

Mrs. Tilton is in Ottawa and we regret to say will not visit Cragsmoor this season.

Mrs. Thos. S. Ogden and the Misses Ogden of New York and Washington, who were guests at Herrnhut last year have now become bona fide cottagers, residing at Hillcrest.

Mr. and Mrs. Henry returned to the mountain on May 8th. During the second and third weeks of June they visited in Albany and Johnstown. Mr. Henry Collins Brown, author of the continuation of Valentine's Manual of the City of New York, was their guest on the 23d and 24th of June.

It is a pleasure to welcome Mrs. Ernest Wood back to the mountain from her four years sojourn in the Philippines, China, and Texas. She is accompanied by the Misses Katharine and Gretchen, and Ernest Wetherill Wood, born January 31, 1916. The Rev. Wood is serving as army chaplain on the Mexican border.

Mrs. Compton and children joined Mrs. Sturdevant the first part of May. Miss Winifred Sturdevant arrived on June 24th and Mr. Compton is expected for over the Fourth.

-224-

Carroll Butler Brown

ENTER, CARROLL BUTLER BROWN, V.I.P.

For the amount of $200.00 on September 4, 1917, I, living in New York City at the time, purchased land from Emilie H. Keene of the Roseville section of Newark New Jersey, and also on the same date, a separate parcel from Mollie V. Leavitt of Manhattan, New York, for which I paid one dollar. (Liber 462 Pages 221 and 222)

My mother, Mrs. Theodore (Frances M.) Brown and I first summered in Cragsmoor in 1908, staying at the Hartshorn's "Pines Casino". We revisited the Casino each summer during the years of 1909 (according to The Cragsmoor Journal, Vol. VII, No. 1), 1910, 1911, 1912, 1914 and 1916. (Appendix B Houses of Cragsmoor 1903-1928 does not show the Browns in Cragsmoor the summer of 1909.) There is no information available regarding visitors to the area from 1916 through 1928. Is it possible that this lack of information could possibly have been due to World War I which began on June 28, 1914 and ended June 28, 1919??

According to Ulster County tax records, taxes were paid by myself on land only (no building) and referred to on the Assessment Roll of the Town of Wawarsing, as lots formerly owned by Keene and Leavitt. The lots were valued at fifty dollars ($50.00) each. (Again, no tax records were found for the year 1919.) There are however, tax records for the year 1920, which in reality are for the 1919 taxable year.

About this time, I built my beautiful cottage. And....the tax roll now shows a house and lot owned by myself and assessed at $1040.00, with a real value of $5000.00. The Assessment Roll for the Town of Wawarsing until 1923 shows my home and land to remain in my name until my demise in 1923. But....this is getting ahead of my story!

Appendix B Houses of Cragsmoor 1903 – 1928	1903	1904	1905	1906	1907	1908
Albert cottage (Built in 1889)	O- Rev. Martin Albert family	→	(Mrs. Albert died)	—→	Misses Albert	Misses Albert
Alsop cottage		O- Mrs. Alsop of Phila.	(For Sale)	→		
Barnacle	O- Mrs. Hartshorn	O- Mrs. Hartshorn	(For Sale)		Sherman Family	
Blythewood (Blithewood) (Built in 1908)						O- Mr. + Mrs. William Halsey Wood
Boulders (Bowlders) (Built in 1898)		O- Judge + Mrs. Addison Brown	→	Closed this summer	→	
Breezy Brae (1898)	O- Mr. + Mrs. Edward Clay	Mrs. Witter + Mr. Norris	Mrs. Nix, Miss Nix, Dr. La Favre	Mr. + Mrs. Peck and Misses Peck	Misses Weston, Elliott + Flood	
Brodhead Cottages	O- Miss Kate Brodhead	1) Prof. Wm. G. Luhr	1) Dr. Harley + father 2) Dr. Lewis + Dr. McIntyre 3) Prof. Wm. G. Luhr	1) Miss Belnap 2) Mrs. Wilson + Miss Wilson 3) Mrs. von Eltz + family 4) Dr. Lewis + Dr. McIntyre	1) Miss Turner 2) Mrs. Eaton	Mr./Mrs. Fred. Baker
The Bungalow (Built c. 1897)						O- Mrs. Fox + Miss Marian Fox
Casino (O- Mrs. Hartshorn)	Miss Katherine Chipman	Miss Chipman Miss Bisbee + Miss Varmilye		Miss Dennison		Mrs. T. Brown + son Carroll
Chetolah	O- Mr. + Mrs. George Inness, Jr.	→	→	→	→	→
Cragsmoor Inn Cottage					Mrs. + Miss de Teresa	
Crow's Nest (Built in 1908)						
Edith-a-ker						
Edithiea (opposite The Pines)	O- Miss Edith Mason	Dr. Mary Harley Dr. Joseph Harley		Mr. + Mrs. Haskin of Buffalo	Miss Mason + family	
Eltzruhe (Built in 1907)		—			O- Mrs. von Eltz + family	→
Endridge		O- Mr. + Mrs. Frederick S. Dellenbaugh	→	→	→	
Eyrie (one of Miss Kite's cottages)		O- Mr. + Mrs. W. A. Polk	→			
Fletcher cottage	O- Mrs. Fletcher	—→	Mr. + Mrs. Webster	→		
Gayland (In Xanadu)			O- Mr. + Mrs. Edward Gay + family	→	→	→
Hamlet Built in ____		O- Miss Annette Hom	—→	—→	Misses Dudley	Miss Ham

Owners and Residents (as listed in *Cragsmoor Journal*)

1909	1910	1911	1912	1913	1914	1916	1928
Rev. Miss Albert	Miss Hilda Albert	?	The Alberts	Miss Hilda Albert (Rev. Albert die)	Mrs. Hard; Mrs. Atmerman + daughters		
Mr. Eliz. V. + Fredrick Baker						Mr. + Mrs. Sutton + family	Mr. + Mrs. Meredith B. Langstaff
?	Mrs. Wood, Miss Emily, Messrs. Halsey + Alex	Mr. + Mrs. Halsey Wood + Miss Emily	Mr. + Mrs. Halsey Wood, Miss Emily + Mr. Alexander	Misses Trend back (renting)	Miss Sellers; Miss Howe Mrs. W.H. Wood (Sept.) + Tobi	Mrs. Hoffman + daughters	
→	→	→	→	Judge died in Ap ?	Mrs. Addison Brown Miss Elinore and Mr. Ralph Brown	+ Stanley Brown	Mrs. Helen C. Brown
Mrs. Nat. B. Foote, Isiel + Hastings	Mme. Demetries Son Andrew + family	Mr. Demetre	Mrs. Hobbie + family		Mrs. Clay + Miss Gladys Clay	Mrs. + Miss Clay	.
1) Mr. Browning + daughters 2) Mises Turner		1) Mr. Baker + family 2) Dr. + Mrs. Lewis + family → 3) Mr. + Mrs. Munson + family 4) Mrs. Hitchings + daughter Marjorie 5) Mr. + Mrs. Maltby + family	1) Mrs. Lewis 2) Hoffmans 3) Maltbies	Mr. + Mrs. Baker	Miss Gabay	Dr. + Mrs. Hill	
	Mrs. Bloodgoody of Long Island	Mrs. Fox	Mrs. Fox + Master Jack Hillard	Mrs. Fox et a		Dr. + Mrs. Duncan Browne + children	
★ See note	Mrs. Theodore Brown + son Carroll	Mrs. T. Brown + son Carroll	Mrs. T. Brown + son Carroll		Mrs. Brown + son Carroll	Mrs. Brown + son Carroll	.
dexter Mrs. B. Ellsworth in cottage	→	→	→		Mr. + Mrs. Inness Miss Isabel Inness	→	Mrs. Inness Sold it + left Cragsmoor
Mr. + Mrs. Compton							
O—Mrs. Walter Long	→	→	+ Miss Edna Aller	→	Mr. + Mrs. Long	Mr. + Mrs. Krebs	Mrs. Long
	O—Mr. + Mrs. A.I. Keller + family	→	→	→	Mr. + Mrs. Keller	.	
							J. Corona Sutton, Billy + Julie S.
→	→	→	→	→	von Eltz family	→	
→	+ Miss Otis	→	→	→	Mr. + Mrs. Dellenbaugh + Miss Otis		→
→	Mrs. Anderson Polk + family		→	→	Mr. + Mrs. Stuart Polk + family	Mrs. Polk	
		Mr. Edward Tichenor + family			Mrs. E. Tichenor (of Middletown) + Misses Constance + Margaret	Mrs. James F. Sanborn ed family	
→	→	→	→	→			
→	Dr. + Mrs. Northrup	Miss Ham + Miss Ruth Dudley	Miss Ham	→	Mr. + Mrs. Gay + 3 daughters (Misses Helen + Ingovar + Mrs. J.S. Coker)	Mr. + Mrs. Gay + Miss Ingovar G. + Mrs. Larned.	
					Miss Ham	Misses Phinney of Newport	

★ According to The Cragsmoor Journal Vol. VII, №1, Mrs. Brown & Carroll summered in Cragsmoor in 1909

A LI'L BIT OF OWNERSHIP HISTORY

Going back as far as we can determine, the original owners of the property on which Carroll Butler Brown built his home, were Alexander Terwilliger and his wife, Harriet J. Terwilliger of Wawarsing, who on June 10, 1893 sold to Eliza G. Hartshorn, a widow of Providence, Rhode Island, for $800.00. (Liber 315 Page 39 - Ulster County Building, Kingston, New York)

On July 29, 1895, one parcel of this land was sold to Emilie H. Keene of the Roseville section of Newark, New Jersey, for the amount of one dollar (Liber 324 Pages 630 and 633): and another parcel of the land was sold, again for the amount of one dollar, to Molly V. Leavitt of Manhattan, New York on July 29, 1895 (Liber 324 Pages 630 and 633).

Legend has it that quite often in those days that a homemade pie or cake could be used as "bartering chips" for a small piece of land. Many parcels of land in the area are not square and many property lines come together. (This legend/story has been handed-down from Helen Clark, who in turn, heard it from local folks.)

Note: All Liber references were located in the Ulster County Building in Kingston, New York, and all Libers mentioned throughout this writing refer to Libers of Deeds.

This Indenture made this 29th day of July in the year of our Lord one thousand eight hundred and ninety five

Between *Eliza G Hartshorn* of Providence Rhode Island party of the first part and *Emilie H. Keene* of Roseville New Jersey party of the second part Witnesseth That the said party of the first part in consideration of the sum of One Dollar to her duly paid has sold and By These Presents does grant and convey to the said party of the second part her heirs and assigns All that certain lot piece or parcel of land situate lying and being on the top of Shawangunk Mountain in the town of Wawarsing Ulster County New York and which is bounded and described as follows.

Beginning at the most northerly corner of a triangular lot sold to *Rebecca C Fox* at a stake and stones and runs thence north 5° 35' West one hundred and thirty nine and 6/12 feet to a stone thence north 80° West one hundred and seven feet and four inches to a stone near a marked chestnut tree thence south 6° west one hundred and ninety four feet to an oak tree marked on the northerly edge of a ravine thence about north 16° East one hundred and forty three feet to the place of beginning the same more or less

Together with a right of way along and over the proposed new road on the westerly side thereof.

Together with a right of way over Schuyler Avenue to the public highway. the above described premises being a part of the premises heretofore conveyed by *Alexander Vermilyea* to *Eliza G. Hartshorn*

175

With the Appurtenances and all the estate
Title and Interest therein of the said party of
the first part

And the said _Eliza G Hartshorn_ does
hereby covenant and agree to and with the
said party of the second part her heirs and

324

assigns that the premises thus conveyed in the
Quiet and Peaceable Possession of the said party of
the second part her heirs and assigns she will
forever Warrant and Defend against any person
whomsoever lawfully claiming the same or any part
thereof

In Witness Whereof the party of the first part
has hereunto set her hand and Seal the day and
year first above written

Sealed and delivered }
in presence of
James B Keeler

Eliza G Hartshorn P

State of New York } SS
County of Ulster }

On this 5 day of August in the
year one thousand eight hundred and ninety
five before me the subscriber personally came
Eliza G Hartshorn to me known to be the person
described in and who executed the within instru
ment and she acknowledged that she executed
the same

A true record entered
August 7 1875. 1030. A M

James B Keeler
Notary Public

Jno S Sleight
Clerk

176

This Indenture made this 29. day of July in the year of our Lord one thousand eight hundred and ninety five

Between Eliza G. Hartshorn of Providence Rhode Island party of the first part and Mollie V. Leavitt of Providence Rhode Island party of the second part

Witnesseth That the said party of the first part in consideration of the sum of One Dollar to her duly paid has sold and By These Presents does grant and convey to the said party of the second part her heirs and assigns

All that certain lot piece or parcel of land situate lying and being on top of Shawangunk Mountain in the town of Warwarsing Ulster County ny and which is described as follows Beginning at the east side of the gate at a stone on the bounds of lands of Abbie Kite running thence north along her bounds North 41° 45 West (357) three hundred and fifty seven feet to a stake thence north 38° 50' West further along the bounds of said Abbie Kite (285) two hundred and eighty five feet to a white oak tree marked on both sides and from said white oak tree thence south 18° 50' West about (263) two hundred and sixty three feet to a stake and stones thence south 80° East twenty two

feet to the most northerly of a lot of Emelie H. Keene at a pile of stones near a marked chestnut tree thence same course along said Keene lot (107½) one hundred and seven and ½ feet to the northerly corner thereof thence along said Keene lot south 5° 30' East (139 6/12) one hundred and thirty nine and 6/12 feet to stones north of a large maple tree the northerly corner of the triangular lot of Rebecca C. Gox thence along the same south 70°

50' East (89) eighty nine feet to the northerly corner of the Rebecca Crq_{th}^{b} lot thence along the northerly side thereof South 78° 35' East (761) feet to a post thence in a straight line north easterly about (19) nineteen feet to the place of beginning.

Containing about three acres of land.

Reserving a road about (30) thirty feet wide along the northerly and westerly side of said lot to lands of said Eliza G Hartshorn and others.

Together with a right of way over Schuyler Avenue to the public highway the above described premise being a part of the premise heretofore conveyed by Alexander Deroulejie To the said Eliza G. Hartshorn ᵗ

With the Appurtenances and all the estate Title and interest therein of the said party of the first part.

And the said Eliza G Hartshorn does hereby covenant and agree to and with the said party of the second part her heirs and assigns That the premise thus conveyed in the Quiet and Peaceable Possession of the said party of the second part her heirs and assigned She will forever Warrant and Defend against any person whomsoever lawfully claiming the Same or any part thereof

In Witness Whereof the party of the first part has hereunto set her hand and seal the day and year first above written

Sealed and delivered }
in presence of }
           Eliza G. Hartshorn Ⓞ

James B Keeler

324

State of New York } SS
County of Ulster

On this 5th day of August in the year one thousand eight hundred and ninety five before me the subscriber personally came Eliza G Hartshorn to me known to be the person described in and who executed the within instrument and She acknowledged that she executed the same

A true record entered
August 7, 1895,

James B. Keeler
Notary Public
10 40 A M

Geo J Sleight
Clerk

LIBER 462 page 221

THIS INDENTURE, Made the Fourth day of September, nineteen hundred and Seventeen,

BETWEEN EMELIE H. KEENE, of Roseville, Newark, N. J., party of the first part, and CARROLL B. BROWN, of Cragsmoor, Ulster Co., N. Y., party of the second part.

WITNESSETH, that the party of the first part, in consideration of TWO HUNDRED ($200) DOLLARS, lawful money of the United States, to her duly paid by the party of the second part, does hereby grant and release unto the party of the second part, his heirs and assigns forever,

ALL THAT CERTAIN LOT, PIECE OR PARCEL OF LAND, situate, lying and being on the top of Shawangunk Mountain in the Town of Wawarsing, Ulster County, New York, and which is bounded and described as follows: Beginning at the most Northerly corner of a triangular lot sold to Rebecca C. Fox at a stake and stones and running thence North 5° 30' West one hundred and thirty nine and 6/12 feet to a stone, thence North 80° west one hundred and seven feet and four inches to a stone near a marked chestnut tree; thence south 6° west one hundred and ninety four feet to an oak tree, marked, on the Northerly edge of a ravine, thence about North 76° East one hundred and forty three feet to the place of beginning, be the same more or less, together with a right of way along and over a proposed new road on the westerly side thereof, together with a right of way over Schuyler Avenue to the public highway, the above being the same premises as were conveyed to the party of the first part by Eliza G. Hartshorn, Widow, by deed dated July 29, 1895, and recorded in Ulster County Clerk's Office August 7, 1895, in Liber 324 of Deeds on page 630.

TOGETHER with the appurtenances and all the estate and rights of the party of the first part in and to said premises.

TO HAVE AND TO HOLD the premises herein granted unto the party of the second part, his heirs and assigns forever,

AND said Emelie H. Keene, party of the first part, does covenant as follows:-

FIRST:- That said Emelie H. Keene is seized of the said premises in fee simple, and has good right to convey the same;

SECOND:- That the party of the second part shall quietly enjoy the said premises.

THIRD:- That the said premises are free from incumbrances.

FOURTH:- That the party of the first part will execute or procure any further necessary assurance of the title to said premises;

FIFTH:- That said Emelie H. Keene, will forever warrant the title to the said premises.

IN WITNESS WHEREOF, the party of the first part has hereunto set her hand and seal the day and year first above written.

In presence of
Edith M. Peck.   Emelie H. Keene,   (Seal.)

STATE OF NEW YORK,
COUNTY OF NEW YORK,   SS:

On the Fourth day of September, Nineteen Hundred and Seventeen, before me, came,
-----EMELIE H. KEENE, (widow), ----

to me known to be the individual described in, and who executed the foregoing instrument, and acknowledged that she executed the same.

(Seal.)   Wm. Halsey Peck,
                                 Notary Public, N. Y. Co., No. 26,
                                 Cert. filed in County Clerk's
                                 and Register's Office No. 8041.
                                 Commission expires March 30, 1918.

STATE OF NEW YORK,
COUNTY OF NEW YORK,   SS: No. 52683 Series B.

I, WILLIAM F. SCHNEIDER, Clerk of the County of New York, and also Clerk of the Supreme Court for the said County, the same being a Court of Record, do hereby certify, that

----WM. HALSEY PECK, ---

whose name is subscribed to the deposition or certificate of the proof or acknowledgment of the annexed instrument, and thereon written, was, at the time of taking such deposition, or proof and acknowledgment, a Notary Public in and for such County, duly commissioned and sworn, and authorized by the laws of said State, to take depositions and to administer oaths to be used in any Court of said State and for general purposes; and also to take acknowledgments and proofs of deeds, of conveyances for land, tenements or hereditaments in said State of New York. And further, that I am well acquainted with the handwriting of such Notary Public, and verily believe that the signature to said deposition or certificate of proof or acknowledgment is genuine.

IN TESTIMONY WHEREOF, I have hereunto set my hand and affixed the seal of the said Court and County, the 12 day of Sept. 1917.

(Seal.)   W. F. Schneider,
                                 Clerk.

A true record entered
September 27, 1917, at 8 A. M.

                                                                        Clerk.
//

THIS INDENTURE, Made the 11th day of September, in the year Nineteen Hundred and Seventeen,

BETWEEN MOLLIE V. LEAVITT, of Borough of Manhattan, New York City, N. Y., party of the first part, and

CARROLL B. BROWN, (an unmarried man), of Cragsmoor, Ulster County, N. Y., party of the second part.

WITNESSETH, that the said party of the first part, in consideration of ONE DOLLAR, ($1.00) lawful money of the United States, paid by the party of the second part, does hereby grant and release unto the said party of the second part, his heirs and assigns forever,

ALL THAT TRACT OR PARCEL OF LAND, situate in the Town of Wawarsing, County of Ulster and State of New York, and being on top of the Shawangunk Mountain, said parcel of land being described as follows:- BEGINNING at the East side of the gate at a stone on the bounds of lands of Abbie Kite; running thence north along her bounds North 41 degrees 45 minutes west three hundred and fifty seven feet, (357) to a stake; thence North thirty eight degrees 50 minutes west further along the bounds of said Abbie Kite, two hundred and eighty five feet (285), to a white oak tree marked on both sides, and from said white oak tree; thence south 18 degrees 50 minutes west about two hundred and sixty three feet, (263) to a stake and stones; thence south 80 degrees East twenty two feet to the Northeasterly corner of a lot of Emelie H. Keene at a pile of stones near a marked chestnut tree; thence same course along said Keene lot, one hundred seven and 4/12 feet, (107 4/12) to the Northerly corner thereof; thence along said Keene lot south 5 degrees 30 minutes east one hundred and thirty nine and 6/12 feet, (139 6/12), to stones; North of a large maple tree, the Northerly corner of the triangular lot of Rebecca C. Fox, thence along the same south 70 degrees 50 minutes east eighty nine feet, (89) to the Northerly corner of the Rebecca C. Fox house lot; thence along the Northerly side thereof south 78 degrees 35 minutes east 261 feet to a post; thence in a straight line northeasterly about nineteen feet (19) to the place of beginning. Containing about three acres of land.

Reserving a road about thirty feet (30) wide, along the Northerly and Westerly side of said lot to lands formerly of Elisa G. Hartshorn, now Daniel I. Odell and others, together with a right-of-way over Schuyler Avenue to the public highway. Being the same parcel of land conveyed by Elisa G. Hartshorn to Mollie V. Leavitt, by deed dated July 29th, 1895, and recorded in the Ulster County Clerk's Office in Liber 324 of Deeds at page 633. The above described premises being a part of the premises heretofore conveyed by Alexander Terwilliger and wife to Elisa G. Hartshorn, by deed dated June 10th, 1893, and recorded in Liber 315 of Deeds at page 39.

TOGETHER with the appurtenances and all the estate and rights of the party of the first part in and to the said premises.

TO HAVE AND TO HOLD the above granted premises, unto the said party of the second part, his heirs and assigns forever.

AND the said Mollie V. Leavitt, party of the first part, does covenant with the said party of the second part as follows:-

FIRST:- That the party of the second part shall quietly enjoy the said premises.

SECOND:- That the said Mollie V. Leavitt, party of the first part will forever warrant the title to said premises.

IN WITNESS WHEREOF, the said party of the first part has hereunto set her hand and seal the day and year first above written.

In presence of
Benj. J. Bayle   Mollie V. Leavitt,   (L. S.)

STATE OF NEW YORK,
COUNTY OF SUFFOLK,   SS:

On this 11 day of Sept. in the year Nineteen Hundred and Seventeen, before me, the subscriber, personally appeared,

----MOLLIE V. LEAVITT, ---

to me known and known to me to be the same person described in, and who executed the within Instrument, and she duly acknowledged to me that she executed the same.

George T. Reeve, Jr.,
Notary Public, Suff. Co.

STATE OF NEW YORK,
COUNTY OF SUFFOLK,   SS: No. 2418.

I, JAMES F. RICHARDSON, Clerk of the County of Suffolk, and also Clerk of the Supreme Court for the said County, the same being a Court of Record, do hereby certify that

-----GEORGE T. REEVE, JR., ---

whose name is subscribed to the deposition or certificate of the proof or acknowledgment of the annexed instrument, and thereon written, was at the time of taking such deposition or proof or acknowledgment, a Notary Public, in and for such County, duly commissioned and sworn, and authorized by the laws of said State to take depositions and to administer oaths to be used in any Court of said State and for general purposes; and also to take acknowledgments and proofs of deeds of conveyances for land, tenements or hereditaments in said State of New York. And further, that I am well acquainted with the handwriting of such Notary Public, and verily believe that the signature to said deposition or certificate of proof or acknowledgment is genuine.

IN TESTIMONY WHEREOF, I have hereunto set my hand and affixed the seal of the said Court and County the 11 day of Sept. 1917.

(Seal.)   James F. Richardson,
                                                        Clerk.

A true record entered
September 27, 1917, at 8 A. M.   Clerk.

Item 1	LOCATION OF PROPERTY 2	DESCRIPTION 5	QUANTITY 6	7
	Name of Owner, Last Known or Reputed Owner	Name of Villages and Name or Number of School Districts and Special Districts Where Property is Located	Insert in this Column the Names of the Abutting Property Owners on Each of Four Sides, Respectively. For Example: N.—Brown; (E.—Jones; S.—Smith; W.—Robinson	Amount of Land or Linear Dimensions	Full Value of Such Real Property

					$
1	Benedict Thos E.	Napanoch		45	800
2	Brown Elizabeth H	Cragsmore		2 H+L	350
3	Brown Sarah	Cragsmore	5 Houses + Barn	73	4000
4	Brown Addison Est	Cragsmore		H+L	2000
5	Brown Addison Est	Cragsmore		Lot	100
6	Brown Helen E	Cragsmore	Alex Terwilliger	10	500
7	Bunting Wm.	Briggs Street		Lot	20
8	Budd Anderson	Ellenville		45	500
9	Brodhead Harry	Laurenkill		140	2400
10	Burham Alfred Est	Laurenkill		85	800
11	Dove Eugene	Cantonville		47	600
12	Benson Rosetta Est	Spring Glen		Lot	20
13	Bollin Martin	Napanoch		6	150
14	Brown Carol B.	Cragsmore	Levett Lot	Lot	50
15	Brown Carol B	Cragsmore	Keen Lot	Lot	50
16	Bennett Charles H. jr	Irish Cape		36	200
17	Braysmer C. C.	Cragsmore		Lot	30
18	Brodhead Kate	Cragsmore		50	600
19	Bouton Charles W	Cragsmore		Lot	50
20	Browning Alice + Edith	Cragsmore		H+L	350
21	Bell Martha	Cragsmore		H+L	250
22	Benedict M. S.	Cragsmore		70	500
23	Baker Fred +	Cragsmore		H+L	250
24	Boyce George	Cragsmore		Lot	50
25	Braysten May D.	Cragsmore		H+L	400
26	Butterick H. S. K.	Cragsmore	Russell Est.	Lot	100
27	Bishop Mary	Cantonville		H+L	200
28	Durlison John	Ellenville	Fuller Place	90	800
29	Blackberry May	Cantonville		30	500
30	Brocksnyder H.	Laurenkill	Smith Farm	200	3200
31					

182

Assessment Roll of the Town of Wawarsing

Ulster County for 1920

FIRST COLUMN	SECOND COLUMN		THIRD COLUMN	FOURTH COLUMN	
Item 1	LOCATION OF PROPERTY 2		DESCRIPTION 5	QUANTITY 6	7
Name of Owner, Last Known or Reputed Owner	Name of Villages and Name or Number of School Districts and Special Districts Where Property is Located S.D.		Insert in this Column the Names of the Abutting Property Owners on Each of Four Sides, Respectively. For Example: N.—Brown; E.—Jones; S.—Smith; W.—Robinson	Amount of Land or Linear Dimensions	Full Value of Such Real Property $
Braxton Mary D	Cragsmore	7	Kite Road Henry Henry	H+L	52
Boyer + Halperin	Leuren Kill	3	Francisconia R.R. Griswold Road	108	455
Boyer + Halperin	"	3	" " "	178	26
Boyer + Halperin	"	3	" " " "		19
Bornstein Hockgen	Spring Glen	20	Brodkin Creek Hoyt Corlland	82	260
Brodkin + Cohen	Leuren kill	20	Lice R.R. Bornstein Road	260	429
Benedict Thos. E.	State Road	2	Young Road Cemetery Intermonate	35	91
Browne Elizabeth M	Cragsmore	7		2 H+L	52
Browne Addison Est Helen C. Brown		7		H+L	525
Browne Addison Est Anna M Brown		7		Lot	130
Browne Sarah		7		73	585
Browne Helen E. Helen C Brown		7	Road Road Morgan Tichnor	5	65
Bauting C.R.	Briggs St	9	Power Co Tenenbaum Power Co Pow Co	Lot	80
Benson Georgetta	Spring Glen	20	Thornton Canal Road Brown	Lot	3
Bollin Martin	Insh Cape	2	Road Road Hoornbeck Watson	6	260
Brown Carol B.	Cragsmore	7	Road Road Fox Road	H+L	1040
Chapman P. G	"	7		Lot	58
Brodhead Kate	"	7		50	780
Bouton Charles W	"	7		Lot	66
Bishop Mary	Cantonville	29	Percher Kye Mountain Henneman Road	H+L	260
Burlison John	Ellenville	3	Cemetery Creek Wygant Road	90	1040
Browning Alice + Edith	Cragsmore	7		H+L	455
Ball Martha	"	7	Brodhead Henry Road Brodhead	H+L	394
Benedict B. F.	"	7		70	650
Baker Fred	"	7	Road Road Suydam Terwilliger	H+L	390
Boice George	"	7		Lot	65
Blackberg Max	Cantonville	29	Leimon Mountain Road	30	650
Babcock Theodoro	Leuren kill	3	Wygant Wygant Lane Road	H+L	180
Badash Ben	"	3	Miller R.R. Slutsky Clunsky	N+L	390
Buttrick Mrs	Cragsmore	7	Road Delenbaugh Sturdevant Road	Lot	130
Brackstone Anna	Cantonville	29	Porcier Cop Road Liedman	H+L	780

183

Assessment Roll of the Town of Wawarsing

Ulster County for 1921

	FIRST COLUMN	SECOND COLUMN		THIRD COLUMN	FOURTH COLUMN	
	Item 1	LOCATION OF PROPERTY 2		DESCRIPTION 5	QUANTITY 6	7
	Name of Owner, Last Known or Reputed Owner	Name of Villages and Name or Number of School Districts and Special Districts Where Property is Located		Insert in this Column the Names of the Abutting Property Owners on Each of Four Sides, Respectively. For Example: N.—Brown; E.—Jones; S.—Smith; W.—Robinson	Amount of Land or Linear Dimensions	Full Value of Such Real Property
1	Braxton Mary D	Cragsmore	7	Kier Road Henry Henry	H+L	52
2	Boser + Halperin	Vernon Kill	3	Franciscomia R.R. Griswold Road 208		455
3	Boser + Halperin	"	3	Franciscomia R.R. Griswold Road 175		26
4	Boser + Halperin	"	3	Franciscomia R.R. Griswold Road Lot		19
5	Bornstein + Hockner + Beckie	Spring Lien	30	Frodskin Creek Hoyt Corliard 82		2600
6	Benedict Thomas C	Wildmere	2	Long Road Cemetery Monmouth 55		910
7	Brown Elizabeth H	Cragsmore	7		L+L	520
8	Brown Sarah	"	7		S H+L 73a	585
9	Brown Helen C	"	7	Lit Road Morgan Tichner	H+L	325
10	Brown Helen C	"	7	Van Road Morgan street 10		65
11	Bunting C. R.	Briggs st	9	River to Shenandoan Creek Pavel Lot		36
12	Benson Georgetta	Spring Lien	30	Thornton Canal Road Rosen Lot		30
13	Brown Carrol B	Cragsmore	7	Road Road Fox Road	H+L	1040
14	Brassee P.G.	"	7		Lot	55
15	Brodhead Kate	"	7		50	780
16	Bouton Charles W.	"	7		Lot	68
17	Bishop Mary	Centreville	29	Chickerpen Brustein Reineman Road	H+L	260
18	Burlison John	Vernon Kill	3	Cemetery Creek Wyguat Road 90		1040
19	Browning Alice + Edith	Cragsmore	7		H+L	455
20	Ball Martha	"	7	Brodhead Mary Road Brodhead	H+L	390
21	Benedict B. F.	"	7		70	650
22	Baker Fred	"	7	Road Road Suydam Terwilliger	H+L	390
23	Boyce George	"	7		Lot	68
24	Blackberg Max	Centreville	29	Reineman Mountain Road	50	650
25	Babcock Theodore	Vernon Kill	3	Stern Stern Road Road	H+L	195
26	Buttrick Mrs	Cragsmore	1	Road Delenbaugh Stuntwart Road	Lot	180
27	Baller George	"	7		H+L	390
28	Budd Anderson	State Road	2	Tauber Road Hoom Edlison 45		585
29	Burhans Alfred Est	Vernon Kill	3	Fuller Road Levine Myers 35		1040
30	Boor August	Centreville	31	U.R. Wine R.R. Bethany 27		780
31	Bernstein + Spielen	Spring Lien	5	Canal Line R.R. Canal	H+L	195
32	Bergman Joseph	Centreville	29	Golding Mountain Lake Road	H+L	320

184

Assessment Roll of the Town of _Wawarsing N.Y._ ,

Ulster County for 1922

	FIRST COLUMN	SECOND COLUMN	THIRD COLUMN	FOURTH COLUMN	
		LOCATION OF PROPERTY	DESCRIPTION	QUANTITY	
	Item 1	2	5	6	7
	Name of Owner, Last Known or Reputed Owner	Name of Villages and Name or Number of School Districts and Special Districts Where Property is Located	Insert in this Column the Names of the Abutting Property Owners on Each of Four Sides, Respectively. For Example: N.—Brown; E.—Jones; S.—Smith; W.—Robinson	Amount of Land or Linear Dimensions	Full Value of Such Real Property $
1	Buxton Mary D	Cragsmoor 7	Kier Road Town Jury	Hse	520
2	Boice Jacob	Lawrenkill 3	Deyo francouis Whitaker Road	208	7000
3	" "	" 3		178	260
4	" "	" 3		Lot	195
5	Bronston & Hockya	Stone Ridge 20	Rondout Creek Fogt Leonard	82	3000
6	Rowe & Fire Co	Napanoch 2	Sams River Delaware Sentry	35	910
7	Brown W H	Cragsmoor 7	Benedict Mulberry Road Moss	Hse	400
8	Brown Sarah	" 7	Little Village Road Kier	73	5850
9	Brown Fire Co	" 7	King and Morgan Street	Hse	2800
10	" " "	" 7	Road Town Morgan Tulmor	13	600
11	Bunting C H	Ellenville 2		Lot	35
12	Bunce Georgette	Kerhonkson 20	Fontner river Rose Rose	Lot	30
13	Brown David B	Cragsmoor 7	Road Road Fogt road	Hse	1050
14	Brazier R L	" 7		Lot	55
15	Morehead Kate	" 7	Harry Bennett Road Jarrett	50	780
16	Bouton Charles W	" 7		Lot	65
17	Bishop Max	Centerville 29	Bishop Morton Thirsen Road	Hse	200
18	Burleson John	Lawrenkill 3	Sentry creek stone Road	70	1040
19	Browning Alice & Edith	Cragsmoor 7	Kollmer Harry Road Morehead	Hse	755
20	Bell Martine	" 7	Kollmer Jury Road Kollmer	Hse	590
21	Benedict B F	" 7	Road Road Suydam Terwilliger	70	650
22	Baker Fred	" 7	Road Road Suydam Terwilliger	Hse	390
23	Boyce George	" 7	Man Mumm	Lot	65
24	Blackberg Theo	Centerville 29	Simson Mountain Road	35	650
25	Babcock Theodore	Lawrenkill 3	Stone stone Road Road	Hse	195
26	Butrick Kire	Cragsmoor 7	Road Disenbaugh	Lot	130
27	Bauer George	" 7		Hse	390
28	Budd Anderson	Ellenville 2	Brodsky Erkin Brown	45	585
29	Burhans Alfred Est	Lawrenkill 3	Fuller Road Levine Mendelson	35	1040
30	Boon August	Centerville 29	RR RR Wise Perdusky	27	780
31	Bernstein Jacob	Stone Ridge 5	Levine Z OO Canal	Hse	250
32	Brown & Edward		Levine	"	250
33	" "		Kollmer Goldstine 2 Lots	50

MY LIFE

It began in 1868 when I was born in New York City on February 17th and named Carroll Butler Brown, a name which has often been mispelled. There have been discrepancies regarding when I was born, however, a memorial to me which took place one year after my death states my correct birth date as shown above. (The memorial program contains this information.) Some believe that I was born in 1860, however, my obituary reads that I was fifty-five (55) years old at the time of my passing, which would make my birth year 1868.

As a youngster, I had been seriously injured during a shooting accident which left me paralyzed. (Unfortunately, it was one of my brothers who was unintentionally responsible for this tragic occurrence.) I was unable to stand erect or ever walk again. The remainder of my life was spent confined to a wheelchair. Due to my mother's compassion for me and to help my time pass more quickly, she encouraged me to learn to paint. And, so I did!

It was soon clear that I had a definite ability where art was concerned and so I began taking private painting lessons.

When mother and I first came to Cragsmoor during the summer of 1909 or 1910, while staying at The Casino owned by Mrs. Hartshorn, other members of the artist's community welcomed me as an outstanding addition to their colony. I was so well liked that I was included in the weekly meetings of artists which met at various homes including THE FALCON, which was the name I chose for my residence. The reason for these gatherings was to engage in discussion about art. Often times these talks became very animated.

With an attendant and the aid of a horse and carriage or litter, I was transported to a place of my choice on the mountain. It was at these scenic areas where I'd capture the beauty of the landscape on canvas, thus creating the paintings for which I was so well known. The spectacular beauty of mountain sunsets often became the target of many of my paintings -- and

I just loved to paint to my heart's content. All of Cragsmoor felt a great tenderness toward me, being a man of such great perserverance.

Some of my paintings were exhibited at the National Academy even though I was not a member.

My vividly colored landscape scenes of Cragsmoor became so in demand that one of my paintings was the very first to be sold at the first art exhibit ever held in Cragsmoor.

Today my works are more valuable than ever.

The following is a partial listing of my works.

1. Cragsmoor Landscape
   Oil on canvas, 23" x 31"
   Ellenville Public Library

2. October Birch Trees in Cragsmoor
   Oil on canvas, 16" x 22"
   Ellenville Public Library

3. The Tichenor-Miller Home in Cragsmoor (Home of H. T. Miller)
   Oil on canvas, 18" x 24"
   Ellenville Public Library

4. The Cottage
   Black and white wash, 10" x 14"
   Mrs. KayCee Benton, Cragsmoor, New York

5. Landscape
   Oil on canvas, 8" x 10"
   Mrs. E. Wall, Cragsmoor, New York

6. Autumn Sunset
   Oil on board, 18" x 25"
   Marbella Gallery, New York

7. View of Ellenville From Cragsmoor
   Oil on canvas 31" x 32"
   Ellenville Public Library (Painting on display)

8. Windy Moonrise
   Oil on panel, 15½" x 22½"
   Mr. and Mrs. Paul Sehrig

9. Red Sky at Sunset
   Oil on board

10. View From the Stone Church
    Oil

11. An October Afternoon at Cragsmoor
    Oil on sketching board, 21" x 26"
    Signed lower right "Carroll Brown 1921"

12. Title unknown
    Oil on board, frame is 12" x 14" overall
    Inscription on back of painting reads "Painted by
    Carroll Brown for his valued friend Aline Werner,
    August 1921 Cragsmoor, N. Y.
    Inscription on reverse side of wide frame, believed
    to read, Metal V.J. 11   10057   31212
    Stamped on back of frame, Newcomb Macklin & Co., New
    York

All Artists: **A B C D E F G H I J K L M N O P Q R S T U V W X Y Z**

Biographies: LOGIN   REG

Carroll Butler Brown

				-Color Key-
▣ Artist's Summary Page	❑ Artwork For Sale	❑ Museums for this Artist	▣ His Auction Records	
▣ Books on this Artist	❑ Art Wanted	▣ Bulletins	❑ Graphical Analysis	▣ = Members' Area
❑ Periodicals	❑ Exhibits for this Artist	▣ Artist's Keywords	▣ The Images	▣ = Freely Accessible
▣ Biography	❑ Dealers for this Artist	❑ His Upcoming Auctions	❑ Magazine Ad Archives	❑ = No Content availa

Birth / Death	**Strongest Affiliation:**	**Often Known For:**
- 1868 (New York, New York) - 1923 (Cragsmoor, New York)	NY	landscape, skyscape

Subject to Copyright, Courtesy of
Cragsmoor Library

1 Active Bulletins   **Participate in Biographies**

Would you like to discuss this artist?

Biographical information for Carroll Butler Brown

This biography from the Archives of AskART:
The following, submitted March 2005, is from Christina Clark and Marie Bilney of Hamburg, N.J. They have been researching Carroll Brown's life in the Cragsmoor, New York Art Colony. Mrs. Clark and her husband presently own the house that Carroll Brown built when he was a resident of the Art Colony. Much information has been gathered from previously written material including public records, the artist's obituary, Kinston Court houses, etc.

Carroll Butler Brown was born in 1868 in New York City, son of Theodore and Frances M. Brown. His siblings included brothers F. Herbert, Harold P. and sisters Harriet and Martha. As a youngster he had been severly injured during a shooting accident which left him paralyzed, unable to stand erect or ever walk again. The remainder of his life was spent in a wheelchair. Due to his mother's compassion for him and to help time pass quickly, she encouraged him to paint. It was soon clear he had a definite ability in that field and began taking private painting lessons.

He first went to Cragsmoor, New York in 1908 where there existed an Art Colony started in 1882 by Edward Lamson Henry. Other members of this group, some of whom were members of the National Academy, included Edward Gay, Charles Curran, George Inness, Jr. Helen Turner, Frederick Dellenbaugh, LeGrand Botsford and Arthur Keller.

They welcomed Carroll Brown as an outstanding addition to their colony. He was so well liked that he was included in weekly meetings held for the purpose of discussing art. In 1919 he built his own home in Cragsmoor for summer living. These artists occasionally met at his home which he named "The Falcon". Although not a member of the National Academy, he exhibited some of his paintings there.

On Sunday, June 3, 1923 he and his mother came again to Cragsmoor for the summer. He died Monday June 4th in his home at the age of 55. Some of his paintings are: "Cragsmoor Landscape" - oil, "View from the Stone Church" - oil, "October Birch Trees in Cragsmoor" - Oil, "Tichenor-Miller Home in Cragsmoor" -oil (property of Ellenville NY Museumand Library), "The Cottage - Black & White Wash, Landscape" - oil, "Autumn Sunset" - oil, "View of Ellenville from Cragsmoor" - oil (property Ellenville Museum & Library), "Windy Moonrise" - oil, "Red Sky at Sunset" -oil.

* It is our intention to give accurate credit to our sources. If you see credit omissions or have additional information to add, please let us know at Registrar@AskART.com.

Active Bulletins (1)

Carroll Butler Brown (1868 - 1923)

➤ G℄

Research : Carroll Butler Brown		Marketplace : Carroll Butler Brown		Login f℄
Summary	Examples of his work	For sale ads	Auction results*	**Login**
Quick facts	Exhibits - current	Wanted ads	Auctions upcoming for him*	View Asl
Biography*	Museums	Dealers	Auction sales graphs*	
Book references	Magazine references	What's my art worth?	Magazine ads pre-1998*	
Discussion board	Send me updates	Market Alert - *Free*	Place classified ad*	

*may require

Lived/Active: New York   **Known for:** landscape, skyscape

QUICK FACTS AND KEYWORDS for Carroll Brown

Birth/Death	Lived/Active	Often Known For
- 1868 (New York, New York) - 1923 (Cragsmoor, New York)	New York	landscape, skyscape

Methods
* Painter/Artist

Mediums
* Oil

Styles
* Impressionism Before 1940

Subjects
* Landscape
* Skyscape

Geography/Places Visited
* Cragsmoor, New York

Associations
* Cragsmoor Artist Colony

Exhibitions
* Art Institute of Chicago-Exhibited
* Boston Art Club-Exhibited
* National Academy of Design-Exhibited
* Pennsylvania Academy-Exhibited
* Society of Independent Artists-Exhibit

Chronology
* Late 19th Century-After Civil War

Home

Artist Last Name

First Name (optional)

Artist Se

Image Gallery:

LOGIN   REG

Carroll Butler Brown

				-Color Key-
▦ Artist's Summary Page	❑ Artwork For Sale	❑ Museums for this Artist	❑ His Auction Records	
▦ Books on this Artist	❑ Art Wanted	▦ Bulletins	❑ Graphical Analysis	❑ = Members' Area
❑ Periodicals	❑ Exhibits for this Artist	❑ Artist's Keywords	❑ The Images	▦ = Freely Accessible
❑ Biography	❑ Dealers for this Artist	❑ His Upcoming Auctions	❑ Magazine Ad Archives	❑ = No Content availa

Image Gallery

2 of 2 images for Carroll Butler Brown

1

"Valley View" 12 by 14 in pastels by Carroll B. Brown

Search Options

Available to Members

Mediums
Hold the Ctrl button to select multiple mediums

-Choose All-
Oil

Title Contains:

Auction Date:
Show All

Images per Page:
5

Sort Options:
◉ High Estimate
◌ Auction Date
◌ Sale Price
◌ Size

New Search

(All artwork is copyright of the respective owner or artist.)

Subscribers and Premier Dealers may Login to view all available images or complete details. If you are not a Member, you may Click Here for informatio

Subscribers and Premier Dealers may Login to view all available images or complete details. If you are not a Member, you may Click Here for informatio

All Artists: A B C D E F G H I J K L M N O P Q R S T U V W X Y Z

Home Page | **Terms and Agreement**

Ask ART
Home

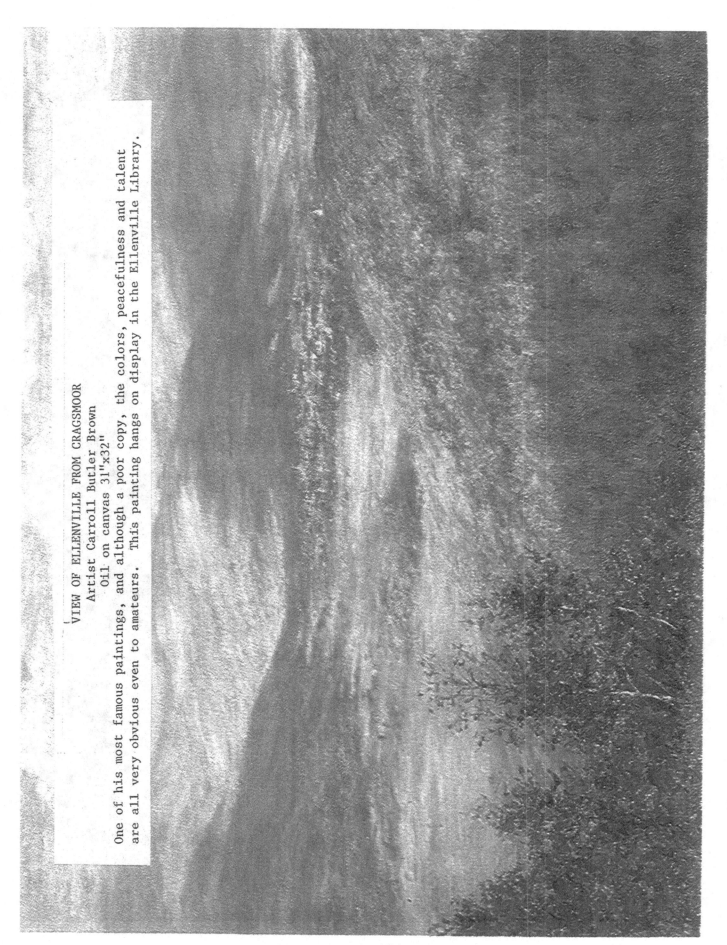

VIEW OF ELLENVILLE FROM CRAGSMOOR
Artist Carroll Butler Brown
Oil on canvas 31"x32"

One of his most famous paintings, and although a poor copy, the colors, peacefulness and talent are all very obvious even to amateurs. This painting hangs on display in the Ellenville Library.

Carroll Butler Brown, 1868 - 1923

Carroll Butler Brown was born in New York City around 1860* He was injured in his youth and confined to a wheelchair for the remainder of his life. To make time pass more quickly, his mother encouraged him to take up painting as a hobby. It soon became evident that he had a true talent for art, and he began serious study privately for a number of years. In 1908 Brown and his mother first came to Cragsmoor where they stayed in one of Mrs. Hartshorn's homes called the Casino. He was immediately accepted as a pleasant addition to the artist colony. Once a week the different artists gathered at his home, called the Falcon. At these weekly gatherings lively discussions on art took place. With the assistance of an attendant, he was transported by litter or horse and carriage to paint at different locations on the Mountain. Powerful sunsets dominate many of the numerous scenes he painted. Brown was not a member of the National Academy, although he did exhibit there on occasion. He died here at his home in Cragsmoor around 1923.

Copied from: Terwilliger House Museum
40 Center Street
Ellenville, New York

Pendaflex – MVF–Cragsmoor Art Exhibit
Booklet entitled – An Exhibition of
Cragsoor Artists 1870's through
1930's

*He was born in 1868.

Several prominent summer residents gather at a luncheon at Belle Dellenbaugh's Orchard Cottage. From left to right: Frederick S. Dellenbaugh, Edward L. Henry, Charles C. Curran, George Inness Jr., Miss Dellenbaugh, Arthur I. Keller, Dr. William Northrup, Edward Gay, James Cowing and Carroll Brown.

Note: Copied from Cragsmoor – an Historical Sketch
Compiled by Margaret Hakan & Susan Houghtaling
Published by the Cragsmoor Free Library 1983

Artists Group on back porch of Orchard Cottage c. 1909. (l. to r.) Frederick Dellenbaugh, E. L. Henry, Charles C. Curran, George Inness Jr., Bell Dellenbaugh, Arthur I. Keller, a Dr. Northrup, Edward Gay, a Mr. Cowing, and Carroll Butler Brown (from the November 1978 issue of the Antiques magazine)

Caption on reverse side: Carroll Brown's house
now owned by John Flynn

Note: The Flynns owned this home from May 1934
until it was sold to the Clarks in November 1951.
However, John Cashman Flynn died on November 23,
1947.

Note; The authors believe that the house looked
like this during Carroll Butler Brown's ownership - or possibly his mother's.

Copied from: Terwilliger House Museum
              40 Center Street
              Ellenville, New York

              Pendaflex - MVF-Cragsmoor
              Art Exhibit
              Booklet entitled - An
              Exhibition of Cragsmoor
              Artists 1870's through
              1930's

THIS OL' HOUSE

It was presumably built in the summer of 1919 and was undoubtedly designed by Frederick Dellenbaugh, as were many homes of that era, including the Cragsmoor Library. Doors and windows were often salvaged from buildings being demolished in New York City, then floated up the Hudson River by barge, dragged by oxen for the two or more hour trip to the top of the mountain where they were utilized in the construction of new buildings -- this house being just one example. In most rooms there are no two windows alike, nor doors either.

A very distinctive feature above the two front doors, are elliptical web-like designs called fan-lights, which were apparently "treasures" from New York City.

Dellenbaugh was noted to use any extra space to build a closet, yet he often forgot to allow space in which to erect a stairway leading to the second story. Often times stairways were steep, curved and very narrow. Not so in the Brown cottage! Perhaps because of Carrolls's disability! The beautiful stairway, made of chestnut, is wide and straight with posts,

newels and a hand rail on one side and a wall-mounted railing on the other. Is it possible that Carroll used both rails to hoist himself up the stairs to the bedroom area?

At the top of the stairway there is a difference in the level of the floors, perhaps an over-sight by Mr. Dellenbaugh. This has been adjusted by the addition of one step as shown at the right.

The master bedroom is a very large room which has six windows, making for a bright and cheerful room. Under one pair of windows is a cushioned storage seat. Many of the windows are crank-out style, but not all. Many are double-hung and, as before mentioned, vary greatly in size and design.

An observation which we find most unusual, are turn-knob style locks on the outside of all upstairs doors. We believe they were not in the house originally, but were installed by a later owner, perhaps the Flynns.

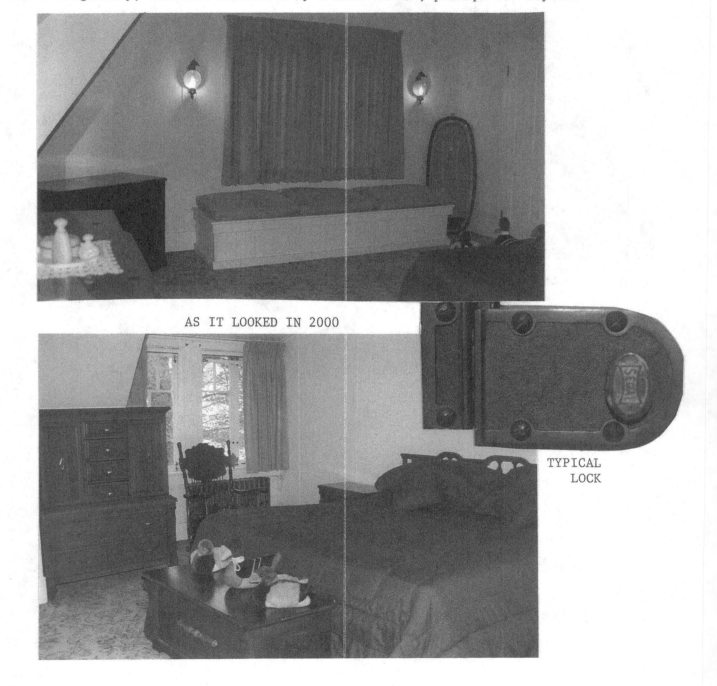

AS IT LOOKED IN 2000

TYPICAL
LOCK

Upstairs, in addition to the large bedroom are three smaller rooms. Today, two are used as bedrooms and one as an office. There is also a large bathroom which of course, was obviously added at a much later date, since outdoor plumbing was strictly in vogue at the time. That fairly well covers most of the highlights of the upstairs. The following photos show it far better than words can ever describe. The following photos were taken in 2000.

THE OFFICE

THE OFFICE

THE SMALLEST GUEST BEDROOM
(Above and below)

THIS IS THE LARGER
OF THE TWO UPSTAIRS
GUEST BEDROOMS.

The living room's most impressive features are the massive American chestnut hand-hewn posts and beams which span the entire room from floor to ceiling. To the best of our knowledge, the Cragsmoor Library is the only other building on the mountain which can boast the same type of beams. It is possible, however, that the same type of construction can be found in other homes and that we are simply unaware of them.

Also gracing the living room is a large and beautiful fireplace built with local stone. For reasons unknown, the fireplace has no damper. Could it be that because of Carroll's disability, he was unable to reach under/into the fireplace opening to use a damper handle?

There are four Dutch doors in this room. Originally, all led outdoors, however, today two of them are used as entryways to the "added-on" sunroom. Two of them lead from the living room to the outside front of the house, (One of them to the front porch).

STILL THE LIVING ROOM –
THE DUTCH DOOR WITH THE
FANLIGHT LEADS OUT TO THE
FRONT PORCH.
IN THE BOTTOM PHOTO, THE
ARCHWAY ON THE FAR RIGHT
IS THE ENTRY HALL TO THE
BATHROOM AND KITCHEN.

The visible flooring (that which is not carpeted today), is original, made of yellow pine and is in excellent condition. This flooring can be seen both downstairs and upstairs.

Now, still in the living room, there are built-in bookcases in three corners of the room. They are L-shaped and are original to the cottage also. Each section of shelving is between three and six feet long and four shelves high. Many shelves harbor books which were owned by several Cragsmoorians, from Carroll Butler Brown and family to the Edward Gay family, John Cashman Flynn and Kenneth and Helen Clark.

THIS BOOKCASE IS JUST TO THE LEFT OF THE FRONT DOOR WHICH LEADS TO THE PORCH.

THIS ONE IS ON THE OP-POSITE SIDE OF THE ROOM. UNFORTUNATELY, THE THIRD IS NOT PICTURED. IT IS SITUATED "KITTY-CORNERED" ACROSS FROM THE ONE NEXT TO THE FRONT DOOR.

207

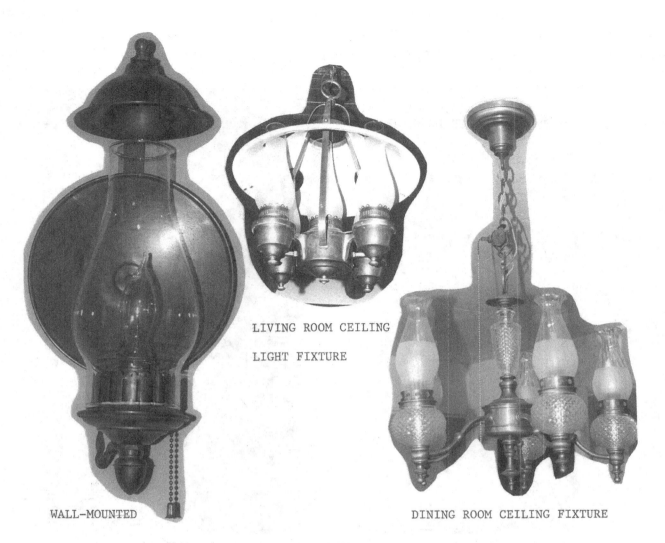

LIVING ROOM CEILING

LIGHT FIXTURE

WALL-MOUNTED   DINING ROOM CEILING FIXTURE

    There are many wall-mounted light fixtures throughout this home, both up and downstairs, which are in all liklihood original and were at some point in time, converted to electric. Ceiling fixtures found now in the living and dining rooms were also original and converted. They, no doubt, also came from razed buildings in New York City. By the way, the type of wall fixtures shown above can be found in almost all rooms of the house, excluding bathrooms, kitchen and sunroom. All of these rooms were either add-ons or renovations.

    Between the dining room and living room is a pocket-door, the only one in the house. Between the dining room and the kitchen there was a narrow glass swinging door, which to this very day may still be stored somewhere in this old house. That door was replaced in the 1980's by a large archway. (On the right.)

POCKET DOOR AND DUTCH DOOR LEADING TO

SUN ROOM IN REAR OF HOUSE.

In the kitchen was a chimney which had a stove pipe opening in it. Presumably, there was a stove for cooking and heating. A door leading outdoors was on the northwest wall of the room. The kitchen windows still today have the original wavy glass panes, as do all windows in the house.

On the southwest side and adjacent to the kitchen is a porte cochere, which we believe to be original. Until fairly recently there remained a hitching ring embedded in the stonework under the porte cochere, but it is no longer there.

This home was built with a cellar which remains much the same today and the interior steps leading from the first floor to the basement are original.

In the attic, yet today, there remains a large tub which, more than likely, collected rainwater which was gravity-fed to supply water for the house.

A fairly large porch, approximately seventeen feet by seven feet adorns the front of The Falcon and is graced by three large Tuscan columns. Those in addition to the two at the main front entrance of the house. Two more support the roof structure of the porte cochere. At the rear of the house, off the living room and dining room, was a patio whose roof was supported by three of these columns.

According to the National Register of Historic Places, Section number 7, page 27, there was a carriage house built on a slab just across from the cottage and being on the same parcel of property. There are several construction similarities between it and The Falcon, such as the fan-light above the central classical doorway, the fireplace (which does have a damper), the exterior shingles and trim, the trademark narrow Dellenbaugh stairway, assorted syles of windows throughout. These are all reminiscent of the main house. (See following page.)

Carroll Butler Brown loved summering at The Falcon and so it was on Sunday, June 3, 1923 when he and his mother arrived in Cragsmoor to enjoy another glorious summer. It just wasn't to be, for his mountain-top stay ended abruptly the very next day. He died on Monday morning, June 4, 1923, at home.

At this juncture, we have not been able to learn any particulars regarding his death, such as cause, burial place, etc. We have, however, at the Ulster County Building in Kingston, been able to procure a copy of his Last Will and Testament. (Copy of same follows.)

Upon Carroll's passing, his mother Mrs. Theodore T. (Frances M.) Brown inherited The Falcon which she owned until her death in 1930. The property stayed in the Brown family until 1934.

NOTE; Since all of the photographs have been taken in recent years, we can only suggest how the house looked in Carrol Butler Brown's day.

Sketch by Emily August - 2006

The carriage house front entry as it looks today. But take away the fancy
front door and decorative fan-light (which we have recently learned is strictly
decorative and certainly not original), and add a large enough barn door through
which a horse or horses may pass.

The picture below clearly shows the additions that made this carriage house
into a house. But more on that later.

—Artist Carrol B. Brown, a well known summer resident at Cragsmoor, died at his summer home there Monday morning. Mr. Brown, accompanied by his mother, had just come to Cragsmoor Sunday. He was 55 years of age. 6-7-1923

ELVL JOURNAL
6-7-1923

In the Name of God Amen!

I, Carroll B. Brown, of the City and State of New York, being of sound mind and memory and considering the uncertainty of life, do make, publish and declare this to be my Last Will and Testament as follows: —

First: I direct my Executors hereinafter named to pay all my just debts and funeral expenses as soon after my decease as practicable.

Second. All the rest, residue and remainder of my estate, both real and personal and wheresoever the same may be situate, I give, devise and bequeath to my Mother Frances M. Brown. In case my mother shall not be living at the time of my death I give, devise and bequeath all my property as follows: My stock in the Davis Machine Tool Company of Rochester, New York, I give to my brother J. Herbert Brown and his wife May E. Brown. The rest, residue and remainder of my estate, I give, devise and bequeath to my brothers J. Herbert Brown and Harold P. Brown and my sister Harriet B. Wright share and share alike. —

Lastly. I nominate, constitute and appoint my brothers J. Herbert Brown and Harold P. Brown, Executors of this my Last Will and Testament, without bonds, hereby giving and granting unto them full power and authority to sell any real estate that I may own at the time of my death. —

————

In Witness Whereof, I have hereunto set my hand and seal this twenty fifth day of March, in the year of our Lord, One thousand nine hundred and Sixteen —

Carroll B. Brown   (L.S.)

The foregoing instrument was signed, sealed, published and declared by the above named Testator, Carroll B. Brown, as and for his Last Will and Testament, in the presence of us, who, at his request, in his presence, and in the presence of each other, have hereunto subscribed our names as Witnesses this twenty fifth day of March, A.D. One thousand nine hundred and Sixteen.

Travis M. Pickner 75 Forsta ave. Mt Vernon New York

215

IN THE NAME OF GOD, AMEN

I, CARROLL B. BROWN, of the City and State of New York, being of sound mind and memory, and considering the uncertainty of life, do make, publish and declare this to be my LAST WILL AND TESTAMENT as follows:-

FIRST:- I direct my Executors hereinafter named to pay all my just debts and funeral expenses as soon after my decease as practicable.

SECOND:- All the rest, residue and remainer of my estate, both real and personal and wheresoever the same may be situate, I give, devise and bequeath to my mother, FRANCES M. BROWN. In case my mother shall not be living at the time of my death, I give, devise and bequeath all my property as follows: My stock in the Davis Machine Tool Company of Rochester, New York, I give to my brother F. HERBERT BROWN and his wife MAY C. BROWN. The rest, residue and remainder of my Estate, I give, devise and bequeath to my brothers F. HERBERT BROWN and HAROLD P. BROWN, and my sister HARRIET B. WRIGHT, share and share alike.

LASTLY:- I nominate, constitute and appoint my brothers F. HERBERT BROWN and HAROLD P. BROWN, Executors of this my Last Will and Testament, without bonds, hereby giving and granting unto them full power and authority to sell any real estate that I may own at the time of my death.

IN WITNESS WHEREOF, I have hereunto set my hand and seal this twenty-fifth day of March, in the year of our Lord, One Thousand Nine Hundred and Sixteen.

CARROLL B. BROWN, (L. S.)

The foregoing instrument was signed, sealed, published and declared by the above named Testator, CARROLL B. BROWN, as and for his Last Will and Testament, in the presence of us, who, at his request, in his presence and in the presence of each other, have hereunto subscribed our names as Witnesses this twenty-fifth day A. D. One Thousand Nine Hundred and Sixteen.
FRANK M. TICHENOR, 75 Forster Avenue, Mount Vernon, New York.
JOSEPHINE B. TICHENOR, 75 Forster Avenue, Mount Vernon, New York.

PETITION TO PROVE WILL.

Surrogate's Court.
COUNTY OF ULSTER.

In the Matter of Proving the Last Will
and Testament of

Carroll B. Brown

Deceased,

As a Will of Real and Personal Property.

To the Surrogate's Court of the County of Ulster:

The Petition of F. Herbert Brown _____ residing
Newark ____ Wayne County New York in said County, respectfully showe
that your Petitioner is an Executor ____ named in
the Last Will and Testament of Carroll B. Brown ____ late of Cragsmoor
of ____ County of Ulster, deceased:

That said Last Will and Testament, herewith presented, relates to both real and perso
property, and bears date the 25th day of March, 1916, and is signed at the
thereof by the said testator and by Frank M Tichenor
and Josephine B. Tichenor ____ as subscribing witnes
The Petitioner does not know of any ____ codicil to said Last Will
Testament, nor is there any to the best of his information and belief.

That the said deceased was at or immediately previous to his death, a resident of
County of Ulster, and departed this life at Cragsmoor in said county
on the fourth day of June 1923

So far as they can be ascertained with due diligence:

The names, relationship, places of residence and postoffice addresses of the husband or w
if any, and all the heirs at law and next of kin of the testator, are as follows:

Frances M Brown, mother of decedent, residing at Cragsmoor
Ulster County - New York

F. Herbert Brown, petitioner, brother of decedent,
residing at 50 Prospect Street, Newark, Wayne County

Harold P. Brown, brother of decedent, temporarily residing a
55 Russell Square, London England

Harriet B. Wright, sister of decedent, residing at 231 West
Ellsworth Street, Denver, Colorado

That said decedent was unmarried and left no heirs
____ or above.

Property situate in Cragsmoor, in the township
of Wawarsing, County of Ulster, State of New
York, conveyed to decedent by two certain deeds
recorded in the Ulster County Clerk's Office on
September 27th, 1917 in Liber 462 of Deeds at
page 221 and 222, respectively.   Assessed value
$1040, real value $5,000, subject to mortgage of
$3,000, equity $2,000, made by decedent in his
lifetime with interest at 6%. $2,000   ✓

SCHEDULE A. 11

Savings Bank Account in American National Bank of
Mount Vernon, New York, including interest to date
of death, in joint name of decedent or Frances M.
Brown   2,500
Chequing account in American National Bank of
Mount Vernon, New York, including interest to date of
death.   625.00 ✓

SCHEDULE A. 111

1000 Shares of Davis Machine Tool Co. par value
$10 per share.   This company went into the hands
of the Receiver and the assets were sold, and there
was not realized from the sale, enough to pay the
debts.

SCHEDULE A. V

Nothing

SCHEDULE A. VI

Nothing

SCHEDULE B. 1

Funeral Expenses   272.68 ✓

SCHEDULE B. 11

Expenses of Administration and Councel fees   250.00 ✓

SCHEDULE B. 111

Note of Decedent for $400, dated July 1st, 1919 to the
order of Frank M. Tichenor, payable on demand. Paid   200.00 ✓
on account, December 27th, 1920, $200, leaving a balance   29.36 ✓
due to June 4th, 1923, including interest at 6%   229.36
Interest on $3,0 0 Motge on property at Cragsmoor at
6% from March 27, 1923 to June 4th, 1923   33.50 ✓

SCHEDULE B. 1V

Nothing

218

Third -- I further report that I found the property left by the decedent herein or in which said decedent had any beneficial interest or appointed or transferred in contemplation of death. by decedent. to consist of the items set forth in the annexed affidavit for appraisal, and that the fair market value of each of the said items at the date of decedent's death is the amount set down by me opposite such item in the column designated " Value as appraised in this proceeding," and that the sums properly to be allowed as deductions herein for funeral expenses, expenses of administration, debts of decedent, etc., are the amounts set down by me after the several items claimed in the column designated "Allowed in this proceeding," as a result of which I find the said assets and deductions to be as shown in the following summary:

Assets.

Schedule A — Real Estate.....................................	$ 2,000.00
Schedule B — Cash...	625.00
Schedule C — Personal Effects...............................	50.00
Schedule D — Mortgages, Notes and Accounts...................	
Schedule E — Insurance......................................	
Schedule F — Stocks and Bonds...............................	
Schedule G — Partnerships or Business Interests.............	
Schedule H — Gifts and Transfers...........................	
Schedule I — Powers of Appointment.........................	
Schedule J — Interest in other estates.....................	
Schedule K — Other property................................	
Gross assets...	$ 2,675.00

Subject to Deductions as follows:

Schedule L — Funeral and Administration....................	$ 522.68	
Schedule M — Debts...	262.86	
Schedule N — Other deductions.............................		
Commissions...		
Total deductions......................................		$ 785.54

The total of all property passing upon the death of the decedent, I appraise at.... $ 1,889.46

Fourth— I further report all the beneficiaries entitled at the time of decedent's death to an interest in this estate pursuant to the provisions of Law, and of the said decedent's Last Will and Testament, the relationship of such persons to decedent, the amount of the share or interest of each, and whether such share or interest is taxable in this proceeding, to be as hereinafter set forth, all of said beneficiaries being of full age and sound mind except as otherwise designated.

BENEFICIARIES Relationship	Amount of interest	Amount of exemption	Amount of interest taxable
Frances M. Brown Mother 30 Claremont Avenue, Mt.Vernon, N. Y.	$1,889.46		
1/2 Joint account amounting to $2,500.00	1,250.00		
	$3,139.46	$3,139.46	

SURROGATE'S COURT : ULSTER COUNTY.

In The Matter Of The Probate

Of

The Last Will and Testament

Of

CARROLL B. BROWN,

Deceased.

FRANCES M. BROWN, the undersigned, being of full age and being one of the heirs and next-of-kin of Carroll B.Brown, late of the County of Ulster, deceased, named in the petition, do hereby appear in person, and waive the issuance of service of a citation in the above-entitled matter, and consent to the Last Will and Testament of said Carroll B. Brown, deceased, bearing date the 25th day of March, 1916, to be admitted to probate forthwith, and that Letters Testamentary may be issued

thereon to F. Herbert Brown of Newark, Wayne County, New York.

Frances M. Brown

STATE OF NEW YORK)
: SS.:
County of Ulster)

On this **20** day of August, 1923, before me the subscriber personally appeared, FRANCES M. BROWN, to me known to be the same person described in and who executed the foregoing waiver and consent to probate, and duly acknowledged that she executed the same.

3

W R Garrett
Notary Public

221

10

That there is no other Will of said Testator on File in the

Surrogate's Office of Ulster County. ————— ——

That the value of the real estate left by the decedent does not exceed $ **5000**
and the value of the personal property left by the decedent does not exceed $ **100**

That personal service of citation cannot with due diligence be made upon the above named non-residents within the State of New York, and your Petitioner prays for an order directing the service thereof without the State, or by publication, pursuant to Chapter 18 of the Code of Civil Procedure.

That no petition for the probate of said Will, or for Letters of Administration on said estate, has been heretofore filed in this or any other Surrogate's Court of this State.

Your Petitioner further prays that a citation issue to the above named persons to attend the probate thereof, and that the said Last Will and Testament of _Carroll B Brown_

————— may be proved as a Will of real and personal property, and that Letters Testamentary may be issued thereon to the Executors who may qualify thereunder. ————

Dated _August 15_ 192_3_

J Herbert Brown

Petitioner.

State of New York, } ss.:
Wayne COUNTY

J Herbert Brown

the Petitioner named in the foregoing Petition, being duly sworn deposes and says that he has read the foregoing Petition subscribed by him and knows the contents thereof; and that the same is true of his own knowledge, except as to matters therein stated to be alleged on information and belief, and that as to those matters he believes it to be true.

Sworn to this _15th_ day
of _August_ A. D., 192_3_

J Herbert Brown
Petitioner.

B C William
Notary Public.

222

(No. 9).

I, C. K. Loughran, Clerk of the said Surrogate's Court of the County of Ulster, do hereby certify that, at a Surrogate's Court held in and for the County of Ulster, in the State of New York, at the City of Kingston, in said county, on the ____27th____ day of ____August,_____1923____, the annexed original Will of_____Carroll B. Brown_____ late of the ____Town____ of ____Wawarsing_____ in said county, deceased, upon due proof, was admitted to probate, as a Will valid to pass real and personal property, and directed to be recorded, by a decree of said Court duly made and entered in Book No.__19__ of Minutes of Wills, at page__361.___

Witness, my hand and the seal of the Surrogate's Court of said County, this ____27th_____ day of _____August,_____1923.

_____
Clerk of the Surrogate's Court.

4

223

STATE OF NEW YORK)
)ss.
County of Ulster)

BERT H. TERWILLIGER and H. WESTLAKE COONS
being duly sworn, depose and say, that they reside in the
Village of Ellenville, Ulster County, New York, and are
acquainted with real estate in the Town of Wawarsing, Ulster
County, New York, and have seen the same bought and sold,
and they are acquainted with the real estate owned by the
late CARROLL B. BROWN at the time of his death, and that
they are acquainted with the value thereof, and that in
their opinion the value of the same at the time of the
death of said CARROLL B. BROWN was as follows:

Parcel #1-ALL THAT TRACT OR PARCEL OF LAND, situate in the
Town of Wawarsing, County of Ulster and State of New York,
and being on top of the Shawangunk Mountain, said parcel
of land being described as follows:

BEGINNING at the East side of the gate at a stone
on the bounds of lands of Abbie Kite; running thence North
along her bounds North 41 degrees 45 minutes West three
hundred and fifty seven feet (357) to a stake; thence North
thirty eight degrees 50 minutes West further along the bounds
of said Abbie Kite, two hundred and eighty five (285) to a
white oak tree marked on both sides, and from said white oak
tree; thence South 18 degrees 50 minutes West about two hundred
and sixty three feet (263) to a stake and stones; thence South
80 degrees East twenty two feet to the Northeasterly corner
of a lot of Emelie H. Keene at a pile of stones near a marked
chestnut tree; thence same course along said Keene lot, one
hundred seven and 4/12 feet, (107-4/12) to the Northerly
corner thereof; thence along said Keene lot South 5 degrees
30 minutes East one hundred and thirty nine and 6/12 feet
(139-6/12) to stones North of a large maple tree, the
Northerly corner of the triangular lot of Rebecca C. Fox;
thence along the same South 70 degrees 50 minutes East eighty
nine feet. (89) to the Northerly corner of the Rebecca C. Fox
house lot; thence along the Northerly side thereof South 78
degrees 35 minutes East 261 feet to a post; thence in a
straight line Northeasterly about nineteen feet (19) to the
place of beginning. Containing about three acres of land.
Reserving a road about thirty feet, (30) wide along the
Northerly and Westerly side of said lot to lands formerly
of Eliza C. Hartshorn, now Daniel I. Odell and others,
together with a right of way over Schuyler Avenue to the
public highway. Being the same parcel of land conveyed by
Eliza GL Hartshorn to Mollie V. Leavitt, by deed dated July
29th., 1895, and recorded in the Ulster County Clerk's office
in Liber 324 of deeds at page 633.

34

224

The above described premises being a part of the premises heretofore conveyed by Alexander Terwilliger and wife to Eliza G. Hartshorn, by deed dated June 10th.,1893 and recorded in Liber 315 of deeds at page 39.

Parcel #2.-ALL THAT CERTAIN LOT, PIECE OR PARCEL OF LAND situate, lying and being on the top of Shawangunk Mountain in the Town of Wawarsing, Ulster County, New York, which is bounded and described as follows:

BEGINNING at the most Northerly corner of a triangular lot sold to Rebecca C.Fox at a stake and stones and running thence North 50 degrees 30 minutes West one hundred and thirty nine and 6/12 feet to a stone; thence North 80 degrees West one hundred and seven feet and four inches to a stone near a marked chestnut tree; thence South six degrees West one hundred and ninety four feet to an oak tree marked; on the Northerly edge of a ravine, thence about North 76 degrees East one hundred and forty three feet to the place of beginning be the same more or less, together with a right of way along and over a proposed new road on the Westerly side thereof-together with a right of way over Schuyler Avenue to the public highway, the above being the same premises as were conveyed to the party of the first part by Eliza G.Hartshorn, widow, by deed dated July 20th.,1895 and recorded in Ulster County Clerk's office August 7th., 1895 in Liber 324 of deeds on page 630,

assessed value $1040.00, real value $ 5000.00

Sworn to before me this
30th.day of October
1925.

Notary Public.

225

JOHN LEVY GALLERIES

Five Hundred Fifty-nine Fifth Avenue

New York

MEMORIAL EXHIBITION

of

PAINTINGS

By Carroll Brown

February Twenty-fifth to March Eighth

1924

The John Levy Galleries

PAINTINGS

Ancient and Modern

559 Fifth Avenue, New York

———

28 Place Vendome, Paris

MEMORIAL EXHIBITION OF PAINTINGS BY CARROLL BROWN

---

1. AN OLD BIRCH ON THE MOUNTAIN TOP
2. OCTOBER, CRAGSMOOR
3. NOVEMBER HAZE
4. OVER THE HILLS AND FAR AWAY
5. MORNING IN AUGUST, CRAGSMOOR
6. THE SHADOW OF THE MOUNTAIN
7. GOLDEN OCTOBER
8. THE NORTH-WEST WIND
9. MY TREES
10. WIND-SWEPT
11. LATE OCTOBER
12. THE VALLEY OF DREAMS
    (LOANED)
13. WIND STORM
14. FROSTY NOVEMBER MORNING
15. RONDOUT VALLEY, END OF SEPTEMBER
    (LOANED)
17. APRIL MORNING IN THE MOUNTAINS

CARROLL BROWN

Born, February 17, 1868—Died, June 4, 1923.

Due to circumstances, the result of an early accident, Carroll Brown was physically handicapped and was thus cut off in a great measure from association with other painters. Consequently isolated and apart from much he longed for, he was little known by his fellows.

His early studies were made under William Sartain and one summer he enjoyed the privilege of Winslow Homer's criticism on his work. But he was largely self-taught and continuously and untiringly searched for ways and means of expression.

He was naturally sensitive and diffident, with a true appreciation for the fine things in literature, music and painting. His mind was gifted and alert and he had a sincerity of purpose which always reached the heart. Being a lover of work and a lover of beauty, his ambition was to record something of the enchanting world, especially as he found it at his beloved Cragsmoor.

Tree forms he rendered with exquisite feeling. The loveliness of flowers, the breadth of hills, the far reach of valleys, and above all, the glory of the sunset skies awakened his most ardent expression. He approached his work with the reverence of a religious rite.

A group of his paintings is assembled here as a memorial to him. In their simplicity, charm and sentiment, they speak to all sympathetic souls and reveal the pure spirit which evoked them.

Augustus Vincent Tack

18. LAUREL AND SUNSHINE
19. THE BRIDGE IN THE WOODS
20. OCTOBER MIST
21. THE HILLS WHENCE COMETH MY HELP
22. THE FALLING OF NIGHT (Water Color)
    (LOANED)
23. DESOLATE NOVEMBER
24. MOONRISE OVER CITY ROOFS
25. LAUREL
26. THE HOLLYHOCK PATH
27. AZALIAS, CRAGSMOOR
28. VILLAGE IN THE VALLEY
29. AUTUMN SUNSET
30. OCTOBER EVENING
31. WINDY MOONRISE
32. AN AFTERNOON IN JUNE
33. APRIL, SENECA FALLS
34. BRIDGE IN THE WOODS (II)
35. EVENING ACROSS THE VALLEY
36. EARLY OCTOBER

37. MY TREES (II)
38. SUMMER AFTERNOON, CRAGSMOOR
39. SUNSET AFTER STORM
40. MIST IN THE VALLEY
41. THE PEACE OF EVENING
42. SPRING SUNSET
43. JULY
44. SEPTEMBER SUNSET
45. GOLDEN EVENING
46. TWILIGHT
47. A MOUNTAIN SUNSET
48. AFTERGLOW
49. SUNSET AFTER A STORM

Note—Paintings not on view for lack of wall space can be seen on application.

228

House Histories –
Brown to Flynn to
Clark to Clark

MORE REAL ESTATE TRANSACTIONS AND OTHER INFO
(Involving four parcels, for the most part)

Property was originally owned by Alexander Terwilliger and his wife, Harriet J.

1893	June 10	The Terwilligers sold to Iliza G. Hartshorn
1895	July 29	Eliza G. Hartshorn sold to Emelie H. Keene (LIBER 324 Pages 630 and 631)
1895	July 29	Eliza G. Hartshorn sold to Mollie V. Leavitt (LIBER 324 Pages 633,634 and 635)
1917	Sept. 4	Emelie Keene to Carroll Butler Brown (LIBER 462 Pages 221 and 222)
1917	Sept. 11	Mollie Leavitt to Carroll Butler Brown (LIBER 462 Pages 222 and 223)
1923	June 7	Carroll Butler Brown died.
1923	Aug. 8	Probate of that date shows that Frances M. Brown inherited the property and house.
1930		Frances M. Brown died.
1934	May 15	Seller F. Herbert Brown and Kathryn M. Brown, wife, of Scarsdale, New York to John Cashman Flynn for $1.00 (quit claim) (LIBER 570 Page 393)
1934	May 16	Seller Harold P. Brown and Martha T. Brown, wife, of Montclair, New Jersey to John Cashman Flynn for $1.00 (LIBER 570 Page 392)
1934	May 19	Last Will and Testament of Frances M. Brown of New York City, (Frank M. Tichenor, executor) to John Cashman Flynn for $2850.00 (LIBER 570 Page 390)
1937	Jan. 14	Premises conveyed by Pratt Boise (Ulster County Treasurer) to Franklin O'Bryon (LIBER 598 Page 369)
1941	Dec. 8	Deed from Marion McMurtie to John Cashman Flynn (LIBER 622 Page 235)
1943	Apr. 9	Deed to Franklin O'Bryon to John Cashman Flynn (LIBER 632 Page 247)
1946	May 8	DeWitt to Kenneth and Helen Clark (1/2 acre) (LIBER 665 Page 589)
1948	May 20	John Cashman Flynn to Kenneth and Helen Clark (LIBER 530 Page 442)

1951 Nov.21 Four parcels from the late John Cashman Flynn to Kenneth and Helen Clark, wife, for the sum of $1.00 (LIBER 816 Page 228)

1951 Dec. 6 Frances Smith Flynn to Kenneth and Helen Clark (LIBER 816 Page 228)

1961 Dec. 1 Patricia Gay to Kenneth and Helen Clark (LIBER 1116 Pages 593 and 594)

1961 Dec. 2 Ingovar Gay, Dorothy Gordon and Patricia Gay to Kenneth and Helen Clark (LIBER 1116 Pages 591 and 592)

1982 Nov. 4 Estate of Helen Clark to Harold M. Clark (LIBER 665 Page 589)

1985 Mar. 26 (Recorded date) Estate of Helen Clark to Harold M. Clark (LIBER 1524 Page 219)

2000 Feb. 28 Harold M. Clark to Christina Clark (LIBER 3080 Pages 7, 9, 10 and 11)

3527 • 1-51-30M—Bargain and Sale Deed, without Covenant against Grantor's Acts—Individual or Corporation.

THIS INDENTURE, made the 21ˢᵗ day of November nineteen hundred and **fifty-one**
BETWEEN FLORENCE SMITH FLYNN, residing at No. 17 Summit Avenue,
Mount Vernon, Westchester County, New York

party of the first part, and KENNETH CLARK and HELEN CLARK, his wife, both
residing at Continental Road, Napanoch, Ulster County, New York

party of the second part,
WITNESSETH, that the party of the first part, in consideration of One dollar ($1.00) and

other valuable consideration

lawful money of the United States,

paid

by the party of the second part, does hereby grant and release unto the party of the second part,

their heirs and assigns forever.

PARCEL ONE:
ALL that certain lot, piece or parcel of land situate, lying and being on the top of Shawangunk Mountain in the Town of Wawarsing, Ulster
County, New York, and which is bounded and described as follows:
BEGINNING at the most northerly corner of a triangular lot sold
to Rebecca C. Fox at a stake and stones and running thence north 5°
30' west one hundred and thirty nine and 6/12 feet to a stone; thence
north 80° west one hundred and seven feet and four inches to a stone
near a marked chestnut tree; thence south 6° west one hundred and
ninety-four feet to an oak tree marked, on the northerly edge of a
ravine; thence about north 76° east one hundred and forty-three feet
to the place of beginning be the same more or less.
PARCEL TWO:
ALL that tract or parcel of land situate in the Town of Wawarsing, County of Ulster and State of New York, and being on top of the
Shawangunk Mountain, said parcel of land being described as follows:
BEGINNING at the east side of the gate at a stone on the bounds
of lands of Abbie Kite; running thence north along her bounds north
41 degrees 45 minutes west three hundred and fifty-seven feet (357)
to a stake; thence north thirty-eight degrees 50 minutes west further
along the bounds of said Abbie Kite, two hundred and eighty-five (285)
feet to a white oak tree marked on both sides, and from said white oak
tree; thence south 18 degrees 50 minutes west about two hundred and
sixty-three (263) feet to a stake and stones; thence south 80 degrees
east twenty-two feet to the northeasterly corner of a lot of Emelie
H. Keene at a pile of stones near a marked chestnut tree; thence same
course along said Keene lot, one hundred seven and 4/12 feet (107 4/12)
to the northerly corner thereof; thence along said Keene lot, south 5
degrees 30 minutes east one hundred and thirty-nine and 6/12 feet
(139 6/12) to stones north of a large maple tree, the northerly corner of the triangular lot of Rebecca C. Fox; thence along the same
south 70 degrees 50 minutes east eighty-nine feet (89) to the northerly corner of the Rebecca C. Fox house lot; thence along the northerly side thereof south 78 degrees 35 minutes east 261 feet to a post;
thence in a straight line northeasterly about nineteen feet (19) to
the place of beginning.
PARCEL THREE:
ALL THAT TRACT, PIECE OR PARCEL of land situated at Cragsmoor,
Ulster County, New York, and more particularly described as follows:
Beginning at an iron pile set in the line of the lands now of
Flynn and runs from the beginning along the Flynn lands the next two
courses (1) south 87 degrees 50 minutes east 87.0 feet to an iron pipe,
(2) South 78 degrees 35 minutes east 162.0 feet to an iron pipe;
thence along the McMurtrie lands the next two courses (1) south

16 degrees 30 minutes west 176.0 feet to an iron pipe (2) south 68 degrees 30 minutes east 135.0 feet to an iron pipe; thence along the road south 24 degrees 30 minutes west 83.0 feet to an iron pipe; thence along another road north 68 degrees 30 minutes west 417.0 feet to an iron pipe; thence north 18 degrees 50 minutes east 232.5 feet to the beginning and containing 2.0 acres of land.

Being a portion of the premises of which Rebecca C. Fox died seized and possessed and which descended to the party of the first part by the said last will and testament of Rebecca C. Fox.

PARCEL FOUR:

ALL THAT TRACT, PIECE OR PARCEL OF LAND situated at Cragsmoor in the Town of Wawarsing, County of Ulster and State of New York, and more particularly described as follows:

100 x 100 Feet, more or less, described at Lot. Cragsmoor. Bounded North by Henry, South by Piney Lane, east by Fox, West by lands of Gay, against which the words "Peck W.H." appear on the assessment roll of the Town of Wawarsing for the year 1934.

BEING the same premises conveyed by Pratt Boice, Ulster County Treasurer, to Franklin O'Bryon by deed of conveyance bearing date the 14th day of January, 1937, and recorded in the Ulster County Clerk's Office on the 24th day of July, 1937, in Liber 598 of Deeds at page 369.

Said four parcels being the same premises conveyed in his lifetime to John Cashman Flynn late of Mount Vernon, New York, by the following conveyances recorded in the Clerk's office, Ulster County:

1. Deed by Frank M. Tichenor as executor of the last will and testament of Frances M. Brown, dated May 19, 1934, and recorded on June 2, 1934, in Liber 570 of Deeds, page 390.

2. Quit claim deed from Harold P. Brown and Martha T. Brown, his wife, dated May 16, 1934, and recorded on June 2, 1934, in Liber 570 of Deeds, page 392.

3. Quit claim deed from F. Herbert Brown and Kathryn M. Brown, his wife, dated May 15, 1934, and recorded on June 2, 1934, in Liber 570 of Deeds, page 393.

4. Deed from Marion F. McMurtie dated November 12, 1940, and recorded on December 8, 1941 in Liber 622 of Deeds, page 235.

5. Deed from Franklin O'Bryon dated November 5, 1942, and recorded on April 9, 1943, in Liber 632 of Deeds, page 247.

Said John Flynn died intestate on November 23, 1947. By decree of the Surrogate's Court Westchester County dated April 21, 1950 (Index No. 996/1948) said party of the first part was adjudged the sole distributee of said decedent and seized in fee simple of the above described premises. Pursuant to said decree said party of the first part in her capacity as administratrix of the estate of said decedent by deed dated June 7, 1950 and intended to be recorded simultaneously herewith, conveyed the above described premises to herself individually in confirmation of her title thereto.

Reserving with respect to PARCEL TWO above described, a road about thirty (30) feet wide along the northerly and westerly side of said lot of lands formerly of Eliza G. Hartshorn, now Daniel I. Odell and others, together with a right of way over Schuyler Avenue to the public Highway.

Granting with respect to PARCEL ONE above described, a right of way along and over the proposed new road on the westerly side thereof.

TOGETHER with all the right, title and interest, if any, of the party of the first part of, in and to any streets and roads abutting the above described premises to the center lines thereof.

TOGETHER with the appurtenances and all the estate and rights of the party of the first part in and to said premises.

TO HAVE AND TO HOLD the premises herein granted unto the party of the second part.

their heirs and assigns forever,

AND the party of the first part, in compliance with Section 13 of the Lien Law, covenants that the party of the first part will receive the consideration for this conveyance and will hold the right to receive such consideration as a trust fund to be applied first for the purpose of paying the cost of the improvement and that the party of the first part will apply the same first to the payment of the cost of the improvement before using any part of the total of the same for any other purpose.

IN WITNESS WHEREOF, the party of the first part has executed this deed the day and year first above written.

IN PRESENCE OF:

Arthur F.X. Hines.

Florence Smith Flynn (S.)

STATE OF NEW YORK, COUNTY OF **NEW YORK** ss.:

On the 21st day of *November*, nineteen hundred and **fifty-one** before me personally came **FLORENCE SMITH FLYNN**

to me known to be the individual described in and who executed the foregoing instrument, and acknowledged that **she** executed the same.

Arthur F.X. Hines
Notary Public, New York
State Residing Nassau County
Certified N.Y. Co Clk & Reg
30-1803600 Com. Exp. 3/30/53

State of New York, ss.:
County of New York.

No. **5132** Form 1

I, ARCHIBALD R. WATSON, County Clerk and Clerk of the Supreme Court, New York County, a Court of Record having by law a seal, DO HEREBY CERTIFY that

Arthur F.X. Hines

whose name is subscribed to the annexed affidavit, deposition, certificate of acknowledgment or proof, was at the time of taking the same a NOTARY PUBLIC in and for the State of New York, duly commissioned and sworn and qualified to act as such throughout the State of New York; that pursuant to law a commission, or a certificate of his official character, and his autograph signature, have been filed in my office; that as such Notary Public he was duly authorized by the laws of the State of New York to administer oaths and affirmations, to receive and certify the acknowledgment or proof of deeds, mortgages, powers of attorney and other written instruments for lands, tenements and hereditaments to be read in evidence or recorded; to protest notes and to take and certify affidavits and depositions; and further, that I am well acquainted with the handwriting of such Notary Public, or have compared the signature on the annexed instrument with his autograph signature deposited in my office, and believe that his signature is genuine.

IN TESTIMONY WHEREOF, I have hereunto set my hand and affixed my official seal this _____ day of _____ NOV 1951

FEE PAID 25¢

Archibald R. Watson
County Clerk and Clerk of the Supreme Court, New York County

9 .35

233

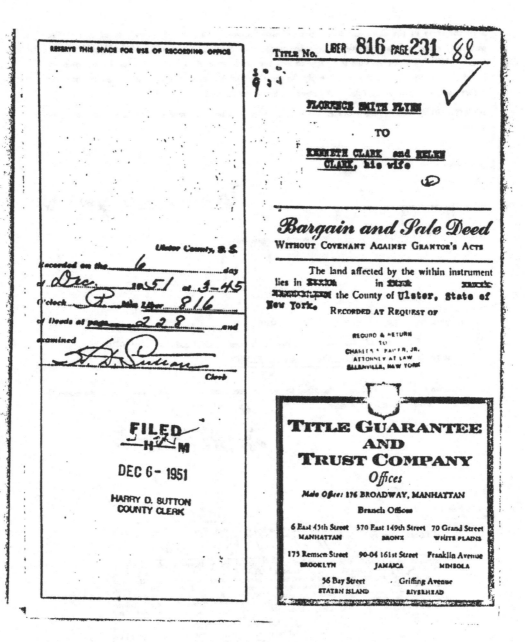

TITLE No. LIBER **816** PAGE **231** 88

FLORENCE SMITH FLYNN

TO

KENNETH CLARK and HELEN
CLARK, his wife

Bargain and Sale Deed

WITHOUT COVENANT AGAINST GRANTOR'S ACTS

The land affected by the within instrument
lies in _____ in _____ _____
_____ the County of Ulster, State of
New York. RECORDED AT REQUEST OF

RECORD & RETURN
TO
CHARLES E. PAPER, JR.
ATTORNEY AT LAW
ELLENVILLE, NEW YORK

Ulster County, S. S.

Recorded on the _____ 6 _____ day
of Dec 1951 at 3-45
O'clock _____ P. _____ in Liber 816
of Deeds at page 228 and
examined
_____
Clerk

FILED
H   M
DEC 6 - 1951

HARRY D. SUTTON
COUNTY CLERK

TITLE GUARANTEE AND TRUST COMPANY

Offices

Main Office: 176 BROADWAY, MANHATTAN

Branch Offices

6 East 45th Street   370 East 149th Street   70 Grand Street
MANHATTAN   BRONX   WHITE PLAINS

175 Remsen Street   90-04 161st Street   Franklin Avenue
BROOKLYN   JAMAICA   MINEOLA

56 Bay Street   ·   Griffing Avenue
STATEN ISLAND   RIVERHEAD

234

six   THIS INDENTURE, Made the 8th day of May Nineteen Hundred and forty-

BETWEEN LOUISE DE WITT, also known as Eliza De Witt, residing at Napanoch, N.Y. (no street or number) party of the first part, and

KENNETH CLARK and HELEN CLARK, his wife, as tenants by the entirety, residing at Napanoch, N. Y. (no street or number) parties of the second part,

WITNESSETH that the party of the first part, in consideration of One Dollar ($1.00) lawful money of the United States, and other good and valuable considerations paid by the parties of the second part, do-- hereby grant and release unto the parties of the second part, their heirs and assigns forever,

ALL THAT TRACT OR PARCEL OF LAND situate in the Town of Wawarsing, bounded and described as follows: Beginning at the west corner of Andrew Rose's house lot running thence North forty four degrees east one chain and seventy seven links to the bounds of the public highway leading from the Napanoch dock to Lackawack, thence along the westerly side of said road North forty four degrees and forty five minutes west two chains and thirty one links, thence north twenty five degrees and twenty minutes west forty eight links, thence South Forty-four degrees West one chain and ninety three links to the bounds of Gabriel W. Lundlum, thence along his bounds forty five degrees and thirty minutes east two chains and eighty one links to the place of beginning.

Containing one half acre of land be the same more or less.

Subject to the right and easement for pole and wire lines granted by Wesley De Witt to Charles P. Dickinson by deed dated July 4, 1911 and recorded in the Ulster County Clerk's office on July 17, 1911 in Liber 431 of Deeds at page 591.

Being the same premises devised by Charles W. De Witt to the grantor herein under his last Will and Testament duly probated in the Ulster County Surrogates Court.

Being the same premises conveyed by Patrick Comfort and Mary P. Comfort, his wife, to the said Charles W. De Witt by deed bearing date November 26, 1901 and recorded in the Ulster County Clerk's office November 30, 1901 in Liber 568 of Deeds at page 246.

TOGETHER with the appurtenances and all the estate and Rights of the party of the first part in and to said premises,

TO HAVE AND TO HOLD the premises herein granted unto the parties of the second part, their heirs and assigns forever.

Subject to a purchase money bond and mortgage for the sum of Fifteen hundred ($1500) Dollars and interest made by the parties of the second part to one Morris Freeman to secure part of the consideration for this conveyance, which said mortgage bears even date and is intended to be recorded simultaneously herewith.

AND said party of the first part covenants as follows:

FIRST. That said party of the first part is seized of said premises in fee simple, and has good right to convey the same;

SECOND. That the parties of the second part shall quietly enjoy the said premises;

THIRD. That the said premises are free from incumbrances; except as above stated.

FOURTH. That the party of the first part will execute or procure any further necessary assurance of the title to said premises;

FIFTH. That said party of the first part will forever WARRANT the title to said premises.

SIXTH. That the grantor will receive the consideration for this conveyance and will hold the right to receive such consideration as a trust fund to be applied first for the purpose of paying the cost of the improvement and will apply the same first to the payment of the cost of the improvement before using any part of the total of the same for any other purpose.

IN WITNESS WHEREOF, the party of the first part has hereunto set her hand and seal the day and year first above written.

IN PRESENCE OF   her
Ethel Kooperman   Louise X De Witt (L.S.)
                                                mark

235

THIS INDENTURE, made the *2nd* day of *December,* nineteen hundred and **sixty-one** BETWEEN

    INGOVAR GAY, residing at 60 Gramercy Park, New York City, and

    DOROTHY GORDON and PATRICIA GAY, both residing at 434 South 2nd Avenue, Mount Vernon, New York,

party of the first part, and

    KENNETH CLARK and HELEN CLARK, his Wife, both residing at

    Cragsmoor, New York,

party of the second part,

WITNESSETH, that the party of the first part, in consideration of Ten Dollars and other valuable consideration paid by the party of the second part, does hereby grant and release unto the party of the second part, the heirs or successors and assigns of the party of the second part forever,

ALL that certain plot, piece or parcel of land, with the buildings and improvements thereon erected, situate, lying and being ~~was~~ at Cragsmoor, Town of Warwarsing, Ulster County, New York, bounded and described as follows:

    BEGINNING at a point on the westerly side of Gardner Lane marked by an iron pipe in the ground, which point is the extreme north-easterly point of said lot of land; and running thence due westwardly to the easterly side of Piney Lane to a point marked by an iron pipe in the ground; thence running along the easterly side of Piney Lane southerly and southeastwardly across the gully as the said lane winds and turns to a stone monument at the intersection of Gardner Lane and Piney Lane; thence running northerly along the West side of Gardner Lane again across the gully as said lane winds and turns to point or place of beginning, which is marked by an iron pipe in the ground as above described;

    Being the same premises conveyed to the parties of the first part and Helen G. Learned by Deeds recorded in the Ulster County Clerk's Office in Liber 531 of Deeds, page 320, and Liber 841 of Deeds, page 01, Ingovar Gay, one of the parties of the first part having acquired the interest of Helen Gay Learned, now deceased, as sole devisee under her Will duly probated in the Office of the Surrogate of the County of New York on November 30, 1960;

TOGETHER with all right, title and interest, if any, of the party of the first part in and to any streets and roads abutting the above described premises to the center lines thereof; TOGETHER with the appurtenances and all the estate and rights of the party of the first part in and to said premises; TO HAVE AND TO HOLD the premises herein granted unto the party of the second part, the heirs or successors and assigns of the party of the second part forever.

AND the party of the first part covenants that the party of the first part has not done or suffered anything whereby the said premises have been encumbered in any way whatever, except as aforesaid.

AND the party of the first part, in compliance with Section 13 of the Lien Law, covenants that the party of the first part will receive the consideration for this conveyance and will hold the right to receive such consideration as a trust fund to be applied first for the purpose of paying the cost of the improvement and will apply the same first to the payment of the cost of the improvement before using any part of the total of the same for any other purpose.

The word "party" shall be construed as if it read "parties" whenever the sense of this indenture so requires.

IN WITNESS WHEREOF, the party of the first part has duly executed this deed the day and year first above written.

IN PRESENCE OF:

[signature]   *Dorothy Gordon*

       Patricia Gay

                                              Ingovar Gay

STATE OF NEW YORK, COUNTY OF   ss:

On the **2nd** day of **December 1961**, before me
personally came **INGOVAR GAY, DOROTHY
GORDON and PATRICIA GAY**

to me known to be the individuals described in and who
executed the foregoing instrument, and acknowledged that
they executed the same.

Lawrence B. Robertson

LAWRENCE B. ROBERTSON
Notary Public, State of New York
Qualified in West. Co. No. 60-3305785
Certificate filed in N. Y. Co.
Commission Expires March 30, 1963

STATE OF NEW YORK, COUNTY OF   ss:

On the   day of   19   , before me
personally came

to me known to be the individual   described in and who
executed the foregoing instrument, and acknowledged that
executed the same.

STATE OF NEW YORK, COUNTY OF   ss:

On the   day of   19   , before me
personally came
to me known, who, being by me duly sworn, did depose and
say that   he resides at No.

that   he is the
of
, the corporation described
in and which executed the foregoing instrument; that   he
knows the seal of said corporation; that the seal affixed
to said instrument is such corporate seal; that it was so
affixed by order of the board of directors of said corporation, and that   he signed h   name thereto by like order.

STATE OF NEW YORK, COUNTY OF   ss:

On the   day of   19   , before me
personally came
the subscribing witness to the foregoing instrument, with
whom I am personally acquainted, who, being by me duly
sworn, did depose and say that   he resides at No.

that   he knows

to be the individual
described in and who executed the foregoing instrument;
that   he, said subscribing witness, was present and saw
execute the same; and that   he, said witness,
at the same time subscribed h   name as witness thereto.

FILED
DEC 21 1961
LAWRENCE D. CRAFT
COUNTY CLERK

Bargain and Sale Deed
WITH COVENANT AGAINST GRANTOR'S ACTS

The land affected by the within instrument
lies in Section   in Block
Land Map of the County of   on the
RECORDED AT REQUEST OF

Ulster County, S. S.

Title No. 2

TO

STANDARD FORM OF
NEW YORK BOARD OF TITLE UNDERWRITERS
Distributed by
**THE TITLE GUARANTEE
COMPANY**

CHARTERED 1883   IN NEW YORK

PLEASE RECORD AND RETURN TO
KAISER & MURRAY
ATTORNEYS AT LAW
ELLENVILLE, NEW YORK

237

THIS INDENTURE, made the 1st day of December, nineteen hundred and **sixty-one**
BETWEEN

       PATRICIA GAY, residing at 434 South 2nd Avenue,

Mount Vernon, New York,

party of the first part, and

       KENNETH CLARK and HELEN CLARK, his Wife, both

residing at Cragsmoor, New York,

party of the second part,

WITNESSETH, that the party of the first part, in consideration of ten dollars and other valuable consideration paid by the party of the second part, does hereby grant and release unto the party of the second part, the heirs or successors and assigns of the party of the second part forever,

ALL that certain plot, piece or parcel of land, with the buildings and improvements thereon erected, situate, lying and being in the at Cragsmoor, Town of Warwarsing, Ulster County, New York, bounded and described as follows:

    BEGINNING at a point on the easterly side of a road now known as Gardner Lane at the division line between the lands of Catherine Chipman, deceased, and the land formerly of Marguerite Schuyler Mason; running thence easterly along said division line to the southwesterly corner of the land now or formerly of Emily H. Keene as conveyed to her by Eliza G. Hartshorn by deed bearing date July 29, 1895 and recorded in the Ulster County Clerk's office in Liber 324 of deeds at page 630; thence northerly along said Keene line about 194 feet more or less to the northerly corner of said Keene lot; thence westerly on the westerly production of the northerly line of said Keene lot to the easterly side of the road called Gardner Lane; thence southerly along the easterly side of Gardner Lane to the point or place of beginning;

    Being the same premises conveyed to the party of the first part by Deed recorded in the Ulster County Clerk's Office in Liber 351 of Deeds, page 319, on May 24, 1928.

TOGETHER with all right, title and interest, if any, of the party of the first part in and to any streets and roads abutting the above described premises to the center lines thereof; TOGETHER with the appurtenances and all the estate and rights of the party of the first part in and to said premises; TO HAVE AND TO HOLD the premises herein granted unto the party of the second part, the heirs or successors and assigns of the party of the second part forever.

AND the party of the first part, in compliance with Section 13 of the Lien Law, covenants that the party of the first part will receive the consideration for this conveyance and will hold the right to receive such consideration as a trust fund to be applied first for the purpose of paying the cost of the improvement and will apply the same first to the payment of the cost of the improvement before using any part of the total of the same for any other purpose.

The word "party" shall be construed as if it read "parties" whenever the sense of this indenture so requires.

IN WITNESS WHEREOF, the party of the first part has duly executed this deed the day and year first above written.

In presence of:

Patricia Gay

LIBER 1116 PG 593

238

STATE OF NEW YORK, COUNTY OF   ss: STATE OF NEW YORK, COUNTY OF   ss:

On the 1ᵈ day of *December* 1961, before me personally came

Patricia Hay

to me known to be the individual   described in and who executed the foregoing instrument, and acknowledged that *she* executed the same.

Lawrence B. Robertson

LAWRENCE R. ROBERTSON
Notary Public, State of New York
Qualified in West. Co. No. 60-3305785
Certificate filed in N. Y. Co.
Commission Expires March 30, 1963

On the   day of   19   , before me personally came

to me known to be the individual   described in and who executed the foregoing instrument, and acknowledged that executed the same.

STATE OF NEW YORK, COUNTY OF   ss: STATE OF NEW YORK, COUNTY OF   ss:

On the   day of   19   , before me personally came
to me known, who, being by me duly sworn, did depose and say that   he resides at No.

that   he is the
of
, the corporation described in and which executed the foregoing instrument; that   he knows the seal of said corporation; that the seal affixed to said instrument is such corporate seal; that it was so affixed by order of the board of directors of said corporation, and that   he signed h   name thereto by like order.

On the   day of   19   , before me personally came
the subscribing witness to the foregoing instrument, with whom I am personally acquainted, who, being by me duly sworn, did depose and say that   he resides at No.

that   he knows

to be the individual described in and who executed the foregoing instrument; that   he, said subscribing witness, was present and saw execute the same; and that   he, said witness, at the same time subscribed h   name as witness thereto.

RESERVE THIS SPACE FOR USE OF RECORDING OFFICE

FILED 2 H —— M
DEC 21 1961
LAWRENCE D. CRAFT
COUNTY CLERK

Recorded on the 21
19 61 at 3:50

Min Liber 1116

Lawrence D. Craft

Ulster County, S. S.

Bargain and Sale Deed
WITHOUT COVENANT AGAINST GRANTOR'S ACTS

The land affected by the within instrument
lies in Section   in Block
Land Map of the County of
RECORDED AT REQUEST OF

TO

TITLE No. 2

409

LINEAGE

Herbert Brown and his wife, Kathryn M. Brown, of Scarsdale, New York, sold the Cragsmoor home to John Cashman Flynn of Mount Vernon, New York on May 15, 1934 (see Liber 570 Page 393). The pictures below show the homes in about 1935. See next page for recent pictures.

MAIN HOUSE - "THE FALCON"

THE CARRIAGE HOUSE - EXPANDED
(This is perhaps a ___ more recent photo.)

TAKEN IN 2003 AND 2004

During the time that the Flynns stayed in Cragsmoor, Helen Clark, who resided in Napanoch with her husband, called on the Flynns one day and said to them, "I'll be buying this house". (It wasn't for sale!)

John and his wife, Florence Smith Flynn, spent summers in Cragsmoor, in the home that he renamed Falcon Mount, until his death on November 23, 1947. Mrs. Flynn inherited the house and owned it until she sold to Kenneth and Helen Clark, making Helen's dream come true!

Since Ken and Helen are of utmost importance to our story, let's become acquainted with them. (Ken was Harold Clark's uncle.)

Kenneth L. Clark was born on March 18, 1910 in Lafayette, New Jersey to Robert and Lucy O'Dell Clark. He and his wife, Helen, lived in Cragsmoor for approximately thirty years. He was a retired plumber and had been "Cragsmoor's plumber", having keys for almost all the homes there. (At that time there were only about seven year-round homes but many summer residences in the hamlet.) He died in Ellenville Community Hospital on February 19, 1981 at the age of seventy. Survivors, besides Helen, included five brothers, William (father of Harold), Jim, John, Clinton and Clifford, all of Hamburg, New Jersey; also two sisters, Dorothy Lozaw and Eunice Don Diego of Wheeling, West Virginia, plus several cousins, nieces and nephews. In addition, there was a young brother George and another infant who died along with their mother during the influenza outbreak of 1918. In memory of Kenneth, donations were made to the Cragsmoor Fire Company.

Helen was born to Amos (B 10-2-1867, D 10-18-1954) and Stella Fredericks Card of Hamburg, New Jersey (B 5-9-1875, D 7-5-1973 at the age of 98). They were married on March 29, 1891. Helen was one of seven children, two boys and five girls, as follows.

THE CARD CHILDREN

George	B. November 23, 1891	D.
Elizabeth	B. November 4, 1893	D.
Edna	B. October 28, 1895	D. September 7, 1955
Ida May	B. July 11, 1897	D.
Frank Amos	B. December 5, 1900	D. September 26, 1901
Janet	B. September 7, 1902	D. August 20, 1956
Helen	B. January 29, 1905	D. November 4, 1982

Her father was a rough and very stern man. Stella too, was stern and also a God-fearing woman, however, she showed another side since, at every chance she got, she went gunning for squirrels, aiming to kill. As Harold remembers Stella, she always wore black clothing. It was in the early 1950's, shortly after the Clarks bought in Cragsmoor, that Amos and Stella moved into the carriage house.

It was while living in Hamburg, on the corner of Vernon Avenue (Route 94) and Card Street, where Helen helped to operate her father's livery business. She was truly a "woman ahead of her time", because by the time she was eighteen years old, and during the depression, that she owned and operated three farms that were local to that area. One farm later became the Joustra farm and another the Silconas farm. The other farm is not known. Helen's farms were dairy farms and milk was taken to the Sheffield Creamery in Hamburg.

She also became involved in another venture, this one being a tavern called Midway, which was located on Route 94 in the McAfee section of Vernon, New Jersey. That establishment became known in later years as Wayside Inn, owned by Steve Zorka.

Helen and Ken met while he was employed by Helen as a farm hand. Their relationship took flight and so did they, as they eloped and then honeymooned in Florida. Her business could not have been very lucrative at the time, because of the depression being a cause for very little cash flow, so before they left to get married, they took the farm money with them. During their absence, Ken's brother Clint worked the farm and needed to buy feed for the cows. Much to his surprise, he discovered a total lack of funds. Of course, that was due to the previously mentioned escapade!

Ken and Helen continued to work farms together, then Ken became a sandhog and worked on the viaducts which enabled water to be transported to New York City. This work kept them moving a great deal. Finally Helen became a housewife and thought that she would like to have a permanent home. They were living in Napanoch at the time that Helen heard of the Flynn home being available and she told Ken, "You can move on, or stay here. I'm staying". They bought. They stayed and loved Cragsmoor!

She was very active in the community and just loved hosting parties, of which there were many, and also entertaining the artists. She was quite fond of Patricia Gay and eventually purchased the Gay home. She once told Harold that she was so well-liked and respected that the local women would approach her and ask for advice as to whether they should become pregnant or not.

Sadly, in later years, after most of her friends passed on, she became a recluse.

Kenneth and Helen (nee Card) Clark, purchased the estate known as Falcon Mount on May 20, 1948 (Liber 530 Page 442) and another parcel on November 21, 1951 (Liber 816 Page 228).

Ken predeceased Helen. At the time of Helen's demise on November 4, 1982, the property and homes were left to Ken's nephew, Harold M. Clark.

The property consisted of the main house and a converted carriage house. The third house, located in the southwest corner of the property, is presently owned by Gerald Felice. It was sold to him during Helen's ownership (see Liber 1116 Pages 592, 593 and 594). This house was built in 1905 by Edward Gay (named Gayland), and had been purchased by the Clarks from the Gays.

During the thirty-plus years that Kenneth and Helen lived in the house, many changes took place. Before we go on to the next phase, let's meet the Card and Clark familes.

Approximately 1941
Kenneth and Helen Clark with her parents, Stella and Amos Card who are celebrating their anniversary.

Cards Mark Anniversary

MR. AND MRS. AMOS B. CARD

Mr. and Mrs. Card, of Hamburg, on Sunday observed their 58th wedding anniversary at a family party at the home of their son-in-law and daughter, Town Engineer and Mrs. M. Hampton Byram, of 87 Main Street, Newton. The party was held two days ahead of the actual anniversary.

The couple were married in Paterson on March 29, 1891. Following the marriage they lived for a few months in Brooklyn, then moved to Hamburg. They have five children, Mrs. Byram, Mrs. Joseph Burgess, Highland Lakes; Mrs. Reginald Phillips, Vernon Township; Mrs. Kenneth Clark, of Naponack, N. Y., and Mrs. Douglas Collins, of Livingston Manor, N. Y.

1949

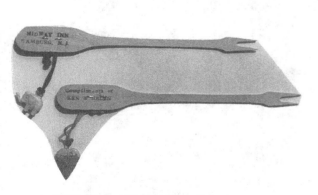

A KEEPSAKE FROM MIDWAY INN

HELEN CARD CLARK

YOUNGER OR A LITTLE OLDER.

SHE'S VERY ATTRACTIVE!

WED 61 YEARS—Mr. and Mrs. Amos B. Card of Hardystonville celebrated their sixty-first wedding anniversary Sunday with a dinner party at the Flo-Jean Restaurant in Port Jervis, for the immediate family. They were married in Paterson March 29, 1891, and for a short time resided in Oak Ridge. Later they moved to Brooklyn, and then to Hamburg, where Mr. Card operated a livery stable and blacksmith shop before going into the road building and contracting business, from which he retired twelve years ago. Mrs. Card is the former Stella Mae Fredericks, daughter of Mr. and Mrs. William Fredericks of Stockholm. Present at the dinner party Sunday were six grandchildren and three great-grandchildren, in addition to the couple's five daughters, Mrs. Hampton Byram of Newton, Mrs. Douglas Cullin of Livingston Manor, N. Y., Mrs. Joseph Burgess of Highland Lakes, Mrs. Reginald Phillips of Sussex R. D., and Mrs. Kenneth Clark of Craigsmore, N. Y. 1952 —Adrien Salvas photo.

THE SEASONS
Taken about 2000,
during Harold Clark's
ownership

PARTIAL FRONT AND NORTH SIDE OF THE MAIN HOUSE-ABOUT 2000

THE BACK (WEST) SIDE WHICH CLEARLY SHOWS THE THREE-CAR ADDITION WHICH
KEN BUILT. IT IS THE VERY LONG AREA WITH NO WINDOWS-ABOVE THE LADDERS
WHICH ARE LYING AGAINST THE FOUNDATION. ABOVE THE GARAGES IS THE OFFICE.
THE PROPERTY SLOPES QUITE A BIT AT THE REAR OF THE HOUSE.

HOME IMPROVEMENTS

Being the plumber that he was, one of the first modern conveniences that Ken added was the addition of oil fueled heat with steam fed radiators. He then hired Shamro Well Drillers to drill a deep well, after which he installed bathrooms -- one small one off the kitchen, which had a metal stall shower and a vertical radiator, which is still there. An outhouse was used prior to these additions.

The second bathroom he installed was upstairs, and much larger. The walls were (and still are) done in yellow formica, the pale colored linoleum floor is bordered in black. This color combination was extremely popular in the late 1940's or early 1950's. The next most noticeable feature is the use of mirrors -- small ones surround the wall lamps over the sink and the medicine cabinet has a large mirror, again with small mirror squares around it.

During the 1950's the kitchen was up-dated with the addition of a few cabinets and a sink. There remained a stovepipe opening in the chimney. Additionally, during this time, he extended the kitchen by adding a pantry with storage shelves and a new door leading outdoors and a small porch with steps leading to ground level.

A three-car garage with workbench area was further added at ground level (rather difficult to explain, but we'll try - also the photo will be

LEFT IS THE UPSTAIRS BATHROOM.

BELOW SHOWS SOME OF "KEN'S
ADD-ONS" FEATURING THE NEW
PANTRY AREA WHICH IS JUST INSIDE
THE BACK DOOR. THE KITCHEN EX-
TENDS ALL THE WAY TO THE FRONT
OF THE HOUSE. ALSO SHOWN HERE
ARE THE SMALL BACK PORCH AND
STEPS. UNFORTUNATELY, ONLY ONE
OF THE THREE GARAGE DOORS IS
PICTURED.

of much greater help.) The property slopes to the rear and therefore, the garage floor level is about eight feet below the back porch level. The roof of the newly constructed garage is very large and flat and is elevated about two feet above the back porch deck.

In the rear of the house there appears to have been an open air "outside patio" whose roof was supported by Tuscan columns. (In Carroll B. Brown's time the view must have been breathtaking, indeed!) Ken, again in the early '50's, enclosed the patio area, thereby creating a beautiful, bright and cheerful sunroom into which he integrated the Tuscan columns and they can be seen as part of the outside wall. (Shown on the next page)

Helen's influence remains throughout the house yet today. Many paintings, including two by Edwin L. Oman, and a variety of antiques have been photographed and appear on the following pages with descriptions and explanations. One item in a corner of the living room is a small corner shelf approximately eighteen inches high, named "Madonna of the Streets". It was obtained from The Vista Maria Convent, formerly known as "Chetola",

ABOVE IS THE SUNROOM WITH ITS

TUSCAN COLUMNS GRACING THE OUT-

SIDE WALL.   (THERE ARE A TOTAL

OF THREE.)

BELOW IS THE SMALL CORNER SHELF

NAMED " MADONNA OF THE STREETS".

AND AN OLD SCHOOL BELL FROM THE

GLENWOOD, NEW JERSEY SCHOOL HOUSE.

TWO PAINTINGS BY EDWIN L. OMAN

the estate which was built by the well-known artist, George Inness, Jr.

Possibly the Tiffany lamp on the marble top table in the living room and other Tiffany pieces, may have been purchased by Helen from neighbor, Patricia Gay (who worked at Tiffany's in New York City). Also, there is an artist's easel in the basement laundry room which belonged to Miss Gay.

Other pieces brought in by Helen include the clock over the mantel, which came from the Glenwood, New Jersey school, as did the school bell. (Helen's sister was a teacher there.) Helen also added the Chinese hanging bells, two marble top tables, and the rocker in the master bedroom, which belonged to her mother.

CLOCK OVER MANTEL

ABOVE

MARBLE-TOP TABLE WITH SIDE

DETAIL SHOWN BELOW

RIGHT -

MARBLE-TOP

TABLE WITH

TIFFANY LAMP

ON THE LEFT ARE THE CHINESE
HANGING BEELS WHICH HELEN
ACQUIRED DURING HER OWNERSHIP.

THE PLATFORM-STYLE ROCKER
ON THE RIGHT BELONGED TO
HELEN'S MOTHER. IT IS IN
THE MASTER BEDROOM. THIS
VERY ROCKER IS AGAIN MEN-
TIONED LATER ON IN THIS BOOK.
REMEMBER IT, PLEASE!

In the dining room, the main focus is on the extremely large wall mural, done in oils and is, unfortunately, in relatively poor condition. The landscape was painted in 1879 by Henry Arthur Elkins, a well-known artist from Colorado who was famous for his western landscapes. This mural was purchased by Helen from the Vista Maria and since it is not a religious painting, it is possible that it came originally from George Inness, Jr's. collection at Chetolah. Perhaps that's just wishful thinking!

THE OTHER SIDE OF THE DINING ROOM

PARCEL ONE:

 All that certain lot, piece or parcel of land situate, lying and being on the top of Shawangunk Mountain in the Town of Wawarsing, Ulster County, New York, and which is bounded and described as follows:
 BEGINNING at the most northerly corner of a triangular lot sold to Rebecca C. Fox at a stake and stones and running thence north 5° 30' west one hundred and thirty-nine and 6/12 feet to a stone; thence north 80° west one hundred and seven feet and four inches to a stone near a marked chestnut tree; thence south 6° west one hundred and ninety-four feet to an oak tree marked, on the northerly edge of a ravine; thence about north 76° east one hundred and forty-three feet to the place of beginning be the same more or less.

PARCEL TWO:

 ALL that tract or parcel of land situate in the Town of Wawrsing, County of Ulster and State of New York, and being on top of the Shawangunk Mountain, said parcel of land being described as follows:
 BEGINNING at the east side of the gate at a stone on the bounds of lands of Abbie Kite; running thence north along her bounds north 41 degrees 45 minutes west three hundred and fifty-seven feet (357) to a stake; thence north thirty-eight degrees 50 minutes west further along the bounds of said Abbie Kite, two hundred and eighty-five (285) feet to a white oak tree marked on both sides, and from said white oak tree; thence south 18 degrees 50 minutes west about two hundred and sixty-three (263) feet to a stake and stones; thence south 80 degrees east twenty-two feet to the northeasterly corner of a lot of Emelie H. Keene at a pile of stones near a marked chestnut tree; thence same course along said Keene lot, one hundred seven and 4/12 feet (107 4/12) to the northerly corner thereof; thence along said Keene lot, south 5 degrees 30 minutes east one hundred and thirty-nine and 6/12 feet (139 6/12) to stones north of a large maple tree, the northerly corner of the triangular lot of Rebecca C. Fox; thence along the same south 70 degrees 50 minutes east eighty-nine feet (89) to the northerly corner of the Rebecca C. Fox house lot; thence along the northerly side thereof south 70 degrees 35 minutes east 261 feet to a post; thence in a straight line northeasterly about nineteen feet (19) to the place of beginning.

PARCEL THREE:

 ALL THAT TRACT, PIECE OR PARCEL OF LAND, situated at Cragsmoor, Ulster County, New York, and more particularly described as follows:
 Beginning at an iron pile set in the line of the lands now of Flynn and runs from the beginning along the Flynn lands the next two courses: (1) south 87 degrees 50 minutes east 87.0 feet to an iron pipe; (2) South 78 degrees 35 minutes east 162.0 feet to an iron pipe; thence along the McMurtrie lands the next two courses (1) south 16 degrees 30 minutes west 176.0 feet to an iron pipe (2) south 68 degrees 30 minutes east 135.0 feet to an iron pipe; thence along the road south 24 degrees 30 minutes west 83.0 feet to an iron pipe; thence along another road north 68 degrees 30 minutes west 417.0 feet to an iron pipe; thence north 18 degrees 50 minutes east 232.5 feet to the beginning and containing 2.0 acres of land.
 Being a portion of the premises of which Rebecca C. Fox died seized and possessed and which descended to the party of the first part by the said Last Will and Testament of Rebecca C. Fox.

SCHEDULE A

PARCEL FOUR:

ALL THAT TRACT, PIECE OR PARCEL OF LAND situated at Cragsmoor in the Town of Wawarsing, County of Ulster and State of New York, and more particularly described as follows:

100 x 100 feet, more or less, described at Lot. Cragsmoor. Bounded North by Henry, South by Piney Lane, east by Fox, West by lands of Gay, against which the words "Peck W.H." appear on the assessment roll of the Town of Wawarsing for the year 1934.

BEING the same premises conveyed by Pratt Boice, Ulster County Treasurer to Franklin O'Bryon by deed of conveyance bearing date the 14th day of January, 1937, and recorded in the Ulster County Clerk's Office on the 24th day of July 1937, in Liber 598 of Deeds at page 369.

Said four parcels being the same premises conveyed in his lifetime to John Cashman Flynn late of Mount Vernon, New York, by the following conveyances recorded in the Clerk's office, Ulster County:

1. Deed by Frank M. Tichenor as executor of the last will and testament of Frances M. Brown, dated May 19, 1934, and recorded on June 2, 1934 in Liber 570 of Deeds, page 390.

2. Quit claim deed from Harold P. Brown and Martha T. Brown, his wife, dated May 16, 1934 and recorded on June 2, 1934 in Liber 570 of Deeds page 392.

3. Quit claim deed from F. Herbert Brown and Kathryn M. Brown, his wife, dated May 15, 1934 and recorded on June 2, 1934 in Liber 570 of Deeds, pate 393.

4. Deed from Marion F. McMurtie dated November 12, 1940 and recorded on December 8, 1941 in Liber 622 of Deeds, page 235.

5. Deed from Franklin O'Bryon dated November 5, 1942, and recorded on April 9, 1943, in Liber 632 of Deeds, page 247.

Said John Flynn died intestate on November 23, 1947. By decree of the Surrogate's Court, Westchester County dated April 21, 1950 (Index No. 996/1948). Said party of the first part was adjudged the sole distributee of said decedent and seized in fee simple of the above described premises, pursuant to said decree, said party of the first part in her capacity as administratrix of the estate of said decedent by deed dated June 7, 1950 and intended to be recorded simultaneously herewith, conveyed the above described premises to herself individually in confirmation of her title thereto.

Reserving with respect to PARCEL TWO above described, a road about thirty (30) feet wide along the northerly and westerly side of said lot of lands formerly of Eliza G. Hartshorn, now Daniel I. Odell and others, together with a right of way over Schuyler Avenue to the public Highway.

Granting with respect to PARCEL ONE above described, a right of way along and over the proposed new road on the westerly side thereof.

BEING the same premises described in a deed by Florence Smith Flynn to Kenneth Clark and Helen Clark, his wife, dated November 21, 1951 and recorded in the Ulster County Clerk's Office on December 6, 1951 in Liber 816 of Deeds at page 228. Kenneth Clark died intestate on February 10, 1981 leaving Helen Clark as sole owner in fee simple. Helen Clark died testate on November 4, 1982, leaving a Last Will and Testament which was probated by Ulster County Surrogate's Court and Letters Testamentary were issued to Harold Clark and Ethel Kooperman on February 6, 1984, the grantors herein. Helen Clark's entire estate was devised to Harold Clark, the grantee herein.

BEING the same premises described in a deed from Harold Clark and Ethel Kooperman as executors of the Estate of Helen Clark to Harold Clark, dated August 14, 1984, and recorded in the Ulster County Clerk's office on March 26, 1985, in Liber 1524 on page 219.

SCHEDULE A - Page 2

HAROLD'S HOUSE

As earlier mentioned, Harold M. Clark of Hamburg, New Jersey and nephew of Kenneth and Helen Clark, inherited this house after the death of Helen. (See LIBER 3080 Pages 0010 and 0011). He had always been extremely kind and caring of Helen and even more so after the passing of her husband, Ken. On many occasions, Harold would drive the hour and a half long trip to Cragsmoor just to visit with Helen or to respond to a "needy" phone call from her.

From the time that Harold took ownership of the house, it became a vacation home and used only as a wonderful and serenely quiet mountain retreat. It remains so today for the most part. The past several years Thanksgiving holidays have been enjoyed by Harold, Christina and their families, especially the younger folks who just love to hike to Bear Hill-- no matter what the weather!! The oldest grandchildren are Emily and Mitchell August who are fourteen and twelve, respectively. They are parented by Scott and Coral. Emily and Mitchell are beautiful beings who are caring, thoughtful, talented and loving. Daughter Colleen and husband Anthony La Banca can boast about their gorgeous off-spring -- namely, Nicholas (nine years), Sophia (four years) and Bella (two years). Even Bella "does" Bear Hill and loves it!! Eldest daughter, Crystal, and son-in-law Jim were instrumental in urging us to continue our efforts to complete this book. At this juncture we'd like to mention that in 2005, Jim made repairs to and painted the exterior of the house. Now, let's go back in time once again.

By 1985 Harold began many major repairs and renovations to his newly acquired cottage, as it was referred to.

One of the first things he did in 1985 was to have a new furnace installed -- just as Ken before him did. It was still oil-fueled and steam fed but so much more efficient, even though the house is not insulated.

This boiler remains in the house today.

The upstairs rooms were all in excellent condition and so all efforts were concentrated on the downstairs rooms.

The bathroom was completely renovated with tile flooring, a large stall shower and double-door vanity with light fixtures above. The vanity houses a single large sink. In addition to being very well lighted, it has a ceiling heat lamp, exhaust fan, etc. (This being the downstairs bathroom.)

By now, it was time to modernize the kitchen and nearby areas, as well, and so work continued in '85. From floor to ceiling the rear entryway and kitchen gained beautiful tile flooring. The kitchen was adorned with many light oak cabinets, enough to store everything one might need. The counter-tops are a very neutral color and everything blends so well, from the built-in wall oven, electric cook-top with range hood and dishwasher, to the micro-wave oven. A Tiffany-style shade hangs from a ceiling fixture above the kitchen table. This room is very bright and cheerful with its four windows and ample lighting, including recessed lights over the sink. It is such a delightful room to work in, read in, or whatever.

VARIED VIEWS OF THE KITCHEN

THE DOWNSTAIRS BATHROOM IS
SHOWN ON THE <u>LEFT</u> WHILE THE
REAR ENTRYWAY AND VESTIBULE
APPEARS <u>BELOW</u>.

The wall leading from the kitchen to the dining room has a very large archway that we previously described.

Helen had painted the living room walls a very dark reddish-burgundy color which made the room quite dark. Harold repainted it a soft neutral cream color which brightened the room dramatically.

In 1991 the Clark residence was listed in the National Registry of Historic Places, as were many homes in Cragsmoor -- at least those homes which were old enough to qualify.

NOTE: In the Cragsmoor Free Library can be found complete volumes of the National Register of Historic Places for the Cragsmoor area.

NPS Form 10-900-a
(8-86)

OMB Approval No. 1024-0018

United States Department of the Interior
National Parks Service

National Register of Historic Places
Continuation Sheet

CRAGSMOOR HISTORIC DISTRICT
Town of Wawarsing
Ulster County, New York

Section number ___7___ Page __26__

property is a small one story clapboard cottage that is said to have been constructed with material from the original third floor of the main house. The windows are two over two as with the main house and a half round window is located in the front.

57. "Herrnhut" Cottage   Before 1900

This is a two story, two bay, house with a central chimney and novelty siding with the gable end facing the street. The front features a one story porch that wraps around to the west and is set on simple square posts. below the porch on the front is a single three part window with a six over one sash flanked by a pair of eight pane sidelights; a typical two over two sash window is adjacent. Above it are a pair of two over two sash and a triangular attic light in the gable peak. The porch extends around to the north where it becomes a deck that is supported on wood stilts. On the east facade is a small shed roof entry and a one story, one bay extension with an open second floor porch under a cross gable. This cottage was initially built for Abbie Kite Herrnhut as a summer rental cottage. In 1904 the property was sold to Mr. & Mrs. Polk who made a number of improvements to the house after relocating the house closer to the edge of the ridge. This cottage remains as one of the few houses at Cragsmoor that are still used solely as a summer cottage. Julia Polk Hunsicker (____-1983) a well known artist, especially for her portraits, was a long time resident of this cottage. Julia Polk was also the subject of many of the paintings by the Cragsmoor artists, especially Curran and Turner. There is a contributing shed with gable roof and novelty siding on the property.

58. "Land's End"   1942

This is a small one story residence on a stone footings and an exterior capped stone chimney centered on an end cross gable. A broad shed roofed enclosed central entry projects from the front resting on block piers. The rear (north) face has a open deck. The windows are one over one. The house was built by Bert Goldsmith.

59. "Locust Lodge"   Before 1899

"Locust Lodge" originally built before 1899, is a one and one-half story three bay shingled house with a set back, two story, two bay gable extension on a stone foundation. The windows are two over two throughout. The principal block has a central gable roof bay dormer over the entry door. There is a further two bay garage extension off the dwelling extension. This house was originally built for Mrs. Abbie Kite as one of her "Hernnhut" rental cottages and was called "Locust Lodge". In the 1950's Mr. and Mrs. Lenox Hodge purchased the deteriorated property and extensively remodeled and enlarged the cottage. The property also includes the "Hernnhut" site. "Hernnhut", built before 1887, was a boarding house that is was torn down in the 1940's. Photos of the clapboard building can be found at the Cragsmoor Library. Piers for the building are all that remain, giving a rough footprint. In about 1885 Miss Abbie Kite, a Quaker, first came to Cragsmoor and stayed at one of the summer cottages of Miss Broadhead. In addition there is a non-contributing pool and associated pool house.

60. "Slab House" Site   ca. 1900

NPS Form 10-900-a
(8-86)

OMB Approval No. 1024-0018

United States Department of the Interior
National Parks Service

National Register of Historic Places
Continuation Sheet

Section number ___7___ Page __27__

CRAGSMOOR HISTORIC DISTRICT
Town of Wawarsing
Ulster County, New York

Stone foundation walls and the stone base of a chimney only remain. Originally this was log building was built for Mrs. Hartshorn who used it as an afternoon retreat and as a guest house. It burned to the ground in about 1915. It was constructed on the exposed slab of slanting rock (hence "Slab House") typical of the Shawangunks and was anchored to it by iron rods.

61. "Gayland"   **1905**

This is a one and one half story side gable house with novelty clapboard siding on a stone foundation. A shed roofed entry extends off the left front. Some six over six windows are present but a number of multipaned picture windows have been installed. A shed roofed, second floor porch extends like a dormer off the rear (west) facade. "Gayland" was built in 1905 for the artist Edward Gay N.A.

62. Clark Residence   **ca. 1920**

MAIN HOUSE: This is a one and one half story, two bay gambrel house with a similar set back extension to the south. Further to the south is a hip roofed port cochere with exposed rafter tails on 3/4 height Tuscan columns on stone piers that extends across the front of the extension. The front has a gable roof entry with a kicked roof that is also on Tuscan columns and is offset to the right. Above, on the kicked roof with a deep overhang is a shed roofed central wall dormer with three casement units. To the rear (west) is a two story cross gable ell with six over one sash. This house was the summer home of artist Carrol Brown. Also found on the property is a contributing carriage house, now converted to a residence. This is a one and one half story converted carriage house with a deep overhanging gambrel roof and shingle siding. The windows are all two over two sash units with board and batten shutters. The gable end features a central classical doorway with an elliptical fanlight and sidelights with a central window above. The east face has a full shed roofed wall dormer. The west face has a full facade, two story, four bay shed roofed enclosed porch, the ground floor having a an offset door. A small one story gable addition extends to the south that is built into the grade of the hill, with a deck below grade on the south end.

63. "Hartland"   **1912**

This is a two story, two bay, shingled frame house with two central brick chimneys, one at each end. The ground floor is shingled in asbestos and is surrounded by a wrap around rustic one story porch on three sides with lattice below. The windows are two over two with some paired units. An original Dutch door is retained on the front. Originally, this was called the Fletcher cottage, but it is better known as being the home of the Sutton family for many years.

64. "Casino"   **1899**

This is a one and one half story shingle home with a new stone front (east) facade. The roof has a gambrel pitch to the front and a gable one to the back. In the middle of the front facade is an exterior stone chimney with a cross gable gambrel cricket. To the left is a small bay window; to the right is a shed roof entry protecting a spindle door. To the rear is a two story ell and a one story enclosed porch with patio doors. A native stone face has been added to east facade. The house, also called the "Pines Casino", was originally built

BUILDING STRUCTURE INVENTORY FORM

NYS OFFICE OF PARKS, RECREATION
& HISTORIC PRESERVATION
DIVISION FOR HISTORIC PRESERVATION
(518) 474-0479

FOR OFFICE USE ONLY
Unique Site No._____
Quad_____
Series_____
Neg. No._____

YOUR NAME: ___Harry P. Hansen___ DATE: 1991/ rev. 4-'95
YOUR ADDRESS: 66 Rest Plaus Road
___Stone Ridge, NY 12484___ PHONE: (914) 687-0854
ORGANIZATION: For the Cragsmoor Free Library, Cragsmoor, NY

* *

IDENTIFICATION
1. BUILDING NAME: "Slab House" Site   060-S
2. COUNTY: Ulster   TOWN: Wawarsing   VILLAGE: Cragsmoor
3. STREET LOCATION: Off the west end of Hillside Road, a
                    private drive.
4. OWNERSHIP: Private
5. PRESENT OWNER: Harold Clark
        ADDRESS: Blair Road, RD 1 Box 240, Hamburg, NJ 07419
6. USE: Original: Residence   Present: Standing Ruin
7. ACCESSIBILITY TO PUBLIC:
   Exterior visible from public road: No, on private road
             Interior accessible: No

DESCRIPTION
8. BUILDING MATERIAL: Stone foundation
9. STRUCTURAL SYSTEM:
10. CONDITION: Site
11. INTEGRITY: a. original site: Yes   b. moved: _____
              c. list major alterations and dates:
                 Cellar hole with walls only remain

12. PHOTO: view toward   13. MAP: Tax Map #: 91.018-1-23
         the [no photo]   USGS: Ellenville Quad.
   Roll: _ Neg.:

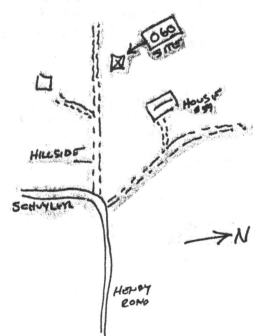

267

14. THREATS TO BUILDING: <u>Deterioration or vandalism</u>

15. RELATED OUTBUILDINGS AND PROPERTY:
    *None

16. SURROUNDINGS OF THE BUILDING:

    The site is overgrown with trees and is a vacant
    unimproved lot.

17. INTERRELATIONSHIP OF BUILDING AND SURROUNDINGS:

    The property is situated in a lightly built-up community
    atop the Shawangunk Mountains. Nearby to the north,
    Minnewaska State Park and the Ellenville watershed offer
    protected open views. Before being overgrown there were
    extensive views to the west over the Catskills. The house
    is about one mile from "Windermere", Mrs. Hartshorn's
    summer house.

18. OTHER NOTABLE FEATURES OF BUILDING AND SITE:

    Stone foundation walls and the stone base of a chimney
    only remain.

SIGNIFICANCE
19. DATE OF INITIAL CONSTRUCTION: <u>ca. 1900</u>
    ARCHITECT: _____
    BUILDER: _____

20. HISTORICAL AND ARCHITECTURAL IMPORTANCE:

    Originally this log building was built for Mrs. Hartshorn
    who used it as an afternoon retreat and as a guest house.
    It burned to the ground in about 1915. It was constructed
    on the exposed slab of slanting rock (hence "Slab House")
    typical of the Shawangunks and was anchored to it by
    spikes.

21. SOURCES:

    Bill Howell, former owner (and distant relative of Mrs.
         Hartshorn) , 12/19/87.
    Ella Stedner, 1983.

22. THEME:

BUILDING STRUCTURE INVENTORY FORM

NYS OFFICE OF PARKS, RECREATION
& HISTORIC PRESERVATION
DIVISION FOR HISTORIC PRESERVATION
(518) 474-0479

YOUR NAME: ___Harry P. Hansen___ DATE: 1991/ rev. 4-'95
YOUR ADDRESS: 66 Rest Plaus Road_____
___Stone Ridge, NY 12484___ PHONE: (914) 687-0854
ORGANIZATION: For the Cragsmoor Free Library, Cragsmoor, NY

* *

IDENTIFICATION
1. BUILDING NAME: "Gayland"_____ 061
2. COUNTY: _Ulster___ TOWN: _Wawarsing___ VILLAGE: _Cragsmoor
3. STREET LOCATION: West side of Gardiner Lane, a private
                                lane.
4. OWNERSHIP: Private
5. PRESENT OWNER: Jerry Felice_____
      ADDRESS: _Box 303, Cragsmoor, NY 12420___
6. USE: Original: Residence_____ Present: Residence_____
7. ACCESSIBILITY TO PUBLIC:
   Exterior visible from public road: No, private road_____
   Interior accessible: No

DESCRIPTION
8. BUILDING MATERIAL: novelty siding_____
9. STRUCTURAL SYSTEM: Wood frame with light members.
10. CONDITION: good
11. INTEGRITY: a. original site: Yes   b. moved: _____
              c. list major alterations and dates:

12.
PHOTO: view toward
         the _____
   Roll: _9 Neg.: 20-21

13. MAP: Tax Map #: _91.018-1-29
    USGS: Ellenville Quad.

269

14. THREATS TO BUILDING: <u>None known.</u>

15. RELATED OUTBUILDINGS AND PROPERTY:
    *None

16. SURROUNDINGS OF THE BUILDING:

    The site is cut out of the woods and sits next to the
    private road that leads to it.

17. INTERRELATIONSHIP OF BUILDING AND SURROUNDINGS:

    The 1.2 acre property is situated at the west edge of a
    lightly built-up community atop the Shawangunk Mountains.
    Nearby to the north, Minnewaska State Park and the
    Ellenville watershed offer protected open views. Open
    cuts in the woods provide views to the west over the
    Catskills.

18. OTHER NOTABLE FEATURES OF BUILDING AND SITE:

    A one and one half story side gable house with novelty
    clapboard siding on a stone foundation. A shed roofed
    entry extends off the left front. Some six over six
    windows are present but a number of multipaned picture
    windows have been installed. A shed roofed, second floor
    porch extends like a dormer off the rear (west) facade.

SIGNIFICANCE

19. DATE OF INITIAL CONSTRUCTION: <u>1905</u>
    ARCHITECT: _____
    BUILDER: _____

20. HISTORICAL AND ARCHITECTURAL IMPORTANCE:

    "Gayland" was built in 1905 for the artist Edward Gay N.A.
    It is another example of the many houses built for the art
    community that thrived in Cragsmoor.

21. SOURCES:
         Ella Stedner,

22. THEME:

BUILDING STRUCTURE INVENTORY FORM

NYS OFFICE OF PARKS, RECREATION
& HISTORIC PRESERVATION
DIVISION FOR HISTORIC PRESERVATION
(518) 474-0479

FOR OFFICE USE ONLY
Unique Site No._____
Quad_____
Series_____
Neg. No._____

YOUR NAME: Harry P. Hansen   DATE: 1991/ rev. 4-'95
YOUR ADDRESS: 66 Rest Plaus Road
             Stone Ridge, NY 12484   PHONE: (914) 687-0854
ORGANIZATION: For the Cragsmoor Free Library, Cragsmoor, NY

* *

IDENTIFICATION
1. BUILDING NAME: Clark Residence   (062)
2. COUNTY: Ulster   TOWN: Wawarsing   VILLAGE: Cragsmoor
3. STREET LOCATION: South side of Hillside Road, a private
                    way off the end of lower Henry Road.
4. OWNERSHIP: Private
5. PRESENT OWNER: Harold Clark
        ADDRESS: Blair Road, RD 1 Box 240, Hamburg, NJ 07419
6. USE: Original: Residence   Present: Residence
7. ACCESSIBILITY TO PUBLIC:
   Exterior visible from public road: Yes
                  Interior accessible: No

DESCRIPTION
8. BUILDING MATERIAL: wood shingle
9. STRUCTURAL SYSTEM: Wood frame with light members.
10. CONDITION: Excellent
11. INTEGRITY: a. original site: Yes   b. moved: _____
               c. list major alterations and dates:

12. PHOTO: view toward   13. MAP: Tax Map #: 91.018-1-32
          the _____   USGS: Ellenville Quad.
    Roll: 9 Neg.: 17-19 (18)

271

14. THREATS TO BUILDING: <u>None known.</u>

15. RELATED OUTBUILDINGS AND PROPERTY:
    *Carriage House converted to a dwelling.
    *Gardens

16. SURROUNDINGS OF THE BUILDING:

    The house and carriage house are located end to end about
    25 yards apart, the secondary structure being behind or to
    the south. A meadow type lawn surrounds the houses and
    the entire property is surrounded by woodland while being
    at the edge of a light residential area.

17. INTERRELATIONSHIP OF BUILDING AND SURROUNDINGS:

    The 4.5 acre property is situated in a lightly built-up
    community atop the Shawangunk Mountains. Nearby to the
    north, Minnewaska State Park and the Ellenville watershed
    offer protected open views. Open lawns and scattered
    patches of woods create an uncrowded atmosphere and views
    to the west over the Catskills. Both houses are sited on
    the sloping land to take advantage of the terrain.

18. OTHER NOTABLE FEATURES OF BUILDING AND SITE:

    <u>MAIN HOUSE:</u> A one and one half story, two bay gambrel
    house with a similar set back extension to the south.
    Further to the south is a hip roofed port cochere with
    exposed rafter tails on 3/4 height Tuscan columns on stone
    piers that extends across the front of the extension. The
    front has a gable roof entry with a kicked roof also on
    Tuscan columns offset to the right. Above, on the kicked
    roof with a deep overhang is a shed roofed central wall
    dormer with three casement units. To the rear (west) is a
    two story cross gable ell with six over one sash.

    <u>CARRIAGE HOUSE:</u> A one and one half story converted
    carriage house with a deep overhanging gambrel roof and
    shingle siding. The windows are all two over two sash
    units with board and batten shutters. The gable end
    features a central classical doorway with an elliptical
    fanlight and sidelights with a central window above. The
    east face has a full shed roofed wall dormer. The west
    face has a full facade, two story, four bay shed roofed
    enclosed porch, the ground floor having a an offset door.
    A small one story gable addition extends to the south that
    is built into the grade of the hill, with a deck below
    grade on the south end.

SIGNIFICANCE
19. DATE OF INITIAL CONSTRUCTION: _____
    ARCHITECT: _____
    BUILDER: _____

20. HISTORICAL AND ARCHITECTURAL IMPORTANCE:

This house was the home of artist Carrol Brown. The house
is another example of the many houses built for the art
community that thrived in Cragsmoor.

21. SOURCES:

22. THEME:

NOTE: The Clark residences address had always been Henry Road until recent

years when the official address became Hillside Road.

Strange Happenings

STRANGE HAPPENINGS

In 1992, Christina Clark (Harold's wife) and Marie Bilney of Hamburg, New Jersey along with two other lady friends began staying at the Clark home for long weekend retreats. Our friends are Eleanor Cacchio of Vernon, New Jersey and Margaret ("Sue") Kervatt of Morris Plains, New Jersey.

On one of our very early visits, after getting out of bed in the middle of the night to answer "nature's call", I, Marie, was amused upon returning to the master bedroom where I slept, to see the platform rocker (remember the rocker?) rocking away. No one was sitting in it!! And there was no breeze or wind that night! The room was well lit being softly illuminated by the moon and the outdoor area light. I did not become alarmed believing that it was just Aunt Helen (Clark) paying a visit. This manifestation has not happened again.

During the next several years, the battery operated wall clock in the kitchen has played tricks on us. It has stopped and started some twenty or more minutes later, all by itself. That means untouched by human hands! Several times brand new batteries were installed in this clock and still it continued to stop and go on it's own. Guess Aunt Helen's at it again! A few years ago, Harold was given a brand new kitchen clock. Upon opening his gift, he asked what the reason for the new clock was. When told that it was to replace the one in the Cragsmoor kitchen that didn't work properly, he simply stated that there was nothing wrong with the one that was there. Isn't it strange that these "occurrences" only happened while we were there? Well anyway, it is now 2005 and we have the same old clock, same batteries, no problem!!

In 2002, after having had breakfast in Napanock, the four of us ladies arrived back at the house and upon entering the kitchen, Christina Clark found on the floor two small fabric objects which had fallen from a shadow-box type wall decoration. Using Crazy Glue, she replaced the items back in their proper places. But the very next day, history repeated itself. It was, however, another shadowbox and a different piece was found lying on the floor. Again, Crazy Glue to the rescue. Helen again???

The strangest of all "happenings" occurred in early November 2003. Having arrived for our long weekend, we unloaded the car, turned up the heat, put our luggage in our respective bedrooms, then left the house and went down the mountain to have dinner at Miranda's Restaurant at the Shawangunk Country Club in Ellenville. About two and a half hours later we returned to the house and decided to put our pj's on. Eleanor's alarming outburst from her bedroom found us all running to her aid. Lo and behold, around the entire perimeter of her small bedroom were dry brown fall leaves.

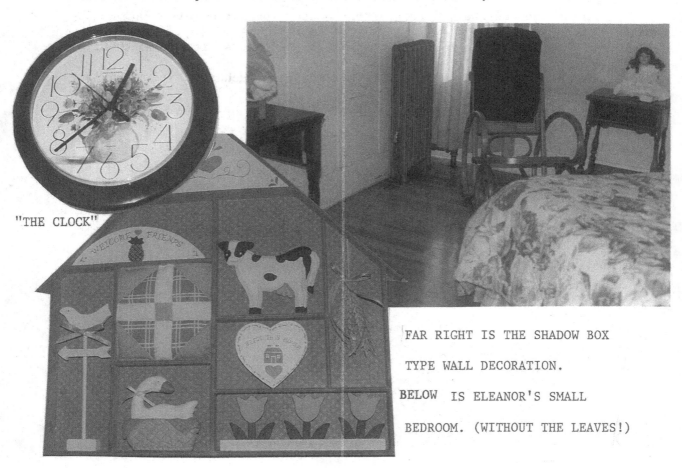

"THE CLOCK"

FAR RIGHT IS THE SHADOW BOX
TYPE WALL DECORATION.
BELOW IS ELEANOR'S SMALL
BEDROOM. (WITHOUT THE LEAVES!)

The floor in that room was absolutely clean when we left. The windows in the room were all closed since they do not open and cannot be opened. There were no other windows open because of it being so cold outdoors. The trees were barren of all leaves. Where did those leaves come from? Who made this mess? And, let it be known, we're not talking about a few leaves but at the very minimum, a shopping bag full!

At least on one or two occasions, people outside who happened to glance up at the house during a time when it was unoccupied, have noticed certain interior curtains fluttering. At these particular windows, there are no radiators underneath or nearby to cause the "fluttering" of these curtains or draperies.

From June 2002 through April 2003, Marie and her husband, Dick Bilney enjoyed living in the ol' house. During their residency there, nothing in the way of strange occurrences took place other than the "thing with the clock". (Dick even witnessed that, also.)

There was a weekend in October of '02 when Dick was invited to vacate the premises so that "the girls" (as we refer to ourselves), could enjoy the peacefulness, seclusion and serenity of a retreat weekend in this wonderful mountain home and the surrounding area.

During that weekend, the final phenonomen happened when we again returned from breakfast in Napanoch. Much to our surprise we found the downstairs toilet seat and lid up! One of us urgently needed to use the toilet. Never dreaming that the seat was not in it's proper position (since we are all ladies only in the house), Marie "fell in"!! Wow, what a shock!! We immediately checked with our very nearby neighbor as to whether anyone had been in the house in the past two hours or so since we'd left. The firm answer was a definite "NO".

Later that day, we had occasion to visit the Cragsmoor Library and it was in telling Eileen Kolaitis, the then Cragsmoor Library Director, of our strange and wierd happenings at "the house". We asked her specifically, who had died in that house. Her answer quite surprised us. She said that Carroll Butler Brown, the artist who built it died in the house. That information opened a whole new avenue of thoughts for us! Without having given much thought to "who" up until now, we just assumed that it was Aunt Helen trying to get our attention. Furthermore, both Kenny and Helen passed away while in Ellenville Hospital. Little, if anything, did we know of Carroll Brown until now. The "toilet seat" episode made it obvious to us that our frequent and friendly visitor was not a female spirit, but a male.

Theory has it that spirits are most likely to manifest themselves when an unexpected and/or violent death takes place. In Carroll's case, it certainly was unexpected! In cases of an untimely death, the spirit of the person so very often has a tendency to make itself known to others in the same area where the passing took place.

This knowledge began our quest for information regarding Carroll Butler Brown, his life and the home he built and summered in with his mother, Frances M. Brown, for about four years, until his death. It is so sad that he was only able to enjoy four brief summers in the home he loved so much.

Since our journey back in time, and our research began in 2002, we regret to say that we no longer have any "ghost stories" to tell!

Because of the newly found information about Carroll, our interests have also spread to his peer group of artists, who were all an integral part of the original art colony in our beloved Cragsmoor.

We have brought Carroll Butler Brown home again by framing and hanging copies of his photograph and paintings in the home which he built and named "The Falcon".

Could it be that since we have acknowledged and validated his life and accomplishments, that his spirit has been set free? We will miss him.........

THE END

A TIME TO GIVE THANKS

Without the help of every one of the people mentioned below, this project would not have come to be. We are greatly indebted to all the wonderful folks who so generously gave of themselves and their time to assist us in our quest for knowledge. Our heartfelt thanks go to --

Emily August, granddaughter of Harold and Christina Clark, for her beautiful poem entitled "A Hard Road To Travel; Harold M. Clark for his excellent remembrances of "the house"; Patricia Christian and Marian Erheardt of the Ellenville Library and The Terwilliger House Museum; Ruth Diem and Jeffrey Slade who officiate at The Stone Church; Hattie Grifo, Director of the Cragsmoor Free Library; Eileen Kolaitis, former Director of the Cragsmoor Free Library; Lisa Krom, clerk in the Tax Assessor's Office in Wawarsing Town Hall in Ellenville; Steve Krulick, Editor of Wawarsing.Net Magazine; Sally Matz, President of the Cragsmoor Historical Society; Laun Maurer for his computer expertise; Mary Ann Maurer, President of the Board of Directors of the Cragsmoor Free Library; Janet McDonnell, Executive Secretary of the Ellenville Chamber of Commerse; Maureen Radl, a deeply involved citizen and an active member and coordinator of Cragsmoor activities; Katharine Terwilliger, Historian and author (deceased); Rudy Travali, former Cragsmoor Postmaster; John Unverzgat; all the wonderful employees at the Hall of Records in the Ulster County Building in Kingston, New York. whose help we so desperately needed to enlighten us in how to look-back Libers, Wills, etc. and whose names were not notated by us (accept our apologies, please); to all the tireless and dedicated residents of Cragsmoor who helped us to get to this point and who help to make Cragsmoor such an active, interesting and fascinating community.

Thanks to all of you, from the bottom of our hearts!!

READ ON

The following books/booklets have been most helpful to us in gleaning information, and references have been made throughout our writings to many of them. It is suggested to those of you who have not yet read these, we do believe that there is much to be learned from them.

1. Cragsmoor Artists Past and Present 1885-1975
   By Gragsmoor Free Library

2. Cragsmoor - An Historical Sketch
   Compiled by Margaret Hakam and Susan Houghtaling

3. Cragsmoor Journals (from 1903 - 1916)
   Cragsmoor and Ellenville Libraries have copies of these.

4. Historical Review of the Cragsmoor Playhouse 1936 - 1957
   Recollections and Research by William R. Howell

5. The Mountain Echo 1928
   Cragsmoor and Ellenville Libraries have copies of these.

6. The Life and Work of Edward Lamson Henry N.A. 1841 - 1919
   By Elizabeth McClausland M. A.
   New York State Museum Bulletin Number 339
   Published by The University of the State of New York, Albany, N. Y.
   September 1945

7. Wawarsing, Where The Streams Wind
   By Katharine T. Terwilliger 1977

8. Windy Summits, Fertile Valleys
   By Cragsmoor Free Library 1982

9. Antiques Magazine (Cragsmoor, an early American art colony)
   November 1978

10. Wawarsing.net magazine
    Steve Krulick, Editor
    December 2002 through September 2005

NOTE: As seen by the dates above regarding publication of Wawarsing.net magazine, Steve Krulick's final edition was September of '05. The many articles contained therein were of varied interests for one and all to enjoy -- and enjoy we did! Mr. Krulick was always most helpful and courteous in our dealings with him. Thanks again, Steve, and good luck to you in the future.

ABOUT THE AUTHORS

Marie Bilney (left) and Christina Clark have been friends for many, many years. Along with husbands, each raised three daughters. They now enjoy time spent with their daughters, sons—in law, grand children and great grandchildren.